THE CORRESPONDENCE OF
LORD ACTON
AND RICHARD SIMPSON

VOLUME III

THE
CORRESPONDENCE OF
LORD ACTON
AND
RICHARD SIMPSON

VOLUME III

EDITED BY

JOSEF L. ALTHOLZ

DAMIAN McELRATH

AND

JAMES C. HOLLAND

CAMBRIDGE

AT THE UNIVERSITY PRESS

1975

Published by the Syndics of the Cambridge University Press
The Pitt Building, Trumpington Street, Cambridge CB2 1RP
Bentley House, 200 Euston Road, London NW1 2DB
32 East 57th Street, New York, NY 10022, USA
296 Beaconsfield Parade, Middle Park, Melbourne 3206, Australia

Library of Congress catalogue card number: 75–112466

ISBN: 0 521 20552 2

First published 1975

Printed in Great Britain
at the University Printing House, Cambridge
(Euan Phillips, University Printer)

CONTENTS

INTRODUCTORY NOTE

This third and final volume of the Acton–Simpson correspondence, somewhat larger than the other volumes, contains 328 letters, from July 1862 until Simpson's death in 1876. Over three-fifths of the letters date from the period of Acton's editorship of the *Home and Foreign Review*, until its suppression in April 1864. The correspondence is intermittent after that date, but there are spurts of activity in connexion with the publication of other periodicals, Acton's candidacies for Parliament, Simpson's researches and the Vatican decrees controversy of 1874. With this volume, the publication of the known surviving correspondence is complete, and the ghost of Gasquet[1] may at last be laid to rest.

After the first draft of the edited correspondence had been prepared, further research by Professor Holland uncovered some twenty hitherto-unknown letters in the Shropshire County Council Archives, Shrewsbury. These have been inserted in the text without renumbering the original letters, and they are indicated by a capital letter following the number (e.g., 694A, 734A, 734B, etc.). Two letters from the period covered by Volume II are given in an appendix, as is the letter from Mrs Simpson to Acton announcing her husband's death.

There has been a change in the specific responsibilities of the editors, occasioned by Father McElrath's assumption of the office of President of St Bonaventure University.[2] He was responsible for the preliminary preparation of the text, but the final editing was undertaken by Professor Holland, who also prepared the Index. Professor Altholz undertook the annotations and the Bibliography.

Readers of the first two volumes will be familiar with the format of this series, which continues unchanged. Where a person, book or article has been adequately footnoted in an earlier volume, the Index to this volume will indicate the location of that footnote.[3]

Readers are reminded that the originals of the Acton letters are

---

[1] Abbot Gasquet, *Lord Acton and his Circle* (London, 1906), may now be regarded as superseded. Among other defects, it contained no Acton–Simpson correspondence between March 1864 and January 1874.

[2] Before assuming his new position he published the biography, *Richard Simpson 1820–1876: A Study in XIXth Century English Liberal Catholicism* (Louvain, 1972).

[3] Two corrections to Volume I should be noted. On p. 180, 'Swarbrick' should read 'Scarisbrick'. On p. 218, the work of 'Williams' is erroneously identified; it should be Canon John Williams, *Letters on Anglican Orders and Other Matters* (London, 1859). We are indebted to the Dean of Christ Church, Oxford, for this last item.

located at Downside Abbey; the originals of the Simpson letters (except for the new discoveries) were in the possession of Mr and the Hon. Mrs Douglas Woodruff. These latter have recently been acquired by the library of Cambridge University.

Additional acknowledgements are due to the Graduate School of the University of Minnesota for a grant to Professor Altholz, to his research assistants David Horgan and Steven Strandmark, to Mr R. K. Browne, librarian at Farm Street, for his generous assistance, to Mary C. Hill, Salop County Archivist, and her staff, and to Mary Griset Holland for her proof-reading and other assistance.

THE CORRESPONDENCE

SIMPSON TO ACTON · 15 JULY 1862

Chez the good Lafontaine
Rue de Grenille St. Germain.

Dear Acton

Williams & Norgate have sent me certain letters—one from G. R. Kingdon S.J.[1] thanking you on behalf of the Rector for the H.&F.[2] & begging you to tell the publishers to send a copy regularly, directed to the Revd. Joseph Johnson,[3] Stonyhurst Coll. Whalley Lancashire. The other is the enclosed from your Bishop.[4] You see that Roberts had reason when he told us that there was a disposition at Rome to require the Bps. to condemn the R. The rich thing is, that whereas the true reason is your politics, the only reason they can assert for wanting to condemn it is Newman's heresy.[5] Could you not, occasionally, let Newman know of this manoeuvre, in order to increase his too cordial attachment to the Bps.?

I had a long talk with Frank Amherst this morning. He declares that he forgets the circumstances I have mentioned,[6] in the review of Marshall though he has no doubt that I am right. He has been very ill at Lyons, so he was not in case to be bullied, else I would have told him that there was a traitor amongst them, who had warned us of the dispositions of Rome, & had told us of the pretended reasons for our proposed condemnation. And that, thanks to his kindness, we had been a trifle too sharp for their Lordships. I told Amherst that I wd not for the world have lugged him in, or mentioned his name; that he had only to thank Coffin & Northcote for that, who had for long been looking out for some false step on our part, & had at last, as they thought, found one—

Will you tell Wetherell that I have a letter from Wilberforce, which I have not answered, nor shall I—It is simply this—"I hear from Mr. Macaulay with very sincere regret that there has been something unpleasant between Prendergast & you. What, I do not know, except that it is about some letter he published. I am sure I need not tell you that

---

[1] George Renorden Kingdon (1821–93), converted and entered Society of Jesus 1847, taught at Stonyhurst and Beaumont schools, author of school books.
[2] *Home & Foreign Review.*
[3] Joseph Johnson (1826–91), entered Society of Jesus 1844.
[4] Brown of Shrewsbury.
[5] The article 'On Consulting the Faithful in Matters of Doctrine'.
[6] In 'Marshall on Christian Missions', which had been attacked by 'Pudens' in the *Weekly Register*.

had I been here nothing should have appeared which could annoy you. I suppose it was about the Rambler. I came back here after leaving the office to ask P. about it, but he is gone, & I do not like to wait in telling you this." Wetherell was quite right in prophesying how Wilberforce would treat the quarrel when he came back.

Paris is quite empty. Gratry is out, so I asked for Perraud[1] & gave him a copy of the H.& F. for G. Augustin Cochin out. Melun,[2] for whom I have a letter, I missed today, & he is gone South. So I give up all thoughts of finding people at home, & spend my days in the Campana Museum & the Louvre, and in admiring the improvements, under which Paris is losing all individuality, & becoming a fine city with miles of handsome houses, all alike, wide streets, & good drainage. If the eye is disappointed, foot & nose are forced to acknowledge the improvement.

I suppose that you will deal with your Bishop. I find Paris as bad a place for news as Rome was in 1848. There is more in one Times than in a whole weeks' Moniteur & Monde—the only papers of this pious Hotel.

Ever yours faithfully
R Simpson

Tuesday Night—June[3] 15.
Wilberforce complains that he has not received the "New Rambler", & wants it sent regularly to him at 77 Onslow Square. If you have it sent, he will probably give you a puff,[4] since he will evidently take all kinds of indirect ways of getting out of his scrape. I have sent his letter to my lawyer, & told him to answer it.

469

SIMPSON TO ACTON · 16 AUGUST 1862

4 Victoria Road,
Aug. 16. 62

Dear Acton
I returned on Monday, & received Block's article[5] on Tuesday, I have translated it, & it went to Wetherell yesterday evening. It is com-

---

[1] Adolphe Perraud (1828–1906), entered Paris Oratory 1852, ordained priest 1855, professor of church history at the Sorbonne 1865, bishop of Autun 1874, cardinal 1895.

[2] Vicomte Armand de Melun (1807–77), leader of French social Catholicism, edited *Annales de la Charité* from 1845, active in numerous societies.

[3] This is an error by Simpson. He was in England on 15 June, and the context of this and related letters indicates that he spent parts of July and August abroad.

[4] In the *Weekly Register*.

[5] 'Poor-Relief in England and France' (communicated), *Home & Foreign Review*, I (October 1862), 312–34.

4

municated & signed, Maurice Block. I don't think he understands the principles of our poor law as well as he does those of his own *bienfaisance*. Thus he persists in calling it legalized *charity* in spite of the principle that to take from others what is necessary for ourselves ceases to be a sin when self-preservation demands its being done. Our poor law, it seems to me, is only a legalized acknowledgement of this right of the destitute, which it surrounds with all kinds of tests & safeguards. On this view the poor law is the most perfect expression of Catholic morals that can be, & the substitution of voluntary bienfaisance for it is only either a denial, or a shirking of the Christian Doctrine. I have sent B. only 200 ffr, though his article will be much more than the 20 pp. wh he promised.

Buck does not promise, but he lent the H.&F. to all the Bollandists in turn, & he says they all agree that it is the best Review in Europe. He thinks however that the literary notices—all of them—are as weak as water, & has the same opinion about the Review of Trollope.[1] He is especially delighted with the current events, & is translating them for the Journal de Bruxelles.

So the Cardinal has pitched into my Italian affairs.[2] It is a pity that W. left the one sentence "the opening sentences of the address are unfortunate", when he cut out the reasons I gave for saying so. The misfortune is, that the Bps. first claim to speak by the Holy Ghost, & then go on to speak of the Pope in terms wh. are about as true as those used by the Eng. Bps. to our James I.

To return to Buck—he considers the review of Prat to be horribly unjust, & only admits the truth of one criticism—that about the *nepos*.[3] Of course I threw the blame upon you.

I send you by this post two short notices of books which I read in Brussels—they both want your corrections & additions—after making wh perhaps you will send them on to Wetherell.

The affair with the Weakly is settled. Wilberforce has paid the costs, £17 odd, & I have forgiven him the debt of £22 w. he owed me for my articles &c—nevertheless he complains of being the most ill used man, & summons me before God's tribunal to answer for the injustice with which I have treated him & his.

[1] 'Trollope's North America.'
[2] In 'Current Events', *Home & Foreign Review*, I (July 1862), 251, Simpson had reported a rumour of a disagreement among the bishops assembled in Rome in the spring of 1862 on the terms of their address to the Pope. Wiseman, interpreting this as an attack on his own conduct, publicly denounced the *Home & Foreign* in *Rome and the Catholic Episcopate: Reply of His Eminence Cardinal Wiseman to an Address presented to him by the Clergy Secular and Regular of the Archdiocese of Westminster* (London, 1862), pp. 26–7.
[3] In his review of Jean Marie Prat, *Histoire du Père Ribadeneyra*, *Home & Foreign Review*, I (July 1862), 242–3, Acton had criticized Prat's description of Pope Paul III's grandson as his 'nephew'.

Roberts wont write for this number after what the Cardinal has said. But he will write for an early number.

I have seen no one but Wetherell for a quarter of an hour, & so I know nothing about the terms &c of the Cardinals attack. W. comes here tomorrow & I shall know all about it.

What articles have we got? Had you not better do Italy, to save my getting you into more mess? I have read up something of the Danubian provinces, & may perhaps be able to make something of them, by the light of Laguérronnière's pamphlet.[1]

Ever yours faithfully
R Simpson

470

ACTON TO SIMPSON · 17 AUGUST 1862

17th August

My dear Simpson,

I hope you enjoyed your tour and am delighted at your return with Block.[2] It is not strictly speaking right to take from *others* what we want, in case of need—but it is a claim of the individual on the whole community, in order that he may continue to form part of it. It will not be needful, I presume, to modify him much, as the interest of his paper will be in the fact of its coming from a well known French Economist, whose peculiarities and errors may be curious. We ourselves must work out the thesis of the Catholicity of the Poor Law some day ourselves.

I have not seen what the Cardinal said, nor the text of the Roman document denouncing the Rambler—I am told the ill feeling between bishops and Cardinal is stronger than ever, and will be a difficulty for the new Dublin,[3] and perhaps an opportunity for us. My bishop wants a talk with me, which I will try to avoid, and to inveigle him into a correspondence.

Wilberforce writes to me declaring his devotion to our cause, and grumbling at you for doubting it, and for robbing him of his earnings.

If you like I will do Italy, and leave France, Danube, Laguéronnière and *Belgium* to you. The debates on the treaty are important, showing the position of the Catholics.[4]

---

[1] An ironical reference to a book by Vicomte Louis de la Guéronnière: either *L'Abandon de Rome* or *De la Politique intérieure et extérieure de la France* (both Paris, 1862). La Guéronnière (1816–75), French journalist, senator 1861, was believed to have written under the inspiration of Napoleon III.

[2] 'Poor Relief in England and France.'

[3] H. R. Bagshawe had finally resigned as editor of the *Dublin Review* and a new editor was to be appointed.   [4] This refers to the October 'Current Events'.

My house is full of people who go away in a few days. I have not been able therefore to decypher Jack Morris's paper,[1] which, to save time I send you. Otherwise we have Paley,[2] who is heavy, Block, Ffoulkes immediately—Renouf lately re-promised, saying he was nearly ready.[3] I have no Germans yet, but I did a little business for the future literature, in Germany. Cannot anybody who knew Lucas[4] make an article of his life? Stokes seems to me the sort of man, subject to correction, but this Wetherell denies. I never knew him, and do not therefore appreciate him. I will send up your notices as soon as read. This is Dedication Sunday, and I have no time before post.

Your's ever truly
J D Acton

Paley
Morris
Darnell
Block
Hayti
O'Hagan
Early history[5]
Lucas
Ffoulkes

A political article and an article on light literature still wanted.

471

SIMPSON TO ACTON · 19 AUGUST 1862

4 Victoria Rd Clapham
19 August 1862

Dear Acton

Block had gone to the printers before your letter came—I had successfully resisted all alteration, except the suppression of one sentence, of no argument, wh. W.[6] insisted on.

W. caught at the idea of having at the same time a short notice of Lamarque's Traité des établissements de bienfaisance[7] in wh. we might state broadly our fundamental differences with Block.

[1] Not published.
[2] 'Manuscripts at Cambridge', *Home & Foreign Review*, i (October 1862), 471–500.
[3] 'The Earliest Epochs of Authentic Chronology', *ibid.* 420–49. Ffoulkes did not publish.
[4] Frederick Lucas (1812–55), converted 1839, founded the *Tablet* 1840, moved to Dublin and became an Irish nationalist, M.P. 1852.
[5] Of these, Darnell did not publish; Thomas Arnold, Jr, wrote 'Hayti', *Home & Foreign Review*, i (October 1862), 361–91; 'O'Hagan' is John O'Hagan, 'Perraud on Ireland'; 'Early History' is Renouf's article.   [6] Wetherell.
[7] Jules de Lamarque, *Traité des établissements de bienfaisance* (Paris, 1862).

To my mind they come to 2.

1. Our poor law is not charity, but an admission of a right—socially dangerous, & only admissible when guarded with extreme cautions,—of the pauper, not on the community but over such of the goods of the community as are absolutely necessary to preserve his life. The canon law is strong on the point

a Extrema necessitas eo redigit, ut censeantur omnia communia.

b *Tempore* necessitatis omnia sunt communia, et maxime cibaria.

c Necessitas facit licitum quod alias est illicitum.

a. Extreme necessity suspends the meum et tuum with respect to necessaries of life.

b. This suspension becomes general in *times* of general necessity, & by parallel inference in *places* of such necessity, & only in those places—So that the poor law must always be limited to circles like Unions or similar divisions.

c. This necessity as it changes some illicitum (viz. certain helping yourself to other mens loaves) into licitum, so correlatively it must change some duty of charity into a duty of obligation—This is the mere religious view. Then the state comes in—acknowledges the justice of the view, but recognizes its extreme practical difficulty— solves the knot by a poor law, in wh. the principle is acknowledged, but surrounded with tests & penal machinery to prevent the lazy robbing the rich under the title of a wilful distress & destitution.

N.B. my canon law is simply *index* learning.

2. Block's imperialism.

a admiration of centralization.

b denial that the demolitions & reconstructions in Paris, Rouen &c must be taken into account when comparing the English & French systems of relief, *though* the French system does not extend to able-bodied unemployed poor.

It seems clear to me that the work & relief wh. we supply in Work-houses, is supplied by the French government in the demolitions & buildings; in the forcing manufacturers to keep open their mills at a loss, the state paying the difference; in the bakers maximum &c &c—

Just write me a few lines on this, tracing the political dangers of warding off a poor law by giving the unemployed the right, in bad seasons, of rebuilding gentlemen's seats at the expense of the gentry.

I enclose Block's letter for your edification.

I have told Williams[1] to get for you the Moniteur of July 17 in wh. I read an account of the campaigns of the South written by a polemo-graph of first rate powers. I thought it would help your current events.

---

[1] The publisher.

As for Lucas. The new life,[1] for all Catholic purposes, stops with his conversion. the writer knows, & pretends to know, nothing about his intestine controversies. Therefore a short notice, embodying all that is really valuable in the life, viz, the account of the progress of his mind up to his conversion seems all that is at present necessary. What do you say to this?

I have written to Buck to help me with Belgium, & have sent him, at the expense of the Home & F., Rees' Welsh Saints, price 10/6, wh. he is in much want of, as a sort of payment before hand for favours to come—

Wetherell is off today for Malvern—direct—care of Ld Charles Thynne[2]—How is Pythagoras?

Ever yours truly
R Simpson

472

ACTON TO SIMPSON · 20 AUGUST 1862*

Wednesday

My dear Simpson,

You seem to me quite right about Poor Relief, always sticking to the distinction between pillaging your neighbour and the community. The rate and the relief must be local, in order that the atomic system prevail not, which would be the result if it was not communal—if rates were entirely equalized. On the other hand by making the area of a rate too small, as the parish often is now, the evil is often aggravated, as the poor must pay for the poor, and the machinery for the relief of paupers increases the number of paupers, and spoils with one hand the good it does with the other. The parish has ceased to be the economic unit in the distribution of the population.

The use of the word bienfaisance is detestable. It means charity, not relief—one is personal, and INDIVIDUAL, private, voluntary, and a channel of spiritual influences—the other, impersonal, official, mechanical, unconnected with any spiritual end or action. One is merely negative, keeps men alive—The other occupies itself in detail with their condition, raises them up, stops the supply of paupers, whilst the other combats not poverty, but starvation—

The avoidance of a Poor Law by means of public works, not actually

---

[1] Christopher James Riethmüller, *Frederick Lucas. A Biography* (London, 1862), reviewed in *Home & Foreign Review*, I (October 1862), 552–7.

[2] Lord Charles Thynne (1813–94), canon of Canterbury 1845, converted 1852.

* Gasquet, Letter cxxxv, pp. 290–1, with one paragraph omitted.

necessary, is characteristic of a centralized absolutism. It nurses artificially, a proletariate, a classless community, which, instead of being absorbed in its own places, is permanently relying on the state to provide for it, not by barely keeping it alive, and leaving to vice and improvidence all its natural effects, but by raising it up to the level of those who are able to provide for themselves, as far as present profits go, only depriving it of the possibility of becoming independent and normally selfsupporting. Thus a constant danger menaces society, and the need of a strong hand perpetually saving society, and converting dictatorship into a regular form of government, is kept always before it, as private individuals cannot constantly go on with this kind of benevolence without ruin, the labourer turns from the proprietor to the state as his protector and refuge, and the antagonism of property and labour is made more irreconcilable, to the great advantage of the civil power—

Why should there not be an article completing Riethmüller's life of Lucas? I could perhaps get his letter to the Pope, with his theory of indep. opposition,[1] for publications. I have however no clear estimate of his proportions.

Ever truly Your's
J D Acton

Hayti[2] comes next Tuesday

473

SIMPSON TO ACTON · 26 AUGUST 1862

Dear Acton

Wetherell (to whom direct care of Ld Charles Thynne, Malvern Wells,) complains that he gets neither proof nor copy, & that Acton is silent as the grave. I sent him yesterday a short notice of a volume of the Bibliotheque de l'administration Francaise, containing ideas about French & English poor law compiled in part from your note to me.

I send you by this post a short notice by Buck, who also half promises a lot about Belgian affairs in the first fortnight of September—It might perhaps be made an article of, if we run short.

In talking to him about you & your library, I told him how you had given me some duplicates, & that you had sold some. This seems to have stuck in his memory, & he has sent me a list of Spanish & Portuguese works wh. the Bollandists want, asking me to find out whether you have any of them in duplicate to dispose of, or if not, if you could put

---

[1] Lucas had been a member of the Irish Independent Party, which adopted a policy of 'independent opposition' to all ministries in the 1850s.
[2] Arnold's article.

10

him on the way to get them cheap. Such books, he says, are horribly dear in Belgium. I dont know how many francs appear dear to a Belgian.

What about the Cardinal?[1] You have seen what he says—it is printed in the Tablet of Saturday, first leader—Buck says he is quite right—il s'est permis de dire un mot sur votre Revue puisque vous vous êtes permis de dire votre avis sur l'adresse—I asked him to write us a review of Grossetête's letters—he says Je n'ai pas du tout envie de faire un travail à part sur Robert Go: on me lapiderait dans les conjonctures actuelles. Mais je répète que je voudrais avoir l'occasion d'insérer sa vie dans les *Acta SS.* ou il ferait inouis de bruit.

He advises us to say nothing about the Roman question—but he is a Jesuit, however liberal.

Roberts was going to write me a letter about the kind of reply we should make to the Cardinal—He wants us to own that the *tone* of the Rambler was sometimes not all that could be desired. Perhaps it would be as well to say this, & that it was our consciousness of this fact, & our determination to change our tone, that was one reason why we changed the name & the form of the Review, & turned over a new leaf. Give me a line, if it is only to let me know that you are not dead of diphtheria typhus or cholera.

Ever yours faithfully
R Simpson

Tuesday, Aug. 26.

474

ACTON TO SIMPSON · 27 AUGUST 1862*

Wednesday

My dear Simpson,

I am very sorry to say that I have looked in vain among all my Spanish books for those on the enclosed list. There is little Portuguese literature here, and most of the Spanish books mentioned are rare. The more recent works, such as DeCastro's history of Cadiz, would be supplied by Bauthes and Lowell in London, or by Garnier at Paris. The former probably have some of the older books, such as Pulgar's Palencia. They are however very expensive people to deal with. It might be worth while to send a list of Desiderata to Quaritch who has often Spanish books, or to Stewart, who knows where to get ecclesiastical history, and also how to turn an honest penny.

---

[1] Wiseman's denunciation of the *Home & Foreign Review*.
* Gasquet, Letter cxxxvi, p. 292, with major omissions.

I am strongly against noticing the Cardinal. His attack on our narrative is a tissue of lies.[1] Let us rather submit to an unjust accusation of error than subject him to a true accusation of falsehood. Also I disagree with Roberts. 1° The tone has nothing whatever to do with it. The antagonism of principles is so enormous that it overwhelms all the lesser questions of disagreement. But our principles, method, and objects are unchanged.

2° We cannot separate our Rambler from Newman's. Any surrender about the past must involve more or less the paper on consulting the Laity—which is, theologically, the most offending thing of all.

3° Newman's school, the future University[2] (whether our own or at Oxford) and the whole interest of thought and science, are mixed up in our cause. In order to save them I am persuaded that patience and a duck's back are the only safeguards.

How is Darnell getting on?

Your's ever truly
J D Acton

475

SIMPSON TO ACTON · 29 AUGUST 1862

Dear Acton

Here is the Moniteur's account (July 17) of the Battle of Richmond. Here also is Robert's letter,[3] which is unjust—We have always spoke of the teaching Church with the greatest respect. That wh we dont respect, I presume, is a clique of reverend gentlemen who maintain in pulpit & pamphlet a system of political morality wh they dare not enforce in the confessional—Like Manning —

I have a great boil on my abdomen wh is as bad as the toothache, & I have not begun my article on Döllinger[4] yet—but I know what to say.

Ever yours
R Simpson

Aug. 29.

[1] Gasquet (p. 292) says 'mistakes' for 'lies'. He also omits the last two words of the next sentence.
[2] Acton refers first to Newman's Edgbaston school and second to his own idea of a Catholic university or college in England.
[3] J. W. Roberts to Simpson, 27 August 1862, criticizing the *Rambler* for a lack of 'loyalty to the Church' and urging that the *Home & Foreign Review* dissociate itself from the *Rambler*. ('T. W. Roberts', cited in Letter 442 [II, 305], is Simpson's error for the same person.)
[4] 'Döllinger on Heathenism and Judaism.'

ACTON TO SIMPSON · 30 AUGUST 1862

Aldenham
Saturday

My dear Simpson,

Your translation of Block[1] is excellent—I have just read the proofs. Thanks for Moniteur.

Roberts' letter shows how strong the moral effect of the Cardinal's address must be, as he is evidently trying to reconcile himself both with the attacks and with the R. itself. You ought, I think, to bring him to book, when you have an opportunity, and make him try to precipitate his amorphous criticisms.

Take care of yourself and swallow a little pill. I am off to see the Bishop on Monday, who wants to see me before he issues his pastoral.[2]

Your's ever truly
J D Acton

Green has just brought me the Register.[3] How Wilberforce enjoys his revenge. Is there no Horsepond?

477

SIMPSON TO ACTON · 2 SEPTEMBER 1862

Tuesday

To be read by Wetherell *see end*

Dear Acton

I send you my article on Heathendom & Jewdendom[4]—It is very rough, because written in a hurry, but perhaps it has more unity on that account. I send it you before sending it to Wetherell, because the judgment of its substance is more important than the judgment on its style. Therefore, if you have little to alter, or only obliterations to make, will you send it on to Wetherell as soon as possible, telling him

---

[1] 'Poor Relief in England and France.'
[2] Bishop Brown of Shrewsbury, along with other bishops, was going to follow Wiseman in criticizing the *Rambler* and the *Home & Foreign Review*.
[3] *Weekly Register.*
[4] 'Döllinger on Heathenism and Judaism.' Simpson plays on Döllinger's title *Heidenthum und Judenthum.*

also that he must be merciful, because I really will not write the affair over again.

Moreover it is clear to me that this article, & Morris on development cannot appear in the same number of the Review.[1] Hence if anything is to be prepared out of the MSS wh. I have, it must be something from the history of German philosophy, wh. must be cut in two—divided into two periods, or two subjects, or the like—but I lack the English translation of the first 30 pp. or so, as I wrote to you when you first sent it. How are they to be replaced?

Like the brazen Bell you have devoured all the tow & pitch balls I have administered to you in the shape of short (?) notices &c, & have not returned them either digested or indigested—Let us have some back to correct, or I shall suppose that they are all bosh, & are in the waste paper basket.

Wilberforce sent me an impertinent letter on Friday, enclosing one from Marshall to him, in w. the poor beggar acknowledges himself Wilberforce's debtor to the extent of 17£ (the Solicitor's bill) & asking time for payment. Whereupon I wrote a civil letter to Marshall, explaining how Wilberforce had been a gainer of £5 by the process, & telling him that he wd be a great fool if he ever thought of repaying W. a farthing. I told him he was quite at liberty to show my letter to W. So I had a little bit of revenge for Saturday's Weakly impotence. If Marshall receives it civilly we may proceed to ask him to write an article—

Ever yours truly
R Simpson

Dear Wetherell

I find that Acton is out for a day or two, so I send you this letter instead of to him. Send it on to him with the art. RS.

478

SIMPSON TO ACTON · 3 SEPTEMBER 1862

Dear Acton

I finished my article on Döllinger yesterday, & sent it on to Wetherell, with a letter intended for you, which I transferred to him when I remembered your visit to your Bishop.

---

[1] Morris' article was not published; neither was the other material referred to in this paragraph.

This morning the Redemptorist to whom I confessed asked me to call on him—It was the same story as with a former Redemptorist.[1] He could not hear my confessions after the Cardinal's address. I asked him what he wished me to do in order that he might be able to continue hearing me, but I could not bring him to book. After he had made an ultimatum wh. he accepted, I saw there was always something behind, wh. he wd not bring out—of course a promise from me that I wd write no more in the H.&F.—but when I plumply asked him whether this was it, he disclaimed all right of such dictation. I gave him to wit that he was a mere tool in the hands of a gigantic tyranny wh. wanted to force on us not only the dogmas & laws of the Church, but eke its own "instincts" & "tones" & "old womanisms", & that I should stand on my rights—That the Cardinal had not had the politeness to send me a copy of the writing denouncing me, that I had not bought it, & certainly should not, & should take no notice whatever of it till it was formally communicated to me. Finally I said that I was infamously treated, &c on wh. he went down on his knees—to prevent his forthwith scourging himself I also went down on mine, assured him that my answer was no consequence of *his* personal clownishness, but that I should have answered anybody else in the same way, &c. I finished by assuring him that the treatment I was receiving was infamous, but that he personally enjoyed my highest consideration—So there is a nice quarrel with these fools. What I am to do next I know not. I have thought of writing to the Bishop to appoint for these parts some parish priest who should be obliged to hear my confession according to the rules of the Confessional, & not according to his own fancies—

I have sent to Wetherell Block's corrections[2]—here is his letter, so you may see what they are. I have written an account of our objections to his "manner of to see", in wh. I have proposed to him to have the general principles of opposition stated in a short notice—probably he will say that he should like to see it—

What of Buck's short notice?

Ever yours sincerely
R Simpson

Sep. 3.

---

[1] The Redemptorists, led by Fr Coffin, had charge of the mission at Clapham, where Simpson resided. The 'former Redemptorist' may have been Coffin.

[2] To 'Poor-Relief in England and France'.

ACTON TO SIMPSON · ?19 SEPTEMBER 1862

Friday

Dear Simpson,

As we have not got the proofs we cannot correct Victor Hugo[1] or current events, and must exhort you to correct them, the last on Monday morning. Also OHagan has made additions on his proof. We tell Robson not to adopt them till you have seen them.

Pray remember that there is no harm in abundance, and that even after cutting several things away from Paley[2] we may still be 320 pages.

I hope you arrived safely.

Your's ever truly
J D Acton

ACTON TO SIMPSON · ?26 SEPTEMBER 1862

Friday

My dear Simpson

Those rogues the publishers continue to exact eighteen pence from old subscribers for the remainder of this year. I thought they had consented to forego the money. Green, who tells me this, is much perturbed by my use of the word Popish Plot.

A friendly letter from Lord Stanhope[3] came this morning. He is much pleased with Paley,[4] and thinks me right about Charles II.[5]

Reeve[6] writes: "I wish I had had the good fortune to attract you and your friends to enlist in my corps, instead of forming another battalion: but I acknowledge that there are points connected with church matters on which you require a more complete independence than any of the old Reviews could afford you".

Consider therefore whether it may not be well to take advantage some-day of his good fellowship, to write a paper in the Edinburgh on "church

[1] Simpson, 'Victor Hugo's *Misérables*', *Home & Foreign Review*, I (October 1862), 392–419.
[2] 'Manuscripts at Cambridge.'
[3] Philip Henry Stanhope (1805–75), previously known as Lord Mahon, succeeded as Earl Stanhope 1855, historian.
[4] 'The Science of Language' in July.   [5] Concerning Charles II's alleged bastard son.
[6] The editor of the *Edinburgh Review*.

parties among the English Catholics" of course quite between ourselves—or on any other subject that would swamp the H&F.

Has Roberts begun his article and does Waters promise his archaeology for October?[1]

Ever truly Your's
J D Acton

Saturday

Jack[2] says the corrections of his article give him a better idea of the type wh. we wish an article to be cast in. I hope there is not any reason for alarm in the last sentence of his letter. Don't show it to anyone 'I shall do what I can for your uncle's[3] soul, BUT great trials within and without continue to harrass me.'

Capes[4] writes amiably, and is highly pleased with the Conservative Reaction[5]

Yrs. ever
JDA.

481

SIMPSON TO ACTON · 26 SEPTEMBER 1862

23. Great New Street. Fetter Lane
London. E.C. Sept 26. 1862

Dear Acton

Your messenger will not be of much use unless you send him by the train I came by, 4.50 PM, & on Saturday in which case he will arrive here[6] at 11.30 on Saturday night, *before the men have gone*, & they may be kept till early on Sunday, & made to do all the corrections & set up all the copy you send. But if you send a messenger on Sunday morning, how can he get here before 3 or 4 P.M.? In that case you must send a telegram to Robson in the course of Saturday, to say *when* your man would arrive, & *what* he would bring, in order that he may have the proper staff in attendance to receive the work.

This latter course would not be very profitable, because of the difficulty of getting men in condition to work, & the consequent slowness of

---

[1] Roberts did not publish. Waters published 'Parish Registers', *Home & Foreign Review*, II (April 1863), 433–55.
[2] J. B. Morris.
[3] Sir Robert Throckmorton, Acton's uncle-in-law.
[4] J. M. Capes.
[5] Simpson's article in the July *Home & Foreign Review*.
[6] The address of the printer, Robson.

their progress. The difference between Sunday in the middle of the day, & Monday morning, for receiving the last proofs, would be the difference between Tuesday night & Wednesday morning in the delivery of the Reviews to Williams & Norgate—not worth the trouble of a messenger & the expense of Sunday's work.

This calculation about time assumes that the proofs of Hayti, Döllinger,[1] & short notices will arrive on Saturday morning.

I shall make my few corrections of Hugo[2] & send them here, to be added to Wetherell's, Wetherell's to be preferred if the two happen to clash, or to be in the same sentence—

I finished Servia[3] yesterday, & sent it up here—It is rather rotten; not like your Potomac.[4] You see that Mac:clellan says he has licked Lee,[5] & Wall street believes him.

Ever yours
RS——

482

SIMPSON TO ACTON · 29 SEPTEMBER 1862

23 Great New Street. Fetter Lane.
London. E.C. Goose day 1862

Dear A.

I hope you keep Michaelmas as above without running the risk of being bilked of the goose as I shall probably be, by missing the train that should convey my famished body to Mitcham, all along of having to wait for the last proofs.

The Review will be in the hands of the publishers at 2 PM tomorrow, exactly—just 28 hours too late; the nuisance is that a review in its beginnings depends so much on the good will of the trade, & this goodwill is lost by nothing sooner than by dealers not finding the review they ask for forthcoming at the exact time. We must be more punctual next time—28 hours is so small a gain for idleness & procrastination that we shall find no difficulty in making the sacrifice & giving up that small

---

1 Respectively, 'Hayti' and 'Döllinger on Heathenism and Judaism'.
2 'Victor Hugo's *Misérables*.'
3 Simpson, 'The Slave Provinces of Turkey', in 'Current Events', *Home & Foreign Review*, I (October 1862), 593–7.
4 Acton, 'The States of North America', *ibid*. 598–602. Neither of these attributions is in Walter E. Houghton, ed., *The Wellesley Index to Victorian Periodicals 1824–1900* (Toronto, 1966), I, 550.
5 The reference is to the battle of Antietam (17 September), a less than decisive Northern victory.

fraction of pleasure—I was delighted with a sentence of yours[1] about the K of Prussia[2] (while prince) "the monarchical party *regularly drove* him into the camp of the liberals"—I made some foolish alteration, under the more foolish impression that regularly was a vulgarism of the first class—ask Wetherell whether it is so.

I have told Robson to send you 25 copies by Tuesday's rail—You will thus get them quicker—also 25 for me—I will send Blocks affairs with 6 copies—I have told Robson to keep up Riley's[3] type till we know whether he wants more copies. Old Robson says that the article is the best he has ever seen on a very difficult subject,—& that he has written to his correspondents in Australia to call their attention to it—If it is so, Riley had better distribute as many as he can with our covers. I have now done all the proofs, & must make haste to Mitcham—I have not lost the goose—

Yours ever truly
R Simpson

483

ACTON TO SIMPSON · 29 SEPTEMBER 1862[*]

Michaelmas Day

My dear Simpson,

Ought not Roberts to review Villari's life of Savonarola[4] which is translated, and will make much sensation in anti Catholic circles? It is an excellent book, and I will send Roberts everything he can wish for on the subject. It would be important to use it as an occasion to exhibit scientific honesty, and at the same time to meet the theological conclusions enemies will draw from the story. S. Charles[5] might follow in a later number.

Why should you not write an article for the January Edinburgh on the present state of Catholic parties in England? It would not only

---

[1] This suggests that Acton wrote 'The Ministerial Crisis in Prussia' in 'Current Events', *Home & Foreign Review*, i (October 1862), 570–80, not previously attributed.

[2] William I (1797–1888), prince regent of Prussia 1858, king 1861, German emperor 1871.

[3] Edward Ryley, 'General Average', *Home & Foreign Review*, i (October 1862), 335–60, dealing with marine insurance.

[*] A. Watkin and Herbert Butterfield, 'Gasquet and the Acton–Simpson Correspondence', *Cambridge Historical Journal*, x (1950), 92–3.

[4] Pasquale Villari, *The History of Girolamo Savonarola and of his Times*, tr. Leonhard Horner (London, 1862), was reviewed not by Roberts but by Acton, *Home & Foreign Review*, ii (April 1863), 616–17.

[5] Borromeo.

enlighten Catholics as to their faults but Protestants as to some of their merits, and would excite curiosity, besides drawing attention to our position. Think of this and answer affirmatively as soon as you can, that I may write at once to Reeve to bespeak thirty pages.[1]

The advertisement[2] in the 3 Catholic newspapers appeared very opportunely, and will no doubt disturb quiet minds, to judge by the excitement of the verdant[3] yestere'en.

I hope Waters is undertaking Salop, DeBuck Grosseteste, you Deutinger[4] —

Your's ever sincerely
J D Acton

Arnold has been paid for his article.[5] There will remain only his three short notices.

484

SIMPSON TO ACTON · 30 SEPTEMBER 1862

Tuesday. Sep. 30.

Dear Acton

Your idea of the Edinburgh deserves consideration, especially if we could get up a concerto a tre like the "Cardinal & the H.&.F."—many things could be said, especially if the article professed to be a dispassionate estimate of the quarrel from an external stand-point. But then it must not be what Wetherell suggested—an asylum for all my rejected wickednesses.

I talked with fatuous Father Coffin today—we were very good-natured, & I tried upon him the argument of the article on the C. & H&F. He did not know what to say, but evidently had a glimpse of a principle, which frightened him much more than any former view he had taken—which was, in the main, that we were very good fellows, kicking up a row and bonneting authorities out of mere gaity of heart.

In fear & trembling I made a few verbal corrections out of many

---

[1] Watkin and Butterfield (p. 79) regard this as a conspiracy to undo the effect of the bishops' condemnation of the *Home & Foreign Review* by 'secretly' appealing to a wider audience. The article was eventually not published in the *Edinburgh*, but much of its substance appeared in the *Home & Foreign* as 'Milner and his Times'.

[2] Of the new management of the *Dublin Review*.

[3] A play on Green (Acton's chaplain).

[4] Of these, only Waters, 'Parish Registers', was published.

[5] 'Hayti.'

suggested by old Robson in the art on the Card.[1] Some were necessary—one especially, where three "mosts" came in two lines.

I enclose a letter from Hecker, partly that you may see the spirit of the man, partly to show you the abominable wickedness of Williams & Norgate,[2] who were going to do such great things for us in America, & have not yet distributed the first number to our friends—

Coffin elaborately brought out all his papers & letters upon the Hecker affair, to convict me of error—he made three complaints—one was that I called the Paulists a branch of Rpsts.[3] 2. that I said the new general had introduced a new policy—3 that I said that H. & the American fathers had made a "separation perfect in order"—To convince me he showed me a copy of the *decretum* of Pius IX, wh. recited that Hecker & Co having asked (after the quarrel) to be allowed either to continue to be Redemptorists with a superior of their own, independent of the Rector Major, but dependent immediately on the Pope, or, in default of this to be dispensed with their vows—the Pope took the latter alternative, dispensed them, & allowed them to set up a congregation for giving missions, subject to the ordinary jurisdiction of the *Bps*—This is entirely justificatory of what I said—I showed C. also that I said "branch from" & "separated", w^h was not "branch of" or "united", & ad 2^{dum}, that if the new general had not introduced a new policy, at least he had in a "shameless" way refused to allow a single adherent of de Held to hold office, though Held & another German had at first all the votes for the Rectorship, & the present man was only a compromise —C. answered. 1. that that question had nothing to do with the American secession; 2 that I had no business to use my knowledge of this fact to say a thing damaging to the order—I told him that I was much obliged to him for giving me an opportunity of seeing how accurate I had been in every word that I had said.

We were very civil, not to say affectionate but we each had our tails up, & walked on the tips of our toes—or sat on the t— of our b— as you please.

Grant has sent round a private circular to the clergy, quoting the Cardinal, & telling the clergy to take opportunities privately to warn their flocks against publications, which are not Catholic—Coffin would not show it to me.

An argument that had much effect on him was that the Cardinal ought both as a gentleman and as a judge, to have relinquished all interest in the Dublin before he performed an ecclesiastical act which

---

[1] Acton (assisted by Wetherell and Simpson), 'Cardinal Wiseman and the *Home & Foreign Review*', *Home & Foreign Review*, i (October 1862), 501–20.

[2] The publishers.

[3] Redemptorists. The subject is the secession of Hecker and his followers (the Paulists) from the Redemptorist order.

might be interpreted as a mere mercantile act of touting for his Review —The way he winced under it shows that it will be one very proper for the Edinburgh—

After all, I got no goose yesterday—I only got wet through.

Ever yours truly
<u>R Simpson</u>

485

ACTON TO SIMPSON · 1 OCTOBER 1862*

Wednesday

My dear Simpson,

I much rejoice at your conversation with Coffin. In a day or two you will hear a good deal said against us which will gratify you. Old Green is knocked completely off his legs by the new world opened out before him where he expected that we were going to make everything comfortable.

Clifford[1] has sent round a very short circular privately to his clergy, saying 'we agree with the Cardinal', and exhorting the clergy prudently to prevent people from being led astray by dangerous teachers like the H&F. Jack Morris consequently begs to have his Ms sent back to him, which pray do, to Shortwood Temple Cloud Bristol.

This bishop has done nothing yet, but I suspect they have all adopted the same form.

Can you find Bunbury? He could get at Watson, who is a friend of his, and make him write for us.

I will write at once to Reeve. The article[2] ought most decidedly to give a full description of the internal state of Catholics, and end with our quarrel, but by no means be confined to it. What are the influences and traditions in the Catholic body? The old school, Milnerites, Lingardites &c.[3] The Cardinalician reform—The Italian movement—Irish influences—Earlier converts, like Digby[4] & Phillipps—Then the fragments of converts—converts in no sense a party by themselves, and yet not absorbed in the old lot. How marriage of new zeal with old Cardinalism has produced Romanism, Faber—Manning, and the Wardian fear

---

* Watkin and Butterfield, pp. 93–4.
[1] The Bishop of Clifton.
[2] Simpson's intended article for the *Edinburgh Review*.
[3] This portion of the article emerged as 'Milner and his Times'.
[4] Kenelm Digby (1797–1880), converted 1823, author of the medievalist *Broad Stone of Honour* (1822).

22

of advancement. French and Roman influences—Failure to unite with the Irish (University) Estimate of Newman's position in the Catholic world—Why so different from what it was of old. Position of clergy & laity to each other. Feelings of all parties towards each other. Their principle in judging common questions. One broad question—sincere love of truth on one side—craven dread of it on the other—both in church, state, school, literature, even industry. Believe me it will be useless if the H&F is the chief topic.

I am sorry for your goose, for our's was very good. Is there not a rather illogical tone about Hecker?

Your's ever truly
J D Acton

486

SIMPSON TO ACTON · 2 OCTOBER 1862

Thursday Morning

Dear Acton

Here is William Clifford's circular;[1] I will try to get Grant's. Your friends of Clytha will help you to get Brown's.[2] He will probably have a harder fling at us, unless they have taken counsel together & agreed to quote the Cardinal, with such heading and tailing as each may see good. We ought to get the whole collection, so keep the copy on the other side. This tallies so with what Coffin told me of Grant's that I suspect a common formula has been fixed upon.

I am sending off letters & copies to Block's friends. I hope they all understand English. I ask Don Emilio de Santos[3] if he can put us in the way of some one to give us periodical information upon the current events & contemporary literature of Spain.

If an article on Catholic parties is written for the Edinburgh ought the starting point to be the quarrel between the Cardinal & the Home & Foreign Review? If so, it would be much better to cram some other person & get him to do it. If not, & if no mention is to be made of this quarrel, what is the use of taking this occasion to write the article?

Ever yours truly
R Simpson

---

[1] The circular (24 September 1862) is enclosed with the letter. The major part of it is reprinted in Altholz, *The Liberal Catholic Movement in England* (London, 1962), p. 189.

[2] Thomas Joseph Brown (1798–1880), Benedictine, bishop of Newport and Menevia 1850, a very conservative bishop who had denounced Newman's 'On Consulting the Faithful in Matters of Doctrine'.

[3] José Emilo de Santos, Spanish writer; cannot be identified further.

The Bp of Plymouth[1] told Dr. Clifford in the hearing of Case,[2] my informant, that he believed, since the Cardinal's condemnation, the H.&F. was looked upon with favour by the laity of England. But that he did not know how it wd be after all the Bps. had spoken—

Ward[3] I discouraged as not significant enough—I suggested Brownson, but I dont think he will do. Also Gioberti's posthuma, but Roberts seems not very willing—Cannot you suggest some subjects for a man strong in theories & in logic, & rather weak in facts?

487

ACTON TO SIMPSON · 3 OCTOBER 1862*

Friday

My dear Simpson,

The article on the Catholic parties can do no good unless it goes into the whole question, and only discusses our position as a part of it, and the latest and most significant phase in the conflict of adverse elements. I cannot make out why you think there is no alternative between speaking only of our quarrel, and omitting us altogether. The article would be good at any time, most of all now that it can be a diversion in our fight.

Wetherell exhorts you to nickname each of the 3 great divisions of English Catholics. The names would probably stick to them. You have an exquisite opening, if you do it with dignified moderation and not apparent malice. A few mistakes, natural to a Protestant reviewer, would be excellent. As that the Cardinal rebuked laymen meddling with theology after Ward's publication.[4] I shall not wait for your answer to write to Reeve, without naming you. Absolute secrecy is of course required.

I believe the bishops must have acted in concert, and all probably will say the same thing. Mine has sent nothing to Aldenham, but I have sent him the H&F. with a letter requesting his opinion, and intimating that he will not find anything to complain of *there*.

How as to Waters & Roberts?

Your's ever truly

J D Acton

---

[1] William Vaughan (1814–1902), bishop of Plymouth 1855.
[2] George Case (1823–78), converted 1850, a priest in the diocese of Clifton, later had difficulty in accepting the Vatican decrees of 1870.
[3] This paragraph is a fragment, very possibly belonging to an earlier letter.
* Watkin and Butterfield, p. 94.
[4] Wiseman had in fact supported Ward, a layman teaching theology.

ACTON TO SIMPSON · 6 OCTOBER 1862[*]

Monday

My dear Simpson,

I believe you will find only 3 *parties*. 1°. The old school, not warmed up by the C^{11} into devotion to Rome, and not intellectual or progressive —descendants of Milner,[2] Lingard, and even Butler,[3] so far as they all refuse, like chaos, to be converted. Their strength is in the North and in the midland counties. 2° Ourselves. 3° The zealous converts and those of the old set who are under $C^{1's}$ influence, the Romanists, lovers of authority, fearing knowledge much, progress more, freedom most, and essentially unhistoric and unscientific. But the elements are very various and the leaven of different sorts.

ad 1um The very old school of Berington,[4] the 'Staffordshire clergy,' long ago vanished. Something of its spirit survived in the Butlerites, who were simply Gallicans, and lovers of lay influence. Milner had almost succeeded in prevailing over these tendencies before Emancipation. The idea of the liberty of the *Church* was his, as distinguished from the liberty of *Catholics*, which they all desired. Liberty of the Church in the State involves authority of the Church in her own sphere—all liberty means the free exercise of authority in whatever is its right sphere. This separates Milner from Butler &c. who disliked the hierarchical system almost as much as the penal laws. To the Milnerite Catholics, pricked up by agitation and emancipation, enter (with a florish of trumpets) Dr Wiseman. Cetera norunt.

Converts are an element, a leaven, not a party. Puseyism sickly, one-sided, maker out of a case, set its stamp permanently on many, making them advocates, workers out of a view, aprioristae,—also devoted to authority, anxious for mental repose and no questions asked. Coming in they met the Roman current of the C^1 and the Dublin, the plausible defenders of everything, so called Ultramontanes, nursed by the spirit of Roman advocacy, and by the strong current setting in that way from France, in the Correspondant first, then in the Univers— and so there was the fusion we wot well of.

Now our party is made up of those converts who escaped the taint of

---

[*] Watkin and Butterfield, pp. 95–6.
[1] Cardinal (Wiseman).
[2] John Milner (1752–1826), ordained priest 1777, vicar-apostolic of the Midland district 1803, opponent of Gallicanism or 'Cisalpinism'.
[3] Charles Butler (1750–1832), lawyer, spokesman of the 'Cisalpine' lay Catholics.
[4] Joseph Berington (1743–1827), priest, also a 'Cisalpine' leader.

Puseyism in one of several ways, and of those natives who without losing the old English spirit of Milner and Lingard are educated enough to follow the advance of knowledge among Catholics abroad and Protestants at home. Preservatives ag^t Puseyism in the character of some men, like Hope,[1] in the historic mind of others, at least in Newman, Robert Wilberforce, Renouf, in the absence of ruling intellects in later Puseyism, which makes the later generation, like Oxenham and Wetherell much better than the older lot, in absence from Oxford, Stokes, Paley, in the impulse to study and research given by a latent scepticism, or by a not thorough heartiness of conversion in others. The more passive element of our party is in the old Catholics who have knowledge and honesty enough not to be humbugs, Tierney, Waterworth, Maguire etc. See: *Berington* on the State of Catholics. *Butler's* memoirs. *Milner's* Supplementary memoirs. *Flanagan. Husenbeth's* lives of Milner and of Weedall[2] (for extracts from *Weedall's* discourses) *Lingard's* Tracts, his A.S.[3] Church, his low views of the Middle Ages in account of Gregory VII, of Becket, of Joan of Arc, behind German Protestants, even behind Berington's Henry II. *The Catholic Journal* 1838–43, by MacDonnell and the Milnerites, Life of *Baines*. Perhaps life of *Doyle. Oliver's* Exeter priests, and his Jesuits.

Ever truly Your's
J D Acton

Which of the above am I to send you? I have not all. You should manage to pump Maguire.

489

SIMPSON TO ACTON · 8 OCTOBER 1862

Dear Acton

Block is not convinced by my arguments in the H.&F. p 416 sqq.[4] C'est trés bien écrit, c'est noblement pensé, mais selon moi (et beaucoup d'autres) le pauvre n'a pas un *droit* à être nourri. Ce n'est pas pour nous un devoir politique, ni un devoir légal de le nourri. mais seulement un devoir réligieux et humanitaire. Nous avons une obligation a remplir, *mais le pauvre ne peut nous y contraindre.* (Does this mean that we have

---

[1] Hope-Scott.
[2] Henry Weedall (1788–1859), ordained priest 1814, taught at Oscott, president of Oscott 1826–40, 1853–9, an 'old Catholic' who had been displaced by Wiseman.
[3] Anglo-Saxon.
[4] The concluding section of 'Victor Hugo's *Misérables*'.

no political or legal duties except to those who can constrain us? or only that the poor ought not to have a remedy in law against starvation?)

He is sorry that his *Puissance comparee* arrived too late (!) to be noticed in the H.&F. he bespeaks a réclame next time,[1] & promises one of us in the 2 Mondes, Debats, Temps, Correspondant, l'Union, & Monde. These last will be excellent, if they can be hoaxed into paying us a compliment.

Buck writes that he & Carpentier[2] (another Bolandist) consider the H.&F. to be "une des revues les plus instructives & les plus variées"— mais, he adds, de grâce, de la prudence, de la reserve, et un peu de misericorde. Hayti, très-bien but not complete enough on its ecclesiastical, or its present state. Renouf trois-fois très bien for Egypt. feeble for China—J'ai lu aussi Mss de Camb. C'est un converti qui doit avoir écrit cela. Un vieux Cat. trouvera cela difficilement intéressant. *Card. W. &c.* C'est une pièce écrite avec infiniment d'art, de prudence, de netteté, de dignité.[3] About Italy & the Pope & Cardinals generally he says—Non licet afflictionem addere afflicto. *Jetons un manteau sur notre père Noé.* He objects to some of my (& your) additions about Belgium, & I must soothe him—

"Pour revenir au Card. Wiseman—je ne pense pas que vous puissiez continuer à adherer à la doctrine qui enseigne qu'il y a en politique et dans toutes les autres sciences morales des principes absolus, autres que le dix commandements de Dieu. Il font y compter necessairement avec l'utilité, les interêts, parceque le but est le *bien* des hommes".

W ᵐ Eyre made almost this same objection. I had to answer suddenly, so I said that in morals as in physical & historical science, the method was a principle, & the method only gave universal results—That Aristotle was before the Church, & the Ethics of the Church were in an unscientific state till Aristotle was rediscovered, & a new method of arrangement & deduction followed; that now it was difficult to divide the two, & to say how much was pure Xtianity, how much Aristotle &c, & passed off the objection—Of course also one could come down with all Ward; that morals is an a-priori necessary science, like mathematics in its method, & near it in certainty—surpassing it in the self-evidence of its first principles &c. This however will be an objection, & it will behove us to have the answer ready.

I have begun to write on the Catholic parties. After I have done the article, I will send it to you; you shall judge where it is incomplete, & where it sins by too much detail. Then I will tell you what books I want.

---

[1] Block, *Puissance comparée des divers Etats de l'Europe* (Paris, 1862), was reviewed in *Home & Foreign Review*, II (January 1863), 266–8.

[2] Edouard Carpentier, S.J., not further identifiable.

[3] This phrase, referring to 'Cardinal Wiseman and the *Home & Foreign Review*', is cited by Acton to Döllinger, 10 October 1863, in Victor Conzemius, *Ignaz von Döllinger/Lord Acton: Briefwechsel 1850–1890*, I (München, 1963), 279.

It will be necessary to have a reference to some printed authority for every fact I advance not generally known.

Buck prays us to ménager him a little about the life of Grossteste—He wont say that he wont do it, but, actually, he has not the time.

Tell W.[1] to send me the *addition* so that I may pay the cheque in to his bankers as we agreed. It should have been done before this.

Yours ever truly
R Simpson

Wednesday—Oct 8.

The Jesuits think our article too complimentary to Wiseman in the beginning, & too independent in the end. Eyre however agrees that in our protest we have said all that any one could say who had had no definite accusations brought against him.

490

ACTON TO SIMPSON · 9 OCTOBER 1862

Thursday

Dear Simpson,

W. is just off to Edgbaston and Malvern.

Do you hear that the Bishops are going to sit in judgment on our article?[2] Shrewsbury[3] writes not angrily about it, and has issued an absurd but not violent address against the Rambler, as if it still existed, without naming the H&F. Cornthwaite's[4] seems the worst of all. Priests have read it from the pulpit in Yorkshire.

Don't forget to send Marisco[5] to F. de Buck. His view of our principles is a marvelous mystery to me.

I don't understand whether you quote Ward's doctrine for or against us. Your instance of Aristotle is quite right. Do they suppose there was no such thing as ἐπιστήμη as long as there was nothing to help the understanding but fragments of early revelation, or that there was no right and wrong in the Roman state?

It would be very curious to see an articulate theory made out of the vague feeling. The least the bishops can do is to produce it, whether by way of definition or of correction.

[1] Wetherell.
[2] 'Cardinal Wiseman and the *Home & Foreign Review.*'
[3] Bishop Brown.
[4] Robert Cornthwaite (1818–90), ordained priest 1844, rector of the English College in Rome 1851–7, Bishop of Beverley 1861, of Leeds 1878; a strong Ultramontane.
[5] Adam de Marisco (Adam Marsh; d. *c.* 1258), Franciscan theologian.

I hope to send you Whiggism[1] by the end of the month. My new agent comes next week. I think Whiggism will soothe the bishops, as on our own new principles it will give the church a more exalted part to play in civil society than any modern writer that I know has attributed to her.

Assure Block of his short notice in January, and of our high consideration. It would be amusing to see his réclames.

I remain
Your's truly
J D Acton

491

ACTON TO SIMPSON · 13 OCTOBER 1862

Monday

My dear Simpson,

Wetherell has probably told you that Ullathorne is writing a pamphlet against certain of your old doctrines,[2] but has not issued any denunciation.

Have you seen Roberts or Waters?[3] All that you gave me of Deutinger[4] is of no avail. It is all preliminary to Kant. Hume is discussed on the last page of it. You must have several pages more that must be left out.

Might not the paper be divided into Protestant Philosophy in Germany, and Catholic d° in a second article.

The first would then prepare the way admirably for the second—and the second would be rich in the account of Günther, of Baader, Kuhn, Kleutgen etc.

I have asked him for current short notices, and an article on Abelard, on whom his friend is printing a stout book,[5] which is likely to be very good.

I hope your Edinburgh paper is going on well. I have no answer yet from Reeve, who is perhaps not in England. Read your Spectator and London of this week.

---

[1] Acton projected a series of articles on his political doctrine, one of which was to be on Whiggism and Burke. This was not published.
[2] Ullathorne, *A Letter on the Rambler and the Home & Foreign Review* (London, 1862).
[3] Roberts did not publish; Waters, 'Parish Registers', was delayed until April 1863.
[4] An article on German philosophy.
[5] Heinrich Hayd, *Abälard und seine Lehre*...(Regensburg, 1863). Deutinger prepared a review of this, but it was not published.

Madden offers a paper on Galileo's torture. I have tried to win the man without pledging myself to the article. Ffoulkes writes on Ozanam.

Your's ever truly
J D Acton

492

SIMPSON TO ACTON · 13 OCTOBER 1862

Monday

Dear Acton

Could you answer the enclosed paper of questions?

I have got together such a lot of matter on Catholic parties that it will scarcely compress into an article—I shall write the affair so as to make it as long as a pamphlet—Then it can be made into an article by excision—And we can perhaps agree with Reeve that instead of his paying for the article, he shall print the whole, but only publish in the Review a portion, leaving Longman to bring out the unmutilated copy "Reprinted with additions from the Edinburgh Review"—

Mudie promises to put on the Home & Foreign[1] in Jan.y—

Have you seen the Spectator? they tell me there is a flamboyant article on the H.&F.[2] I have not seen it.

They have not got the "Catholic Journal" to w.h you referred me at the Museum. I supposed you meant the Orthodox J. but I see that Flanagan refers to the C. J.

Ever yours
R Simpson

Index to *Dublin* —
Reference to article on Digby's Lover's seat (1856)

————

Ib.

Did the Dublin ever write about "Development" before the publication of Newman's Essay in 1845? Did it review his University Sermons, & if so, did it touch upon the one upon the theory of developments?

————

The Tablet
When was it founded?

[1] To have it placed in his Lending Library.
[2] 'The Position of English Catholics', *Spectator*, 11 October 1862, pp. 1138–9, a favourable review of 'Cardinal Wiseman and the *Home & Foreign Review*'.

How did it get into Lucas' hands?

What were Lucas' chief points of programme?

What were his quarrels with the Cardinal?

(In 1848 about the diplomatic relations especially.

When did he go to Dublin & why?

Have you Wallis' prospectus for a return to London

July 17 1858?

After that date I have the Tablet filed.

———

The dates & salient characteristics of the Catholic organs before the Tablet—

Two[1] short notices—The one on Lucas is rather more religious that it should be, by way of protest aganst the suspicions insinuated by the "what next?" of the Saturday Review.

—I suppose you have seen the Article in the S. of Ag. 16 on the H.&F. Riethmüller really gives no data for a Catholic estimate of Lucas—so I think it is better to finish with his summing up, reserving what else is to be said for a future occasion.

I will write to Stokes if you like, but I do not see the slightest probability of his knowing about Lucas. Charles Weld knew him well—also Wallis—Macmullen knew something about him. D[r] Whitty[2] was one of his great allies. His Irish career can only be understood by Irishmen I should think—Perhaps O'Hagan would know about it.

493

ACTON TO SIMPSON · 14 OCTOBER 1862

Tuesday

My dear Simpson,

Here is Reeve's answer.[3] His suggestion about politics is an obvious one, as the political conduct of the Catholics is exactly parallel to their religious divisions, and it is natural for the Edinburgh to inquire into that.

---

[1] It is possible that the following paragraphs (on a separate sheet from the rest of this letter) belong to a letter of late August 1862.

[2] Robert Whitty (1817–95), ordained priest 1840, vicar-general of the archdiocese of Westminster 1850–7 and provost of the pro-cathedral 1852–7, joined Society of Jesus 1857.

[3] Concerning Simpson's projected article on Catholic parties for the *Edinburgh Review* (eventually 'Milner and his Times'), for which Acton supplies the information requested in the previous letter.

Compress, I beseech you, your matter into 32 pages. He will give monies. Whether afterwards it grows into a volume is another question altogether.

The Catholic periodicals I know of are 1. The Orthodox Journal, for which see the Life of Milner. 2 The Catholic Magazine and Review—edited by the priests of Birmingham—Macdonnell[1] C. about 1833—liberal, almost radical—but only in politics—Milnerite in doctrine. 3 Dolman's Magazine—1838–43 or so—conducted, I believe, by Price.[2] 4 The Dublin. 1836—

The Tablet cut no figure before Lucas, who began it 16th of May 1840 —I don't think it existed before. See Riethmüller

I never read it till about 1857, & do not know where to get Wallis's declaration. I don't even know when Lucas carried it to Dublin. It must have been about Xmas 1849. It was Irish politics made him hate the Whigs, and elaborate the theory of independent opposition, out of the ruins of which, being a party of *opportunists*, Catholic Toryism grew up. Lucas's address to the Pope, which I have seen, is the clearest and amplest statement of the whole system attacked in the H&F. However he did not succeed with the Pope, and Newman in a letter to me[3] draws a striking picture of the desolateness of his stay at Rome. So discountenanced Ind. opposition had no resource but to become Tory in the wake of foreign Catholics. All Catholics not men of principle however liberal their profession, have a tendency that way—so Montalembert.

As to your article on Catholics: I am in communication with divers of the Old School for materials respecting Milner. If I get them (I have not asked for a *review*), could you not make them up, with your superabundant materials, into a picture of Milner and his times, with a sort of supplement, touching only on internal matters, down to our's? It ought to be extremely objective and quiet, not making points etc. For April. Taking care not to betray the same hand.

Ever Your's
J D Acton

1 Thomas Michael McDonnell (1792–1869), ordained priest 1817, in charge of St Peter's, Birmingham, 1824–41, editor of the *Catholic Magazine* 1831–6, canon of Clifton 1857; politically active, often in conflict with bishops.

2 Edward Price (1805–58), converted c. 1825, ordained priest 1832, editor of *Dolman's Magazine* 1846–9, of the *Weekly Register* 1849–50, resigned after he criticized image-worship.

3 Newman to Acton, 31 December 1858, in C. S. Dessain, ed., *The Letters and Diaries of John Henry Newman*, XVIII (London, 1968), 561, on Lucas' abortive mission to Rome to defend the Tenant League against Archbishop Cullen.

SIMPSON TO ACTON · 15 OCTOBER 1862

Oct. 15

Dear Acton

Roberts will not be in Town till this day fortnight when he has promised to talk to me about writing. He is "pleased with the article on the Cardinal." Waters dines with me next Tuesday, to talk on a like subject. Macmullen & Wenham were here yesterday. Mac has ratted to the extreme of oscurantism. His reasons are two. 1. Roma locuta est in a way, or at least all the Bps have spoken. 2. He is a tory & hates above all things scientific Whiggism. He liked the Rambler, because it was *personally* independent (the only independence he tolerates) & tolerated it because its sallies were founded on humours, not on principles. It was a toss up whether the offensive statements would not be contradicted next month. Now however the opposition is reduced to a principle, & that principle is detestable. He utterly denies that there are such things as political truths, & avows himself an Imperialist, not democratic on the French system, but autocratic on the Russian or Austrian (?) &c &c He is still disposed to be personally very goodnatured, & promises to defend us as good Catholics, which he says he has done within a week to Manning—but at the same time he has inoculated M. with the notion that the new abomination consists in having formulated in to a principle what was before a series of unconnected sallies. M. told him he was never more taken aback than at the way in which the R. had treated him from top to bottom, when all the time he had been a good friend of the R.

Wiseman had not read the article up to last Saturday—Todd thought it everything that could be desired. Wenham thought it very respectful & so on; but after all my dear Sir &c &c—He was not well influenced by Mac, & especially by F. Capes, who came out in our defence just as our worst enemies might wish.

J. M. Capes thinks that we buttered H.E.[1] too much—that we have a very difficult game—that H.E. does not hold all the trumps—& that we are about to experience *furens quid femina possit.*

Let me keep Reeves letter a few days. I send you by this post a 54 sides of my collections for the article—give me your criticisms upon them, telling me especially what to leave out for the Edinburgh, & what to amplify for a volume—if you think such a vol. worth working at. I am afraid I shall not be able to go on just yet as I have a good deal of Trust business on hand & have to meet lawyers & parsons.

[1] His Eminence (Wiseman).

Many thanks for your notes—How does Pythagoras get on? The art on the Cardinal puzzles every one about its authorship. Your thoughts but not your style—Wenham said "I could never get through an article of A's—this I could not leave off—It can't be his." Mac. a priori said it must be written by the Coryphaeus. No one seems to think of the possibility of one man supplying the stuff another, or rather others, the verbiage.[1] Altogether it is a great success.

Ever yours faithfully
R Simpson

I suppose I am to conclude that you have furnished W. with money to pay the writers, as he will not send in the bill to me.

495

ACTON TO SIMPSON · 16 OCTOBER 1862

Thursday

Dear Simpson,

I think of running up to town tomorrow for some business. Drop a line to say whether I should find you at home before 12 on Saturday, for $\frac{1}{2}$ an hour's chat.

Your article will be extremely good, but much more H&F. than Edinburgh. I do not see why you should not simply make it into an article called Three Generations of English Catholics,[2] using the materials I hope to get on Milner, and the sketch of foreign Catholic parties I propose in the accompanying. It would be very long, at least 40 pages, if complete, as it ought to be, but it would follow up our exposition of principles most effectively. Down to p. 22 It is unfit for the Edinburgh and again farther on. Pp. 26–28 are not suited for us, but the rest would very easily be translated into our language. You could evidently touch upon much in the H&F., that would not do in the Edinbro'. It would define our position better than a more political article. Pray consider this.

Offers and promises of articles are crowding in upon us—

Macmullen is too bad. I expounded the Home & Foreign theory to him a year and a half ago—on the other hand a man who is not *homme*

---

[1] This is conclusive for the joint authorship of 'Cardinal Wiseman and the *Home & Foreign Review*', with Acton supplying the material which was rewritten by Simpson and Wetherell. Cf. *Wellesley Index*, I, 550.

[2] It was eventually entitled 'Milner and his Times' and published, as Acton suggested, in the *Home & Foreign* rather than the *Edinburgh Review*.

d'élite has no business to agree with us. He can only do it from indifference or ignorance.

Have you asked JM. Capes about his article on Oliphants life of Irving?[1] It is a subject for him.

> Your's ever truly
> J D Acton

Indeed I gave W no money, and it is very late. Contributors came to about 40£—I gave him the figures.

496

SIMPSON TO ACTON · 17 OCTOBER 1862

> Friday

Dear Acton

I shall be at home all the morning tomorrow—Saturday—Trains from Victoria to Clapham (L. Chatham & D. Co.[2]) 9.40, 10.35, 11.10, 11.25—

Your notion about the 3 generations of E. Cats.[3] exactly coincides with what was growing to be my opinion. It will be more difficult to adapt the end than the beginning; certain pet characters of mine—the Cardinal, Ward, & Manning, will have to go out. Perhaps however the author may make a pamphlet of it in an enlarged form, "reprinted from the H.&F." with a notice that the conductors of the Review have nothing whatever to do with the reprint, & are in no wise responsible for the additions—

> Ever your faithfully
> R Simpson

497

SIMPSON TO ACTON · 20 OCTOBER 1862

Dear Acton

I have taken Capes to task for what he says about the sale of the Dublin. He has brought a thing to my remembrance that justifies him. In 1858 we were at a fête champêtre at Joseph Hasting's, the lawyer.[4]

---

[1] Not published.
[2] The London, Chatham and Dover Railway.
[3] English Catholics.
[4] Not identifiable.

There we met Bagshawe Senr. I think I attacked him first about the sale of the Dublin, & he then & there offered it to us as Proprietors of the Rambler I think for £1000, & another £1000 for copyright of back numbers, articles in hand & "plant." We said that the price was monstrous, & could not bargain on such terms with a Review wh. notoriously could not pay. So there is no stopping Capes who certainly only tells the truth in the matter—The thing never made much impression on me, because I think I forced the talk on Bagshawe, & therefore he may say he was unprepared, that he spoke without book, & that all was subject to the Cardinal's future agreement. Still no doubt I spoke to him on account of previous overtures made to you—

By the enclosed you will see that I want to find something about the *politiques* among the English Cats, temp Eliz. I am convinced that they were among the hangers on of the French ambassador—The Papists were Exspaniolated. The loyalists were quiet men in their counties. The *politiques* affected the patronage of a court where Bodin[1] was a great man, & an ambassador, or rather attendant on a French Prince, in England. Has Teulet an index? There ought to be something in him. I have borrowed Sir J. Throckmorton's[2] two letters, & from them I shall be able to make a much better account of the real status of the lay-party —But if I can trace them through James II & his Jesuits, through a party of Jesuits *temp* Cromwell, up to the *politiques* who hung about the French court it will be a good foundation to put them on.

Look at the indexes of Barclay—Not his *de Potestate Papae* wh. I have —but any other books.

Ever yours faithfully
R Simpson

Monday.

How about Noggs?[3]

Waters dines here tomorrow to talk about Salop.[4]

I have just read Sir J. Throckmorton's letters 1792. He makes out that from the time of publication of Pius V's Bull to his day there have existed 2 parties among Eng. Cats. The *protesting* or loyal party, and the papists.

To these I must add a third—*les politiques*—who sometimes approached one side, sometimes another, using the natural tendency of Ultramontanes to identify their religion with a political cause, and appealing to the interest of the protesting set at certain conjunctures.

---

[1] Jean Bodin (1529/30–96), French political philosopher, was for a time in the service of François, duc d'Alençon.

[2] Sir John Throckmorton (1753–1819), succeeded to baronetcy 1791; member of the Catholic Committee, opposed to Milner; wrote two letters (1790–1) to the clergy on the appointment of bishops.

[3] Newman.   [4] 'Parish Registers.'

These have from the first, at various times, shown a tendency to unite with the non-conformists against the Ch. of Eng^d, first to extort a toleration, & secondly to destroy it.

Geo. Cranmer,[1] in his lre to Hooker (H's works., ed Keble, ii. p 605) does not identify the "godless politics" with any section of Catholics. But they are so identified in a contemporary book on Catholic parties of the reign of Eliz. of wh. I have notes wh. I cannot find now.

In the library at Brussels is the journal of the English Jesuit House at Ghent; in the time of the Protector the Jesuits are continually writing from Eng^d upon the policy of sacrificing religion for royalism, and recommending making a common cause with the puritans. That ass Flanagan has not a word about the conduct of the Catholics under Cromwell. Have you any books about it?

Then came the first general identification of interests between Catholics & Dissenters under James ii. Do you know anything about this?

Out of this clearly grew the "Protesting Catholic Dissenters" of 1780–91. Sir John Throckmorton was then coryphaeus. Are there no papers w^h w^d throw light on the matters at Buckland? The man who could write those two lres must have made a very good historical collection. Besides, Berington died at Buckland—Are his papers in the possession of the family?

One wants more foundation of this kind to build the first of the 3 generations of Cats. upon.

498

ACTON TO SIMPSON · 21 OCTOBER 1862

Tuesday

My dear Simpson,

I send you a few tracts, but have not time before post to look through everything. I rather suspect the independent party you speak of were not very zealous Catholics—which would reduce their representative value.

James' policy threw Catholics and Dissenters together—see Macaulay —but the later laws fell heavily on the Catholics only. For a wise distinction between them see Burke's speech, imperfectly preserved, on Dissenters, 1791. Burke is always in favour of Catholics tho' differing from their general politics, which he considered Tory.

I greatly doubt the importance of making such profound researches into the 17th century as you would be obliged to do, for matter to which

[1] George Cranmer (1563–1600), pupil and friend of Richard Hooker, wrote a letter *Concerning the New Church Discipline* (1598) which is reprinted among Hooker's works.

you could not give above a page. Could you show any continuity between 1688–1778? I doubt it.

I don't know about Berington's papers. The Throckmorton collection is not rich. I have gone over it.

I suppose you know all about the elder Bellings,[1] and the scheme which some Catholics accepted and others rejected—The position then was exactly the same as that of the lay party 60 years ago. Howley's[2] speech on Catholic Relief might have been delivered in Charles II's time.

Have you looked at Dod-Tierney, Butler, Milner, Arnauld on the Popish Plot, and the State Papers? I find nothing in Teulet but the antagonism of French and Spanish influence. Abundant matter for January—look over the page.

Your's ever truly
J D Acton

We have the following promises to choose from.[3]

Wetherell ——	Volunteers
Monsell–O'Hagan ——	Ireland
Block ——	Spain's Revival
Lathbury ——	Cotton
Arnold ——	Albania
Roscher ——	Perin's Political Economy
Ffoulkes ——	Ozanam
O'Hagan ——	Recent Poets
Sullivan——	Scientific Exhibition
MacCabe——	Christmas
Deutinger ——	German Philosophy
Madden ——	Galileo
Paley ——	English Scholarship
Ephrem[4] ——	Sanctity
Acton ——	Frederic II
Simpson ——	Three Generations

---

[1] Sir Richard Bellings (d. 1677), Irish royalist, wrote a history of the Irish rebellion (not published until 1772).

[2] William Howley (1766–1848), bishop of London 1813, archbishop of Canterbury 1828; an opponent of Catholic emancipation.

[3] Of these, the following appeared: Monsell, 'University Education in Ireland', *Home & Foreign Review*, II (January 1863), 32–58; Block, 'The Material Revival of Spain', *ibid.* 59–83; Lathbury, 'Cotton Cultivation and Supply', *ibid.* 1–31; Wilhelm Roscher, 'Périn's Political Economy', *ibid.* 84–100; Sullivan, 'Scientific Aspects of the Exhibition of 1862', *ibid.* 101–28; MacCabe, 'Christmas Customs and Superstitions', *ibid.* 129–51; Acton, 'Confessions of Frederick the Great', *ibid.* 152–71; Arnold, 'Albania', *ibid.* III (July 1863), 52–70; and Simpson, 'Milner and his Times'. O'Hagan wrote the Irish 'Current Events' for January 1863 (pp. 302–4).

[4] Dom Ephrem Guy.

SIMPSON TO ACTON · 23 OCTOBER 1862

Oct 23

Dear Acton

I send you another 50 sides of my collections[1]—I cannot write on Manning till I have read something more of him, & I cannot read till I have borrowed. I have written to Roberts to point out his most characteristic writings & to lend me them—

Academy[2] next Tuesday at York Place—Manning reads on "the attitude of England towards the Xtian society of Europe"—Has there been any article stuffed with facts on this subject in any German paper lately—If so I would that you would lend it me. I sh^d like amazingly to contradict some fact. I meet Manning & Wiseman at Macmullen's on Sunday—Mullens dined here on Tuesday with Waters

Waters said—If you quarrel with the Cardinal you should make it amusing, like the Saturday. If you make it argumentative everybody who cares to read it will take the Bishops' side. I take the Bishops' side —Mac pricked up his ears, & praised his parishioners greatly—Yes rejoined Waters, for I dont care a button for the Cardinal & all the Bishops to boot. They may quarrel with whomsoever they choose & I certainly shall never read a word they say. Mac was quite shut up by his Gallio. But I shall jeer at him for his excellent disciple—Of course that is the kind of man w^h his system tends to form.

Waters will write on Salop, & on the Catholic members of the College of Physicians[3]—I told him I did not know that either could go in in *Jany*

Ever yours faithfully
R Simpson

If you have sent any tracts, none have come. Not a word from Wetherell to whom I sent our calculations—directed to the care of Ld Charles Thynne—that is right is it not

———

Miss Kavanagh has published "French Women of Letters" & now "English do"—Both parts of one whole "to show how far from the last two centuries & more, women have contributed to the formation of the modern novel in French & English literature? — Who can write an article on the subject?

[1] For 'Milner and his Times'.
[2] A meeting of the Academia of the Catholic Religion.
[3] 'Parish Registers' (dealing with Shropshire) was published; the other article was not.

500

ACTON TO SIMPSON · 24 OCTOBER 1862*

Friday

My dear Simpson,

All my horses and all my men have been busy carting away the trees knocked down by the wind all over the place, so I was not able to send the books till today.

I have received three new articles since I last wrote, one by an Irish landlord on Irish land,[1] one by Woodlock on Irish parties, cookable and acceptable, and one against the Trinity, which I propose to pass on to the Dublin. Clearly we shall reject more than we shall accept for January. Have you seen Ullathorne's pamphlet?[2] Lo! the view of one of his priests, on 2d thoughts I send you Formby's pamphlet[3] instead of his letter.

Your materials are getting superabundant. I hear nothing of Wetherell in reply to my many important letters and fear he must be ill.

I am afraid I have nothing handy for the refutation of Manning. Why not let him have his say? I also have received my invocation to the Academy. Pray don't commit yourself in discussion respecting our future course. Be sure all you say is much and dishonestly repeated. You can't be too amiable to the Cardinal, in the flesh as well as in type.

Waters is profoundly wrong. We don't quarrel with these good people, and don't want to hurt or weaken them – only to be left alone. Therefore no sting and no fun.

But I am very glad he is writing. We might have Salop for April. Does he want any notices? Has he got the histories of Ludlow, Shrewsbury and Bridgenorth?[4] Has he read in Smiles' Engineers the life of the man who built the Ironbridge? Has he traced Charles II from Whiteladies to the Severn ford at Madeley? Has he read Baxter's autobiography for this part of the country? Dugdale for Wenlock and Buildwas? The lives of the Clives and the Hills? Does he know the man who lived 207 years at Bridgenorth? That old man must do good service in founding the University.[5] Has he read Blakeway's Sheriffs of Shropshire, and

---

* Gasquet, Letter CXXXVII, p. 293, misdated 'October 21', with extensive omissions.
1 This may be O'Hagan, 'Tenure of Land in Ireland', *Home & Foreign Review*, II (April 1863), 346–73. The other two articles were not published.
2 Ullathorne, *A Letter on the Rambler and the Home & Foreign Review* (London, 1862).
3 Henry Formby published two books in 1862: *The Life of St. Patrick* and *Pictorial Bible and Church-History Stories*, III: *Church History*. The latter was reviewed by Acton, *Home & Foreign Review*, II (January 1863), 215–19.
4 The detail of this paragraph owes much to Acton's being a Shropshire landowner.
5 Acton was considering the idea of a Catholic University in England, situated at Bridgnorth to take advantage of the proximity of his library.

somebody's all Round the Wrekin, and a history of foxhounds to know about old Squire Forester? And has he got all the ghost stories about Acton Burnall?

If Mrs. Bastard was well she should write on Miss Kavanaugh.[1] But she is quite disabled, I fear. Will Capes do a light article for April on the two first volumes of Kinglake's Crimean War?[2]

Ever Your's
J D Acton

501

SIMPSON TO ACTON · 28 OCTOBER 1862

Oct 28. 62

Dear Acton

Has any report of me, tending to state my determination of the future course of the H.&F., reached Northcote & Ullathorne? If so, it could only have come through Coffin, who sent for me, talked as my parish priest & old friend, & got out of me, not what the H.&F. was going to do, but what *I* was going to do. I told him that for my part I had been so abominably treated by all his party that from henceforth I should never be amenable to the persuasive pressure that they had formerly found sufficient to make me do what they liked, but that I should never think of listening to any thing that did not come to me in official shape, & in canonical form. And I enlarged on this, but without a single reference to the H.&F. solely with regard to my own connection with it, & to my ceasing to write in obedience simply to their hinted wishes, enforced by refusals to hear my confession & the like.

I should like to find out whether Coffin wrote about this to Northcote, as he wrote about the affair of conversions in Syria;[3] because if he has done so, I have power to give him a very hard slap in the face to encourage him—He looked over, corrected, & approved my letters on original sin[4] wʰ Ullathorne pitches into, & the bare mention of the fact, while it would be an element in my defence, would get him into a great row with his superiors. I should not like to do it because it would look vindictive, perhaps might *be* so, but it seems hard sometimes to have to be told of

[1] Julia Kavanagh, *English Women of Letters: Biographical Sketches* (London, 1862).
[2] This article (by no means 'light') was in fact written by Lathbury.
[3] See Letter 449 n. 1.
[4] Simpson ['R.P.S.'], 'The Immaculate Conception viewed in connection with the Doctrine of Original Sin', *Rambler*, 2nd ser. iv (July 1855), 25–37; 'On Original Sin as affecting the Destiny of Unregenerate Man', *ibid.* v (May 1856), 327–45; 'R.P.S. on the Destiny of the Unregenerate, in reply to J.S.F.', *ibid.* vi (July 1856), 28–47.

one's bumptiousness in pulling out, without submitting to a theologian, all kinds of crude theories, without replying that it was done with the encouragement & approval of the man who is trying to take a leading part against us now.

How are we to answer Ullathorne? In the H.&F. or out of it? After our promise of retraction[1] we are obliged to say why we cannot do it in this case. I am much tempted also to apologize to U. for not having put my quotation from the Fathers into inverted commas, so as to have saved him from the accident of condemning St Augustine, and from putting himself within the anathema of the same father—

Robson's bill this time is 104 instead of 84£. 22£ corrections, 12£ night work—About 4£ for reprinting certain copies—I am going to pay it today. Let us hope that Williams and Norgate will let us see some of the proceeds of the sale in January or I shall have to draw upon you again—I shall have paid for this no. 104 + 58 + 33 (paper) + 8 (Block) + 9 (books for Buck & the postage you wot of) = 212: Of this about 20 would have been saved by being ready in good time, & correcting, not so much the proofs as the MSS.

Ullathorne has no right to return to R.P.S.[2] He gave it up when he exacted out of Capes my retirement from the editorship in 1857;[3] & again when we gave up to Newman in 1859; I called upon him with St John, & the understanding certainly was that all byegones should be bye-gones if I then submitted—I did so, & he only knows best how I was forced back into the position w^h I twice sold to him for a condition w^h he has twice infringed. For those letters the Cardinal named a commission of 3 theologians to sit upon me, & the conclusion was that I was to withdraw from the controversy & that he in return would withdraw the commission.[4] Not to mention Ullathornes entire falsification of what I said, he is a manifest treaty breaker in dragging *that* controversy to light again—I should like to publish my letter to the Cardinal on the occasion of my withdrawal from the controversy, in order to show how he was contented with three merely verbal corrections w^h had nothing to do with the real questions at issue.

Ever yours faithfully R Simpson

---

[1] The statement that, if anything in the *Review* was contrary to Church doctrine or disrespectful to Church authority, 'we sincerely retract and lament it'. 'Cardinal Wiseman and the *Home & Foreign Review*', p. 447.

[2] The letters on original sin.

[3] Simpson had been acting editor of the *Rambler* from October 1856 to January 1857.

[4] For the near-condemnation of Simpson in 1856, see Altholz, *Liberal Catholic Movement*, pp. 33–4.

ACTON TO SIMPSON · 31 OCTOBER 1862*

Friday

My dear Simpson,

I have heard no report from Northcote or anybody else. But you surely cannot suppose that everything you say will not be interpreted in the most hostile sense, or that it will not be altered in passing from mouth to mouth, or that it will not be considered to commit the H&F.

If I was you I would use the weapon you have ag^t. Coffin only in terrorem. I have not seen Ullathorne's letter yet, but I suppose the H&F. comes in for its share. Now so far as I see my way I am decidedly against any public answer on the part of the review. I was against answering the Cardinal and see much stronger reason against answering Ullathorne. Newman writes a singularly absurd letter,[1] saying that Ullathorne's is the voice of the church, that there is no opposition or explanation possible, and seems to ask what we mean to do. He tells Arnold he means to submit in the fullest manner. I can only tell him that the Review will not combat or resist the censure.

The only thing I can do is this: Sooner or later I shall either hear from my bishop,[2] or have an opening to write to him about Ullathorne. Now I ought to be able to explain to him why the blunders and faults of his episcopal brother make it impossible to make any public acknowledgement.

Ever Your's truly
J D Acton

Plenty of cash whenever it is wanted.

503

SIMPSON TO ACTON · 31 OCTOBER 1862

Oct. 31.

Dear Acton

Herbert[3] has been here, & asks me to tell you that the greatest favour that could be done him would be to procure him an interview with Lord

---

* Gasquet, Letter cxxxiv (out of order), pp. 289–90, with omissions.
[1] Newman to Acton, 29 October 1862, in *Letters and Diaries of Newman*, xx (London, 1970), 332–3. [2] Brown of Shrewsbury.
[3] Of the several possible Herberts, this is most likely Sir Arthur James Herbert (formerly Jones, of Llanarth) (1820–97), entered army 1839, served in Crimea, lt-col. 1855, served in Corfu until August 1862; quartermaster general 1882–7, knighted 1882, general 1885.

Granville, about his candidature for a Queen's Messenger. I suppose he relies on his own powers, & that he thinks that when he makes the offer of his talents to the country the country cannot but accept it. At least if after such an interview he does not get what he wants he can only blame himself for not getting it. I cannot make out whether he has had any losses, or whether it is only the prospect of another family by his second wife that has reduced him to look about for employment.

Have you read Ullathorne? I never saw a more knavish imposture. Roberts is going to do the answer to the original sin part of the business.[1] The quotations from science & faith[2] are either garbled & misinterpreted, or, only misinterpreted, throughout. The Bishop makes it a practice to omit from the sentences which he condemns just those words which would prevent him from putting upon them the sense which he condemns in them. I am anxious to hear whether the pamphlet is to be answered in the review or not? It would be difficult not to make it over long, but one need not answer all the points—

Ever yours
R Simpson

Have you seen the "London" on O'Hagan?[3] I forsee so much work in Block, the three Generations, the rewriting Pythagoras,[4] & *making the Index* (w[h] I have begun) that I positively can do neither short notices nor current events for the next N°—especially if Ullathorne is to be added to the work.

There have been two schemes of the Dublin[5]—One under a counsel, H Thompson for editor—this broke up chiefly through Wenham, who was on the counsel, & insisted that Bagshawe should be there too. Now Manning & Ward are to be joint editors, & T. W. M. Marshall for sub —at least Ward has taken a house for a month at Brighton, it is suspected for the purpose of offering that place to him. This I heard at Roberts' where I dined on Tuesday. Mac prophesies of the Dublin that it must increase & we decrease, for that an opposition review against all the B[ps] could not possibly succeed in Eng[d] Can we not do something to win some of them?

Send me back the enclosed sketch of Charles Weld's

[1] This was not published.
[2] 'Reason and Faith.'
[3] The *London Review* for 25 October 1862, pp. 364–5, had a favourable review of 'Perraud on Ireland'.
[4] Respectively, 'The Material Revival of Spain' (which had to be translated), 'Milner and his Times' and an unpublished article on Pythagoras.
[5] To provide a new editorship for the *Dublin Review*, now that Bagshawe had finally resigned.

ACTON TO SIMPSON · 2 NOVEMBER 1862

Sunday

Dear Simpson,[1]

I can say nothing before I see Ullathorne.[2] I am obliged to go to town tomorrow on a sick call, but only for a day, and shall probably not be able to see you.

All that seems to me perfectly clear is that U. cannot be *answered* in the H & F.

As to winning over some of the bishops: There are who say that the greatest obstacle to an understanding is your constant introduction of religious topics. I do not say this myself, because I believe my objectivity and indifference is profoundly hateful to the English Catholic mind. For this however there is no hope or remedy, because the one thing needful is to accustom people to the method and spirit of truth-seeking. But they do not learn this from articles written on religious subjects and not in a scientific manner. I say not scientific because I have argued over and over again with you that you cannot speak confidently on the philosophy of mythology, that you have neither overcome all the difficulties of the original authorities, or mastered the results of all modern researches. Now it is perfectly possible to write on subjects of which you will have this complete mastery. These will be useful even if they are offensive, and need not be offensive. The others are always both offensive and of little didactive use.

I do not think I exaggerate the real importance of this element in our difficulties. If it is hard to make a sacrifice of pet inquiries, then I would say that the whole scheme requires grievous sacrifices of us all, sacrifices of time, of our good repute, even of personal influence. Do not underestimate the enormity of the difficulties before us. We are the flying fish who can neither swim with the Protestants or fly in peace with the Catholics. Our ground is fearfully narrow to build up a great literary and political organ upon. The balance must be preserved with exquisite nicety. There is no room for any indulgence.

If you think I have no right to be anxious about this; consider what the past has brought me in one week.

1. A letter from a promised contributor of January declaring his acceptance of Ullathorne's censure, and his horror at what he finds was published in the Rambler.

---

[1] It is possible that this letter was not sent. Much of this matter is repeated in the next letter.   [2] *A Letter on the Rambler and the Home & Foreign Review.*

2. An elaborate critique of about twenty propositions of your review of Darnell[1] by Newman, forwarded by Arnold with the declaration that he thought the article just like Essays & Reviews.
3. Information that the H & F. was taken into the pulpit and preached upon in Birmingham Cathedral last Sunday.
4. Wetherell's resignation on the strength of some remark or report of your's.
5. Newman's assurance that Ullathorne speaks as the voice of the church, and must be believed.[2]
6. My final condemnation by those nearest and dearest to me,[3] in consideration of the evil repute I have acquired at Rome. and in the background my bishop coming up with a profession of sympathy with his Birmingham colleague, and a request for prompt and dutiful submission. So you see there is not much to fall back upon, and no great comfort but the consciousness of having committed no imprudence.

Papers indeed pour in on all sides. We have above 20 offered for January. The last candidate is Döllinger.[4]

I have met all the announcements that were immediately pressing as well as I could. W. and our contributor, and Arnold relent. I have, in Arnold's opinion, sufficiently answered the critique of your article, and I am playing off Brown against Ullathorne[5] in writing to Newman, and hold Döllinger in reserve. I think it however still possible that Newman may repudiate us entirely this time—

In spite of these difficulties of detail I believe we have the game in our hands if we make no false move, and if we fail, the fault will be amongst us three.

There can be no Pythagoras and 3 Generations[6] in one number, so you will not have quite so much work. What you leave undone abroad I will do as well as I can: France, Greece, Mexico ! ! ! ![7]

I will do what Herbert wishes as soon as I get to Town. Did you receive the Catholic Magazine?

Your's ever truly
J D Acton

Have you conferred with W. about the Index? He says the London was Ox.[8]

---

1 'Döllinger on Heathenism and Judaism.' See Newman to Wetherell, 6 October 1862, and to Arnold, 11 October, in *Letters and Diaries of Newman*, xx, 290–2, 294–7. 2 Newman to Acton, 29 October 1862.
3 Acton's relatives, the Arco family of Munich. An attempt appears to have been made by Msgr Nardi of the Curia to prevent Acton's marriage with Marie Arco.
4 Döllinger, 'The Waldensian Forgeries', *Home & Foreign Review* ii (April 1863), 504–30.
5 I.e., Acton's bishop against Newman's bishop.
6 'Pythagoras' was not published; 'Milner and his Times' appeared in April 1863.
7 This refers to 'Current Events'. Acton only wrote 'The Greek Revolution', *Home & Foreign Review*, ii (January 1863), 319–25.
8 Oxenham wrote the review of O'Hagan in the *London Review*.

ACTON TO SIMPSON · 4 NOVEMBER 1862

Brookes'
Tuesday

Dear Simpson,

I have just run up to have myself examined by the Drs. and am off again, too soon, I am afraid, to be able to see you. I called on Lord Granville to prepare him for Herbert's visit, but found that he had gone to Dorsetshire for some time.

I have seen no Ullathorne yet, but cannot conceive that it would be wise to answer him in the H&F.

Don't you think that your determination to write on religious subjects is an obstacle to the conciliation of any bishop? I do not think I exaggerate its importance, for I know that the scientific idea alone would be enough to horrify them. But that is unavoidable, as it is the one thing we are good for, to teach people that faith is no reason not to think. We have so many sacrifices to make of all kinds, of time, of our good name, and even of personal influence that it seems hard to suggest another. But our difficulties are really enormous.

Two January contributors have written about Essays & Reviews,[1] and shown themselves rampageous. These I have pacified. Newman wrote a long criticism on your review of Döllinger, which I dealt with at least to Arnold's satisfaction. But now he is ostentatiously accepting Ullathornes voice as the voice of the Church, and asking what we mean to do. We may lose him altogether this time. Then I have had all manner of difficulty in inducing the obstinate Wetherell to withdraw his resignation.

The only comfort is that we have had above 20 articles offered for January, and shall refuse enough to make a very improved number of the Dublin.

Döllinger promises an early paper on the Waldenses.[2]

Ever Your's truly
J D Acton

[1] I.e., that the *Home & Foreign Review* was repeating the faults of *Essays and Reviews*.
[2] 'The Waldensian Forgeries'.

SIMPSON TO ACTON · 5 NOVEMBER 1862

Wednesday

My dear Acton

We must satisfy Newman if we can. Ullathorne leaves us a way open. He not only quotes, but he explains us. We can abjure his explanations, subscribe ex animo the propositions he brings forward against us, and disclaim the intentions which he fixes on us. We can express our grief that it should be possible to take our words in such a sense. As to the Original sin, we can say that 3 theologians appointed by the Cardinal examined that paper, & none of them read the propositions, in that sense: moreover that the writer took due pains to state the doctrine correctly, and that his propositions are simply & word for word translations from Perrone—whom we may quote. Then may follow the other sentences from St Augustine &c—Then we may say that it is quite possible by collocation &c to make the Fathers say what they did not mean to say, quite as possible in fact as to make us say what we never thought of. And so conclude. It might all be done in two pages without a single retraction in fact, & might be prefixed as an advertisement to the Review & published as a letter in the Catholic papers.

I repeat that nothing can be more disgraceful than Ullathorne's paper—Roberts mocks at it. I wont write a word on religion any more; I have begun to write the article on the 3 generations of Catholics, & I think I shall be able to avoid saying anything of my own[1]—What can be done to push the Review in Ireland?

Ward is sole editor of the D. He is to publish his 1st no. in July. He has three censors. Russell, Manning & Eyre. He is cock-a-hoop about Newman, whom he hopes to catch. N. tells him that unless we retract we must lose all sympathy—that Ullathorne is something like a Bishop, & that he delights in such hard hits.

I hope you are not bad. As for Wetherell, he is almost as difficult as Newman. His resignation was all through my chaffing him about Macmullen's attributing the censured passage to him.

Ever yours truly
R Simpson

---

[1] This remark represents the abandonment of the idea (originally Acton's) of an article on the present state of Catholic parties and its transformation into the historical 'Milner and his Times'.

SIMPSON TO ACTON · 10 NOVEMBER 1862

Nov. 10. 1862

Dear Acton

I send you my translation of Block's article[1]—I have not read it over, so there are probably words omitted here and there—will you alter the phraseology or mark where it wants altering. I send you his letter, in order that you may answer for yourself the question whether any more tables are wanted, & also that you may consider whether at the end we should say something about having so entirely ignored the religious side of the question—The increased N° of bastards—1 in 5—does not argue well for the moral resurrection of the country—I wonder whether Collingridge would give a supplement to this article on "the religious state of the Peninsula", compiled like this from official returns & adding Bishops' pastorals.

Have you read Ullathorne yet, & have you made up your mind how he is to be treated?

I dont know whether the history of the last 90 years *can* be kept off religious topics as much as you would wish—all that I shall bargain for therefore will be that the article[2] should be cut about, altered, postponed, or rejected, exactly as you think best, without the slightest reference to what you fancy I should like—The difficulties are too great & the stake is too valuable for any merely literary feelings to stand in the way. Do you know anyone who knows, & is willing to laugh at, Edinburgh literary coteries? If so, let him do Mrs. Gordon's life of her father, John Wilson.[3] Christopher North seems to me the founder of that mystical Edinburgh school w[h] judges of literature on grounds not merely literary, and adjudges us southerners to be a lot of nincompoops who cannot understand the feelings or the words of a jolly giant who could drink a quart of whiskey at a pull, & whose sentiments were so acute that he made it his habit to go into hysterics before his class whenever he was reminded of his departed wife —The "reign of terror" of Early Blackwood[4] is well illustrated by correspondence—Lockhart[5]

---

[1] 'The Material Revival of Spain.' [2] 'Milner and his Times.'

[3] Mary Gordon, *Christopher North: a Memoir of Professor Wilson, late Professor of Moral Philosophy in the University of Edinburgh*, 2 vols. (Edinburgh, 1862), was reviewed by Simpson, *Home & Foreign Review*, II (January 1863), 260–4. (Not attributed in *The Wellesley Index*.) 'Christopher North' was the pseudonym of John Wilson (1785–1854) in the Tory *Blackwood's Magazine*.

[4] William Blackwood (1776–1834), publisher and editor of *Blackwood's Magazine* 1817–34.

[5] John Gibson Lockhart (1794–1854), contributor to *Blackwood's Magazine*, editor of the *Quarterly Review* 1826–53.

appears as the "scorpion", & carries off his character well. What a thing it w^d be if you could get Hope Scott to do the book, or to give private information from family papers or the like that would help in it. The line to take would be, the necessary connection of the scandalous school with Toryism, as personal disloyalty is the natural counterpart of personal loyalty just as bad principles are the counterpart of good principles. Hence absolutist or Tory controversy must always be black-guardly & vituperative, Whig controversy may be unfair lying, un-principle, but must ever at least pretend to principles. The partizans of an absolute Pope must denounce every one that does not condemn the Italian revolution as a knave & a fool; only the believers in law can afford to allow for both sides—but this example may be suppressed. Wilson is one of the best types of Tory that can be imagined, so genial & yet so violent, & so utterly chartless & compassless that after being Professor 20 years he had still no principles of ethics, but was always talking of putting a bottom to his philosophy. His only lectures that are remembered are busts of ditty rambic rhetoric that have as much to do with ethical philosophy as with rifled guns—

Ever yours faithfully
R Simpson

508

ACTON TO SIMPSON · 14 NOVEMBER 1862

Friday

My dear Simpson,

I have sent Block[1] to Wetherell. There are some things you will correct as a matter of course in revising. It will be well to say a word at the end as to religious &c. statistics and as to their relation with the others. I am sorry he has omitted criminal statistics, but otherwise I think there are figures enough. I would even shorten the early historical part, omit the first account of the Mesta,[2] &c.

Collingridge knows nothing about Spain. I asked Wetherell to ask a Scot for a review of Wilson (Lockhart, de Quincy &c) but he failed. Hope I fear could not do much. Pray make your remarks into a short notice to begin with. I hope the 3 generations[3] are prospering—Of course it is not a subject that can be treated without any reference to theology.

I have seen the substance, I suppose, of Ullathorne's letter, and am as clear as I can be that it is better not to answer it in the H&F. It would

---

[1] 'The Material Revival of Spain.'   [2] The Spanish sheep-herding monopoly.
[3] 'Milner and his Times.'

be necessary to meet every point, or those which we omitted would be admitted. There would be no end to the controversy in which we should be involved with the episcopate. I beseech you not to insist on answering him in the Review. I quite agree with you that it is a most absurd production. My people are here & distract me.

Your's ever truly
J D Acton

How about Spanish measurement? I believe *Fanega* is sort of bushel— and Fanegada is the measurement of surface.

509

SIMPSON TO ACTON · 15 NOVEMBER 1862

Saturday. Nov. 15

Dear Acton

I send you the first part of the three generations.[1] It is only a comparison of the opinions of Berington Butler, Milner, & Wiseman. I am going to add Newman. You see that I have quite omitted the political part, & confined myself to Ecclesiastical politics & tone. I thought that the political part would be quite enough for another article—At any rate, I am too stupid an historical writer to be able to combine the two into one essay of any reasonable proportions. I am very much dissatisfied with it, & am quite ready to have it rejected.

I quite agree about Ullathorne. Shall I send you his pamphlet?

I have written to Block to get the criminal statistics.

Ever yours faithfully
R Simpson

510

SIMPSON TO ACTON · 19 NOVEMBER 1862

My dear Acton

The boys name is Stewart. I cannot find out however whether any cards have been sent round yet, but I will let you know in time—The election is not till March, I believe[2]—

---

[1] 'Milner and his Times.'

[2] This paragraph is not clear; it may possibly refer to a scholarship election.

When you have 10 minutes I should like to know about the H&F.
I have left off work & am idle now till I know your decisions—

Herbert was here yesterday to ask whether he might call on L^d
Granville—

Block has sent some criminal statistics, which I will send to Wetherell
as soon as my idle fit allows me to translate them

Ever yours faithfully
R Simpson

Wednesday

511

ACTON TO SIMPSON · 21 NOVEMBER 1862

Friday

My dear Simpson,

I have written to Ld Granville, but I find he is out of town again. He
will probably pass this way before he returns to town and will be prepared for Herbert's call.

Wetherell has sent off the last of Block's article[1] to the printers, where
you had better insert the criminal statistics.

He has also got Christmas and Ozanam[2]—neither of them satisfactory
articles. I have a paper on political economy: pray send me *Périn's
Richesses*.[3] I have also done 35 pp. of short notice. You know Volunteers[4]
are put off to April, alas!

Why are you idle? Are you not finishing the 3 generations?[5] I like what
I have got very much, and will send you by Monday morning a perpetual Commentary, which I have not had time to finish. The general
criticism would be that you do not write history en masse, but cling to
persons and particulars.

Are you going to answer Ullathorne separately, so far as you are
attacked? If not will you not give me materials for a note to my Bishop,
briefly but pointedly showing up his episcopal brother, and giving the
reasons why we do not answer?

Ever Your's truly
J D Acton

---

1 'The Material Revival of Spain.'
2 'Christmas Customs and Superstitions' was published; 'Ozanam' was not.
3 Roscher, 'Périn's Political Economy'.
4 Wetherell never published his intended article on the Volunteer movement.
5 'Milner and his Times.'

SIMPSON TO ACTON · 24 NOVEMBER 1862

To be shown to y^r B^p if
you like—or to *any one else*

Dear Acton

I enclose a letter about U's pamphlet. On Saturday night I began an answer in detail,[1] & have already written 45 sides. I surprise myself to find how utterly & entirely wrong he is in every single instance.

I will finish the three generations as soon as I have finished this.

Block says—

Si vous voulez avoir un correspondant à Turin, je vous en indiquerai un (je ne sais pas s'il sait l'anglais, mais il sait le français) c'est un directeur au ministère des finances, qui ne manquera pas de m'être agréable s'il en a l'occasion.

Answer by return what I shall say. I think I must print a pamphlet against Ullathorne—It is so very smashing, & yet there is not an injurious word throughout.

Ever y^{rs} R Simpson

Monday

Remember a puff of Block's Comparative Statistics[2]—We have promised, we must perform

513

SIMPSON TO ACTON · ?24 NOVEMBER 1862

Dear Acton

Dr Ullathorne's pamphlet[3] from p 11 to the middle of p. 36 is directed against my articles.

He has entirely mistaken the scope of the two articles on faith & reason;[4] they are directed against the rationalist theory that comes out in such books as "Essays & Reviews" or in Colenso;[5] hence they begin with the mere rudiments, & strive to build up the idea of faith by a

---

[1] This was eventually published as *Bishop Ullathorne and the Rambler* (London, 1862).

[2] A review of Block's *Puissance comparée des divers Etats de l'Europe.*

[3] *A Letter on the Rambler and the Home & Foreign Review.*

[4] 'Reason and Faith' in the *Rambler.*

[5] John William Colenso, *The Pentateuch and Book of Joshua Critically Examined* (London, 1862), was, like *Essays and Reviews* (London, 1860), a controversial work of biblical criticism.

succession of accumulations, ending at last with the supernatural grace which is the chief element of faith. Dr U. takes each of these separate accumulatory parcels as if it were intended to be a complete definition of faith, blames each for leaving out the notion of grace, & when he comes to the passage where I treat of grace, accuses me of not knowing the difference between gratia creatoris & gratia salvatoris—a distinction which I acknowledge, though for my controversial purposes it is sufficient to bring my opponent to own one species, because that granted the other is implied.

This general misapprehension seems to have led him to adopt a prejudice against my statements which has entirely blinded him to the rules of ordinary criticism & grammar, and leads him to garble my words in the most unjust manner. His first quotation from my articles (pp 11 & 12 of his pamphlet) one adduced to show that I begin with eliminating his confidence from the *legitimate* teachers of the Church. In order to make my words bear out his construction he has omitted a sentence in which the names of Dr Cumming[1] & Dr Pye Smith[2] occur as persons against whom I am writing.

He next says it is untrue that "divines have supposed" a certain theory to be true. He seems to forget the logical rule about distribution. When I say that [some] divines do a thing, he does not contradict me when he says that some Popes do not do it.

His interpretation of my words are in *every single instance* unfair. E.g. the expression, the "inward core" of the faith, w^h he supposes I use for the invisible realities of faith only, I use in the only place where it occurs for the central pillar of revealed dogmas round which human opinions are clustered. See his own quotation from me at the top of p 26. The core being the revealed dogma, the rind the popular & changeable opinion. I could go over all his 25 pages, with the same objections to every single interpretation which he puts on my words. His whole deduction I protest against as unfair; illogical, & only to be maintained by garbling my words, applying my sayings to dogmas when I have expressly limited them to evidences, misinterpreting my philosophy of the understanding & reason, and (as in the quotation at p. 27) quoting what I put into the mouth of an objector as my own.

This is what he accuses me of doing in regard to Suarez.[3] I have done no such thing. I understood Suarez when I quoted him; Suarez says that of the species (phenomenon) there is not faith but experience, whereas

---

[1] John Cumming (1807–81), M.A. (Aberdeen) 1827, minister of the National Scottish Church in London 1832–79, D.D. (Edinburgh) 1844; frequent controversialist with Roman Catholics, also wrote on apocalyptic prophecies.

[2] John Pye Smith (1774–1851), congregationalist, tutor at Homerton College 1800–51.

[3] Francisco Suarez (1548–1617), Spanish Jesuit theologian.

faith is of "the truth & Substance of that which is seen". This is all that I say—And St Hilary whom D. Ullathorne condemns in a sentence I quote from him (p. 29. "St Thomas puts his finger &c) says the same. On this subject I try to say that Dr U. is very unjust in concluding that I do not believe the facts of the incarnation &c because I say that the element in the facts which is the subject matter of faith is not the visible phenomenon but the invisible substance.

At p. 31. (bottom) is a sentence w^h Dr U. has put altogether in italics, as being very wicked. This is not mine but St Augustine's.

At p. 32. is another instance of an objection w^h I adduce in order to answer being quoted as my own.

At p. 34 I am condemned for denying that original sin comes by propagation, whereas in the sentence quoted I expressly assert that it is inherited by natural propagation. My sentences which Dr U. condemns are literal & verbal translations from Perrone,[1] & the doctrine which he censures is no other than Spondrati's which Bossuet moved heaven & earth to have condemned, but which Rome persisted in refusing to censure. However, we have in Dr U. a less considerate censor. Dressed in his little brief authority, he plays fantastic tricks which people who know more & are less angry will pause before they play.

I have written a refutation at length of D^r U's pamphlet, so far as it regards me. My only hesitation in publishing it is that it unmasks so very disreputable conduct on the part of a Bishop that some scandal may arise. But I think it is very weak in me to be moved for a moment by such considerations. Melius est ut scandalum oriatur quam veritas tegatur.

Ever yours
R Simpson

514

ACTON TO SIMPSON · 25 NOVEMBER 1862*

Tuesday

My dear Simpson,

Your letter will be useful, and I will use it en temps et lieu. Ullathorne says that he hears he is to be ignored, so, as he has his hand in he will just finish off another pamphlet[2] at once, so as to crush the Review. I

---

[1] Giovanni Perrone (1794–1876), entered Society of Jesus 1815, professor at the Collegio Romano 1824, the leading theologian of the day.

* Gasquet, Letter cxxxviii, pp. 294–5, with omissions and minor errors.

[2] Ullathorne did publish On Certain Methods of the Rambler and the Home & Foreign Review: A Second Letter to the Clergy of the Diocese of Birmingham (London, 1863). Although published after Simpson's reply to his first pamphlet, it takes so little notice of the reply that Ullathorne may well have written it earlier.

don't know whether this will be against the H&F. only—which would in some degree alter our position. If it is also against you, you ought to wait for it, I think. Only keep your plans to yourself, and let not Roberts blab.

I should be in favour of the Turin financier. It ought to be done through Block, not engaging to print off bodily his communications, offering a proportionable remuneration, desiring facts and particulars, explaining that the Review is equally Catholic and liberal, and not of Passaglia's[1] school. Pray use your discretion. Döllinger has just been told by the Nuncio that I have been at Turin concerting measures with Passaglia—whose pamphlet[2] is very unsatisfactory.

I begin to think that the 3 generations may stand over to April[3]— to end our model number, which that is to be. You might then work a little at Events and notices. For we stand thus:

Perin's Political Economy	Roscher
Irish University Education	Monsell
Material Revival of Spain	
Albania	
Cotton	
Three Recent Poets	OHagan
CLASSICAL Scholarship in England	Paley
Confessions of Frederick the Great	
Ozanam	
Stanhope's Life of Pitt	Capes
Christmas	
SCIENCE and Industry	Sullivan

Four are in hand. TWO are due next week[4]
I look forward to a grand April number, for which see next page.

Your's ever truly
J D Acton

Volunteers	Wetherell
Land question in Ireland	OHagan
The Teutonic Alliance	Frantz[5]

[1] Carlo Passaglia (1812–87), Italian priest, formerly Jesuit, leading proponent of the dogma of the Immaculate Conception, professor of moral philosophy at Turin 1861, an opponent of the Temporal Power, suspended *a divinis* 1867.
[2] *Plurimonium ex Italiae Clero ad Pium IX...Petitio* (Turin, 1862).
[3] 'Milner and his Times' was delayed until the April number.
[4] Of this list, 'Périn's Political Economy', 'The Material Revival of Spain', 'Cotton Cultivation and Supply', 'Confessions of Frederick the Great', 'Christmas Customs and Superstitions' and 'Scientific Aspects of the Exhibition of 1862' were published in January 1863; 'Albania' was published in July. The others were not published.
[5] Konstantin Frantz (1817–91), German Protestant political philosopher.

Position of Austria	Price[1]
Revolution in Greece	Finlay
Shropshire	Waters
Lyell on antiquity of Man ⎱ Celtic Literature ⎰	Sullivan
The Waldenses	Döllinger
Mary Stuart	A and Weale[2]
Art at the Exhibition	Pollen
Pythagoras	Acton
Three Generations	Simpson[3]

Besides other things by yourself, Renouf,[4] Block,[5] De Buck, Deutinger, Ryley (Marine Insurance),[6] Monsell and many others.

If the 3 gen. are postponed pray short notice Husenbeth.[7] Don't let us bid against each other at Tierney's sale.[8]

515

SIMPSON TO ACTON · 27 NOVEMBER 1862

Dear Acton

I have written to Block about the Turin Correspondent—This note I write to ask whether it would not be better that I should publish what I say against Ullathorne without you or Wetherell seeing what I write, so that I may say in the introduction that the Editor & Subeditor of the H.&F. have seen nothing & know nothing of what I say, & that the pamphlet is written entirely without their knowledge or concurrence.[9] It is a kind of thing for which I wish to take the sole & undivided responsibility—

I am going to read it over to Coffin, if he will hear it, & to Roberts, &

---

[1] Bonamy Price (1807–88), economist, mathematical master at Rugby 1832–50, Drummond professor of political economy at Oxford 1868–88.

[2] W. H. James Weale (1832–1917), writer on art and architecture, keeper of the National Art Library, South Kensington, 1890–7. His *Bruges et ses environs* (London, 1862) was reviewed *Home & Foreign Review*, II (January 1863), 226–7.

[3] Of this list, the following were published: O'Hagan, 'Tenure of Land in Ireland'; Waters, 'Parish Registers'; Sullivan, 'Lyell on the Antiquity of Man', *Home & Foreign Review*, II (April 1863), 456–503; Döllinger, 'The Waldensian Forgeries'; Simpson, 'Milner and his Times'.

[4] Renouf wrote at least two short notices in *ibid.* 567–70, 596–8.

[5] Block wrote 'The Finances of the French Empire', *ibid.* 374–97.

[6] Ryley, 'Belligerent Rights at Sea', *ibid.* III (July 1863), 1–34.

[7] Simpson did not review F. C. Husenbeth, *The Life of the Rt. Rev. John Milner* (Dublin 1862), the subject of his 'Milner and his Times'.

[8] The sale of Tierney's books.

[9] See Simpson, *Bishop Ullathorne and the Rambler*, p. 3.

then publish it at once, without waiting for any more Ullathorne—He is too great an ass to make one take any pleasure in beating him

Ever y^{rs} truly
R Simpson

Nov. 27.
    Write at once about this.

516

ACTON TO SIMPSON · 27 NOVEMBER 1862

Thursday

Dear Simpson,

What you propose is much the best plan. I would rather neither Wetherell nor I should be a party to your answer, as we ought not then to shirk answering for the Review.[1] I assume you will answer exclusively for your own writings, and in saying that you leave the rest unanswered intimate that the Rédaction has decided not to take part in your answer. But this should be very briefly and barely stated, neither so as to imply contempt on our part for the Bishop, nor a disposition to avoid the difficulty by the pretence of a hypocritical reverence.

Did you say you were doing the Index? I think I told W. so, who is not doing it.

Your's ever truly
J D Acton

517

SIMPSON TO ACTON · 1 DECEMBER 1862

Dear Acton

I send you a Ms. quite worthless in itself, but which by dint of erasures may make a short notice. I will do Husenbeth,[2] & set to work on the Index. But nothing more this time.

I took my answer to Ullathorne[3] to the Printers on Saturday; we shall get it out about Thursday in next week. I have told Robson to send you & Wetherell proofs, which I hope you will have on Thursday. You will see if you have any objection to make.

---

[1] The *Home & Foreign Review* as distinguished from the *Rambler*.
[2] Simpson did not do this.
[3] *Bishop Ullathorne and the Rambler.*

Block you will see does not offer us a correspondent but only a puffer. What answer shall I make to him?

Do you know anything of the life of F. Colombière's[1] doings in England according to the enclosed, from Weld S. J.[2] to Weld of Chideock,[3] who passes on the question to me.

Ever yours
R Simpson

Monday.

About Ullathorne—You would not advise my sending him a proof would you? I have been urged to do so on pious grounds, in order that he may make due reparation without being publickly proved to be a liar & an ignoramus. But it would look like a threat as it seems to me.

Besides, I am afraid I shall never have so sweet an opportunity again of getting a Bishop's head into chancery, & I should not like to spoil it.

518

ACTON TO SIMPSON · 2 DECEMBER 1862

Aldenham
Tuesday

My dear Simpson,

I send you the Index, after having struck out un-numbered p's, and marvelled greatly at the persistency with which you ignore the orthography of the name of Stuart. Wetherell's criticism is that some articles, like Nationality, are regularly analyzed, while for instance Catholicism is cut very short.[4] Mine would be that the titles of books should be given exactly, not in summary or translation.

Is it any use sending you a few Errata? I would put in the titles if I could see any chance of getting through my work this week.

Ever your's truly
J D Acton

P.S. I suppose you have not sent a proof to Ullathorne, which seems unnecessary. I could find nothing about La Colombière when I had all the books about Charles II about me.

---

[1] Claude de la Colombière (1641–82), French Jesuit, assisted St Margaret Mary Alacoque in founding the devotion to the Sacred Heart, court preacher to Mary of Modena, wife of the future James II, 1676–81; beatified 1929.
[2] Alfred Weld (1823–90), entered Society of Jesus 1842, B.A. (London) 1847, ordained priest 1854, provincial 1864–71, held other Jesuit officies, dying on the Zambezi mission; an astronomer, F.R.A.S. 1849.
[3] Charles Weld.   [4] This refers, not to articles, but to subject headings.

Wetherell has your Wilson,[1] which ought to be either longer or shorter, as it is, it is a capriccio, but would squeeze into a very pregnant short notice. I have asked him to do it, but I am afraid he is getting ill again.

I would accept the local services of Block's Turin friend, provided it is made clear to him that we are not of the Piedmontese party, but liberals of a totally different description.

When shall you ask Block about the French finances?[2]

519

ACTON TO SIMPSON · 3 DECEMBER 1862

Wednesday

Dear Simpson,

Arnold offers a review of Venn's Xavier,[3] with Newman's encouragement—I have accepted, and sent him books, and pressed him to send it soon. Albania for[4] April.[5] Monsell (21) Sullivan (25) are at the printers. Cotton (12) so far as it is finished also.[6]

Your's very truly
J D Acton

520

ACTON TO SIMPSON · 8 DECEMBER 1862*

Monday

My dear Simpson,

I could not get through your pamphlet in time to write by today's post, and I am afraid I shall be rather late. I have no difficulty in writing about it, in the presence of what you say about W[7] & me, as I strongly dissent from a very important part of it.

You end by a sort of appeal to Philip sober and to the Holy See. Now the first is only a charitable figure, but the second is, to my mind, an

---

1 The review of *Christopher North*, the life of John Wilson.
2 'The Finances of the French Empire.'
3 Thomas Arnold, Jr, 'Venn's *Life of St. Francis Xavier*' (communicated), *Home & Foreign Review*, II (January 1863), 172–89.
4 Acton originally wrote 'Mar', but deleted it.
5 Arnold's 'Albania' was postponed to the April number.
6 Respectively (with the estimated number of pages), 'University Education in Ireland', 'Scientific Aspects of the Exhibition of 1862' and 'Cotton Cultivation and Supply'.
* Gasquet, Letter CXXXIX, pp. 295–6, misdated 'December 9', with major omissions.
7 Wetherell. The question concerned Simpson's dissociating his own responsibility from that of the editors of the *Home & Foreign Review*.

error. Under circumstances such as these, when the issue lies between the authority, veracity and theology of the whole hierarchy of England, supported already by Propaganda, and people obnoxious in the highest degree because of the temporal power which is in Roman eyes a question of existence, I should think very poorly of the chance of a just verdict. The inducement to decide wrongly would be extremely powerful, and the excuses and modes particularly copious.

1. They do not deem themselves canonically bound to hear or to consult an obnoxious writer that is a privilege of esteemed adversaries.
2. There is an enormous latitude for condemnation of what is offensive to pious ears, dangerous to the weak, open to misinterpretation, intended to bear a double meaning etc etc etc.

I remember how important I thought it to state in reply to the Cardinal[1] that Rome had virtually spoken, and that we were going on in despite of her. We are in a position which obliges us to defy the thunders of the Vatican. Rome defends the political and temporal rights and possessions of the Church by spiritual censures. We say that if there is politically a sound reason against them we must incur excommunication.

In this great point therefore you—in the pamphlet—and the H&F. part company, and you can safely say that there is no combination between us in terms as strong as you like to use.

Your third sentence unnecessarily implies a hazy responsibility which will seem inconsistent with what you say afterwards of W & me.

Proudhon's[2] name is misprinted at p. 23 and 24, and at p. 42. You call Cardinal Borgia[3] Spanish ambassador, which I did not think he was, but director of the Spanish interests.

I have not time or opportunity to look at Venn's Xavier.[4] But from the London Review I see there is an opening for the doctrine that missions require the way to be prepared by the civil power in the destruction of the fabric of pagan society & polity before they can succeed—This w^d be the defence of S. Francis's otherwise very impolitic letter to Portugal.

Your's ever truly J D Acton

---

[1] 'Cardinal Wiseman and the *Home & Foreign Review*.'
[2] Pierre Joseph Proudhon (1809–65), French social radical.
[3] Either Alfonso de Borgia (1378–1458), cardinal 1444, Pope Calixtus III 1455, or Rodrigo Borgia (1431–1503), cardinal 1456, Pope Alexander VI 1492.
[4] Henry Venn, *The Missionary Life and Labours of Francis Xavier* (London, 1862), including general comments on Roman Catholic missions.

SIMPSON TO ACTON · 11 DECEMBER 1862

My dear Acton

About the H. & F. & my pamphlet.[1] I certainly have one kind of responsibility in the article on the Cardinal.[2]—The responsibility of an accomplice. I have not that of Editor or Subeditor. In presence of this, can I honourably do what Wetherell suggests in the following extract from a note to me. "What I should aim at w^d be that you should disclaim *all* responsibility for anything that may have appeared in the H.&F. & that you should refrain from expressing agreement with, or a private knowledge about, the Review". I wish to keep out of Ullathornes spirit—that of lying; & if I disclaimed *all* responsibility I should hardly know how to reply to a cross examination.

I quite agree with you about an appeal. It was with me rather a form of words. I should have let any action go by default; the only thing I would have done would have been to express assent to or dissent from interpretation put upon propositions extracted from my writings. But a protest is as good. I will tell Robson to send you a corrected proof before publication.

I hope that you have a good haul from Tierney's preserves.[3] If you have, you must lend me the Orthodox & other Journals

I am afraid that my Index is a shabby performance. I will send it to Wetherell tomorrow.

Ever yours faithfully
R Simpson

Dec. 11.

522

ACTON TO SIMPSON · 13 DECEMBER 1862

Aldenham
Saturday

My dear Simpson,

I do not think Wetherell carefully considered his words, and it will not do to walk in the footsteps of the Bishop. But as it stands you actually imply a responsibility which can only confuse the minds of honest men,

---

[1] The *Home & Foreign Review* and *Bishop Ullathorne and the Rambler*.
[2] 'Cardinal Wiseman and the *Home & Foreign Review*.'
[3] The sale of Tierney's books.

and which others will think inconsistent with the allusion to the conductors of the H&F.

On the other hand can you stick to the statement that you have not concerted your reply with us if I declare my agreement with your revised text?

As long as I only made objections which I did not know whether you would accept it was well. But if I adopt your corrected proof there will be a slight contradiction. I am very glad however that you have not appealed.[1]

I got very little Catholic literature at Tierney's sale. The orthodox Journal fetched a fabulous price. But I got all Butler's works, and Berington's Tracts. That on Materialism might be interesting to you, as it is dedicated in terms of extravagant compliment to Priestley.[2]

Private

I have received this morning a long and very beautiful letter from Dupanloup, recommending a form of submission founded indeed on a misconception of our doctrine, but quite excellent from its ingenious vacuity. When I have time I shall send him a very nice answer. Moriarty[3] also sent a friendly message to the same effect.

This is a dreadful hard working week, and I have visitors besides.

Ever Your's truly
J D Acton

523

SIMPSON TO ACTON · 17 DECEMBER 1862

My dear Acton

I can have no objection to do what Wetherell recommends in the enclosed part of a letter.[4] Proprietorship implies property. Now the capital of the Rambler is, I suppose, spent, At any rate, Capes has rendered no account of it, & I hardly like to ask him for it, lest the surplus sh^d not be enough to pay off his £50.[5] Hence, there being no property, I can

---

[1] From Bishop Ullathorne to the Pope.

[2] Joseph Priestley (1733–1804), dissenting minister, supporter of the French Revolution; discoverer of oxygen.

[3] David Moriarty (1814–77), professor at the Irish College, Paris, 1839, rector of All Hallows College, Dublin, 1845, coadjutor bishop of Kerry 1854, bishop 1856; Newman's only friend among the Irish bishops.

[4] In order to dissociate the *Home & Foreign Review* from the odium of Simpson's denunciation by Ullathorne, Wetherell proposed that Simpson resign his joint proprietorship of the *Review*.

[5] Frederick Capes had a £50 share (out of £200) in the *Rambler,* and (although he took no part in the management) he presumably had a claim for that sum upon the *Home & Foreign Review.*

have no difficulty in renouncing the empty title of Proprietor. I do not know that Wetherell is right in his description of the arrangement between us; but, anyhow, I never expect or expected to make money as *Proprietor*; I only hoped that, in course of time, the Review would pay well enough to let me pay myself for what I wrote. When Burns made up his account in May 1859 I appropriated 30£ to myself, 30£ to J. M Capes, & 15£ apiece to F. Capes & you; leaving £200 capital to go on with—or rather 215 as you refused to draw your 15£. All this I left in F. Capes' hands. He has paid all the Printers' & Stationer's bills for the Rambler out of it, & the returns wʰ Burns has given him. Williams & Norgate have furnished him with no account yet, & of course he has given me none.

With the money you have given me I have paid the Contributors to the *Rambler*—Sub-Editor of Dᵒ—My expenses out of pocket for Mudie & Newspapers—And the whole expenses of the Home & Foreign except such contributions as you have paid. (from these expenses I of course exclude any charge for what I write, for wʰ I refuse payment till the concern flourishes—)—Williams & Norgate have as yet furnished no account of the H.&F. & paid nothing; so I shall have to ask for more money to pay for the coming number—The Stationers have already sent in a bill for £31, & my assets are much less than that, after paying Block, & Stewart for books for Buck.

Hence it appears that the name of Proprietor only means sacrifice & loss—to you of money & work—to me of work. The rose by any other name would smell as sweet. Let me be a friend of the Property—all that I bargain for is that I may still have the same right of refusing payment for articles till the Review can pay as I have now as Proprietor—For the rest, let Wetherell settle the business as it pleaseth him—

Oxenham's friend Bonus[1] has come to the conclusion which I augured for him. He has given up all missionary work, renounced the title of Revᵈ, & is learning to be a Sawbones at the London University, where, and *not at his lodgings*, he asks me to go & see him. You remember Henry VIII asking Cranmer whether his bed-room would stand the test of the 6 articles[2]—I must say I have some vague suspicion of a similar difficulty in the present case.

Sullivan[3] ought to be whipped for his careless English—in many sentences there is neither sense nor syntax—

Ever yours truly
R Simpson

Dec 17. over

---

[1] To the footnote on Bonus (I, 35 n. 3), it may be added that his Christian name was John, his dates are 1828–1907 and he was converted *c.* 1847.

[2] Thomas Cranmer (1489–1556), archbishop of Canterbury 1533, was secretly married. The Six Articles of 1539 required clerical celibacy.

[3] 'Scientific Aspects of the Exhibition of 1862.'

I beseech you to make a brief notice of Block's comparative Statistics[1]
—I promised him faithfully it should appear in the coming number—
Milner[2] I will not do. It is better that I should have no hand in the
contents of the present number.

524

SIMPSON TO ACTON · 19 DECEMBER 1862

Dec. 19.

I cant find Buck's note but he
says that he has taken great pains
with the notices, that if we dont
want them we are to send them back,
& that he will never write any more for us.

Dear Acton

With the enclosed Buck has sent me three (two) short notices 1. Anti-
quitates monast. S. Martini majoris Colon. Kessel. 2, 3. (in one) Die
Kirchengeschichte von Spanien.   P. B. Gams O.S.B.
Histoire Ecclesiastique de l'Espagne
(Same in French)[3]
As the time is far gone, I will send my translations direct to Robson
on Monday, unless I hear from you to the contrary on that date. They
will make perhaps 5 or 5½ pages. I have not begun them yet, or I would
send you a taste of their quality.

I have inserted the titles into the Index, but I have not analyzed
more articles. I chose for analysis those w^h seemed most H-&-F-ish.
Nationality & Renouf[4] to wit. The others I passed over as ephemeral.

I am in correspondence with Marshall[5] again—Grant got out of
Armenian Abp of Constantinople a denial that there was any Papal or
Episcopal Censure for missionaries receiving the abjuration of
Mahometans.

Marshall sent it to me, saying that it was put into his hands for publication, but w^d no doubt answer the purpose quite as effectually if sent to
me as if sent to the newspapers— "when you have read it you will judge

---

[1] The review of *Puissance comparée des divers Etats de l'Europe* is not attributed to
Acton in the *Wellesley Index*, I, 551.
[2] 'Milner and his Times.'
[3] *Home & Foreign Review*, II (January 1863), 223–5, 208–10 respectively. (Not
attributed in *Wellesley Index*, I, 551.)
[4] 'Nationality' (Acton) and 'The Earliest Epochs of Authentic Chronology'.
[5] T. W. Marshall, regarding the *Rambler* article on 'Marshall on Christian Missions'.

whether it makes any appeal to your conscience.... St Augustine published retractations & his reputation did not suffer by the process."

Hereupon I translated the letter, & added an appendix, showing how carefully the point at issue was evaded; I talked of "excommunication for attempting to convert"; the reply was there was neither Papal nor Episcopal censure against receiving abjuration—a thing w^h I had always distinguished.

I also quoted the authority of F. de Buck to show that such censures were sometimes made, not by Pope or Bishops, but by a religious order— as the Franciscans at Jerusalem are—

"When the Jesuits were in Russia they had a college in St Petersburg attended by the chief of the young nobility. The society made rules for the college, in w^h it was prohibited under pain of mortal sin, to attempt to make conversions."

Such a bye-law of the Franciscans, coupled with a prohibition of aliens from attempting to make converts within the Franciscan mission—such as the Jesuits had in Japan—would be quite consistent both with the veracity of Amherst & Whitgreave & with that of the Armenian Abp.

Grant replied that he had given Marshall the letter for the new Editor of his book, & deprecated the publication of my Ms. as it was only likely to lead to fresh discussions in w^h the merits of the question at issue w^d be forgotten.

I sent my Ms. & the Bps letter to Marshall, from whom I have another letter, full of the same preachments, & attributing the same offensive motives, but unable to see the point of my reply.

I have answered him in his own coin, telling him that my motive for criticising him, not the Holy See, was a belief that the cause of God was not served by want of truth, fairness, & equity, or by attacking others for what under another name we do ourselves.

One more point—I hope that you & Wetherell will not forget to maintain some point of moral, or if you like it, sentimental interest for me in the H. & F. when you do away with my shadowy material interest as proprietor. Otherwise, in spite of myself, I shall never prevail over my natural idleness to take the same trouble for it as I have done. There is much point in what Shakespeare makes the Clown say of Audrey— "A poor thing sir, but mine own"[1]—There are four positions that I can imagine

 Partner }
 Friend }
 Hack with pay }
 Hack without pay }

I will not be either of the two last. The difference between the two first,

---

[1] *As You Like it*, V, iv (inexact).

as we have always treated each other, is absolutely nil. But what would it be in case of some passing difference—for we are both men—? In that case the second would have the insecurity of the position of *amica* as opposed to *uxor*.

I think then that I had better give up the nominal proprietorship for a definite time, just as we let the Rambler on lease to Newman. We remained proprietors without any control over the Magazine. Wetherell wants me to cease to be proprietor. Well, let me deposit in your hands all my interest, control, &c &c for 6 months; subject then to a review of how we get on.

I cannot help feeling that in some respects I am *de trop*—Now I do not know how far, or by whom this is felt to be the case. While I am partner, of course I need not care a rap for such feelings. But once out of partnership, it would be my duty to care for them, & not to intrude, under pretence of the rights of a friend, where I have no right to be & am not wanted. What I should desire then is definiteness in any new position that may be assigned me. I could easily bear a position to be indefinite while I had rights. Where I have none, I must know exactly the extent of the charity on which I have to draw. You shall determine what this shall be—withdrawal for six months, for a year, for ever—or a position in all respects like that w^h has hitherto been mine, except the nominal withdrawal of the name of proprietor—

Ever y^rs
R Simpson

525

ACTON TO SIMPSON · 21 DECEMBER 1862

December 21

My dear Simpson,

I am sorry I have been too busy to write to you for several days, and that I am not in time to save you from the annoyance you must feel at your interpretation of Wetherell's letter, and from falling into the fault —not your own—of being unjustly suspicious.

Wetherell's notion is that the arrangement regarding the proprietorship is beneficial to nobody, and detrimental to the review. He takes this view more strongly perhaps than I do for several intelligible reasons. He gathers from Todd's letter that people play us off ag^t each other, and say things of us which in no way apply to him—Feeling himself innocent he thinks this irksome, injurious and unjust. Then he has a notion that our arrangement looks like a dodge, and that he is used as a mask to disguise our offensive alliance. He conceives therefore that a change might be made affecting in no way the reality of your influence or interest in the thing, but altering only what is at present merely nominal.

Although the reasons strike my more patient mind less strongly than Wetherell's, I have not opposed his plan, because I thought it might possibly do some good, and because I thought it out of the question that you could suppose I should be a party to any scheme really to diminish your influence, or to make the Review less your organ than it is.

The letter of Bishop Ullathorne[1] supplied a case in which it would have been very troublesome if you had not been able to distinguish broadly between yourself and the Review. The silence of the Review would justly have appeared cowardly and dishonest if it had put forth a partial answer in your name, and tried to unite the incompatible merits of having demolished the Bishop and having spared him.

All that I ever contemplated, or has ever been in Wetherell's thoughts, would be an understanding preserving your present position really intact, and sacrificing only the name of proprietor. I hoped this might be attained if I engaged to restore your property to you whenever you please. If then there should arise any question of conscience, or of opinion or of interest in which the free, voluntary, friendly relations between us failed to secure to you the power you would have had in the other character, you would have a right to resume it, and to suspend the arrangement now proposed. In that we are men the plan might prove defective. In that we are men of honour we should have the means of remedying it. The surrender would be on your part now, not on my part when you choose to return to the old plan.

There is an operation well known to those who embark in the Austrian crédit mobilier, which is called *arroser les fonds*, and consists in paying when the funds are low, so as to have a glorious return when they rise, at the Greek Calends. I only propose to discharge the functions of an *arrosoir* until the Review pays its way. I don't for a moment propose to produce the money you have invested in the concern.

But on the other hand you alarm me by hinting that any change would slacken your active interest in the Review, and by your extraordinary reason for not noticing Husenbeth.[2] I see no security against this unless you will give me the comfort of seeing you pay yourself for all you write. This is the second part of the scheme I should propose. I retract however the whole proposal at once if there remains on your mind the impression you speak of, that we cannot pull together now as

[1] *A Letter on the Rambler and the Home & Foreign Review.*
[2] *The Life of the Rt. Rev. John Milner.*

well as ever. All that I meant is, in your words—a position in all respects like that which has hitherto been your's except the nominal withdrawal of the name of proprietor.

Do I understand aright that De Buck is grumpy, or does he only say he will not write any more if his notices are omitted? There is no reason against inserting them, but I do not see how they exhibit particular care. As to the notion of Niehues'[1] nationality making him unfair to the popes it is preposterous. The only wise things written on the medieval papacy were written by Germans, and generally by Protestants. You might have appended a hope that his priesthood would not make him unjust to the secular authority.

We shall have 80 or 90 pages of notices, but a very dismal number on the whole.

I suppose you will take an opportunity of going to see Bonus. What an ass he must be?

I have half the Current Events to do before tomorrow night, so I write in grievous haste.

I remain
Your's ever truly
J D Acton

526

SIMPSON TO ACTON · 23 DECEMBER 1862

Dear Acton

Many thanks for your letter—I have done what I wanted, & given you the opportunity, for the good of the H. & F. to say the word which would decide my departure, which would I know in some respects be beneficial to the Review. But as that word is not said then let me have "a position in all respects like that which has hitherto been mine except the nominal withdrawal of the name of proprietor"—And let this position be kept quiet between you & me, so that Wetherell may not be annoyed at any uncertainty of his position with regard to me—i.e. let him be told that I have ceased to be "proprietor", but nothing further—

On these terms I will work as hard as I can for you, provided you will always *clearly* tell me what you want & what you do not want, so that I may not be troubled with suspicion that I am forcing things upon the Conductors which they do not really want.

As to being payed for what I write, I cannot stand it. I would take the

---

[1] B. Niehues, *Geschichte des Verhaltnisses zwischen Kaiserthum und Papsthum im Mittelalter* (Münster, 1862), reviewed by Acton, *Home & Foreign Review*, II (January 1863), 220–1.

money willingly if it came from legitimate profits. But I will not be watered so long as the waterpot is only filled from your private pump. On the contrary, I have rather hoped to bear some small share, out of my improved income—I have just raised it from 500 to 700—in the expenses.

As to not doing Milner[1]—I will show you my reason when we meet in the shape of a letter—I thought after it that Wetherell would much rather be able to say that I had written nothing, & had no share in this number, than that I should have made an insignificant contribution of a few pages.

You & I can pull as well together as well as ever, & I sincerely hope & trust that no cloud will ever rise between us. I & Wetherell could also pull together, but somehow it seems that Wetherell & I cannot & I suspect that Newman thinks, & has persuaded him that I am the black sheep & the terrible infant of the whole concern. I am a great fool for letting suspicions act upon me as they do, but I have a nervous temperament & cannot help it, however I conceal it in general; & in order to make me able to work I must be quiet in mind.

Your short (?) notices are excellent, & will redeem the number—Why did you not do Frederick ii?[2]

A happy Christmas to you

Ever yours truly
R Simpson

Dec. 23.

527

SIMPSON TO ACTON · 1 JANUARY 1863

Clapham Jany 1. 1863

Dear Acton

A happy new year to you.

Block writes—

Un article sur les finances de l'Empire[3] me va bien parceque j'ai réuni des renseignements extrèmement nombreux (peut-être tout ce qui existe) sur cette question pour un travail que je projette. D'ailleurs je me proposais de faire l'article pour le *Dictionnaire politique*[4] que je

---

[1] Neither the review of Husenbeth nor 'Milner and his Times'.

[2] This probably refers to T. L. Kington, *History of Frederick II, Emperor of the Romans* (London, 1862), reviewed by Acton, *Home & Foreign Review*, ii (April 1863), 613–14.

[3] 'The Finances of the French Empire.'

[4] Maurice Block, *Dictionnaire général de la politique*, 2 vols. (Paris, 1863–4).

publie en ce moment. Vous aurez l'article du 15 au Fevrier.—plutôt avant que apres.

Then he wants you & me to write him each an article for this "Dictionary". To you he assigns 2 or 3 pp. sur l'organisation de comtés en Angleterre—To me 2 pp on the poor laws. May I tell him that you will do both mine & your own?

I have had a talk with Wetherell about the 3 generations.[1] He puts his foot down like Lincoln on the necessity for ending at the hierarchy. from 1780 (Gordon)[2] to 1850 he thinks ample limits. His reason is, the necessity of avoiding any reference to Newman.

Of the paper w^h you have got, almost all that I say about Milner will go into a short notice of Husenbeth.[3] The rest I can make more impersonal & political. A fortnight at the Museum will answer a quantity of questions w^h I have framed.

How many of Plowden's[4] works have you? I bought yesterday his History of Ireland from 1800 to 1810 (3 Vols) for 1/6 — but there are lots more which I ought to look through.

Buck approves of the matter of my Ullathorne pamphlet,[5] but thinks the form & manner deplorable. Formby hopes that I will stick to the said form & manner, & so assert the right of the Xtian person to answer whomsoever in the same form as that in w^h he is attacked. Roberts, Macmullen, Doyle[6] approve. The latter, questioned by Grant, said that he thought I was not piquant enough. He told me that the B^p seemed more sorry that Ullathorne had given the occasion, than angry with me for having taken it.

Ullathorne is going to answer in a much greater pamphlet. He is very angry, & so will probably make a greater fool of himself. I have become acquainted with two of his points, & so am going to take the wind out of his sails by a postcript to a new issue. (I only had 250 printed at first, & they are nearly all gone)

I hope that you are hard at work upon Pythagoras. I think I could have improved Fred. the great[7] very much simply by inverting the whole, & beginning at the last page, & so working back. You seem to have exactly inverted the order in w^h the arguments should have been put out—

[1] 'Milner and his Times.'
[2] The anti-Catholic riots led by Lord George Gordon.
[3] Not published.
[4] Francis Peter Plowden (1749–1829), Catholic lawyer, published legal and historical works, including *The History of Ireland from its Union with Great Britain in January 1801 to October 1810*, 3 vols. (Dublin, 1811).
[5] *Bishop Ullathorne and the Rambler.*
[6] Thomas Doyle.
[7] 'Confessions of Frederick the Great.' 'Pythagoras' was not published.

But your Short Notices are first-rate. Old Robson is in raptures with you, & Levey[1] considers you to be an avatar of Bacon.[*2]

Ever yours faithfully
<u>R Simpson</u>

* NB he believes in Hepworth Dixon,[3] so there is no sting in the compliment

528

ACTON TO SIMPSON · 20 JANUARY 1863*

January 20th

My dear Simpson,

I have been losing my time on a visit to a crazy Lord in Cheshire. As it is I am in a fair way to be overwhelmed with work, and cannot see how I can manage what Block wants. Either you, which will be easy, write both articles, and let me annotate them; or let us tell Block where he may find all he wants.

His article on French finance will be most useful—The publication of the Matinées[4] cuts off the hope of Prussian contributors, such as Frantz. I must try to make up for it among the Grossdeutsch.[5]

I trust you will complete the Three Generations,[6] down to 1851, for April. It will be of the greatest importance to have that article in the next number if you can manage it. I cannot find anything of Plowden, but I will try to get you a pamphlet or two when I come to town.

Will it not be possible to get Waters's Salop[7] for April? It would be very desirable, if you can bring any pressure to bear on him. April ought to be a model number.

Of ten men who wrote 63 notices in January, I wrote 31. This must be more equally divided. I beg of you do as many as you can conscienciously. If you are doing a light article, let not that prevent you.

---

1 Robson's partner in the printing firm.
2 Francis Bacon (1561–1626), philosopher and scientist, lord chancellor 1618–21.
3 William Hepworth Dixon (1821–79), journalist, popular historian, and traveller; editor of the *Athenaeum* 1853–69; wrote *Personal History of Lord Bacon* (London, 1861) and two other works on Bacon.
* Gasquet, Letter CXL, pp. 297–8, omitting the first two paragraphs.
4 Acton had just published, as genuine, the spurious *Les matinées royales ou l'art de regner, opuscule inédit de Frédéric II, dit le Grand, Roi de Prusse* (London & Edinburgh, 1863). This gave great offence to the Prussian royal house.
5 Non-Prussian Germans.
6 'Milner and his Times.'
7 'Parish Registers.'

I read most of Kinglake[1] before it appeared. A splendid, mischievous performance, bottomed on much good political doctrine. It requires a showy article. Shall not Capes write it?[2]

over the page my dreams for April. Lord Stanhope has asked me to review him on human sacrifice[3]—so if I can do it he will talk about it. Shall we get anything from DeBuck?

Ever your's truly

J D Acton

Ultramontanism	S & A
Past and Future of the Volunteers	W
Present Position of Parties	Price
Tenant Right	O Hagan
Finances of the French Empire	Block
Albania	Arnold
The Art Exhibition of 1862	Pollen
Lyell on the Antiquity of Man	Sullivan
Human Sacrifice	Acton
The Waldensian Forgeries	Döllinger
Kinglake's Invasion of the Crimea	Capes
Three Generations of English Catholics.	S[4]

Also Waters on Salop,[5] Monsell on Irish politics, Sullivan on Celtic Lore, Capes on Pitt, Helfenstein on medieval education, Deutinger on German philosophy, Renouf, Simpson &c &c &c.

---

[1] Alexander William Kinglake, *The Invasion of the Crimea*, 8 vols. (London, 1863–87).

[2] Capes did not. Lathbury wrote 'Kinglake on the Causes of the Crimean War', *Home & Foreign Review*, II (April 1863), 398–432.

[3] This refers to Lord Stanhope, *Miscellanies* (London, 1863), one part of which dealt with the question of human sacrifice. Acton's review became a separate publication: Acton, *Human Sacrifice* (London, 1863).

[4] Of this list, the articles by O'Hagan, Block, Sullivan, Döllinger and S[impson] were published in April, along with Lathbury's 'Kinglake on the Causes of the Crimean War'. 'Albania' was published in July, along with 'Ultramontanism', *Home & Foreign Review*, III (July 1863), 162–206. Simpson's notebook observes that 'Ultramontanism' is 'much more Acton than Simpson'.

[5] 'Parish Registers' was the only article in this list to be published in April.

SIMPSON TO ACTON · 21 JANUARY 1863

4 Victoria Road
Clapham Common
Jan 21. 1863

Dear Acton

You have my sketch of the 3 generations;[1] send it to me with your annotations, & I will finish it forthwith.

I dont think Capes will do Kinglake. It wants a man who was up in the preliminaries of the war. Besides, C. is sure to disappoint you. What of the new current event man?[2] He did Cotton[3] so well that he might be trusted to do Kinglake too—except for the *showy*.

One Captain Robert Hall, just home from the Pacific is here—He has some ideas on the discipline of the navy that seem to me excellent—We have just been talking over the plan of an article[4] w^h strikes his fancy much, & w^h will I think come out well—it is

Comparison of regulations of 1844
    with those of 1862
History of the more important changes—
Tendency of these changes, with regard
to discipline & service, on
    officers
    crews
    manning the navy
    general efficiency

He is a great friend of Coles,[5] & will be able to get us full materials for an article on plated & cupola ships[6]—this for July—
W. on Volunteers[7] wont make our naval article out of place will it? I am rather anxious to book Hall, & make him strike while the iron is hot because he probably wont be at large long; he is beginning to look after another Ship, & then his pen will be wiped.

Wetherell must look after Waters. I am afraid that he overheard Mac-

1 'Milner and his Times.'
2 Lathbury, who did write 'Kinglake on the Causes of the Crimean War'.
3 'Cotton Cultivation and Supply.'
4 Hall, 'Naval Discipline and Efficiency', *Home & Foreign Review*, II (April 1863), 327–45.
5 Cowper Phipps Coles (1819–70), entered navy 1831, captain 1856, designed methods of applying armour plate to ships.
6 Hall, 'Iron-clad Ships', *Home & Foreign Review*, III (July 1863), 71–83.
7 Wetherell's article on the Volunteer movement was never published.

mullen telling me of his antecedents. Mac. is a horrid fellow for talking of his neighbors almost before they are out of sight, & long before they are out of earshot.

I suppose I may buy whatever blue books & pamphlets Hall wants.

I suppose from your signing "Ultramontanism" S & A. that you write as you wrote the Cardinal & H. & F.[1]

I have not known where to find you or I would have sent you some of my 2nd edition against Ullathorne[2]—

Roberts promises for October—an article on necessity[3]—

Ever yours faithfully
R Simpson

Can you help me with the enclosed? I wrote to Romilly[4] at the suggestion of Duffus Hardy[5] to ask for the publications of M. Rolls[6] for Buck & the Bollandists. Here is his answer. Hardy tells me that Romilly w[d] have done it at once, but Turnbull's matter[7] had made him so timid on all points of Catholic politeness, that he will do nothing except he is ostensibly ordered by his superiors. As soon as I can get anything like this from Buck I will ask him for the current events of Russia. But I have shocked him so by my treatment of Ullathorne that I am afraid I have estranged him for the present from the H.&F.

530

ACTON TO SIMPSON · 22 JANUARY 1863[*]

January 22[d]

My dear Simpson,

I have written to Gladstone to get Romilly the requisite authority.

I send the 3 generations.[8] Pray finish it carefully, and spare no pains. It will be a capital article.

---

[1] The article was to be primarily by Acton, with Simpson's assistance, as in the case of 'Cardinal Wiseman and the *Home & Foreign Review*'.

[2] *Bishop Ullathorne and the Rambler.*

[3] Not published.

[4] John Romilly (1802–74), barrister 1827, M.P. 1832–5, 1846–52, solicitor-general 1848, attorney-general 1850, master of the rolls 1851–73; created Lord Romilly 1865.

[5] Sir Thomas Duffus Hardy (1804–78), archivist since 1819, deputy keeper in the Public Record Office 1861; edited medieval sources, first editor of the Rolls Series, 1857–63.

[6] Master of the rolls, in charge of the public records.

[7] The dismissal of Turnbull as a result of anti-Catholic prejudice.

[*] The first part of Gasquet, Letter CXLI, p. 298, misdated 'January 23', with several omissions.

[8] 'Milner and his Times.'

Captain Hall on Naval Discipline by all means. Get him all official books and publications he may want, and encourage him in every way. Also on Coles's shield &c. for July, an excellent idea. Nothing can be better than these two articles.[1]

Tell me Waters's direction, and I will write to him.

I will supply materials on Ultramontanism,[2] and you literature and wisdom. Roberts on necessity, October, to be booked. Duffus Hardy crops up from time to time in your and Wetherell's letters. Will he ever be of any use to us?

Will you give me back those men whom you describe as the founders of our school in the 3 generations? I want them for Ultramontanism, where I propose tracing the true and the spurious pedigrees.

Your's ever truly
J D Acton

531

SIMPSON TO ACTON · 23 JANUARY 1863

Dear Acton

E. Chester Waters Esq
1 Wilton Crescent
W.

Of course you may have your pedigrees[3] back—I dont suppose that you want the Ms. but I send you back the sides. It will be more convenient for me simply to mention the three schools, with a reference perhaps to the "Card. Wiseman & the H.&F.R."[4]

I am cultivating Duffus Hardy, but I have not asked him to write. I don't quite feel my way to do so yet:

Hall went away to Southampton this morning, & promised to set to work at once—Wetherell imagines that he can get copies of the printed orders of the Admiralty through Lᵈ De Grey. It will not do for Hall to let it be publicly known that he writes, therefore he cannot apply for a sight of of the papers directly. For the rest, Wetherell says that Hall's paper cannot appear in the same no as the Volunteers.

---

1 'Naval Discipline and Efficiency' and 'Iron-clad Ships'.
2 The joint article on 'Ultramontanism'.
3 The sources of Ultramontanism and Liberal Catholicism. Acton was fond of constructing intellectual 'pedigrees'.
4 The article in October 1862.

Tell me where to find what Block wants; I will try to do two pp on each head,[1] & you shall correct them—Block is so civil to us that it will be politic to be civil to him.

Wetherell is very positive on the doctrine that Kinglake[2] must be done, & that you must do him—Why not?

Ever yours
R Simpson

Jany 23.

532

ACTON TO SIMPSON · 24 JANUARY 1863*

Saturday

My dear Simpson,

I don't want to deprive you of the men bodily, but only to avoid their coming twice over.[3]

I hope you will get Duffus Hardy some day. Bergenroth[4] would be the right man for us. I wish we could get a scrap from Brewer.[5]

Don't let Volunteers (which must come in April)[6] prevent the Captain from writing his two articles, for July and October. W will easily, I should think, get him the admiralty papers.

Gladstone has not answered yet. Perhaps he is not in town.

I have written to Waters. Renouf offers an April paper on Orientalism in the early Church,[7] with new light on Manichees and Gnostics. I accept, as it may stand over for July.

When I come to town I can put down some notes on the preliminaries of the Crimean war. But somebody else must write the article and read the book. Perhaps Cotton[8] is best after all. He will do a lot of Current Events and Notices, but I have declined an American article.

Do I reckon on you for Greece, Russia, Egypt, France and Spain?[9]

---

[1] The articles for the *Dictionnaire politique.*
[2] *The Invasion of the Crimea.*
* The second part of Gasquet, Letter CXLI, p. 299, misdated 'January 23', with several omissions.
[3] This refers to the 'pedigrees' of 'Ultramontanism', which should not appear both in that article and in 'Milner and his Times'.
[4] Gustav Adolf Bergenroth (1813–69), exiled German historian, since 1860 working in the Spanish archives at Simancas.
[5] John Sherren Brewer (1810–79), professor of classical philology at King's College, London, 1839, professor of modern history 1855; edited letters and papers of Henry VIII. [6] It did not.
[7] Renouf, 'Orientalism and Early Christianity', *Home & Foreign Review,* III (July 1863), 118–61. [8] Lathbury.
[9] 'Current Events' for April. None of these were written.

Your couple of pages for Block can be done out of two German books and two English, which I will send you.

Ever Your's truly

J D Acton

533

ACTON TO SIMPSON · 25 JANUARY 1863*

January 25

My dear Simpson,

You see it is not to be done.[1] Do you think the Bollandists would allow me to make them a handsome present of the medieval series published and to come? If you do, pray direct all that has appeared to go to them, and order the continuation, in my name. Stewart will manage it if you like. Let Paley have the Speculum;[2] he will review it, and Stewart shall give us advertisements. Will not De Buck review De Rossi?[3] Here it is, and I don't know what to do with it.

Your's ever truly

J D Acton

534

SIMPSON TO ACTON · 26 JANUARY 1863

Dear Acton

Greece is yours; therefore also Egypt—Russia & Poland[4] only mind provided Buck comes to, & accepts your munificent offer which I will make him at once. France & Spain,[5] alas, I must take. I will ask Buck again to do de'Rossi. But he refused once, last August, on the ground of having too much to do.

I will also tell Wetherell to write to Paley about the Speculum.[6]

I send you a short notice—will it do?—I will write what I can, but you must remember that I shall be hard worked with Block (translation

---

* The first part of Gasquet, Letter CXLII, p. 299, with omissions.
[1] The Master of the Rolls would not send his publication series to the Bollandists.
[2] J. Ph. Berjeau, ed., *Speculum Humanae Salvationis* (London, 1861), published by Stewart, reviewed in *Home & Foreign Review*, II (April 1863), 606–8.
[3] J. B. de Rossi, ed., *Inscriptiones Christianae Urbis Romae septimo saeculo antiquiores* (Rome, 1861), also published by Stewart, reviewed in *ibid.* 598–604.
[4] Of these 'Current Events', Acton only wrote 'Poland', *Home & Foreign Review*, II (April 1863), 677–95.
[5] Not written.
[6] *Speculum Humanae Salvationis.*

& poor laws)¹ 3 Generations, Ultramontanism,² a possible reply to Ullathorne, France & Spain, notices, & my own idleness to satisfy. E.G. I must go to London today to hear Spohr's Nonetto³—

Ever yours faithfully
R Simpson

Jany 26.

Ward (fat)⁴ has an article in hand "more or less adverse to you gentlemen of the H&F." for wʰ he seeks information "There were some remarks wʰ struck me as very good in an art. I think by Acton, on the Roman government⁵ in regard to the mistake made by Suarez and others in placing the supreme civil government with the people & regarding Kings as merely the peoples' delegates—could you refer me to said article"—

So far W. I hand him over to you. Write to him about it. It is rather fine to have the new Dublin⁶ begin by being a disciple of the R.

535

ACTON TO SIMPSON · 27 JANUARY 1863*

Tuesday

My dear Simpson,

Ward alludes to an article on the Roman States in March 1860, and the passage he means is vol. II p. 315. 316. The allusion to Suarez refers chiefly to his Defensio against James I. The treatise De Legibus is not quite in the same degree open to this objection. Ventura afterwards wrought out this system in his Pouvoir Chrétien, not always happily. Pufendorf⁷ quotes some writer who had died shortly before, I forget whom and calls him beatus so and so. Ventura sees this in Pufendorf, and without acknowledgment, pretending to have read the book referred to cites *Le Bienheureux so and so* as an authority on his side.

Ward must settle the question with Manning, who agrees with Suarez, and alludes to this theory when he says that he is in reality a Radical.

---

¹ The translation of 'The Finances of the French Empire' and the article for the *Dictionnaire politique*.
² 'Milner and his Times' and Simpson's share in 'Ultramontanism'.
³ A chamber music piece by Ludwig Spohr (1784–1859), German composer.
⁴ W. G. Ward was always stout; perhaps he was more so than usual.
⁵ 'The States of the Church' in the *Rambler*.
⁶ Ward had finally taken over the editorship of the *Dublin Review*.
* The second part of Gasquet, Letter CXLII, pp. 299–300, with an omission.
⁷ Samuel Freiherr von Pufendorf (1632–94), German jurist and historian.

The most extreme development of Suarez's views is in Spedalieri,[1] whose book is not very common, and who is a sanctimonious Tom Paine.

Will you suggest to Ward that a very good book has been lately published on the Life and System of Suarez by Werner,[2] an Austrian theologian of note. If he has some German reading friend who would review the book, and would add his own thoughts on Suarez it would be interesting.

I sent you a parcel of books yesterday.

Ever truly your's

J D Acton

536

ACTON TO SIMPSON · 8 FEBRUARY 1863

Sunday

My dear Simpson,

Capes says you have told him we want his Pitt.[3] I told him at Xmas that it could not appear later than January, and I incline to that opinion still. We have to choose from:

Volunteers	Antiquity of Man
State of Parties	Human Sacrifices
Land Tenure in Ireland	
Emigration	Waldensian Forgeries
French Finance	Orientalism in early Xty
Albania	Three Generations—
Kinglake[4]	Pitt comes rather late.

But let me know, that I may answer him.

I hope we have made a decent advertisement out of the Berlin academy. The London has a good article on the Matinées,[5] and the

---

[1] Nicola Spedalieri (1740–95), Italian apologist against the *philosophes*. The work referred to is *Dei diritto dell'uomo* (Rome, 1791).

[2] Karl Werner, *F. Suarez und die Scholastik der letzten Jahrhunderte* (Regensburg, 1861).

[3] His review of Stanhope's *Life of Pitt*.

[4] Of these, 'Tenure of Land in Ireland', 'Finances of the French Empire', 'Kinglake on the Causes of the Crimean War', 'Lyell on the Antiquity of Man', 'The Waldensian Forgeries' and 'Milner and his Times' appeared in April; 'Albania' and 'Orientalism and Early Christianity' in July; and Henry Moule, 'Emigration in the Nineteenth Century', *Home & Foreign Review*, III (October 1863), 472–96. *Human Sacrifice* was separately published.

[5] The spurious *Matinées royales* of Frederick the Great.

Athenaeum quite a frantic attack. The Smyrna merchant[1] looks to me rather suspicious.

Ever Your's truly

J D Acton

Emigration, a review of a very learned and exhaustive book by a French economist, is offered by Moule,[2] a Saturday reviewer, and may perhaps do for July.

537

SIMPSON TO ACTON · 9 FEBRUARY 1863

Clapham Feb 9. 63

Dear Acton

Capes wrote to me in the beginning of the year to say that he was extremely vexed not to have sent the Pitt—that the cause was, your not having sent him the books he asked for in time, for w[h] reason he concluded that you did not want it *at present*. I forget what I answered, but something urging him to finish what he had begun, as I had no doubt that it would be useful. He knew at the same time that I was not any longer connected with the H.&F. so he had no business to take my exhortation for more than it was worth, or to weigh it against your express declaration that it could not appear later than Jan[y].

If any difficulty occurs lay it all upon me. Say at once that I was not authorized to make any such offer as he implies that I made—sed non credo—

When shall you be back? I have a long communication from Buck which is to be talked over with you—or written about if you do not come soon.

My letter to Capes must have been written Jan[y]. 5.—When I sent him my pamphlet about Ullathorne[3]—so if you had told him the contrary as late as Xmas he had no business to let me override yours—Shall I write to him, taking the matter on myself?

Where has your Ultramontanism vanished to?—& where is Pythagoras?[4] Can't you make notes of the latter, such as I can work up for you

Ever yours sincerely

R Simpson

[1] James William Whittall (1838–1910), merchant in Smyrna 1854–61, in Manchester 1861–73, in Constantinople from 1873; wrote anonymously in London papers on Oriental questions; published another edition of the *Matinées royales* in 1901.
[2] Henry Moule (1801–80), vicar of Fordington 1829–80, sanitary reformer and inventor.   [3] *Bishop Ullathorne and the Rambler.*
[4] 'Ultramontanism' was delayed until July; 'Pythagoras' was not published.

81

I congratulate you on your letter to the Times.[1] It w^d have been a good article—Have you not some friend in Great Dutchland who will contradict Ranke's statement that all Germany was agreed upon the forgery?[2]

Do you give up Deutinger?[3]

538

ACTON TO SIMPSON · 10 FEBRUARY 1863

Tuesday

My dear Simpson,

Capes's allusion to your letter is only a sign that he is still willing to do Pitt. But I really think it is too late, unless we are quite sure he will do it extraordinarily well. The Dublin received the book[4] at Christmas.

My notion about Deutinger is that, if we have not Salop[5] for April—and I can get no answer out of your friend—it will be a very good, but not a buoyant n° and that metaphysics require something light to float them. April has nothing lighter than Albania[6]—unless Kinglake[7] turns out very successful. I have written to a very wise experienced and well informed gallant officer for his notes on the military operations.

Pray forget Pythagoras for a long time to come. It is really too serious a matter—Ultramontanism for July[8]—It is half done, that is, half ready for you.

If you think it worth while I will give you human victims[9] to cook. I have put together a great lot of matter on the question, and as soon as I finish it I will come up, in about a week. For my short notices I have to stay too, till I have got through all the work that requires looking out for marks in other books, and withal I am busy with my agent who is going away at Lady Day—

There is such a raging disturbance in Germany that Ranke's statement was impudent—The whole thing is being translated at Freiburg, and

[1] *The Times*, 3 February 1863, p. 10, signed 'The Home and Foreign Reviewer'.

[2] Ranke's statement that the *Matinées royales* was a forgery was printed in *The Times* 30 January 1863, p. 8, and provoked Acton's letter. See Victor Conzemius, ed., *Ignaz von Döllinger/Lord Acton: Briefwechsel 1840–1890*, I (München, 1963), 286–7, n. 4.

[3] The article on German philosophy was not published.

[4] Stanhope's *Life of Pitt*.

[5] 'Parish Registers' was published in April.

[6] Not published until July.

[7] 'Kinglake on the Causes of the Crimean War.'

[8] 'Ultramontanism' appeared in July, 'Pythagoras' not at all.

[9] The paper on 'Human Sacrifice', later separately published.

controversy is much excited. At Berlin of course Ranke has it all his own way, but a Person of Quality[1] fights my battles for me.

It will be a bore if De Buck won't notice De'Rossi.[2] You know Oxenham has handsomely accepted a subscription at Mudie's to do notices for us.

Ever Your's truly
J D Acton

539

SIMPSON TO ACTON · 11 FEBRUARY 1863

Buck has sent his *de phialis*
& the hymns of Ferrerius for
you. I suppose the last is *a
treasure*

Feb. 11. 63

Dear Acton

As you are not coming up in any haste, I send you, with Buck's permission, his letter to me on w[h] I was going to consult you. I have spoken to Wetherell about it—He is very adverse to having any article of the kind[3] in the H.&F., but thinks that I could publish a short pamphlet, which might be noticed in the H. & F. I might embody all that Buck says, & something more, in about 16 pp. However we will talk of that when you come up.

I am now waiting for Wetherell to return me the 3 generations,[4] reduced by about one half by excisions, so that I may know how much it wants to finish it. Also for Block's article,[5] promised for the 14th Then there is Buck's pamphlet. Also the 2 pp. on the poor laws will develop into an article for July,[6] of w[h] Wetherell approves highly.—It will be thus—

Nicholls,[7] in his history of the genesis of the poor law, like Nolan & the rest whom he quotes, look only at one side, i.e. the statutes of the realm, & accordingly find that the first poor laws were simply repressive & penal—

---

[1] Lord Granville. See Acton's *Essays on Church and State*, ed. Douglas Woodruff (London, 1952), pp. 473–4.
[2] *Inscriptiones Christianae Urbis Romae* was reviewed in April.
[3] Probably dealing with the question of the signs of martyrdom in the Catacombs.
[4] 'Milner and his Times.'
[5] 'The Finances of the French Empire.'
[6] Simpson wrote the article a year later: 'The Rise of the English Poor Law', *Home & Foreign Review*, IV (April 1864), 609–22.
[7] Sir George Nicholls, *A History of the English Poor Law*, 2 vols. (London, 1854).

But they forget the whole machinery of Poor law *relief*, set up in Lanfranc's[1] constitutions, & claimed by the Church as its own prerogative in Canon law &c—

Hence the principles of the Ecclesiastical law "de personis miserabilibus" should first be considered.

Then a parallel account of the progress of legislation from the statute book, & of ecclesiastical injunctions from Wilkin's concilia[2] should be made—

Then the first attempt of the state to unite the two in its own hands Temp Hen. IV.—Completed by Henry VIII *two* years before the suppression of Abbeys—& developed by Elizabeth—

Lots of minor questions come in—e.g. The anxiety of the Church to *settle* the poor in the 6th Century, & her anxiety to give privileges to vagrancy under colour of pilgrimage in the 12th 13th & 14th, when feudal servitude was breaking up—

The law of usury, considering the borrower simply as a "miserabilis persona"—

The way in wh the state borrowed from the Church the *Obligation* & *compulsion* of benevolences & poor-rates—

To treat the poor law as the solitary good result of the absorption of the Church by the State in Engd.

—Have you any books on this matter? Collections of authorities, without views I mean.

I will work at your human sacrifices[3] when you bring it up. But I shall have to get a dispensation for Lent, for I write only with full stomach.

Ever yours
R Simpson

540

ACTON TO SIMPSON · 12 FEBRUARY 1863*

Thursday

My dear Simpson,

When I come up you shall see my dissertation,[4] and decide whether it is worth your while to make it decent. If not I will rewrite it in London.

---

[1] Lanfranc (c. 1005–89), archbishop of Canterbury 1070.
[2] David Wilkins, ed., *Concilia Magnae Britanniae et Hiberniae*, 4 vols. (London, 1737).   [3] *Human Sacrifice.*
* Gasquet, Letter CXLIII, pp. 300–1, with several omissions. 'H & Fical' is given as 'heretical'.   [4] *Human Sacrifice.*

Pray thank Father DeBuck for his present—I shall be very curious to see the hymns, which appear to be in the style of Bembo[1] who implored Sadolet not to read S. Paul, che vi corrompe il gusto. I presume you have told Stewart to send and continue sending the books.

As to the insertion of a treatise on the Corpi SS.[2]—in the shape of a review of De'Rossi[3]—it would be so good an advertisement in ecclesiastical quarters that I think it deserves consideration. I will bring up my De'Rossi for you, as I conclude you will not put the matter into Northcote's hands. As a review of the Inscriptions there would be a favourable prejudice in the minds of readers, and De'Rossi and his friends would puff it. This would be quite consistent with omitting his name in that portion of the paper which will be offensive piarum aurium.

Pitra's[4] elevation is really creditable, for he is as learned as so great a goose can be. The Solesme people all believe in the spurious Acts of Martyrs, and think that Tillemont, Arnauld and Ruinart rejected them in a sort of H & Fical spirit. So they would of course multiply the number of martyrs by here and there an odd ten thousand. Döllinger's demolition of the Laurentian legend carries criticism a stage farther than Mabillon.[5]

Your idea of the Poor Laws is truly admirable. A dissertation of Mone's will help you, if W & N. can get it for me. You won't forget Eden's history of the Poor.

I hope under any circumstances you will dispense with fish this Lent.

Dunne,[6] who is much in the confidence of every Irish bishop, but testibus Newman and Renouf a very clever fellow, offers literary or historical articles. I have dangled Bossuet's new works before him at a distance, and proposed Limerick at once. Lathbury is on Kinglake,[7] and an illustrious Crimean hero has promised military criticisms. So it will be: "We can only say we saw nothing of the kind". "We can appeal to every man present on the left wing whether we are not right in stating"... "No historian has yet done justice to...".

Ever Your's truly

J D Acton

---

[1] Pietro Bembo (1470–1547), cardinal 1539, humanist.
[2] The bodies of martyrs in the Catacombs.
[3] *Inscriptiones Christianae Urbis Romae.*
[4] Jean Baptiste Pitra (1812–89), Benedictine monk at Solesmes 1841, liturgical scholar, cardinal 1863.
[5] Jean Mabillon (1632–1707), Benedictine monk 1654, founder of the scientific study of historical sources.
[6] David Basil Dunne (1828?–92), D.D. and Ph.D. (Rome) 1852, did not take orders, lecturer in logic at the Catholic University of Dublin 1854, later professor of law and logic, joint secretary of the Royal University 1879.
[7] Lathbury wrote 'Kinglake on the Causes of the Crimean War'.

ACTON TO SIMPSON · 20 FEBRUARY 1863

Friday

My dear Simpson,

I have read the letters in the Miscellanies[1] over & again, and they suggest only one point. Julius Caesar had 2 men sacrificed and one executed after a meeting. Peel[2] imagines the 2 were in fact executed. It must be pointed out that the one execution proves the 2 to have been a sacrifice—as they are mentioned distinctly together by Dio.[3] To make the priests the executioners of the army, for a mutiny in w^h many had taken part, out of a demoralized and not reverent soldiery, would have put the priests in a very unpleasant predicament—and there is no sign of any feeling such as would have arisen.

You will see that the phenomena of of h.S.[4] are gone through, both in their variety, and in the uniformity of various nations, and I think you will agree with the theory.

The Roman part, after 97 B.C. is exhaustive. the Greek is sketchy because it has been done by others, and I have only classified the modes —Besides there was no room—But Peel, Macaulay, Liddell, Preller, Lewis, &c &c &c &c—all deny that there was such a thing in Rome in civilized, classical times—So it was necessary to be very full.

Ever Your's truly
J D Acton

ACTON TO SIMPSON · ?25 FEBRUARY 1863

Wednesday

Dear Simpson,

We are oppressed with Woodlocks. I send you one of the oppressors,[5] who wants us to enrich him. Do you think Block will answer him?

I have heard the beginning of Parish Registers,[6] which is very good— I have encouraged him to give us short notices.

---

[1] Lord Stanhope's *Miscellanies.*
[2] See *Were Human Sacrifices in Use among the Romans? A Correspondence...between Mr. Macaulay, Sir Robert Peel and Lord Mahon* (London, 1860). The correspondence dates prior to 1850, when Peel died; Mahon later became Lord Stanhope.
[3] Dio Cassius (c. 150–235), Roman historian.
[4] Human Sacrifice.
[5] Proposed articles from Woodlock.
[6] Waters' 'Parish Registers'.

The Pope repudiates the idea of reforms, and declares the announcement a French ruse.

Ever Your's truly

J D Acton

543

ACTON TO SIMPSON · 2 MARCH 1863*

Halfmoon S^t

Monday

My dear Simpson,

Flahault[1] has sent to Paris to know whether Frederic's MS. is in the archives where the letter was. So we shall be well provided with facts.

I hope Poland is getting on well. Have you got your information?[2] Don't forget to describe the iniquitous tendencies among the Poles, and the general inclination to be independent, on the basis of the Polish nationality, which involves Posen and Galicia is quite revolutionary, and justifies the hostility of Prussia. It also is a great excuse for Russia, who knows that a constitution, self gov^t &c. would become the means of a new agitation. Hence importance of European intervention, and the determination of Russia to put down the revolt at all hazards, of course you read the debate of Friday. The gov^t was very near getting beaten, if the animus against them had not too obviously predominated over love of the Poles.

Dunne offers a paper on the Louvain University,[3] not worth having, I think.

OHagan wants to be released for April. I refused of course, but gave him his choice between rewriting Woodlock's article on Parties,[4] and sending us that on Tenant Right.[5]

I hope Beaumarchais[6] is giving you the wish to do Epigrams for July.[7]

---

* Gasquet, Letter CXLIV, pp. 301–2, with most of the text omitted.

[1] Charles Auguste Joseph, comte de Flahaut de la Billarderie (1785–1870), French soldier, ambassador to Vienna 1841–8, to London 1860–2; better known for his *amours*.

[2] Information for 'Poland' in 'Current Events' was supposed to be forwarded by de Buck.

[3] Not published,

[4] Not published.

[5] 'Tenure of Land in Ireland.'

[6] Pierre Auguste Caron de Beaumarchais (1732–99), French dramatist, author of *Le Barbier de Seville* and *Le Mariage de Figaro*.

[7] Simpson wrote 'Epigrams', *Home & Foreign Review*, III (July 1863), 84–117.

It would be much wanted. If we have Volunteers and Convicts,[1] which are timely. Poor Law,[2] not being particularly timely, might come in October. I think that would be better economy than to sacrifice the chance of a July light article for the publication in July of the paper on the Poor Law.

I believe there is no better thread for epigrams than philology: seeing how different languages, and therefore the spirit of different nations, adapted themselves to the construction of pointed sayings: Greek, Latin, Italian, French, English and German. The beginning is however in the Sapiential books. They say Lady Herbert of Lea[3] has been received at Rome.

Ever Your's truly
J D Acton

544

SIMPSON TO ACTON · 2 MARCH 1863

My dear Acton

Hall has almost finished his article,[4] w^h will take the place of Volunteers—I am to have the first half of it early this week. Here is a note from him that came this morning—Will you see about it? Probably you will take Hay's[5] side in the H.& F. so you had better be consistent & do the same at Westminster.

Buck has sent off by Rail Martinof on Poland[6] & himself on Russia[7] —so I shall have lots on those parts of current events.

Whatever you have to send me on Human Sacrifice send at once, for I am going to write my addition to you. I am going to say—hitherto we have considered the rite of human sacrifice combined with the dogma of a personal & supreme deity. In the pantheistic degeneration to w^h polytheism led it came to have a cosmical & magical instead of moral meaning, an extorting instead of impetratory power, and a medicinal instead of expiatory force. So I shall only add a paragraph to w^h I shall add your extract from Bähr about the Macrocosmus & Microcosmus—

---

[1] 'Volunteers' was not published; 'Convicts' is Lathbury, 'Gaol Discipline in England and Wales', *ibid.* (October 1863), 407–35.

[2] 'The Rise of the English Poor Laws' was not published until April 1864.

[3] Elizabeth A'Court (d. 1911), married 1846 Sidney Herbert (1810–61), created Baron Herbert of Lea 1860, converted 1863.

[4] 'Naval Discipline and Efficiency.'

[5] Sir John Charles Dalrymple Hay (1821–1912), 3rd baronet 1861, entered navy 1834, captain 1849, rear admiral 1866, retired 1870, admiral 1878; M.P. 1862–5, 1866–85, lord of the admiralty 1866–8; a frequent critic of the navy.

[6] Polish 'Current Events' were forwarded by de Buck but written by Ivan Mikhailovich Martynov (1821–94), a Russian Jesuit then stationed in Brussels, author of works on the Eastern churches.

[7] Not published.

1 am incorporating most of your notes with the text, & giving little more than references in the notes—

Shall I send you the little that I have done, to see how you like it

Ever yours
RS.

Monday Morning

545

ACTON TO SIMPSON · 2 MARCH 1863

Monday

Dear Simpson,

Hall's article[1] will be very timely, as Volunteers[2] are quite uncertain. They may come in July with iron ships,[3] pace our friend at the War office.[4] I will be faithful to our naval principles in the House tomorrow.

Poland[5] will be capital.

Many of the extracts in notes will probably not work in, as they illustrate the question but don't carry it further. There is very little that is new in Bastian, and no proper distinctions. My notion of the beginning would be simply to allude to Lord Stanhope's Miscellanies, and the controversy therein, with Peel and Macaulay, which is odd as showing a disinclination to admit h.S.[6] in civilized Rome from ignorance of the real nature of the thing quite as much as from ignorance of the facts.

I must break off to vote at Brookes's[7] at 3—

Ever Your's truly
J D Acton

546

SIMPSON TO ACTON · 3 MARCH 1863

Dear Acton

I found here last night Buck's parcel. Not a word about Poland. A review of the state of Russia from the point of view of a Russian parliamentary-legitimist. Also a valuable statistical table of the Russian population in 1862 drawn up by M. Pauly (sic. Pauli)—It seems to me

---

[1] 'Naval Discipline and Efficiency.' [2] Wetherell's article was not published.
[3] 'Iron-clad Ships.' [4] Wetherell.
[5] For 'Current Events'. [6] Human Sacrifice.
[7] Brookes' Club.

to be rather materials for an article on Russia in July, than for current events in April.[1]

Buck asks me to forward to you the enclosed.

He sends me also the prospectus of a new edition of the Acta Sanctorum, 54 vols, at 25 ff the vol, to subscribers before June 1. I shall send it to Stewart that he may make as good a thing of it as he has of Rossi. Does the thing tempt you?

A note from Hall, promising the end of his article[2] by tomorrow, & pleading for your permission to retain the contrast not of *pay* but of *rewards*, between the military & naval services. He expresses great gratitude to me for washing the brine out of his article.

As my Poland people have failed me, try to get what you can to help me elsewhere[3]—

Ever yours
R Simpson

Tuesday Mg.

547

ACTON TO SIMPSON · 3 MARCH 1863

Tuesday night

Dear Simpson,

I have struck out the references[4] to moderns when their ideas, but not their words are taken. The text contains one's own thoughts and researches. The notes contain the proofs and illustrations. An idea not at all one's own, not taken from the originals, and not proceeding from them, ought not fairly to go into the text of any independent, original enquiry. That's the principle on which I stick so many things into the notes, so as to give other men their due. It is not very unfair to borrow ideas in an article, so we'll take the benefit of your iniquity. But I should not like to republish a paper so constructed.

I presume you don't know of anybody who has defended h.S. before Wuttke[5]—tho' Wuttke forgets the distinctions. At p. 7 you give the beginning of a passage of Nägelsbach; I would give all of it or none, as you like.

Lycurgus is not the legislator, but the orator, which makes a dif-

---

[1] The materials on Russia were not published in any form.
[2] 'Naval Discipline and Efficiency.'
[3] Simpson (with Acton's assistance) thus undertook the writing of 'Poland', *Home & Foreign Review*, II (April 1863), 677–95, credited to Acton alone by both the *Wellesley Index*, I, 551, and Conzemius, I, 299.
[4] In *Human Sacrifice*.
[5] Karl Friedrich Adolf Wuttke (1819–70), German Protestant theologian, professor at Berlin 1854, at Halle 1861.

ference of 400 years. I should like to intercede for Rougemont, and should have thought it a pity not to give the whole of the great passage in Oedipus at p. 28—

You have really made the whole quite charming and readable.

I have just seen old Lady William Russell,[1] of whom I am a favourite, and she promises to give me all the details about the incident Odo.[2] I dine with Flahault on Saturday, and shall get more out of him.

We shall have[3] Ranke's collection at Berlin, the Princess's[4] extracts from the Gotha MSS. & the French imperial archives, all in our short notice—Also, probably, a letter from Buffon,[5] and from Whittall. I am told the Princess is determined to have it out with me en tête à tête, and am meditating a precipitate flight.

I shall not ask Hayward[6] until I hear from you about Epigrams,[7] for I really think it would amuse you, while doing Poor Laws.[8] Begin with the Latin (not Martial's) which I have in the Anthologia, then Owen and other modern Latinists, some English and Italian, a few I can give from Göthe and Schiller and W. A. Schlegel, and then some of the best French, which are the best of all.

Ever Your's truly
J D Acton

548

ACTON TO SIMPSON · 5 MARCH 1863

37 Halfmoon S^t
Thursday

Dear Simpson,

Read Gladstone's speech on qualification for offices[9] yesterday. It is a great event. He has jumped with both feet into Home & Foreigndom.

---

[1] Elizabeth Anne Rawdon (d. 1874), married 1817 Lord (George) William Russell (1790–1846), converted 1862; mother of Odo Russell.

[2] Through its agent Odo Russell, the British government had invited the Pope to take refuge in Malta in case the Papal States were overrun.

[3] This refers to the controversy over the spurious *Matinées royales* of Frederick the Great. Apparently a short notice was planned; it was not published.

[4] Victoria (1840–1901), princess royal of Great Britain, married 1858 Frederick (1831–88), crown prince of Prussia 1861, German emperor 1888. Princess Victoria was indignant at Acton's publication of the *Matinées royales*.

[5] Henri Nadault de Buffon (1831–90), editor of *Correspondance inédite de Buffon* (Paris, 1860), a collateral descendant of the naturalist Comte Georges Louis Leclerc de Buffon (1707–88), whose son Georges Louis Marie (1763–93) had obtained possession of one of the manuscripts of the *Matinées royales*.

[6] Abraham Hayward (1801–84), barrister and essayist, contributor to the *Edinburgh* and *Quarterly Reviews*.

[7] Simpson wrote 'Epigrams'.   [8] 'The Rise of the English Poor Law.'

[9] The oaths imposed as religious tests for offices.

He asked me to dine in the evening to discuss Kinglake[1] with him & Duke of Argyle,[2] but I could not, being bound to the Speaker.[3] I see Gladstone as the subject to morrow. Lord Clarendon[4] talked to me for two hours yesterday, only too confidentially, telling me many things he wants me to keep to myself. I sent the rest to Lathbury, give him your notes too.

I made Merivale's[5] acquaintance yeste'even and thought him rather a goose.

I went to my ball last night, and much comforted Ladies Camoys and Castlerosse, because of my notorious rigorism.

Thanks for DeBuck's letter. By all means put me down a subscriber for the reprinted Acta SS.

I decidedly think the comparison, if deliberately made, as it stood, dishonest. Pray insert[6] a line of reservation—about purchase in the army.

An excellent paper by Renouf on early orientalism in the Western world.[7] Have we room for it? I am rather doubtful. It is a paper particularly adverse to certain of your combinations. Do you see all about Kenealy[8] in the Times.

I heard great praise of Waters last night from Childers,[9] MP. for Pontefract.

You shall have the Telegraph for Poland.[10] Pray exhibit very prominently the strictly revolutionary element mixed up with the good cause, for therein lies the virtue of the analogy with Italy.

Ever Your's truly

J D Acton

[1] Lathbury, 'Kinglake on the Causes of the Crimean War'.

[2] George John Douglas Campbell (1823–1900), duke of Argyll 1847, lord privy seal 1852–5, 1880–1, postmaster general 1855–8, secretary of state for India 1868–74; amateur scientist.

[3] John Evelyn Denison (1800–73), M.P. 1823–30, 1831–7, 1841–72, speaker of the House of Commons 1857–72, created Viscount Ossington 1872.

[4] George William Frederick Villiers (1800–70), earl of Clarendon 1838, ambassador to Spain 1833–9, lord-lieutenant of Ireland 1847–52, foreign secretary 1853–8, 1865–6, 1868–70.

[5] Charles Merivale (1808–93), dean of Ely 1869; Roman historian.

[6] In 'Naval Discipline and Efficiency'.

[7] 'Orientalism and Early Christianity.'

[8] Edward Vaughan Hyde Kenealy (1819–90), barrister 1847, Q.C. 1868 (disbarred 1874), M.P. 1875–80. His *New Pantomime* was severely reviewed in the *Weekly Review*, whereupon he brought a prosecution against the owner and editor for libel. *The Times*, 5 March 1863, p. 14. The suit was dropped after a rebuke by a *Times* leader on 6 March.

[9] Hugh Culling Eardley Childers (1827–96), M.P. 1860–85, 1886–92, first lord of the admiralty 1868–71, war secretary 1880–2, chancellor of the exchequer 1882–5, home secretary 1886.

[10] Copies of the *Daily Telegraph* as source material for 'Poland' in 'Current Events'.

Naval Discipline
Irish Parties
Finances of the Empire
Kinglake on the causes of the War
Parish Registers
Albania
Antiquity of Man
Human Sacrifice
Orientalism
The Waldensian Forgeries
Milner and his Times[1]

I hear for certain that Sidney Herberts' widow has been received by Talbot.

549

ACTON TO SIMPSON · 5 MARCH 1863

Thursday night

My dear Simpson,

I have just come home and found Hall.[2] Of course there will be gorgeous illuminations on Saturday. I have promised to escort a friend who is coming up from the country, and fear I shall not get rid of him so as to be able to join you; but you must come and see them, at the risk, of course, of your life. We shall never see such a sight again in this country. Milman[3] tells me S. Paul's will be splendid.

I find from his conversation that he is not prepared for the Roman part of human sacrifice.[4] By great good luck I got Flahault to write to the Paris archives about Napoleon's MS. and find it was something quite different from the Matinées.[5] We should have been for a laughing stock to the grave Prussians.

Ever truly Your's
J D Acton

---

[1] 'Naval Discipline and Efficiency', 'Finances of the French Empire', 'Kinglake on the Causes of the Crimean War', 'Parish Registers', 'Lyell on the Antiquity of Man', 'The Waldensian Forgeries' and 'Milner and his Times' were published in April. 'Irish Parties' turned out to be 'Tenure of Land in Ireland', also in April. The two items not in italics appeared in July. *Human Sacrifice* was separately published.

[2] 'Naval Discipline and Efficiency.'

[3] Henry Hart Milman (1791–1868), dean of St Paul's 1849, liberal historian of the Jews and the Latin Church.

[4] The assertion that the Romans practised human sacrifice.

[5] The manuscript from which Acton edited the *Matinées royales* had allegedly been copied for Napoleon I in 1806.

ACTON TO SIMPSON · 6 MARCH 1863*

Friday morning

My dear Simpson,

I send you the Daily Telegraphs from the end of January. You will find all details about the Polish revolution in the field. Of course you have seen Montalembert in the Correspondant.

You have filled me with a misgiving about your doctrines. The conspirators of the Emigration, who for many years have been getting up a movement, aim at independence, at a restored Poland, and as it would be Catholic, and would deprive Austria of a great province, the French liberal Catholics of course desire it. But from the point of view of right what is to be insisted on is the establishment of just government & gradual freedom, there as everywhere else. National independence must not come into competition with this, or be preferred to it, as it of course is by all men of ambitious views, all democrats, believers in the sovereign nationality, lovers of a Catholic Power. There is no security for good government in a restored Poland, with the revolutionary party supreme,—either in the principles of that party, or in Polish traditions, or in the chance of union with Austrian and Prussian Poland. Now on the principle that arbitrary power must be put down we must think not of a restored Poland, but of a converted Czar. The wrongs of Russia are also very great, and only part of the work would be done by taking away Poland. The principle requires us to defend the Russians also— If we appeal to the Treaties of 1815 as a security for the liberty of Poland, they are a security also against its restoration. The same claim the Poles have for the old, promised constitution, secures Galicia to Austria, & Posen to Prussia. It is not enough to stick up for that constitution. The evil is not that Poland is oppressed, but that Petersburg oppresses—The claim of Poland to a constitution is not greater than the claim of Russia. Seu vetus &c.[1] The position of the Russians is not improved by taking away Poland, but the right to care for them is yielded up; and so the principle would be abandoned.

I do not see how we can be consistent if we urge a separation of Poland, or a restoration of the ancient territories, on true legitimate principles the revolution is to be justified by Russian despotism, and is therefore on behalf of the Russians also. The crime that destroyed Venice was greater than that of the Partition, for Poland was unable to preserve

---

* Gasquet, Letter CXLV, pp. 302–4.
[1] 'We seek the truth, whether it be old or new.'

her independence without being a nuisance. The abomination of the last generation of her independence cannot be over estimated. Yet we do not wish Venice to be restored, at the expense of Austria or of Italy. We really cannot build up a right now on the basis of the iniquity of the Partition.

From a religious point of view, which will not do as a guide, but with which one ought to cover one's rear, the striving of Poland to be independent is a great evil for the Catholics in Russia, as it connects Catholicity with insubordination. But a reconciled Poland, selfgoverning, and carrying the necessity of self gov^t into Russia, would be a great support to Russian Catholics. I remember I saw nobody so earnestly opposed to Polish independence as the good Polish monks in Russia.

Your notice of Colenso[1] will be of great importance. Pray do it carefully, without allusions.

Ever Your's
J D Acton

551

SIMPSON TO ACTON · 6 MARCH 1863

Friday March 6. 63

Dear Acton

The enclosed will show you how enchanted Block is with 15£. I have told him that our new tariff to him is 8£ a sheet; that possibly the 15£ may be something over, & that the surplus goes towards paying the next article.

What say you to his Enfants Trouvés[2] for July? I should have thought that a non-French subject would be one for July, but this you see he promises to make in some measure European.

What think you of Hall?[3] As for Renouf[4]—put him in instead of 3 generations[5]—never mind my combinations I am not in love with them.

You see Block absolves you from your chapter on County organization[6]—I gave him a touching picture of your literary—dino—danceo—legislative late hours.

Ever yours faithfully
R Simpson

---

[1] Simpson reviewed *The Pentateuch and Book of Joshua critically examined*, *Home & Foreign Review*, II (April 1863), 561–3.

[2] Block wrote 'Foundlings', *Home & Foreign Review*, III (October 1863), 497–521.

[3] 'Naval Discipline and Efficiency.'

[4] 'Orientalism and Early Christianity', delayed until July.

[5] 'Milner and his Times.'   [6] For the *Dictionnaire politique*.

How many pp do you reckon Human Sacrifice[1] at? Albania of course you will leave out.[2] As for the rest it is a question for your speculation—Each sheet additional costs in printing something less than

5£—say	— — — — — — — — — — — — — — —	4. 17. 6
Paper	— — — — — — — — — — — — — — — —	2. 0. 0
Writer	— — — — — — — — — — — — — — —	5. 0. 0
		11. 17. 6

Also each 500 copies sold bring in 100£—when Williams & Norgate please to open their flood-gates & let us have the benefit of the fertilizing flood.

552

ACTON TO SIMPSON · 6 MARCH 1863

Halfmoon S^t
Friday night

My dear Simpson,

Foundlings are not a bad subject if he[3] will treat them comprehensively. One of our many administrative articles may fail us in July, so I would agree with a hint that may induce him to deal more with the marrow and less with the visible phenomena of his subject than he sometimes does. Many thanks for saving him and me from my county organization. Get him, if possible, not to overlook the rules that determine the religion of foundlings in the various lands. If he dealt with the historique of foundling hospitals, and the moral controversy it w^d be also interesting.

I think Hall makes a good first article.[4] Make quite sure of his perfect war ships for July.[5] I imagine that the starting point should be the American experience.

A long and charming talk with Gladstone to day. We have materials for demolishing Kinglake.[6] I am to see two more of the cabinet of 1853 on the subject, and then we may fairly say that the survivors of the Aberdeen administration speak through the H&F.

Nothing could induce me to omit Milner.[7] Renouf[8] may come in if

---

[1] *Human Sacrifice* was still intended to be an article.
[2] 'Albania' was held over (perhaps it was not ready) until July.
[3] Block.
[4] 'Naval Discipline and Efficiency' was the first article in April.
[5] 'Iron-clad Ships.'
[6] 'Kinglake on the Causes of the Crimean War', though written by Lathbury, contained information collected by Acton.
[7] 'Milner and his Times.'
[8] 'Orientalism and Early Christianity.'

Waters,[1] who is sick, or OHagan, who rejects my alternative and re-promises his article,[2] should fail us.

Lewis I find a reluctant and most unlikely convert to the Matinées,[3] while Lord Stanhope resists. I think my man on the whole the best.

Illuminations for Tuesday.[4]

Ever truly Your's
J D Acton

553

SIMPSON TO ACTON · 6 MARCH 1863

Friday Night

Dear Acton

I will take care not to tread upon your corns on the Polish question; and you attribute to me radical notions which I dont hold. If I wish for an independent Poland, it is not because I am a nationalist, but because I fear the bigness of Russia, which would be still more terrible to Europe if it was as well governed & contented as it is homogeneous. I suppose that to wish to carve out a new Kingdom in the interest of the balance of power is very different from the wish to do so in the mere interests of nationality. Is there or is there not a just reason why the Poles should wish to separate from Russia & to refuse to trust the promises of a power w^h has so often broken them? Is there or is there not just reason why Europe should wish to weaken Russia by dividing Poland from it? And if such a reason exists, it is valid for demanding of Prussia & Austria such minor sacrifices as may make the great sacrifice of Russia a permanent check upon her aggression? Especially if it is possible to compensate Austria by equivalent territories elsewhere? I only put these questions to show on what grounds my interior sympathies would go with a reconstructed Poland; but I dont mean, & never meant, to bring these notions into the Current events,[5] which I intend to make as far as possible a mere analysis of the events that have happened—leaving you to do the doctrine at some future time. But it seems to me as likely that a divided Poland would fall into a course which would at last conduct to freedom, as that the same result would come by the conversion of the Czar to H. & F. & the consequent free development of all the Russias.

Ever yours faithfully
R Simpson

[1] 'Parish Registers.'
[2] 'Tenure of Land in Ireland.' Acton had proposed a revision of Woodlock's 'Irish Parties', which was not published.
[3] A believer in the genuineness of the *Matinées royales*.
[4] On the occasion of the marriage of the Prince of Wales.
[5] 'Poland' was part of 'Current Events', not an article by itself.

SIMPSON TO ACTON · 8 MARCH 1863

Dear Acton

I send you a short notice of Colenso, Stanley & the Oscott Divines[1]—
You may see that I have read the two latter, & not seen the former—
except in quotations. If the review is of the kind you want, & if you
think it would be safer to see Colenso, send the paper back to me, with
observations.

I went up to Piccadilly on Saturday at 3 o'clock, & pushed into an
excellent place under the D. of Cambridge's,[2] whence I saw the proces-
sion of Westminster Potwallopers[3] headed by two Baubles, in all their
comicality, & also the young lady, with great content, & got home by
6 o'clock, laughing at many who had gone up to the city at 9.30 & were
not home before me.

Ever yours truly
R Simpson

Sunday Night—

555

ACTON TO SIMPSON · 9 MARCH 1863

Halfmoon S[t]
Monday

My dear Simpson,

Bodenham[4] has just left me. We had a very long talk on Poland, and
you would have been amused to hear me, enemy of restoration, discussing the characters of various candidates for the vacant throne.
I told him that I could not properly ask him for information, not being
able to pledge myself to support all his views, but that if he chose, in
his discretion to give me any, it would be used with joy. He promises
heaps of papers &c. As I did not know whether he knew you I spoke for
myself only, although you would probably suit his politics better. He
will tell Zamoyski,[5] and we are sure to get valuable matter. I dwelt

---

[1] In addition to his notice of Colenso, Simpson reviewed A. P. Stanley, *Lectures on
the History of the Jewish Church*, and J. S. Northcote and C. Meynell, *The Colenso
Controversy considered from the Catholic Stand-point*, *Home & Foreign Review*, II
(April 1863), 565–7 and 563–5.

[2] Prince George William Frederick Charles (1819–1904), duke of Cambridge 1850,
general commanding-in-chief 1856–95, field marshal 1862.

[3] Householders.

[4] Charles de la Barre Bodenham (1813–83), of Rotherwas, Herefordshire, married
1850 Countess Irena Maria Kray-Morawska.

[5] Count Wladyslaw Zamoyski (1803–68), Polish patriot, in exile in England.

largely on the impropriety of doing as Montalembert does, treating it as a Catholic question, dwelling on the restored balance of power by a Catholic state,—also on the hopelessness of recovering Galicia, on the inevitableness of a purely revolutionary element—on all which points he more or less cordially agreed, especially on the first. So I think it will do. He seemed overjoyed at the prospect of discussing these matters confidentially with the H & F. and I shall go to see him as soon as I have got rid of my sore throat, and recovered my voice after the relapse I shall have to morrow night.

I think, considering that Colenso[1] is under the impression that we are in the same boat with him, that it would be worth while for you to spend an hour over his prefaces and his second volume. Then I would take care to part the three, not so as to leave no allusions from one to the other, but so as to make three distinct notices. Surely you need not treat the Erasmian view as so peculiarly Erasmian—for it is not a good name—and may speak of it more as a true view than as a tolerated view. I don't know how many years it is since any noted Catholic defended any other view. Your quotation from Newman very timely. I am sorry you have not a good word for Meynell. Has he no merit of any kind? But what you have written is very good, and it ought to be made as clear and as precise as possible.

I remain
Ever truly Your's
J D Acton

556

SIMPSON TO ACTON · 9 MARCH 1863

Dear A.

These erased lines[2] are Hall's pet comparisons between the *pay* of the various branches, civil & military of the Navy, & the *rewards* of the two services, army & navy. He made so great a point of having something of them in that I hope you will be able to persuade W. to allow something. Why not compare the pay of captains & commanders with that of surgeons, paymasters, & Admiralty clerks? Why not compare the percentage of colonels who are CBs[3] with that of Captains in the same moist situation? The only thing to provide against is an unfair selection of figures. I have asked Hall to refer me to the pamphlets where these

[1] John William Colenso (1814–83), Anglican bishop of Natal 1853, questioned the historical accuracy of the Pentateuch, deposed 1869 for heresy.
[2] In 'Naval Discipline and Efficiency'.
[3] Companions of the Bath.

comparisons are made, so that, if possible, we may at least make some reference to them, leaving the responsibility of the figures to the authors. Do what you can with convenience, for I committed myself to Hall, that you & I would defend him against the "Quil-driver"—Hall gives up the comparison between the army & navy *pay*.

I have borrowed the 2 vols of Colenso[1] of Stewart, to whom also I have given the prospectus of the new Ed of the Bollandists, & I have told him that you had authorized me to put down y^r name.

Jack Cocks[2] & I pushed our way through Bond St Saville Row Regent St Pall Mall, Trafalgar Sq. Strand, Temple Bar, Fleet St St Paul's Ch Yd, Cheapside Queen St Mansion House, K. William St London Bridge, & back to Victoria Station—We were home by ½ past 11. Capes,[3] who paid £5.10.0 for an omnibus, got to Westminster Bridge at 2.30 AM. & returned over Vauxhall Bridge at 3.30 having seen nothing.

Ever Y^{rs} RS

557

ACTON TO SIMPSON · 16 MARCH 1863

Monday night

Dear Simpson,

Confabs today with my Polish friend,[4] with Lewis[5] & with Gladstone. The Journal confutes Kinglake on Sinope.[6]

Mrs. Bodenham says Andre Zamoyski's[7] friends were against rebellion, and in favour of mere material progress and gradual national organization. He is even now against the movement, and won't come here because of his promise to the Emperor. But the aristocracy is by degrees carried away by the rest, and serving as privates. They marvel at the moderation and wisdom of Langiewiz[8]—and at Dembinski's[9] wonderful letter.

The Prussian convention *is* secretly but rigorously executed. Austria

1 *The Pentateuch and Book of Joshua critically examined.*
2 John Somers-Cocks.
3 Frederick Capes.
4 Mrs Bodenham.
5 Sir George Cornewall Lewis.
6 The Russian bombardment ('massacre') of Sinope, 30 November 1853, was a decisive point in the diplomatic preliminaries of the Crimean war.
7 Count Andrzej Zamoyski (1800–74), brother of Wladyslaw, Polish leader.
8 Marian Langiewicz (1827–87), Polish soldier, commander in the revolt of 1863.
9 Count Henryk Dembinski (1791–1864), Polish soldier, general in the insurrection of 1830–1, fought for the Hungarians in 1849, refugee in France.

evidently holds the balance that prevents the movement becoming revolutionary. The aristocratic party thinks of the old constitution of 1815 &—for the kingdom—The rest, nearly all her correspondents, wish for restoration of the old territories. She says: Last week Francis Joseph[1] privately told Prince Sapieha[2] that he waited only for England to take the lead—he did not care for France. If by their interposition Poland could be reconstituted, Galicia should be made free immediately. This she heard today from Sapieha's brother in law. As it suits you I send it that you may let it influence your description—

Sullivan[3]—very good—will be 50 pages. Waters[4] about 20—not bad.

After a long talk with Owen[5] on Saturday I gather that he will some day write for us.

Ever Your's truly
J D Acton

558

ACTON TO SIMPSON · 26 MARCH 1863

Wednesday night

My dear Simpson,

I have just got through Poland.[6] All the beginning is very good. But surely when Andre[7] has been throbbing for weeks with excitement at the performances of Langiewiz you don't mean to throw him over in this way. I can't conceive anything more disappointing to the casual reader of newspapers. We see the people flying to the woods from the conscription, in great detail. Then all at once the scene enlarges itself, events become serious, fright turns to fight, there is war, success &— and you choose this moment to drop the curtain. I am sure you know how much I want the rest inserted, for I remember saying that the accounts of battles, which you were prepared to insert, were not wanted. By how much more therefore the account of the campaign— how the thing spread. How the Russians were discomfited—&c—otherwise the event is really not intelligible—I really have not time to insert

---

[1] Francis Joseph (1830–1916), emperor of Austria 1848.
[2] Leon Sapieha (1803–78), Polish leader, speaker of the Galician parliament 1861–75.
[3] 'Lyell on the Antiquity of Man.'
[4] 'Parish Registers.'
[5] Sir Richard Owen (1804–92), naturalist, Hunterian professor in the Royal College of Surgeons 1836, conservator 1849, superintendent of the natural history department of the British Museum 1856–84, knighted 1884; the leading British biologist until Darwin.
[6] Simpson's contribution to 'Current Events'.
[7] Andrzej Zamoyski.

it—as my Roman events[1] (8 days) are lost, and I must supply them from memory. But you have the materials—pray don't throw the thing up in that way, if you possibly can help it.

Ever Your's truly
J D Acton

559

SIMPSON TO ACTON · 30 MARCH 1863

Dear Acton

This[2] is begining betimes for July. Dont read it now, for I only enclose it promiscuously—I write simply to ask you what is the size of Block's political encyclopaedia,[3] & how much a page is in terms of a page of the H.&F. short notices. I have now to write him his two pages on poor laws—

Ever yours
R Simpson

Monday Morning

560

ACTON TO SIMPSON · 30 MARCH 1863

Halfmoon S[t]
Monday night

My dear Simpson,

Rome[4] turned up at the last moment, and I strove to unite the two.. not altogether discordant texts. Andrewes[5] is very pleasant.

Block's Dictionary is very good, and by first rate contributors. There will be two volumes. Each page contains, in double columns, about 900 words, or two of our common pages. His writers do not give literary references—which is a mistake.

[1] Acton wrote 'Rome and Italy' in 'Current Events', *Home & Foreign Review*, II (April 1863), 695–705.
[2] A sketch of 'Epigrams'.
[3] The *Dictionnaire politique*.
[4] For 'Current Events'.
[5] A. T. Russell, *Memoirs of the Life and Works of Lancelot Andrewes, D.D., Bishop of Winchester* (London, 1863), reviewed by Acton, *Home & Foreign Review*, III (July 1863), 298–300.

Hayward declares he will beat us about Sinope,[1] but he is more defiant than confident. Reeve[2] has the same point.

We have no short notices.[3]

Ever Your's truly

J D Acton

561

SIMPSON TO ACTON · 2 APRIL 1863

Thursday

Dear Acton

I was with Waters last night—he accepts as payment for his article[4] the discharge of his bills for Rambler & H&F at Williams & Norgates— He will write on names,[5] but wants two books w^h I have written on the next leaf, with a note where they may be got 2^d hand—Will you send it to Stewart with directions to get the books for him?

Your "Rome"[6] rejoices the heart—& makes one mourn your absence from America & Poland[7]

Ever yours

R Simpson

562

ACTON TO SIMPSON · 2 APRIL 1863

37 Halfmoon S^t

Thursday

My dear Simpson,

I will get the books for Waters. Don't forget the new books to be reviewed:

Whewell's Lectures on Political Economy

Mill on Utilitarianism

---

[1] Hayward reviewed 'Kinglake's *Invasion of the Crimea*', *North British Review*, XXXVIII (May 1863), 325–65.

[2] Reeve reviewed 'Kinglake's *Invasion of the Crimea*', *Edinburgh Review*, CXVII (April 1863), 307–52, written in consultation with Lord Clarendon.

[3] That is, none were yet on hand for the July issue.

[4] 'Parish Registers.'

[5] Possibly Waters reviewed Charlotte Yonge, *History of Christian Names*, 2 vols. (London, 1863), *Home & Foreign Review*, III (October 1863), 735.

[6] 'Rome and Italy' in the April 'Current Events'.

[7] Simpson had written 'Poland'. 'The States of North America', *Home & Foreign Review*, II (April 1863), 713–16, is in fact attributed to Acton in the *Wellesley Index*, I, 551, following Conzemius, I, 299 n. 1. Conzemius is in error in attributing 'Poland' to Acton.

Gardiner's James I.[1] You must read him, for he has studied carefully, and his treatment of the Catholics is worth examining. If he wants setting right about the Bohemian war I will append a few lines.

The life of Blomfield. Do you do this, or Stokes, or who? It ought to be done. Lo! a list of Epigrams.[2]

Ever Your's truly
J D Acton

P.S. Saturday.

Epigrams when you return. If Emerson Tennent's Story of the Guns[3] is a book of artillery will not one of your Portsmouth friends[4] review it?

563

SIMPSON TO ACTON · 15 APRIL 1863

Ap. 15.

Dear Acton

Pownall[5] says "I have just been in company with D[r] *Errington* & D[r] Goss.[6] I am delighted to hear that it is *proposed* to take immediate steps for the establishment of a Catholic house at one or other of the Universities where Papists may go & get their degrees."

Meynell writes to ask if I wrote the *fishy* notice of the Oscott divines[7] —& says that Newman says he is quite sure it does not represent the opinions of the editors, & is surprised that they inserted it, because it is unfair, ill natured & impertinent. So he writes to Northcote.[8]

The enclosed came to me from the printers last night. I have sent them £60, & told them that when I return I will give them the rest. In the mean time you may meditate profitably over the items.

Do remind Williams & Norgate to pay in something to my account at Hoares,[9] if it is only 50£—

---

1 Of the books listed, only S. R. Gardiner, *History of England from the Accession of James I...*, 2 vols. (London, 1863), was reviewed by Acton, *Home & Foreign Review*, III (July 1863), 296–7.

2 For Simpson's article.

3 Sir James Emerson Tennent, *The Story of the Guns* (London, 1863), dealing with Whitworth's ordnance.

4 Naval officers, such as Captain Hall.

5 Possibly Assheton Pownall (1823–86), rector of South Kilworth 1847, archdeacon of Leicester 1884; active in missionary, artistic and numismatic societies. Or else a relative: the Pownalls were a Liverpool family.

6 Alexander Goss (1819–72), coadjutor bishop of Liverpool 1853, bishop 1856; allied with Errington in his struggle with Cardinal Wiseman.

7 Simpson's review of Northcote and Meynell, *The Colenso Controversy considered from the Catholic Stand-point*, was critical of their feebleness.

8 Newman to Northcote, 12 April 1863, in *Letters and Diaries of Newman*, XX, 431–2.

9 Simpson's bank.

I was going to send you some epigrams which I composed last night but lo, it is time to go to Ryde—

Ever yours
RS

564

SIMPSON TO ACTON · ? APRIL 1863

St Thomas' House
Ryde
I. of W.

Dear Acton

You see that Noel[1] withdraws his offer—Will you send back this Ms. to W^{ms} & Norgate.

W^{ms} & N. also send their account of the Rambler. They owe us 141£. We shall see what is due to Capes[2] out of this; the rest is balance to go down the wide jaws of the H.&F. I am going to convert Telford[3] the Priest here to H.&F-dom. He publishes abroad that the Bp of Newport[4] is on our side —

Y^{rs} ever
R Simpson

565

ACTON TO SIMPSON · 9 MAY 1863*

37 Halfmoon S^t
Saturday night

My dear Simpson,

I am sorry I missed you today. Your Austria[5] was a miracle of speed.

Brewer is evidently meant by Fate to write for us, but he will give us great trouble. I will take advantage of the opening and write as you suggest.

---

[1] Possibly Hon. Baptist Wriothesley Noel (1798–1873), Anglican minister of St John's, Bedford Row, 1827–48, left the Church of England and became a Baptist minister 1849.

[2] Frederick Capes.

[3] Rev. John Telford, parish priest at Ryde; not otherwise identifiable.

[4] Thomas Brown of Newport and Menevia.

[*] Gasquet, Letter cxxvii (out of place), pp. 281–2, misdated 'May 1, 1862', with minor omissions.

[5] Simpson's translation of 'Austria and Germany', *Home & Foreign Review*, iii (July 1863), 35–51. The *Wellesley Index*, ii, 1195–6, identifies the author as Julius Fröbel.

As to the other question I must postpone my answer, rather than reject the offer. The Philobiblon is to have a paper on Richelieu[1] so that is no difficulty.

But the Lingard Society?[2] I meditate a volume by way of inauguration, which ought to contain those papers, the life of Mary Stuart,[3] and many more important papers. For I am in negotiation with Theiner for manuscripts from the Vatican Archives.

He offers to let me have many letters of Henry VIII to four popes, the *acts* of *the trial* of his divorce, letters of Wolsey and of Beatoun, some of Mary Stuart to Rome, inedita all James II's letters to the pope, the answers, letters of Sunderland and Mary Beatrice, of the exiled Irish bishops under William &c.

He says he wants money for the fourth volume on the temporal power, that the pope has none to give, that he will regard payment as a gift to St Peter &c.[4]

To whom I, making many conditions, have made a munificent offer.[5] There would probably be matter for a couple of volumes altogether. If this fails me I think Romilly's idea[6] might be entertained. I would put them off with some allusion to arrangements now pending, but not absolutely. The thing itself I wish to keep very quiet and have told nobody but you and Wetherell.

Keep an eye open *occasionally* for things which might be added.

Will you review: Stanley's letter to the Bishop of London—on subscription? The claims of the Bible and Science letters between Maurice and a layman?
Howitt's Supernatural? The Polish Captivity by Sutherland Edwards? Keble's life of Wilson?[7]

Ever Your's truly
J D Acton

Read Henry Lennox[8] last night?

---

[1] Intended for the Philobiblon Society, but not published.
[2] Acton projected a Catholic historical or record society under this name.
[3] Mary, Queen of Scots (1542–87).
[4] This was a subterfuge.
[5] Approximately £160.
[6] Having a copyist transcribe letters.
[7] Of these, only *The Claims of the Bible and of Science: Correspondence between a Layman and the Rev. F. D. Maurice* (London, 1863) and John Keble, *The Life of the Right Rev. Thomas Wilson*...(Oxford, 1863) were reviewed, *Home & Foreign Review*, III (July 1863), 224–7, 301–3, almost certainly by Simpson, although not attributed in *Wellesley Index*, I, 552.
[8] Lord Henry Charles George Gordon-Lennox (1821–86), M.P. 1846–85, first commissioner of works 1874–6; his speech in Parliament, 8 May, was published as *Italy in 1863* (London, 1863).

SIMPSON TO ACTON · 18 MAY 1863

Monday

Dear Acton

Block has sent me a long article (26 pp.) on "Les Enfants trouvés et les problèmes sociaux qui s'y rattachent"[1]—As time is getting on, I dont want to translate it now unless it is wanted for July—Ergo, will you decide. Do you want to see it before deciding?

I have sent for the books you asked me to notice, but Mudie says they are all unpublished, except Poland,[2] & that is only a reprint of the Times Correspondents' letters.

I have now set to work to write about Epigrams. I have studied so heavily that I am afraid there is but a poor look out for the lightness of the article—

I have not seen Duffus Hardy again. Have you heard from Brewer? Shall you be in doors on the Derby day? OK[3] on Saturday at 3, after my shriving? or when?

Ever yours
R Simpson

Hall is working like a good fellow at Iron Clads, but he is worked so hard otherwise that I fear he will hardly be ready[4]—

Why have you not sent me a copy of human sacrifice?[5]

Can you tell me any publication in w^h I can find the rhyming latin Poetry of the mediaeval ethnical & epigrammatic poets? There were many—Poor Henry, Valdevedus of Saragoza, Cyprian of Cordova, Landenulphus of Cassino, Godefrid of Winchester, Henry of Lincoln (is he the same as "poor Henry") Pinda of Hanenberg, & Richard of London. I can only find S. Malachi & Arnulph of Lisieux, who spoils his points.

---

[1] 'Foundlings', held over until October.
[2] Henry Sutherland Edwards, *The Polish Captivity*, 2 vols. (London, 1863).
[3] This may be the earliest use in England of this phrase, believed to be of American origin.
[4] 'Iron-clad Ships' appeared in July.
[5] *Human Sacrifice* had been published.

ACTON TO SIMPSON · 19 MAY 1863

37 Halfmoon S[t]
Tuesday

My dear Simpson,

I am laid up,[1] and so shall be sure to be at home tomorrow afternoon. If you don't go to Epsom I shall hope to see you here.

Block may, I hope, lie by till October. Especially if Hall[2] is in time; for Wetherell[3]—of course—fails us, and the American article[4] is uncertain.

The books you want, on medieval jingle, are to be found in Grässe's Literärgeschichte.[5] I think two or three collections contain nearly all.

Ever Your's truly
J D Acton

568

SIMPSON TO ACTON · 26 MAY 1863

Tuesday

Dear Acton

I suppose that the arrival of Gräse 3.a.[6] does not mean that the mediaeval part will not arrive.

Can you look into some Cyclopaedia under Anthologies to see whether the Persian & Arabian collections so called or epigrammatic or lyric— Have you written to Brewer?

Revd J.S.B. Kings College London—or Rolls House Chancery Lane (I should think)—or care of Duffus Hardy Esq—to be forwarded.

Does Ultramontanism[7] flourish?

Ever yours
R Simpson

---

[1] With a throat cold.
[2] 'Iron-clad Ships.'
[3] The unpublished article on the Volunteer movement.
[4] Possibly on the Civil War; never published.
[5] J. G. T. Grässe, *Lehrbuch einer allgemeinen Literärgeschichte...*, 4 vols. (Dresden Leipzig, 1837–59).
[6] One part of the *Literärgeschichte*.
[7] The article on 'Ultramontanism'.

SIMPSON TO ACTON · MAY OR JUNE 1863

Dear Acton

I send you an unsatisfactory mass upon epigrams.[1] I have marked parts that may come out with advantage. Some will do in a future article upon proverbs. I should be glad of your observations so as to alter & improve.

Hall has done his article[2] & has sent it off to Coles for additions & corrections. I should like Reed's[3] observations also, if I could get them on the sly—

Ever yours
R Simpson

over

Tell Wetherell that I have not got Maurice's book[4]—It has gone back to Mudie.

Tuesday night

570

SIMPSON TO ACTON · 17 JUNE 1863

Dear Acton

Have you done, or are you going to do, Gardiner's Hist. of Jas. 1. and Phillimore's Hist of Geo^r iii?[5] The latter proves himself a fool by his preface, though I rather like his pitching in to the English character—

Do you still expect me to do France?[6] If so, why have I no materials? I have only the Times, & they are too long to read through. There is a history of Mexico in todays Times w^h w^d furnish dates[7]—Say again on paper what you said at Wetherell's about the salient points of the

---

[1] 'Epigrams' was published in July.

[2] 'Iron-clad Ships.'

[3] Sir Edward James Reed (1830–1906), chief constructor of the Navy 1863–70, M.P. 1874–95, 1900–6, knighted 1880.

[4] *The Claims of the Bible and of Science.*

[5] Acton reviewed Gardiner in July and John George Phillimore, *History of England during the Reign of George the Third,* I (London, 1863), in *Home & Foreign Review,* III (October 1863), 713–15.

[6] 'The Elections in France', in 'Current Events', *ibid.* (July 1863), 385–90, was written by Acton.

[7] Presumably with reference to the French intervention in Mexico.

elections, for I have forgotten the order—Also whatsoever other lights you may have.

What of Ultramontanism?[1]

Ever yours
R Simpson

4 Vict. R^d June 17.

4 Vict. R^d June 17.

571

ACTON TO SIMPSON · 17 JUNE 1863*

I have kicked out Helfenstein's article,[2] in spite of much preaching from Wetherell, who thinks it about our best. So we have only Seven. But if you will do a few short notices more we shall put out everybody's light in that department.

Brewer fears he cannot extricate More from the hands of the National,[3] but is ready to give us an article—yea, articles—on any subject we please. Pray answer by return what you think of Wolsey,[4] for whom he must have lots of not yet registered materials?

In case Roberts fails us[5] will you prepare Deutinger[6] for October? How shall we stand as to supply?

Proverbs	*Emigration*
Names	*Federal Reform*
Foundlings	Italian Historians
Poor Law	
German Philosophy	
*Brownson & Si*mpson	
Wolsey	
Mary Stuart	
Medieval Universities	
English University Education for Catholics*	
The Irish Church	
Celtic Literature	
*Sir Jam*es Graham**	

---

[1] Acton's draft of 'Ultramontanism'.

* Gasquet, Letter cxxxii (out of place), pp. 488–9, misdated 'June 17, 1862', with omissions and slight changes.

[2] Dealing with medieval history; not published.

[3] The *National Review*, for which Brewer was writing.

[4] Thomas Wolsey (*c.* 1473–1530), archbishop of York 1514, cardinal 1515, lord chancellor 1515–29, virtual ruler of England under Henry VIII until his fall.

[5] He did.

[6] The unpublished article on German philosophy.

Volunteers[1]

Belgium,	Italy,	or Poland	or Australia.
(Arendt)[2]	(Lacaita)[3]	(Buddeus)[4]	(Childers)

* I have been corresponding about this article with Renouf, who likes the idea, but cannot yet make up his mind. I have sketched a famous article for him,[5] and he is coming up to talk it over.

Milman, to whom I sent the proofs of his article,[6] is a good deal staggered, and is in a fix, seeing that his book[7] is being reprinted.

** Lathbury wants this subject; but we must know first what Gladstone prefers to write on in October.[8]

I have a learned paper on the places where the 3 Kings stopped on the way from *Milan to Cologne*, ending with some doubts as to its having been the 3 Kings at all: to be civilly returned.

Ever Your's truly
J D Acton

572

SIMPSON TO ACTON · 18 JUNE 1863

Dear Acton

Wolsey[9] is no end of a subject, but delicate. The Dublin has eternally compared him & Wiseman, & I should say they weigh about an equal number of stones. No doubt Brewer would do him quite innocently, but it might be a satire for all that.

---

[1] Of the above list, the October issue had only Moule, 'Emigration in the Nineteenth Century', Block, 'Foundlings', and O'Hagan, 'The Irish Church Establishment', *Home & Foreign Review*, III (October 1863), 436–49. 'Celtic Literature' may be Sullivan, 'Celtic Ethnology', *ibid.*, III (January 1864), 129–64; 'Federal Reform' (in Germany) is one of the articles on Schleswig-Holstein in January or April 1864; 'Poor Law' is Simpson's article in April 1864.

[2] Guillaume Amédée Arendt (1808–65), German-born, converted 1832, professor of archaeology at Louvain 1835; not published.

[3] Sir James (Giacomo) Lacaita (1813–95), Italian politician, friend of Gladstone, refugee in Britain 1851–61, knighted 1859, returned to Italy; not published.

[4] Aurelio Buddeus (1817–80), German journalist, published 'The Revolution in Poland', *Home & Foreign Review*, III (October 1863), 450–71.

[5] See Acton to Renouf, 14 November 1862, in *Selections from the Correspondence of the First Lord Acton*, ed. J. N. Figgis and R. V. Laurence (London, 1917), for Acton's ideas.

[6] Renouf's 'Orientalism and Early Christianity'.

[7] *The History of the Jews*, originally published 1830, appeared in a third edition (London, 1863) reviewed in *Home & Foreign Review*, III (July 1863), 219–21.

[8] Gladstone did not publish in the *Home & Foreign Review*.

[9] No article on Wolsey by Brewer was published.

Fisher[1] is hardly figure enough. I should think that when Brewer has skimmed More for the National, More[2] will remain, even for the H.&F. A monograph on his politics would be most interesting. I don't know how far he was Statesman, or how far Utopian, but it is curious that in his early epigrams he writes, populus consentiens regnum dat et aufert, & that in his latest speech he declares that the title to the English Crown is simply Parliamentary.

I am going to the West of Eng[d] in July, but I will take Block[3] with me, if you will read it first (not till after the July H&F is over) & mark the passages to be omitted or modified—we have *carte blanche* to do all this. Roberts I dont think will fail us; I wish Wetherell w[d] write him a note to ascertain. I dont like bullying him again after his promise to me.

Have you touched up Waters upon Names? Why kick out Helfenstein? The history is good enough (is it not?) & the article is innocent.[4]

I have not read Phillimore,[5] except his preliminary chapter & pref. where the man comes out so ridiculously that I thought him an ass.

Gardiner[6] I will attempt. Are you going to send me *La France*.[7]

Ever yours totally
R Simpson

July[8] 18. 63

OHagan[9] does not defend the Model Schools, but says they will be considered if wrong—and that Peel[10] has shown his willingness to reform them—
So the evil in principle and in practice is not denied, no pledge of a remedy is given, and they are left to the wisdom of Peel who declares the high church ought to convert the people.

---

[1] John Fisher (1469–1535), bishop of Rochester 1504, cardinal 1535, martyred, canonized 1935.
[2] Sir Thomas More (1478–1535), humanist, lord chancellor 1529–32, martyred, canonized 1935.
[3] 'Foundlings.'
[4] Neither Waters nor Helfenstein was published.
[5] *History of England during the Reign of George the Third*, reviewed by Acton.
[6] The review was written by Acton.
[7] French 'Current Events' (not published).
[8] Simpson's error.
[9] The following sentences appear to be in Acton's handwriting. The reference is to John O'Hagan.
[10] The chief secretary for Ireland.

SIMPSON TO ACTON · 23 JUNE 1863

Dr Acton

I thought there was only one Vol of Gardiner published. Mudie has send down the 2^d. Either cancel my notice or send it me back to alter[1]— I cannot see that he refers to the papers in the B.[2] Museum for 1612; but I must look again—

Y^{rs} ever

R Simpson

Monday

574

ACTON TO SIMPSON · 23 JUNE 1863

37 Halfmoon S^t

Monday

6'oclock

Dear Simpson,

As I am a member of the Surtees Society, and as we heavily rebuked Raine[3] in reviewing Brown,[4] I have softened a passage or two in your notice.[5] As to France,[6] I presume you have verified about Soissons & S. Brieuc. I know the last only from a letter in the Times, not from Paris.

Your retouchement was excellent, and I have had the first part of Ultramontanism recopied. I send you a lot more, together with some you have seen, with a prayer for similar correction and speedy return. Pray aim at clearness and brevity. I know their value—etsi deteriora sequat. There remains only the constructive part to finish.[7]

---

[1] Acton evidently cancelled Simpson's notice and reviewed both volumes of Gardiner, *History of England*.

[2] British.

[3] The reference is to William Henry Dixon, *Fasti Eboracenses: Lives of the Archbishops of York*, ed. and enlarged by Rev. James Raine (London, 1863).

[4] John Browne, *Fabric Rolls and Documents of York Minster* (York, 1862), reviewed in *Home & Foreign Review*, I (October 1862), 536–8.

[5] Simpson's review of *Fasti Eboracenses*, *Home & Foreign Review*, III (July 1863), 295–6, is not attributed in *Wellesley Index*, I, 552.

[6] Intended for 'Current Events'.

[7] This indicates the relative shares of Acton and Simpson in the writing of 'Ultramontanism'.

I must tie my choker for an early (fashionable) dinner, and the Prince of Wales afterwards—shirking Poland.

> Ever Your's
> J D Acton

I hope you have recovered your digestion, and that you have put proper numbers to your quotations from Homer. Nobody knows what book Iliad Λ365 means.

575

ACTON TO SIMPSON · ? JUNE 1863

Dear Simpson,

A thousand most sincere thanks for your selfdenying patience. I had sent off all my MS. and will insert a line to connect them in proof. They have now all the articles and quite as many notices as we want.

Ryley[1] is all in order at last.

Price's letter is uncommonly civil and gentlemanlike. I think he would be glad to modify his paper for October.[2] Capital news for the library[3] today from Aldenham.

> Ever Your's truly
> J D Acton

I send you a paper on the ministerial changes in France.[4]

576

ACTON TO SIMPSON · 2 JULY 1863

> 37 Halfmoon S[t]
> Thursday

My dear Simpson,

This[5] is an interesting article of Block's, and very worthy to appear in October. It would be well if the contrast of the Teutonic system could be followed out further; but the French system has been carried to the last point, from the extreme centralization, and so it will seem quite reasonable to study the general question where all the phases and results are most completely shown.

1 'Belligerent Rights at Sea.'
2 Bonamy Price wrote 'The Bank Charter Act', *Home & Foreign Review*, IV (April 1864), 402–32.
3 New acquisitions for Acton's library.
4 Not published.
5 'Foundlings.'

You will at once see the unhistorical treatment of the early centuries. I think a few words might have been wasted on lyingin hospitals, but the question of temptation and infanticide is dealt with very well.

If you write to Block, it might be well to mention the fact that a German work has just appeared on the subject; also that Spain and Russia, presenting the opposite extremes, deserve notice. For in Russia Catherine founded enormous establishments, and all the boys are turned into soldiers; so that the state in a manner rejoices at the number of foundlings.

As to the relative morality of Teutonic and Latin nations it should be spoken of as independent of religion. The pagan Teutons had a better idea of women, slaves, and family life, than the classic nations, and that may be said to show itself still in some respects. Some expressions require softening.

I think, now that money is flowing in, and things are more settled, it is time Wetherell should take a fixed sum, say 100£ a year, instead of that which we devised in reference to the number of sheets. That calculation at any rate is simply deceitful, as the quantities have so much increased.

I have proposed to him a mode of relieving him of the hard work, so as to get more real literary work out of him; but I don't know yet what he says. I also suggested a dodge for my own comfort, as a large part of the foreign work falls to my share, and makes it impossible for me to go abroad as much as I ought, and as, sooner or later, I shall be compelled to do. My notion is that we might get some help from Renouf for this purpose; especially if the Atlantis is likely to collapse.[1]

If Roberts is uncertain—I have asked Wetherell to sound him—shall you be able to prepare Deutinger for October?[2] It seems probable we may have enough on Frohschammer[3] to make an article.

Döllinger's Papst fabeln[4] are full of capital things, and I meditate a very short article upon them.

I remain
Ever truly Your's
J D Acton

[1] Publication of the *Atlantis* was suspended in 1863.
[2] Neither Roberts nor Deutinger was published.
[3] Jakob Frohschammer (1821–93), ordained priest 1847, professor of philosophy at Munich 1855, suspended from the priesthood 1862 for his generationist heresy, refused to submit. The article Acton intended to write on him eventually became a large part of 'Conflicts with Rome', *Home & Foreign Review*, IV (April 1864), 667–90.
[4] Döllinger, *Die Papstfabeln des Mittelalters* (München, 1863), reviewed by Acton, 'Medieval Fables of the Popes', *ibid.* III (October 1863), 610–37.

ACTON TO SIMPSON · ? JULY 1863*

Friday night

Dear Simpson,

Gladstone won't write about politics while in office; but there is some chance of a review of his speeches

1 by *Lowe*.[1] *Lathbury* takes Graham.
2

3 *Arnold* promises Geography; *Moule*, emigration;
4

5 *Sullivan*, Celtic literature;

6 *Buddeus*, Poland; Fröbel, Federal reform;
7

8 *Renouf*, University;[2] we have *foundlings*; I can probably get up an
9 article on the
10 *pope-fables*; we shall have *Frohschammer*
11 or Roberts or Deutinger; there is no decided answer from O'Hagan on the Irish Church, or from Waters about Names, or from Brewer on history.[3]

Will you not write on George Eliot?[4] The subject would suit you exactly, for there is doctrine as well as art in her. There are several French essays about her, which you could look at, and then read, chronologically, Scenes from Clerical Life, Adam Bede, The Mill on the Floss, Silas Marner, and Romola, which is just finished.

There would be an opportunity for going into several questions: how

---

* Watkin and Butterfield, pp. 96–7, misdated (following Simpson's dating) 'September 1863'.

[1] Robert Lowe (1811–92), barrister and journalist, in Australia 1842–50, M.P. 1852–80, joint secretary of the board of control 1852–5, vice-president of the board of trade 1855–8, vice-president of the committee of council for education 1859–64, chancellor of the exchequer 1868–73, home secretary 1873–4, created Viscount Sherbrooke 1880.

[2] This was to have been an article proposing a Catholic university in England. It appeared, instead, as a pamphlet: *University Education for Catholics: a Letter to J. H. Newman* (London, 1864).

[3] Of this list, the *Home & Foreign Review*, III (October 1863), contained: Lathbury, 'Gaol Discipline in England and Wales', 407–35; Arnold, 'The Formation of the English Counties', 550–73; 'Emigration in the Nineteenth Century'; 'The Revolution in Poland'; 'Foundlings'; 'Medieval Fables of the Popes'; and 'The Irish Church Establishment'. Other articles are Lowe, 'Mr. Gladstone's Financial Statements', *ibid.* IV (January 1864), 1–18; possibly 'Celtic Ethnology'; probably Julius Fröbel, 'The Schleswig-Holstein Movement in Germany', *ibid.* (April 1864), 365–78; and 'Frohschammer' as part of 'Conflicts with Rome'.

[4] This is the genesis of Simpson, 'George Eliot's Novels', *ibid.* III (October 1863), 522–49.

men draw women and women men, and whether women drawn by women are much more natural than when done by man. I have no doubt they are, though I cannot discover the superiority of their female characters to those of Shakespeare, or even of Sandeau, in *Marianne.*

Moreover, whence the extraordinary indelicacy of female novelists, and their delight in the defilement of their sex? There must be a reason for this. Why are Mrs. Afra Behn & Mrs. Centlivre the most obscene of our writers of comedies? Why is there so little virtue and so much sensuality in the women of Mme de Stael, George Sand, Currer Bell, Mrs. Norton, in Mrs. Kemble's Diary, and in George Eliot? The personal character of the authoress has nothing to do with it, I am persuaded.

And do women understand what we mean by honour? Not courage, which they understand very well, but veracity. I can't help thinking their modesty prevents them hating all untruth. Also some kinds of responsibility all unintelligible to them, and also some kinds of masculine selfishness—all which detracts from their skill in portraiture.

Can they describe madness???

George Eliot is worthy of your pen, and will be very valuable in October, if you can superadd her to Block[1] —

Renouf, having seen Newman, reports, *secretly*, that he spoke without any reserve or qualification of his admiration of the H&F. I hope you are on your travels. I hope to begin mine this day week.

> I remain
> Ever truly Your's
> J D Acton

578

SIMPSON TO ACTON · ? JULY 1863

> Bridgewater, Wednesday Night—
> Write to me at Clapham—I am
> on the wing for another week—
> Get your Pope-fables well forward—
> How about your short notices?

Dear Acton

I am at your disposition—if you think that I shall be able to do Geo. Eliot,[2] and will provide me with the criticisms upon her which have appeared in France & Germany, besides giving me your ideas & hints,

---

[1] The translation of 'Foundlings'.
[2] Mary Ann Evans ('George Eliot'; 1819–80), novelist.

I may possibly get up an article about as good or as bad as that on Victor Hugo.[1]

Have you ever read Miss Afra Behn & Mrs Centlivre? If not, where does one find a discussion of them? Have you any list in your head of powerful & original female characters created of late years by men & women respectively—such as Becky Sharpe—Callista—Ellen Middleton: Mary Thorne—I know of no others; but for my own part I prefer the mens creations. Women's characters, like those of Lady Harriet (?) Lewis, are full of amusing photography but they have not often the complete womanhood of the best of the men's.

I have a letter from Buck—shall I ask him for some short notices, or his remarks on the late Belgian elections—There is no more question of putting him on the Index,[2] only of refuting him—Rossi he says is in a great funk & is thinking of turning round—Patrizi[3] is firm to distribute no more corpi till the controversy is decided.

In Paris get a pamphlet by Schedo-Ferrotti (?) (Baron Fierseu) on Russia[4]—it is the inspiration of Orlof,[5] ambassador at Brussels, who expects to stand in the shoon of Gortchakof,[6] when that man's got shook off—

Father Martinez'[7] prophecy—La réussite probable de la Pologne, et le bouleversement politique certain de la Russie dans deux ou trois ans.

The new edition of the Acta Sanctorum will not be brought to the level of modern criticism because (1) tout le mond wants the primitive work, & (2) because it w^d want to be entirely rewritten—Ever yours most faithfully

R Simpson—

---

[1] 'Victor Hugo's *Misérables.*'
[2] For his questioning the authenticity of alleged saints' bodies in the Catacombs.
[3] Costantino Patrizi (1798–1876), cardinal 1834, cardinal-vicar of Rome 1841–70.
[4] D. K. Schédo-Ferroti (pseud. of Baron H. E. C. F. E. W. von Fircks), *La question polonaise*...(Paris, 1863).
[5] Prince Nikolai Alekseevich Orlov (1827–85), Russian ambassador to Brussels 1859–69, to Paris 1871–82.
[6] Prince Aleksandr Mikhailovich Gortchakov (1798–1883), Russian foreign minister 1856–82, chancellor 1866–82.
[7] Not identifiable with certainty. Considering the sagacity of this remark, it is tempting to identify this Martínez with the one who, as *professeur de théologie* at Paris, published in 1890 *Le Juif, voilà l'ennemi!* More possibly, this may be Narciso Martínez Izquierdo (1831–86), then professor at the University of Madrid, bishop of Salamanca 1874, of Madrid 1885, also a deputy and senator.

ACTON TO SIMPSON · ? JULY 1863

37 Halfmoon S^t
Friday

My dear Simpson,

I am off on Monday to Aldenham for a fortnight, and afterwards abroad.[1] You shall have as soon as may be any French critiques I can find. I cannot call any German ones to mind.

I have Mrs. Behn's plays, which you can have all you like, but you will be none the better or wiser. There is nothing but indecency in them. Mrs. Centlivre I know only from your report.

What says Aristotle concerning the female mind? Surely they lack creativeness, and describe only incomplete men.

All Bulwer's women, that I remember, are badly drawn—Alice, I suppose, is the most elaborate. Dickens's Nancy, and Trollope's Lily Dale, have only one side to their faces, like the women in the Greek plays. How different are Manzoni's male characters from his female! Very few men have taken an inside view of any female character and analyzed it, as they do men's, like Lewis XI in Quentin Durward, James I in Nigel, Cromwell in Whitehall. Really I know hardly one but Becky, and Marianne in Sandeau's wonderful novel of that name.

They tell me, said Talleyrand to Mme de Staël, that you and I are both in Corinso, disguised as women—rather a good test.

There must be good things in Schlegel's dramatic art, in Coleridge passim, in Göthe, St Beuve, Vinet &c. which I will seek.

Are not the great queens &c. in history the crux of historians? Isabella, Mary Stuart, Elizabeth, M^m de Maintenon—and are not women unskilled in history? &c. &c. &c.

Barlow[2] has sent a dry but good and sound article on the Commentators of Dante.[3] Waters promises something light. Frohschammer will be a longish article, which Döllinger says will make us similar to the orthodox. I hope Lowe will review Gladstone's speeches, as he promises.[4]

You can't do too many short notices. We shall not have many from Renouf, as he is in Guernsey, away from his books.

---

[1] Acton planned to go to the Continent during this summer, but was unable to do so.

[2] Henry Clark Barlow (1806–76) had done research on Dante since 1844.

[3] Barlow, 'Dante and his Commentators', *Home & Foreign Review*, III (October 1863), 574–609.

[4] Waters did not publish; 'Frohschammer' was delayed until 'Conflicts with Rome' in April 1864; 'Mr. Gladstone's Financial Statements' appeared in January 1864.

Our Mohamedan contributor[1] seems to me tending strongly to Catholicism. But meantime he is a strict observer of the law. He has translated the Essai sur l'Indifférence,[2] and is trying to cajole W&N.[3] into publishing it. I think he will give us his notes on Croatia for October Events.[4]

I have a good prospect of getting matter for a January article on the internal gov[t] of the Confederate States[5]—a rare subject.

Lathbury has resigned American Events. I will do them if you will get up Mexico. He will give us a chapter on India.[6]

By all means get notes and notices from DeBuck.

I remain
Ever Your's truly
J D Acton

580

SIMPSON TO ACTON · 27 JULY 1863

Dear Acton

I have translated Block[7] & given it to Wetherell who wants to know where Frohschammer is,[8] & when you expect it, & whether you are going to put it out to nurse, or to keep it yourself & translate it at the last moment, as you did with Döllinger[9] He much wants you to make use of Mrs Appell[10] or her like.

Do you know whether Lewes[11] did or did not publish a compendium of Comte, & whether he did or did not leave out the Positivist religion —the worship of Mother Wife & child—from the end? Have you got Lewes' history of Metaphysics. I have only read one vol. of Geo. Eliot, & I suspect that one may find pages of plagiarism of ideas from L.

---

[1] Probably William Gifford Palgrave (1826–88), convert, Jesuit 1853–65, missionary in Syria until 1861, in British diplomatic service from 1865, when he left the Roman Catholic Church, to which he returned in 1885.

[2] Félicité de Lamennais, Essai sur l'indifférence en matière de religion (Paris, 1817).

[3] Williams and Norgate.   [4] This was not published.   [5] Not published.

[6] Simpson wrote 'France and Mexico' in 'Current Events', Home & Foreign Review, III (October 1863), 758–63. This establishes Acton's authorship of 'The States of North America', ibid. 763–8, and Lathbury's of 'Indian Financial Statements', ibid. 751–2, neither attributed in Wellesley Index, I, 552.

[7] 'Foundlings.'

[8] Acton's intended article on Frohschammer ('Conflicts with Rome', 1864).

[9] 'The Waldensian Forgeries.'

[10] Probably a translator; possibly the wife of Johann Wilhelm Appell (1830–96), superintendent of the exhibition of 1862, assistant keeper, South Kensington Museum, 1865–93.

[11] George Henry Lewes (1817–78), positivist philosopher, published among other works Comte's Philosophy of the Sciences (1855).

Frederic Weld proposes writing an article about New Zealand,[1] w^h we may expect in about a year. He is against Grey, & though not approving Browne, laments that his policy, once begun, was not carried out,[2] as the change gives the brownies[3] an idea of ones weakness, which it will be necessary to wipe out in blood—will produce a war of extermination,—he says—His article will be full of local knowledge, & can be made an *I* art.[4] if you dont agree; so I hope you wont be angry with me for accepting it.

I have as yet no notion whether or no Roberts is getting ready—but with him & Froschhammer in bud, I dont see why I should spend time in forcing Deutinger into bloom.[5]

The article on Ultramontanism is said—I suspect at Hill S^ts[6]—to be "special pleading" & "crying stinking fish"—

I have packed up two little cases of your books; shall I send them by goods train to Aldenham. I have I suppose about $\frac{1}{2}$ as many more, w^h I dont send, because I think I may still want them—

Ever yours faithfully
R Simpson

Clapham
July 27, 1863

581

ACTON TO SIMPSON · 17 AUGUST 1863*

Monday

My dear Simpson,

I have had the house full of guests. I have been instructing a local architect to build my library, and I have effected a revolution on the management of the estate involving an immediate increase of rent— besides all of which I am obliged to take care of poor old Green, who has had a paralytic stroke. So don't be too hard on me if I have postponed a great many other things.

---

[1] Not published.
[2] Sir George Grey succeeded Thomas Gore Browne as governor of New Zealand in 1861 with the intention (not fulfilled) of pacifying the native uprising which Browne had provoked.
[3] Maoris.
[4] An article in the first person ('communicated' rather than 'editorial').
[5] In fact, none of these was published.
[6] Presumably this refers to the Jesuits of the Farm St chapel.
* A small part of this letter is in Gasquet, Letter cxlvi, pp. 304–5, with omissions and errors.

I send you Scherer[1] on George Eliot and Heine[2] on Shakespeare's womankind. Heine is a man you ought to delight in. I know nothing of Lewes's Comtism, and I have not got his biographical hist. of Phil;[3] of w^h there is a new ed. in 1 vol. I hope your Eliot studies are getting on. There is no need of Deutinger. Frohschammer seems to have been delayed[4] because I was expected in Munich. You shall have some Grimm for Mrs Appell if you can find her.[5]

Here is what has been given or recently promised, for I have written to make sure.

4	Foundlings	
10	Dante's Commentators	at Robson's
3	Poland	Buddeus
5	Geography	Arnold
6	George Eliot	Simpson
11	Frohschammer	
12	University Education	Renouf
8	Papst Fabeln	half finished
1	Prison rules & ministers	Lathbury
7	Primitive myths	Paley
2	Emigration	Moule
9	Celtic Literature	Sullivan[6]

The Irish Church,[7] Sir Thomas More.

Federal Reform in Germany,[8] Lowe on Gladstone's still unpublished speeches,[9] and a light Waters[10]— —are all uncertain.

Roberts only asks for time. New Zealand excellent, Childers on Victoria in January, Bowen on Queensland in April, and Weld on New Zealand in July would be well.[11] Do you know Ward's father in law

[1] Edmond Scherer, *Etudes critiques sur la Littérature contemporaine* (Paris, 1863), reviewed by Acton, *Home & Foreign Review*, III (October 1863), 718–20.

[2] Heinrich Heine (1797–1856), German poet and publicist.

[3] G. H. Lewes, *A Biographical History of Philosophy*, 4 vols. (London, 1845–6); 2nd ed. (London, 1859).

[4] Deutinger was not published; the article on Frohschammer was delayed until 'Conflicts with Rome' in April 1864.

[5] This never materialized.

[6] Of this list, there appeared: 'Foundlings'; 'Dante and his Commentators'; 'The Revolution in Poland'; 'The Formation of the English Counties'; 'George Eliot's Novels'; 'Medieval Fables of the Popes'; 'Gaol Discipline in England and Wales'; Paley, 'Classical Myths in Relation to the Antiquity of Man', *Home & Foreign Review*, IV (January 1864), 103–28; 'Emigration'; and possibly 'Celtic Ethnology'. The numbers represent the proposed order of publication.

[7] 'The Irish Church Establishment.'

[8] An article (which one is not certain) on Schleswig-Holstein.

[9] 'Mr. Gladstone's Financial Statements.'

[10] Not published.

[11] None of the Australasian articles was published. 'Bowen' is Sir George Ferguson Bowen (1821–99), colonial administrator; 'Weld' is Frederick Weld.

Wingfield?[1] I met him the other day and found him strongly liberal despite the Dublin. Can he write? Old Waterworths a devoted adherent and admirer, but in fear of bishops. However he told me in all secrecy, that Newport[2] was overcome by our last number, and declared to him privately, and at Spetchley quite openly, so that it might reach the ears of the bishop of that diocese, that there has never been anything so good in England.

This was on a visit last week to Worcester and Malvern, where W[3] pitched into the Dublin, which I have not had time to read. The notice of Villari[4] seemed to be carefully done.

I dined and slept at Hornyholds[5]—such a sleepy party. Walker S.T.P. of Oscott was there, vacantly amiable.

I suppose you know that your damages and Hodge's[6] iniquity combined have brought Wilberforce to his last legs. He wrote to me on Saturday that he meant to sell the WR and would come to terms with the Tablet if the liberals did not take some measures. And he wrote also to Monsell, T. O'Hagan, & More O Ferrall.

This is a very serious matter; and I have written to T OHagan in order that something may be done. Whatever happens it is certain that I must not appear in any shape or capacity. Wetherell you know has a great belief in the efficacy of newspapers and an ardent desire to have one as a support to the H&F. So that he is prepared to die the death by carrying on the WR if it can be obtained. I think he underrates the effect of an H&F name in the management, from his absurd belief in the existence of just men. He talks of subeditors and secretaries, of making nothing by it himself, provided the proprietors will spend all but a strict percentage on their outlay in improving the paper, and he thinks that if there were 50£ or 100£ shares, returning 5 per cent, a number of good and true men, F&R. Ward,[7] Case, Cocks, and yourself would like the investment.

Of course he privately reckons on the political and literary resources of the H&F, on my getting good foreign correspondents, on articles and reviews from yourself and Renouf, O'Hagan, Oxenham, Stokes &c— and on getting an opening for many well-wishers who cannot or dare not commit themselves to the H&F.

As a jointstock concern the Register cannot thrive unless so many grandees take shares that it can be said to have passed into the hands

---

[1] William Wingfield (1813–74), converted 1845.
[2] Bishop Thomas Brown.
[3] Waterworth.
[4] Review of Villari, *The History of Girolamo Savonarola*, in *Dublin Review*, n.s. I (July 1863), 232–8, by Edward Healy Thompson and Harriet Thompson.
[5] A misspelling of John Vincent Gandolfi Hornyold (1818–1902) of Blackmore Park.
[6] The former sub-editor of the *Weekly Register*.
[7] Francis Ward.

of the distinguished laity. It cannot thrive as a treble to our bass. But if Lord Petre, Castlerosse, Monsell, Monteith, Hope Scott were shareholders, that would be a cover for H&Fdom as far as it is necessary that it should penetrate the WR. As the editor of such a group of indifferent men Wetherell would be possible. The situation would be so very different from our's, the public exclusively Catholic, and not exclusively composed of educated men, that the abominations of our doctrine could be kept in the background. Pray revolve these matters in your mind. Whatever happens it will be very convenient to strengthen our editorial hands, and if you see no objection I should much like to adopt Renouf into the Rédaction.[1] To me in particular, very selfishly speaking, his foreign lore would be an immense support and relief. I think I could make the idea acceptable to him, but it would probably be best to keep it quite to ourselves. Every contribution would then pass through five pair of hands, and there ought not to be many oversights.

Have you ever told Wetherell that we are reckoning him, for the second year, at 100£ a year?

I remain
Ever Your's truly
J D Acton

582

SIMPSON TO ACTON · 18 AUGUST 1863

Clapham, Aug. 18. 1863

Dear Acton

Imprimis—many thanks for an excellent Haunch of Venison—

Secondly engage Renouf by all means, & give him any powers you like. There could not be a better man.

As to the WR.[2] supposing all the difficulties of a subsidiary H.&F. were, far impossible, overcome, do you believe for a moment that Wetherell, who is knocked up every Quarter by the Review, could stand the Weekly pull of the Newspaper? To put him there would be to drive him from us, into a position where he must fail in a little while. His determination would be to withhold all floss-doodle from an audience who are determined to swallow nothing else, or nothing that is not involved in such masses of the vehicle as to be absolutely unperceived. Now ideas that are unperceived are useless. *Paullum sepulto* &c. The best thing for us would be that the W.R. should be in the hands of men who would criticize us fairly up to their lights, without having

---

[1] The editorial staff of the *Home & Foreign Review*.
[2] *Weekly Register*.

124

one easy explanation for every difference, viz. our *conceit*. This is the only thing the Tablet can say of us. We are conceited. The W.R. carried on quite independently of us, under Petre, Hope Scott, &c might reason against us, might consider us to be grazing the edges of the abyss, but would not be calumnious, & would give some opening for thought & conviction. I certainly shall not throw away any money in it, partly because I don't see the use of it, partly because I am in want of every penny I can get to set free my property at Mitcham from the claws of lawyer Trustees.

Waters called here the other day, & I dine with him this evg. He will not do any *article*, but will do a heap of notices, if we *give* him the books. I have asked for a list, which I suppose he will furnish tonight. His specialty seems books of learned & antiquarian societies, and anything relating to the genealogy of families & historical characters. For an article to be ready at Xmas, he seems to take to the series of Catholic MDs., some of whom, having been foreign physicians to the English Court, or to English Nobles, have many anecdotes appended to their names. This I think would be good light reading.[1] He says he has taken a large place close to Poole, Dorset, & means to be MP. for Poole next Election, of which he makes no doubt whatever.

Newport[2] is very good for the centre of a reaction. Miss Wood[3] tells me that Telford of Ryde has converted four priests to H&Fdom by reading to them the article of last Oct. on the Cardinal & H&F.[4]

I have read all G. Eliot, & now am reading Lewes on Göthe, his Biograph. hist of Phil, & his Physiology of Common Life. He wrote an abstract of Comte in Bohn's Scientific library 1853. He also wrote two novels, the names of which I know not. I have seen quite enough to show the elective affinities between the two minds

Ever yours faithfully
R Simpson

Condole with poor old Green⎫
    in my name—   ⎭

---

[1] This was not published.
[2] The bishop of Newport and Menevia.
[3] Charlotte Wood, daughter of Charlotte Wood (1789–1873), widow of Canon William Wood (1768/9–1841). Both mother and daughter were converted 1845 and lived at Ryde, Isle of Wight.
[4] 'Cardinal Wiseman and the *Home & Foreign Review*.'

SIMPSON TO ACTON · 19 AUGUST 1863

Clapham Aug. 19. 63

Dear Acton

I forgot to say yesterday that I have not said a word to Wetherell about the 100 a year. I thought that you & he managed his pay between you. I think he prefers direct to mediate action in the matter. But I will write if you like.

Waters is Wilberforce's Trustee.[1] He assures me that the W.R. is improving rather than otherwise; that Wilberforce received 300£ out of it last year without in the least anticipating income or infringing capital; that he is sure Wil's only notion is to sell the concern for more than it is worth, himself being retained either as Editor or as French correspondent at a fixed salary; & that his "coming to terms with the Tablet" did not in the least mean his divesting himself of all functions, but simply his chopping round, changing sides, & making an amalgamation with Wallis.

Waters was making all sorts of indirect offers aiming at getting some share in the H.&F. I was very guarded, I told him that you certainly would never let any one else share the expense (!) but that possibly he might have a department—English history to wit. Then he told me in strict confidence a story which I suspect to be only of a cock & a bull. I cannot enter into details, but the general conclusion is this. The Cardinal is highly dissatisfied with the New Dublin. He wants to secede, to set up a new Review, to be called the Catholic Review, on the model of the H.&F. except that it should contain in each number two theological articles, strictly orthodox. He offers to leave all the rest of the number to the Editor. He would try & make terms with the H.&F. if it had not showed clearly that it inherited the personal antipathies of the Rambler.

Is this pure invention? It may indicate to you a line for enquiries. The Dublin is certainly weak. Ward's article on civil government[2] is weak as water. The fundamental assumption is that we know all the spiritual consequences of every political act: & he gets into dilemmas like the following. The C^h has no right to punish with the civil sword. The state has no right to interfere with conscience. Therefore we may suppose there is no Divine institution which may punish sins of conscience with the civil sword. But no. The two may unite & do it. By some process

---

[1] For the sale of the *Weekly Register*.
[2] W. G. Ward, 'Intrinsic End of Civil Government', *Dublin Review*, n.s. I (July 1863), 66–111.

of generation the union of the two produces a new right, the elements of which preexisted in neither. As the article is all a priori & scholastic this seems to be a fatal objection to his theory; he takes the lowest kind of animal view of the state. The article is radical.

Manning on the wants of the Church[1] sh^d be read. It contains his arguments *pro & con* a Cath. College at Oxford. They are badly put but Renouf should read them.

Ever yours sincerely
R Simpson

No books arrived.

584

ACTON TO SIMPSON · 19 AUGUST 1863

Wednesday

My dear Simpson,

I did not like to stop W[2] in what might be the way to emolument. While on the one hand I do not agree with him in thinking that the sort of acquiescence a newspaper can command is of any real value, and fear the agreement of people who have not the means of mastering difficulties more than opposition, at the same time I cannot conceive the state of mind in which a man would be such as you describe, neither for us or against us. He must have honesty and knowledge, and I don't know what else goes to the definition of H&Fism.

We must not delude Waters into the belief that he can fill his shelves with rare new books at our expense by merely writing notices of them. He can have the books for review, and his 6^{s}4^d a page, but we can't give him the books.[3] His MDs[4] by all means at Christmas. The membership for Poole is one of his reasons for hesitating to write for us.

Miss Bowles's Mme Swetchine[5] goes to Malvern to day. I am, on the whole, favourably struck. It is like the first article in the Dublin,[6] picked out with the strong things of the old lady. W will probably consider it unworthy of a serious answer.

---

[1] Manning, 'The Work and the Wants of the Catholic Church in England', *ibid.* 139–66.

[2] Wetherell.

[3] Books for review were usually borrowed from Mudie's.

[4] The unpublished article on Catholic doctors.

[5] An article (not published) by Emily Bowles (1818–1904), converted 1843, writer and translator of religious books, about Anna Sophie Soymonoff Swetchine (Svechin; 1782–1857), Russian convert 1817, kept a salon in Paris frequented by Catholics.

[6] Herbert Vaughan, 'Popular Devotion in Spain', *Dublin Review*, n.s. i (July 1863), 1–32.

I sent you Longman,[1] thinking you might wish to notice him.

I remain
Ever Your's truly
J D Acton

585

SIMPSON TO ACTON · 2 SEPTEMBER 1863

Dear Acton

I am terribly late with my Article,[2] but here it is, with 3 short notices —Make haste to suggest any alterations you think of, & tell Wetherell also to be quick about it.

I dont yet know a bit about Mexico. Have you no French pamphlets to send me? If not I must go to the Burlington arcade, or to W^{ms} & Norgate to get materials—

Nothing from Waters yet.

Wont you say something civil about Montalembert & the contrary about the other congressionists at Malines?[3]

What have you done about Wilberforce?[4] nothing, I should hope—

Printers bill 160£—including 12.12.0 for Human Sacrifice[5]—next time it will be increased by "Parties";[6]—is not that article to be used at all? From what I hear, I think the opinion is that we give too many short notices; people are frightened at ther bulk, & are afraid to attack the mass.

The Jesuits, I gather from Christie, are astonished at the weakness of Manning's reasons against a College at Oxford. C. said. Fathers will send their sons there; that being the case, is it safer to have a Catholic Hall or not.

I wont argue what I said about the W. Register on paper; it is not worth the trouble—I dare say I expressed myself badly, but my meaning was quite orthodox & H&Fish.

How about Pope-fables?[7]

Ever yours faithfully
R Simpson

Clapham, Sept 2. 63.

---

[1] Possibly *The Nullity of Metaphysics as a Science among the Sciences* (London: Longmans, 1863), reviewed in *Home & Foreign Review,* III (October 1863), 667–8.
[2] 'George Eliot's Novels.'
[3] This refers to the Catholic Congress at Malines, Belgium, 18–21 August 1863, at which Montalembert delivered his liberal speeches on 'A Free Church in a Free State' and 'Liberty of Conscience'.
[4] The purchase of the *Weekly Register*, which did not in fact take place.
[5] Acton's pamphlet, separately published.
[6] Woodlock's article on Irish parties had been set in type but was not published.
[7] 'Medieval Fables of the Popes.'

ACTON TO SIMPSON · 4 SEPTEMBER 1863

Aldenham
Friday

Dear Simpson,

Deutinger[1] & Mexico[2] are all that is important. I have seen no serious report of Malines, but you will find something in the *France*.[3] I send the beginning of Deutinger.

I will let you know before I come up to Town where I can have a chance of meeting you. Your notices are all right—Many thanks—

Ever Your's truly
J D Acton

ACTON TO SIMPSON · 8 SEPTEMBER 1863*

Tuesday

My dear Simpson,

The bishop of Shrewsbury[4] under pretence of making his visitation has spent a week here, for the purpose of demolishing the H&F. Wetherell, Arnold and Roger Vaughan[5] came to meet him; and I have been too busy to do anything.

The time was not lost however, for I converted the Bishop, who came to curse, and went away yesterday after giving his blessing to the review, and expressing himself gratified at my explanations, and satisfied with the principle non lac sed escam. At this moment he is at a great meeting at Sedgleypark, where he announced his intention of proclaiming his altered views. He assured me that in spite of the strong feelings of some bishops a reaction has been setting in among them, and that he would try to promote it.

Pray take care not to overuse this fact in conversation. It will be best to let it work out its own effect, and not to provoke others to drive

---

[1] The unpublished article on German philosophy.
[2] For 'Current Events'.
[3] A French newspaper.
* Gasquet, Letter CXLVII, pp. 305–8, misdated 'Sept. 9', with omissions.
[4] James Brown.
[5] Roger William Bede Vaughan (1834–83), brother of the future cardinal, Benedictine monk 1851, prior of Hereford 1862, coadjutor bishop of Newport and Menevia 1873, archbishop of Sydney 1877.

back the Bishop, Arnold and Vaughan to whom the Bp opened his mind, will carry the matter.

At the same time Cullen's organ[1] has a flaming eulogy of the last number.

The episcopal conference was diversified by the study of your article on George Eliot, which is one of the most excellent things you have ever written. Even our stern critic[2] was mollified, and moved to frequent choking. I sent 30 pages to printers today. He has carried off the rest to Malvern.

My review of Döllinger has long been in the printer's hands, as also Emigration, and Wetherell will send up Paley on the ancient myths immediately. I read nine good but severe pages of Arnold on English Boundaries, which will be original, and soon ready. Lathbury is finishing Prison Discipline, and I expect Poland[3] daily.

Renouf and Sullivan[4] are postponed till January. The first I have not pressed, as an interval after Manning[5] is not to be regretted. The latter could hardly come in the same number with Dante,[6] which cannot be put off. The materials on Frohschammer are very incomplete, and contain nothing about what has been done. I go to Munich on the 25th and shall get all particulars for Jan[y] It is no use doing it now very imperfectly. So we stand thus:

1 *Prison Discipline* (incl: Prison Ministers)
2 *Emigration* (very fairly good & solid)
3 *Poland*
4 *English Boundaries*
5 *George Eliot's Novels*
6 *Ancient Legends* (wants another title)
7 *Medieval fables of the Popes* ⎱ invert order
8 *Dante and his commentators* ⎰

As Irish Church is doubtful, and Foundlings cannot well come with Prisoners,[7] could you fashion *Deutinger*[8] for the last article? We should then be right enough.

---

[1] The Dublin *Freeman's Journal*.   [2] Wetherell.

[3] The references are respectively to: 'Medieval Fables of the Popes'; 'Emigration in the Nineteenth Century'; 'Classical Myths in Relation to the Antiquity of Man'; 'The Formation of the English Counties'; 'Gaol Discipline in England and Wales'; and 'The Revolution in Poland'.

[4] Renouf's article on a Catholic university was separately published; Sullivan wrote 'Celtic Ethnology'.

[5] Manning had written 'The Work and the Wants of the Catholic Church in England'.

[6] 'Dante and his Commentators.'

[7] All three articles appeared in October: 'The Irish Church Establishment', 'Foundlings' and 'Gaol Discipline in England and Wales'.

[8] The article on German philosophy was not published.

Materials abound for Mexico[1] &c. You should look up Chevalier, & one or two pamphlets spoken of in the newspapers. Let me know if you would like to look through the *France*.

After Mexico turn for a moment to French internal affairs, the anti episcopal edict—and so by an easy transition to the absence of all the French clergy from Malines, to the spirit of that assembly, the unexpected effect of Montalembert's speech[2] &c. The new Correspondant has an article on it.

I have your notices safe. Can you also do Chevalier, and Cousin's history of Philosophy?[3] I am busy with the splendid new Acta SS.[4] Sullivan & Renouf promise immediate Notices. Arnold also a few. How as to Waters?

Wetherell goes up to town this day week. Have you seen Darnell? Green all right again?

For January.

Volunteers (He[5] is well, and eager to do them)
Lowe on *Gladstone*
The Irish Church
Federal Reform in Germany
Foundlings
Browning's Poems (Arnold)
Celtic Philology
Sir Thomas More (charming letter from Brewer)
Frohschammer
Catholic University[6]
Besides Waters, Lathbury &c.

Would it suggest itself to you to do Vinet[7] for January? Besides the two little volumes I can send you half a dozen exquisite works, and a few criticisms. He is a portent in the history of Calvinism, and would be a capital subject for such a pen as your's.

Wednesday

Here is your letter from Lathbury's. The printers are absurd. It is of no use sending them copy when they return no proofs. If they had done

---

[1] For 'Current Events'.
[2] On 'A Free Church in a Free State' at the Catholic Congress at Malines; reviewed, possibly by Simpson, in *Home & Foreign Review*, III (October 1863), 726–9.
[3] Simpson reviewed only Michel Chevalier, *La Mexique, ancien et moderne*, in *ibid.* 721–2.
[4] Acton reviewed the latest *Acta Sanctorum* in *ibid.* 682–5.
[5] Wetherell.
[6] Of this list, 'The Irish Church Establishment' and 'Foundlings' were published in October. The January number contained Lowe, 'Mr. Gladstone's Financial Statements' and Sullivan, 'Celtic Ethnology'. 'Frohschammer' eventually appeared as part of 'Conflicts with Rome' in April 1864.
[7] No article on Vinet was published.

Emigration and the Pope-fables when you saw them on Monday how is it I have no proofs today? I sent no half articles, except your's yesterday.

Your doctrine and exhortation are sound and I will do my part as well as I can. You see I am trying all dodges to get help which may make me a little superfluous and enable me to get abroad for a few weeks. Don't talk of rich men's hobbies. It is impossible for me to spend anything on the review from *income*.

If you go to printers for your article will you order Molinari[1] in passing W&N's?

I think we cannot expect Renouf to do editorial work till our arrangements are made with him, and he comes to Town.

I have put the W Register question into the hands of the Attorney General,[2] together with much good advice.

Did you read that very remarkable trial of Fillion[3] which I sent you?

Ever Your's faithfully
J D Acton

588

SIMPSON TO ACTON · 10 SEPTEMBER 1863

Dear Acton

I send you some short notices—too long I am afraid, but perhaps containing things worth saying—if you think not, cancel them—

Send me La France—I did not read the trial[4]—I thought you were amused with the Frankfort gastronomy—I hope I shall find the leaf somewhere—I will do what I can, but whether I shall do half of what you ask me I don't know. I won't promise about Deutinger, but as a preliminary you must send me the article which I prepared, in order that I may see where to begin—I have some lucubrations upon Malines from De Buck—very sensible—Send me some paper that contains a rational account of the effect of Montalembert—also the second part of his speech—The Correspondant only gives the first day, & gives nothing of his "liberté des cultes"[5]—

---

[1] Acton reviewed M. Gustave de Molinari, *Cours d'Economie Politique*, in *Home & Foreign Review*, IV (January 1864), 313–15. 'W&N' is Williams and Norgate.
[2] Thomas O'Hagan.
[3] This appears to refer to Charles Fillion, bishop of St Claude 1858, of Le Mans 1862.
[4] Of Fillion.
[5] Montalembert's second speech at the Catholic Congress of Malines.

Can you let me see you on your passage through London on the 25th
I want particularly to say something w[h] I have not time to write—

Ever yours most truly
R Simpson

Sep. 10.

589

SIMPSON TO ACTON · 12 SEPTEMBER 1863

Sept. 12. 1863

Dear Acton

I have read over the rest of Deutinger,[1] & I cannot see my way to do anything with it in less than a fortnights hard work, to which I am not well up, in consequence of my usual autumnal stomachic ailments. But if I could do it, & make it readable, by the 25th, just see how late we should be; Wetherell would want 2 days to go through it;—27th;—& the 28th is the day of publication;—So cannot you fall back on Block?[2] I assured him solemnly, when we left Foundlings out in July, that they should appear in October; & the likeness of the Prison discipline to Foundlings is not more than I suppose that of Paley's Ancient legends to your excellent Pope-fables[3] to be. It would be a charity to take this burden from my shoulders, & a point of wisdom not to overwork a willing ass.

But if you decide that it must be, tell me what you want—Do you want the criticism of Schopenhauer & Herbart, & the a-religious idealists & materialists who have followed them, or that of Günther & Baader— which so far as I see cannot stand without a preliminary sketch of the whole development—& the attempts of the religious school since their day? The article as it stands is at least 4 times too long; Three parts must be left out—which be they? or rather, what exact period or school do you want?

I told you I think how I had been in correspondence *at* Browne of Newport and Menevia[4] in May. The affair closed in June, with a letter of his in which he says "I can go much farther with M[r] S. than I should have been disposed to go a few years back...Altho' to my judgment many of the conclusions said to be come to (in the H.&F.) are by no

---

[1] The article on German philosophy.
[2] 'Foundlings.'
[3] The other articles are 'Gaol Discipline in England and Wales', 'Classical Myths in Relation to the Antiquity of Man' (January 1864), and 'Medieval Fables of the Popes'.
[4] Bishop Thomas Brown.

133

means adequately established, *yet place must be made for them, & for the conviction of those who believe in them*". Thus acknowledging our right of existence as guides to this *place*—"Dr Ullathorne, with whom I have had some correspondence on the above matters lately seems to fear that I am joining those on the edge of infidelity"—Such was the result of B's of Newport endeavour to convert U.; let us hope that B of Shrewsbury will do better—Newport afterwards told my medium that he was well satisfied with the July N° & that he meant to proclaim the fact at a conference at Sedgley—so curiously do facts double themselves —Shall I assault Grant? If so, shall I tell him of the two traitors?

W.&N. know of no new ed. of Cousin's history of Phil:—what you do mean by asking me to notice it? They had not your Chevalier on Mexique,[1] but are to let me have it next week.

Ever Y^{rs} aff^y
R Simpson

590

ACTON TO SIMPSON · 13 SEPTEMBER 1863

Sunday

My dear Simpson,

I am very sorry for the disturbance of mind I have caused you. I had no idea that there would be above a day or two's work in Deutinger. Pray dismiss him from your thoughts. With an altered title, if you can devise one, Block might come after the political articles, before Boundaries.

1	Gaol Discipline	2	Emigration		
3	Poland	4	Principle of F. hospitals		
5	Boundaries	6	Eliot	7	Mythology
8	Dante	9	Pope Fables[2]		It is even a question

whether we might not put off Paley. Only we shall not be *very* rich in Notices, unless you have a few more in hand. Cousin's is a new book, and has been reviewed in the Saturday. I have sent up La France.

I wonder how the 2 Browns did at Sedgley, or whether they were done.

You had better approach Grant very cautiously. Remember what

---

[1] See p. 131, n. 3.

[2] The order of articles in the October *Home & Foreign Review* varies slightly from this. 'Mythology' is Paley's 'Classical Myths in Relation to the Antiquity of Man', held over to January.

Don Abbondio says of the Saints.[1] My experience of them is still more discouraging. It will be best to take the ball on the bound, when we know something of the encounter at the Park gathering.

Lathbury,[2] as much as I have seen is very good—

Ever Y^{rs} most truly

J D Acton

591

ACTON TO SIMPSON · 20 SEPTEMBER 1863

Sunday

Dear Simpson,

I hope you are flourishing and have defeated Ember week. Don't lose time by sending me Mexico—Malines;[3] only pray don't endorse Montalembert's fundamental delusion of the incessant progress of democracy —an error derived from Lamennais, & confirmed by Tocqueville, who expounds it in the opening of his American book.

Renouf practically accepts our proposal,[4] but his plans are uncertain, and I am not sure whether he can help us next time, except of course by sitting upon Manning,[5] which he says he can very thoroughly, and yet very pleasantly for Manning.

I don't think we shall have a bad number. But you ought to relieve me of English notices rather more, as I have no end of foreign books to do. I expect nearly half the notices this time will be mine.

The ambitious colleague[6] has been worrying me ever so long about an annual Register, to be called the H&F. Chronicle, ed. by the conductors of the H&FR. containing the general history, politics, religion, literature & science of the year, faithfully recorded by good men and true, which we are to find in all lands and branches of learning—to appear every April, for the foregoing year, similar in type &c to the H&F. and equal in bulk to a whole vol. of it.

I don't want to spend money on anything but the review, but it might be a good advertisement, or it might even pay, or the publishers might take it on spec. I think it would be possible to find the men, and if successful it might certainly do manifold good. Revolve it in your

---

[1] Don Abbondio is a character in Manzoni's *I Promessi Sposi*. The statement is probably 'Do you think one may say without caution, even to saints, all that passes through one's mind?' (Ch. XXX). Grant was well known for his saintliness.

[2] 'Gaol Discipline in England and Wales.'

[3] 'Current Events.'

[4] To join the editorial staff of the *Home & Foreign Review*.

[5] 'The Work and the Wants of the Catholic Church in England.'

[6] Wetherell.

mind; I have not matured the plans yet, only because I don't want to dissipate our money—resources. If that can be avoided I will work out my idea of it.

I shall pass through town on Friday. Can you meet me at Wetherell's a little before 6 and come and eat a farewell fish at the Wellington?

Ever Your's faithfully
J D Acton

592

SIMPSON TO ACTON · 21 SEPTEMBER 1863

Sept. 21

My dear Acton

I will meet you at Wetherell's on Friday a little before 6.

I have not my bankers book here, so I cannot tell the exact state of H.&F. accounts. But as far as I remember they stood as follows. After paying for April, I had £60 left. I received 119 from W.&N. & I paid 160 to the printers, & 40 odd to the stationers, for the July No. leaving me a little less than nothing. W.& N. still owe for 3 N^{os} & they ought to pay up after every two; but perhaps it is better not to hurry them.

The reason that I have done so few notices is the difficulty of getting books. Mudie has treated me very badly this quarter, I have been away a good deal, & when he treats me well, perhaps for the week the book is here I am not disposed to read it, & then it gets sent back without my looking at it. It is so much harder to get up a borrowed book that you cannot mark & in which you cannot scribble at the end as you (I) walk round the garden reading it, that if I am to do many more notices I must have the books to scribble in, & to keep as long as I like during the operation. Fullerton used to pay Toovey 20 or 30£ a year, & have all new books of importance sent down to Newbury, he keeping what he wanted *up to* the publishing price of 20£ or 30£ (the amount of the subscription) & paying for all books he damaged. I.E. he used to have his reading & use of the difference between the 20£ or 30£ worth & what was sent down to him at the price of Toovey's profit on the 20£ or 30— ie. for 5£ or £7.10 a year—But we ought also now to get books from publishers; at least on loan, if not on gift—or on gift on the condition of review. Then, if we get such books, some arrangement must be come to by w^h they should be sent to me regularly by W.&N.

Perhaps it would be better in the long run if I were to leave off Mudie, & spend some 8 or 10£ annually in buying, at trade price, the books I

136

intend to review.—as I do now. I bought a lot of books to serve me for *epigrams*, & also G. Eliot's novels.[1]

I wonder whether Wetherell's objection to my taking an ostensible share in the management[2] is over yet. I am put into a position in which I often don't know whether I am telling truth or falsehood—& this, it seems to me, for no solid reason at all. Understand me that this no point I am going to make a business of. I only speak to you about it, to give you a hint that it is a kind of discomfort to me, & that, when any thing riles me, the thought of it is sure to come up with some bitterness. However, if there is the slightest real use in it, I will go on contentedly. But I want the assurance that it is utility & not caprice that keeps things as they are. As things are, I often feel sorely tempted to insist upon some trivial point with W. which w^d lead to a row. E.G. I had actually written a letter to insist upon keeping the expression "passion of justice" in George Eliot—but I saw my way to attain my end by a compromise— We will talk of this when you come back from the Continent.

Ever yours faithfully
R Simpson

593

ACTON TO SIMPSON · 22 SEPTEMBER 1863*

Tuesday

My dear Simpson,

I was too busy with preparations for departure to write to you today before post time. There is no doubt that we can make with the booksellers some arrangement such as you describe. But you had better think of some more serious man than Toovey. The worst of having books from publishers is that they expect them to be noticed, and one is not quite free to choose. Now the selection of books for notice is a most important element. There is a dodge which consists in scribbling on a loose bit of paper at the end of one's book. I have heard Lewis did this, but I don't know whether he was the sole inventor and patentee. It is of no consequence this time. We have only too many notices, and too fat a number.

---

[1] The two articles by these titles.

[2] Simpson had officially withdrawn, at Wetherell's suggestion, from the management of the *Home & Foreign Review* in December 1862 in order to dissociate it from his *Rambler* writings. Simpson, but not Wetherell, had understood that this was a merely formal arrangement.

* Watkin and Butterfield, pp. 97–9, misdated (following Simpson's dating) 'September 2'. Gasquet prepared this letter for publication but did not publish it.

It has often occurred to me when my pet ideas have been changed or inverted either for no good reason, or as it seemed to me, on mistaken grounds, by Wetherell, that the same process must be sometimes annoying to you who are on the entirely different footing of a man who cares for the expression of his thoughts. For my part I generally acquiesce partly because you can't teach people what they don't know, and partly as a set off against more important points of difference on which I am obliged to have my own way. If, as you imply, you have not the latter consolation in its full extent, there is certainly a defect in our institutions which I have never contemplated. I was persuaded in the winter, that you had understood the purport of our correspondence in its natural, honest and straightforward sense, and that you did not mean to impose upon me the further duty of 'occasionally' explaining that I had in fact only meant what I had said, and had not ingeniously contrived a device to wrest your own weapon from your hand, or to substitute the merely formal dexterity of our colleague for your astonishing resources, in the management of the Review. For this is what you have silently imputed to me if by your greater reserve in our deliberations you intended to signify that you thought you were not wanted, or that there was a lurking jealousy of your influence. I did not imagine that this was in your thoughts, but rather supposed that we both found comfort in our companionship in the unlimited snubbing we undergo. If I have rejoiced at it beyond this it was for a reason which has never been a mystery. You know that I have always disliked anything polemical in our policy and tone, and that nothing in the world can ever entirely subdue the fight that is in you; and also that with our opposite theory respecting the scientific treatment of subjects I am very glad not to have perpetually to meet proposals for diverse sorts of articles with impertinent objections. I did not dream that there would be difficulty in finding a medium between having your fling—which no old fogy in England regards with more horror than I do—and combining in a constitutional system. If there really is any difficulty it is infinitely better that Wetherell and ourselves should part company. But with reference to this alternative let me remind you of what occurred last number. You know I thought Gladstone wrong about charities, and tried to expound my view in opposition to a clever sketch by Stokes. Lathbury put my notes as a hypothetical argument, and then put his own argument in such a way as to appear that of the Review. This I slightly modified in MS. and W changed it back again so far as to give us the appearance of cowardly trimming, and to put me into what would have been a sad fix, if there had been a vote on the question later. So it went back to printers, and I saw it only after publication.[1] This is a worse

---

[1] This may refer to 'Current Events' in the July *Home & Foreign Review*.

case than that of passionate justice, though it happens I had taken your view about that. If, even after our cooptation of the most learned Catholic in the country,[1] it is still necessary for your comfort that we should go on without Wetherell, transeat, let him pass away. I had much rather we lost him than fail to reconcile you to the present arrangement. When you say that it is vexatious without being profitable, I am surprised that you who differ from me in nothing more than in your habit of estimating opinion as a reality should think that in this particular nothing can be gained. You can of course say that it is not certain that my connection with the H&F. does not do it as much harm that your's could not add to the damage. As to this I will only say one thing, and I am afraid you will not agree with me about it. As a matter of fact there is a certain amount of—I do not say angry or bitter, or unjust, but—personal, feeling, the result of very old events, partly, which you cannot quite get rid of. Now, if I have no sympathy, or anything of that sort, I really have no antipathy for the people who are in our way. I suppose I exhausted all those faculties in a very different sphere of existence; for I certainly think worse of many people than you do.

But this is not really to the point, because it is a matter we cannot thoroughly discuss. What will strike you on reflection is that it would be a mockery and an unfair dodge to have said at one time that you were not editing the H&F. but that W and I were, and then all at once to set about it again.

I would propose first that you should not hold aloof, from an unjust suspicion which must do harm to the Review, but bully us more than you do, and exert your just influence which you seem to have relinquished from a misunderstanding. Next, that you should consider how the introduction of a new power, exactly on a level with Wetherell, will presently tell—taking into consideration the purely objective, scientific nature of Renouf's mind. Or lastly that you would accept the sacrifice of Wetherell as the condition on which the present arrangement is to continue, quoad the office, but not with regard to the influence you have wrongfully refused to exercise. I do not undervalue his critical assistance, but I estimate it far below the importance of not reverting to the old forms, and of restoring you to that virtual supremacy, which cannot be maintained, in any case, without some trouble and discussion.

Believe me
Ever Your's most truly
J D Acton

[1] Renouf.

SIMPSON TO ACTON · 23 SEPTEMBER 1863

Dear Acton

Can you lend me *Gugenheim* if you think he will be useful for tracing the development of the English poor-law.

Does he trace the influence of the Crusades (?) & Mendicant Orders in the mobilisation of the *adscriptus glebae*? Is there any evidence that the mendicant movement was accompanied by any abolitionist fanaticism? I only want to know whether this is a line of enquiry that promises fruit.

I have had dyspepsia worse than ever this year, & in consequence I have done Mexico[1] so foolishly that I am afraid it will be a *caution*. I shall go abroad next week, to see if I cannot shake it off by travelling— I must consult you about a route—You told me much about Speyer & other places which I have forgotten—

Ever yours faithfully
R Simpson

Wednesday
Are Giunchi's exegetics[2] sent to be translated by Mrs Appel? Dont forget to tell me on Friday..

595

SIMPSON TO ACTON · 9 NOVEMBER 1863

My dear Acton

I came back on Friday night, bringing with me an article in the rough which represents my intended history of the poor law[3]—a history I could not make during my travels, & which it is now too late to complete for January. As it stands—(it is not meant to appear in this form, as much of it is unintelligible to any but very good-natured readers—) it is a sketch of an article which I could make up for January if you want it.

Let me know how things stand for the next number; what you have & what you want. I must put off telling you about Montalembert till I see

---

[1] For 'Current Events'.
[2] Not published.
[3] 'The Rise of the English Poor-Law.'

you—He had never seen more than the 1ˢᵗ no of the H.&F. we had forgotten to put either him or the Correspondant on the free list

Send back the article with your suggestions as soon as may be—
Wetherell says that the Printers & he are open-mouthed for copy—When
are you to be up in Town?

Block proposes an article on Paris, municipal & economical.[1] Shall I
accept? There are others, wʰ he proposes also; I will send you the list
tomorrow; but I am finishing this note chez Wetherells & have it not
here—

Ever yours faithfully
R Simpson

Nov. 9.

596

ACTON TO SIMPSON · 14 NOVEMBER 1863

Saturday

My dear Simpson,

I hope you have enjoyed your journey and are the better for it.
I have been in the midst of festive scenes since my return, and shall be
in London in about a fortnight.

By all means accept the article on 'Paris, a microcosm.'[2] It would
be well to have it for January if possible. We have

1 Lord Palmerston's Second Administration
2 Schleswig Holstein
3 History of Poor Relief
4 Henry Taylor's Dramas
5 Classic legends
6 Celtic Literature
7 S. Ursula
8 The Suppression of the Monasteries
9 Froude's Elizabeth
10 Augury
11 The Munich Congress
12 The University Question.[3]   of these I shᵈ

---

[1] Block, 'Paris, Municipal and Economical', *Home & Foreign Review*, iv (January
1864), 55–78.   [2] 'Paris, Municipal and Economical.'
[3] Of these, the January number contained: 'The Constitutional Question in Schleswig-Holstein' (probably by MacCabe), *Home & Foreign Review*, iv (January 1864),
38–54; 'Classical Myths in Relation to the Antiquity of Man'; 'Celtic Ethnology';
C. H. Pearson, 'The Dissolution of the English Monasteries', *ibid.* 165–90; Joseph
Stevenson, 'Mr. Froude's *Reign of Queen Elizabeth*', *ibid.* 191–208; Acton, 'The
Munich Congress', *ibid.* 209–44. 'The Rise of the English Poor-Law' appeared in
April.

like to postpone 7 and 10. 3 and 8 cannot well come together; but I am not sure how far Pearson[1] is safe. If this is ascertained it ought to determine your proceedings. Should you postpone 3 and succeed in getting Paris, it is well. But if Pearson postpones, Poor Relief would come in with Froude better than the monks. Is there anything coming on Catholic MDs?[2] Pray at least ascertain about Water's short notices.

Perhaps we may have Lowe on Gladstone[3] this time. Our worst trouble is that Lathbury wants to deal only with Home Politics, which will not make a proper article.

Pray try for Paris now, and for French agriculture[4] as soon as may be.

If you keep Poor Relief for April, pray get a lot of Notices done this time. Renouf is cooking Grimm's, and will send some of his own. Have you read Gneist[5] on our system of Poor Relief?

I want to bother you for a kindness of another description. My favourite cousin[6] is going to be married, and I have promised to make up a little note book for her, containing Sententias worth reading and recurring to. I have long supplied her with all manner of lore, and my selection must by no means consist of milk for babes, but of the best things on the outer as well as the inner world. You have two of my books which I should like to look through for the purpose; Gioberti and Vinet. Would you either loan them to me for a fortnight, or better still, suggest, from them and others you wot of, matter for my purpose?

What do you hear of the Oxford schemes and fears of the bishops?[7]

> I remain
> Ever Your's truly
> J D Acton

597

SIMPSON TO ACTON · 16 NOVEMBER 1863

Nov. 16.

Dear Acton

I send you the three books you ask for—I hope you found at Aldenham two small cases of books which I sent you two months ago.

---

1 'The Dissolution of the English Monasteries.'
2 An article by Waters on Catholic doctors was expected but not received.
3 'Mr. Gladstone's Financial Statements.'
4 Block, 'Agriculture in France', *Home & Foreign Review*, IV (April 1864), 379–401.
5 Rudolf von Gneist (1816–95), jurist, professor at Berlin 1844.
6 Emily Throckmorton (d. 1929), married 25 Nov. 1863 Col. Sir Gerald Richard Dease (1831–1903).
7 The proposal to establish a Catholic college at Oxford.

I wrote to Block yesterday to ask him for Paris[1]—he will send it, I have no doubt, in about 10 days. Poor laws I shall work at now, while I have some interest in the subject, to the exclusion of other things. The article will do for some other time if it is not wanted now. Why do you allow Lathbury home politics[2] if it will not make a proper article? I should certainly vote for suppressing that, if I have a vote. Surely he will do other other things, if he is told, and things on which you have not the chance of being grieved, as you were in re Gladstone & taxation of charities. ≠ Would a selection of *proverbs* be of any use for your cousins book?

Every body chooses those which strike his own individual fancy, & fancy that an others selection of them, except they are applied to a particular character, to a Sancho or Mrs Poyser, are most wearisome, flat, & unprofitable. You have not the cue to tell you on what principle the selection was made, & in 999 selectors in 1000 the cue is not worth looking for. So I judge that the selection of proverbs is not worth sending —a conclusion I had not arrived at when I asked the question, or I would not have written it.

Do you seek wisdom pure, or expression—e.g. what of the Yankee saying
—Truth is always invariable; but the Smithate of truth must always differ from the Brownate of truth—? or Temple's
"In the education of the world, as in that of children, first come Rules (peremptory & unexplained), then Examples, then Principles. First the Law, then the Son of Man, then the Spirit."[3]

I have got note books full of little sentences like these, some of which I will copy for you, if you like.

Ever yours faithfully
R Simpson

598

ACTON TO SIMPSON · 17 NOVEMBER 1863

Tuesday

My dear Simpson,

I have urged the importance and shown the way of bringing in foreign politics. One cannot say that the treatment of one part of the government policy would be without precedent. But the moral of the

[1] 'Paris, Municipal and Economical.'
[2] The political sections of 'Current Events'.
[3] A slight misquotation of Frederick Temple, 'The Education of the World', in *Essays and Reviews* (London, 1860), p. 5.

tale, the enforcing of the Whig test in judging their conduct, is incomplete without the application of it to international questions.

Pray take an opportunity of pitching in to him.[1] We cannot do without the article[2] altogether, as we are not certain of Lowe on Gladstone.

Block[3] will be very welcome for January.

Renouf is in full action, translating Grimm, abusing Paley, rejecting a weak thing on Renan, &c. But he is still at Dublin, and remains there till Christmas.

The bishops having consulted Rome about Oxford the answer is likely to be discouraging. If it becomes necessary to wait I have a scheme.[4] I have offered the big house at Morville[5] to Renouf to begin with, and wait for better times, dwelling on the proximity of my library, which makes it the only country place he could live at. There are many collateral advantages I have not dwelt upon as I am afraid he will consider my book resources insufficient. But I have been two posts without an answer, so that he is considering about it. The house is being put into repair, and might hold a staff of professors and a dozen students. I have told nobody but Renouf yet, and fear that the very proximity I represent as an advantage will be injurious if not fatal, unless it can be represented as salvation from Oxford.

Thanks for the books, and many thanks for your kind offer of giving me a contribution of Pensées. They would be very welcome, if, like that of Temple, they are rather wise than witty, and if you would give the author's name. Pray think of the legacy of good thoughts you would like to give your nearest relation going away for good. Her usual reading has been Newman, Döllinger, Pascal, and the gravest historians. Anything reaching me by Friday would be most thankfully received.

What do you say to a paper on Shakespeare's philosophy to celebrate the Jubilee?[6] I cannot help thinking you would do it with a special relish and the greatest success.

I remain
Ever truly Your's
J D Acton

---

[1] Lathbury.

[2] On the poor laws.

[3] 'Paris, Municipal and Economical.'

[4] To found a Catholic university in England. This correspondence (misdated 1862) is given in *Selections from the Correspondence of the First Lord Acton*, ed. J. N. Figgis and R. V. Laurence (London, 1917), pp. 162–5, 125–6. Renouf declined the proposal.

[5] The village on Acton's estate, next to Aldenham Park.

[6] The tercentenary of Shakespeare's birth.

SIMPSON TO ACTON · 19 NOVEMBER 1863

Dear Acton

Block promises an article on Paris by the end of the month.

I send you a few *sententiae*. My books were not made with any view like yours, so the selections are of very dubious use.

I think the subject of Shakespeare will just suit me. I should like to do it very carefully, so let it be for July.[1] What books can you lend me? I must read his contemporaries mostly—Dramatists Poets & Essayists.

I hear nothing of the Oxford scheme. With regard to the 3 Colleges[2] the decision, given, to the Cardinal's great annoyance, by the Pope himself, is against the diocesan Bishops; i.e. All Bishops who have an interest in the three colleges, St Edmunds, Oscott & Ushaw, are entitled to a proportionate weight in the appointments of rulers & professors, in the regulation of studies, & in all questions of government. Ullathorne, I believe, has paid off the B^{ps} who had a claim on Oscott, so "illa se jactet in aula" Aeolus ille. But Westminster & Hexham are balanced, the one by Southwark & other SW. sees, & the other by the Northern sees. It seems the equitable division, but I heard that Propaganda was on the point of deciding in favour of the diocesan B^{ps}, when the Pope interposed with a *motu proprio*, in the literal, not technical sense. About Oxford I have heard nothing; But Morville promises to be an excellent introduction to the Hills just outside the Bridgenorth gate—You have not sold them to make your library, have you?

Ever yours faithfully
R Simpson

Clapham
Nov. 19.

---

[1] Since the *Home & Foreign Review* came to an end in April 1864, this article was never published. It was, however, the germ of Simpson's future Shakespearian scholarship.

[2] The existing seminaries, control of which was disputed between Wiseman and his diocesan bishops.

ACTON TO SIMPSON · 20 NOVEMBER 1863

Friday

My dear Simpson,

There is not one in ten of your maxims and observations that I shall not insert, much rejoicing, in my book, and I am very grateful to you for your kindness in taking so much trouble. One or two there are which I had already. I am off tomorrow to our wedding party, and pray you direct next week Coughton Court Bromsgrove Warwickshire.

I am very glad Shakespeare takes your fancy so decidedly, and am persuaded it will be a famous subject. Coleridge is, I suppose, his best English critic. Read, the best American, Gervinus and Ulrici the best Germans. I can lend you Ulrici. Gervinus is translated. Schlegel's Lectures of course you know, Guizot's book I never saw. Nothing could be better than to get up the background of Shakespeare well, Marlowe, Webster, Peele &c. Bodenstedt has translated some of their plays as Vorschule to him, with commentary. He also instructed me in the beauty of the Sonnets, which I never twigged before. Except the great passage on Hamlet in Wilhelm Meister there is little in Göthe, who certainly understood Shakespeare.

Renouf resists Morville, being sanguine about Oxford. I shall pass by Birmingham tomorrow, and will pump Newman, whose state of mind I do not quite understand.

I have a very satisfactory letter from Bergenroth. His eyes prevent his working at present, but as soon as he can he will give us historical articles with new matter. Of this he gives me a specimen. After 1530 Luther wanted to make his submission, for a Cardinal's hat, and Rome proposed to stop all scandals by compelling the secular clergy to marry. Charles V seems to have prevented the reconciliation. I hope we shall not fall into disgrace with the Habsburgs as we have with the Zollerns.[1]

I remain
Ever Your's truly
J D Acton

---

[1] This refers to the offence given to the Hohenzollerns by Acton's publication of the *Matinées royales*.

601

SIMPSON TO ACTON · 14 DECEMBER 1863

Clapham, Dec. 14.[1]
1863

My dear Acton

With the best wishes in the world, I am obliged to declare that I *cannot* make myself comfortable with the present arrangement. After

[1] A draft of this letter, dated 13 December, is preserved; one sentence is cited by Gasquet, p. liv. Portions of this letter which differ significantly from the final text follow:

'My machine has lost its motive power, and I cannot go on working under the present conditions...The first idea is blown to the winds by the reception of my article on the Poor law...when I was ready with the article I learned that two others had been accepted for the number, both of them probably inconsistent with the reception of my article. On this I thought that I would try your proposition—to bully you more than I have done, & exert my just influence—& I came up to Town the day that we went to the Publishers in order to see what might be done in that line. There was really no opening. I knew nothing about the plan of the number, or about the articles you & Wetherell were discussing. I had seen nothing in Ms, & I felt like a stranger & intruder into your conversation. The literary passion is too weak to withstand the annoyance & disappointment resulting from these discoveries. The motive power is gone. I got off the coach to lighten the load, & it has driven on without me. I am tired of running after it.

However, as I suppose Renouf will be an Editor for the April number, I will not make any disturbance now, but I will see how I get on next time; under a few conditions...But of what use was it to labour to save 6 or 8 pounds, when night-work for some 20 was to be an item in the printers bill? This time again I have laboured in compressing Block, & have made his article less costly by about 30 shillings than it would have been, if I had translated diffusely & carelessly. But what is the use of this pinching & grinding, in the face of our reckless way of sending an article which we can never publish to be printed, because it was easier to correct it in proof than in Ms? If you will pay for everything through the nose in this way, there is no reason why I should labour at short notices or current events, when you can easily get some one else to do them, if you pay him enough. I have always been ready to give my labour to save some of this extravagance; but I have found that whatever trouble I take is so much labour in vain. No editorial work seems worth a rush unless it is paid for....

With reference to the necessity of breaking down our paper constitution—on looking into the letter of Wetherell on w^h our present state is founded I think I see my way out of the wood.

Before that we were a cabinet—
Editor—Subeditor—Joint proprietor.
After that we were also a cabinet.

Editor, Subeditor—& a Cabinet minister holding no office—But in the new arrangement, whatever was Wetherell's intention, & however I have hitherto mistakenly considered myself bound by it, I find nothing that obliges to suppress the fact that I still belong to the cabinet—I have tried it, honestly tried it, & the more I try it, the more dishonest I find it to be—internally degrading & externally insulting—

The truth of the matter is that I am not diplomatical enough to fill one position

your letter of Sept. 23[1] I thought that I would let events determine whether I should be as one of the Editors without the name, or an exceptionally privileged contributor, or the steward & economist of the Review.

The notion of exceptionally privileged contributor was never a very wise one, & I find it will not act. It would have required that, after I had said that if I wrote at all for the Christmas Number it should be on the poor laws, a place should be left for such an article, if I wrote it—As I always intended to do if I possibly could. I see the inconveniences that would result from my always claiming a place to be left open for me, so I must forego this development.

If I am to be as one of the Editors, I must not be left to gather what is being done by laboriously asking questions on each particular, but the Mss must be seen by me before they are sent to the printers;—so I may put a stop to such extravagancies as printing 45 pages of Augury, which I hope we shall never publish.[2] This of course requires that Mss which do not arrive in time for this previous reading should not be published in the forthcoming number. The restriction would be most wholesome, & would not apply to your articles—because you must have some licence—but it should be enforced for every other contributor.

If I am to be Steward & Economus I must be seconded in my attempts to prevent reckless expense. Last Xmas I worked at the Index, & turned out one not good, but not very bad for a first attempt—the next would have been better—but I resolved never to give myself the trouble again if all the saving I made by it was doubly squandered in the item of "night work" in the printer's bill. I am in a state of continual rile on this score, & I see no probable termination to it but the enforcing of the two conditions put forth in the last paragraph—all Mss to be submitted

& to say I fill another—perhaps if I had been I might have remained a parson—I was fool enough to try W's nostrum wʰ he recommended as 'essential for my own personal rehabilitation, & for the success of the Review', without believing in it, but honestly submitting to the Regimen, till now that I find it intolerable besides being unsuccessful, & I refuse to take the dose any longer.

Every thing therefore remains as it was—You Ed.—W. Sub. Ed—I in the Cabinet but without office—I have hitherto generally spoken in doing business for the H.&F. as if I was your simple *alter ego*—an agent of yours, without any rights of my own. This was the only theory on wʰ I could reconcile the new arrangment to myself. But this I see is quite contrary to W's notion of the two mutually interchangeable evil genii—for what could be worse than such a personal identification—& moreover was never accepted by you—For in your letter of Dec 21/62 you in answer to me saw no security except in my being paid for what I wrote—a proposal wʰ I at once rejected & would reject more than ever now.

It remains then that I should once more take up my old position—that I should interpret our paper constitution according to the letter, & not according to the mistaken reasons...'

[1] Letter 593.
[2] It was not published.

to me before printing. No Mss (but yours) to be printed in the forthcoming number, if not sent in by the 15th (?) of the month.

If these conditions are not acceptable, I see nothing for me to do but to withdraw. The literary flame is a lambent kind of light, easily extinguished by a chronic rile; & I find my motive power fast evaporating. I have no heart to work. I am soon snubbed out. You must not wonder therefore at having no short notices & no current events from me.

I wish to make no alterations but the two which I propose. The rest of the arrangement can remain exactly as it is. With them, I shall be able to keep more up with you next number, & "to bully you more" as you invited me to do. Last time I saw you & Wetherell in Town I met you for the very purpose, but you were talking of matters of which I knew nothing. This was partly my fault for having been abroad—but the natural corrective will be that I see all Mss.

Also, Wetherell & you mistake me if you suppose I want to be saved trouble. I am a willing labourer in what I undertake, & I feel it the reverse of complimentary to be relieved. Our friend W. has a discouraging manner, & always seems to pour cold water on my propositions. Some time ago I proposed to look over proofs for him, which he was too ill to do it himself, but my offer was not accepted. He clearly thinks me too careless. Yet I dont think the press was worse corrected in the Rambler than it is in the H.&F. The residuum on my mind is the feeling that I am to be tolerated so long as I confine myself to doing a light article, or one on some fanciful half metaphysical subject. But that in more serious matters I must yield to others. Also that for any editorial business I am thoroughly incompetent—of course this is an absurd exaggeration. It is childish to feel it. My only plea for talking of it is, that the feeling is too strong for the reason to master, & that it has entirely undermined my motive power.

Dont worry me by supposing that I ever entertained a thought derogatory to your honour—or that I fancied that you had "ingeniously contrived a device to filch a weapon from my hand"—I know that you submit to the same snubbing—or nearly so. But the case is altered when I find that the coach from w^h I dismounted to lighten the load is trotting on without me, & that my legs are not strong enough to keep pace with it. My conditions seem to be the least I can make to enable me to keep up with you. If you have any thing to say against them let me hear it forthwith.

Ever yours most truly
R Simpson

ACTON TO SIMPSON · 15 DECEMBER 1863

Tuesday

My dear Simpson,

I wish that it had been possible for you to talk to me on the subject of this morning's letter either some little time ago, or after I had got some of the work which is employing all my time at present off my hands, and was not entirely helpless in the hands of any contributor who disappointed me. If you had known what I have still to do in the way of writing and translating you would not have chosen the 15th of this month to tell me that I must supply the whole of foreign events and your share of short notices.

All that you propose is so perfectly right, and your complaint is so reasonable, with the exception of one point which you do not treat seriously, that I am sure we could have come long ago to an understanding which would have satisfied us both, and organized that system of private but yet open war which is essential to constitutional government. I entirely accept and adopt the rule that you should always see MSS before printing, and that they should be in hand some weeks before the day of publication. The latter condition can be obtained only by having a great number of supplementary articles, and this I think we may soon expect.

As to the other rule I would not make it quite absolute. Of some papers, such as Renouf's, we are quite sure, barring only corrections such as may fairly be made in type. Other articles, such as Lathbury's, are often fully discussed before, or relate to matters that I, at least, know nothing of, so that I feel no inclination to see them in Ms. I don't feel a bit the worse for having seen Block neither in the original nor the MS translation. If I thought you would regard every case of this kind as a slight, I should think our difficulties greater than they now appear to me. As to my own articles they are of all others those I most want you to see, and I really think you are unjust if you accuse me of being unwilling to have either my plans or my compositions altered. If Wetherell has not sent you MSS. it has been from looseness, and from no other reason. He sent me neither Pearson, nor Block, nor MacCabe, nor Lathbury.[1] It is a laxity therefore for which I am responsible, but which is not due to any such design as you suspect.

I think I can explain what seems to you W's reluctance to be helped.

---

[1] Respectively, 'The Dissolution of the English Monasteries', 'Paris, Municipal and Economical', probably 'The Constitutional Question in Schleswig-Holstein' and 'Military Courts-Martial'.

I suspect that he considers himself under a contract and obligation to do all correcting &c himself, because he takes remuneration for it. He was too nervous to let Lathbury share the work even when the difficulty about money was arranged. This is the humour shown in his answer about volunteers, which he thinks may injure his official position. Lathbury suggested that under those circumstances we should not hold him bound. But, he said, I am under an engagement to myself.

I did not gather from our correspondence about Poor Relief[1] that you made a point of its immediate publication. If you had pressed it we should have had no difficulty in going into the reasons. Either you thought it quite compatible with the appearance of Pearson's article,[2] or you did not consider that we ought to go out of our way to gain him over to the Review. But I had no opportunity of discussing the matter, because you did not tell me you attached importance to it. I gather, now, that this circumstance has made an unpleasant impression on you, and I regret it extremely. Still you will certainly agree that we cannot determine the insertion of articles by a sort of legal code, and that we must depend on the existence of a good understanding amongst ourselves. That can only be maintained by fair bullying, and taking one's own part. Everybody likes to get as much power as circumstances allow, and nobody will vote for a Self denying ordinance. We ought all to fight and not be riled; but you are sometimes riled without fighting.

Let us understand therefore that I have nothing to say, beyond what I have alluded to, against the arrangement you lay down. Even if it was not the condition of your active cooperation I should think it the best thing for the Review.

I put on the opposite page the prospects for April, and hope you will add a further paper of your own.

Believe me
Ever Your's faithfully
J D Acton

Palmerston's 2^d administration
Cultivation of land in France (Pray ask Block)
Poor Relief
Celtic Philology and Literature

(For Sullivan's first
article is Ethnology[3]

Present State of chemical Science   Sullivan
The University Question   Renouf
Colonization of Northumbria   Arnold

[1] 'The Rise of the English Poor-Law.'
[2] 'The Dissolution of the English Monasteries.'
[3] It had been expected that Sullivan's January article ('Celtic Ethnology') would have been on Celtic literature.

Cardinal Wolsey
Medieval Universities
S. Ursula[1]

Brewer
Helfenstein
Floss[2]

603

SIMPSON TO ACTON · 16 DECEMBER 1863

My dear Acton

There is nothing more to be written, but much to be said; do let us have some talk when you come up to Town next, that we may remove some misapprehensions which each of us has conceived about the other.

I am quite satisfied with what you agree to. I want to see the Mss for two purposes. Not to print what we cannot publish, & to keep myself posted up in the current business of the Review, without which I cannot enter into discussions about it. The third purpose, to make the Review more punctual & thus to save expense is not such a personal one, & therefore I cannot insist upon it so much, however necessary I may think it. But the rule being established for these special reasons may naturally be dispensed with where they do not hold—as in Renouf's papers, in Lathbury's & in yours, which I excepted, not because I thought you did not like me to see them, but because you are such a chastened libertine of time that to make such a condition would be to put them off to the next N° with the probable fate of Human sacrifice.[3]

I send two little notices; I will try to get two or three more, but my house is full of company, & Mudie sends me nothing; I will go to Waters to night to see whether he has got anything more than an article for our first class reserve—New Zealand, by Hugh Carleton,[4] Chairman of Committees in the Parliament of that ilk, which I am to bring away with me.

Poor Relief[5] may go on the Reserve too, if it so seems good, after deliberation. I wont write the long story of my grievance on that account, now that all my complaints are merged in the acceptance of my two propositions, which I suppose, after Christmas, you will enter in the Institute Medo-Persica of the H.&F. We shall all get on much better if the business is less loosely conducted.

---

[1] Of these, there were published 'Agriculture in France'; 'The Rise of the English Poor-Law'; Sullivan, 'The Progress of Chemical Science', *Home & Foreign Review*, IV (April 1864), 433–75; and Arnold, 'The Colonisation of Northumbria', *ibid.* 577–608.

[2] Heinrich Josef Floss (1819–81), ordained priest 1842, professor of moral theology at Bonn 1858, later turned to church history.

[3] *Human Sacrifice*, written as an article, was separately published.

[4] Hugh Carleton (1810–90), settled in New Zealand 1842, member of the House of Representatives 1854–84.

[5] 'The Rise of the English Poor-Law.'

Any *French* translation you have I shall be happy to relieve you of.
Not German. I cannot do France, but I might do something on Belgium[1]
if it would save you at all. I am really sorry for having added to your
burdens, but out of the evil will come the good of an actual & practical
cure of my false position, which I assure you gave me real & very acute
annoyance, and would in a short time have made me determine to
give up writing altogether—

Ever yours faithfully
R Simpson

Clapham, Dec. 16.

604

ACTON TO SIMPSON · 17 DECEMBER 1863

Thursday

My dear Simpson,

Many thanks for your letter and the short notices.

If I am under misapprehensions regarding you I shall certainly be
very glad to have an opportunity of getting rid of them; and as you
believe in their existence I will not absolutely deny it, but assure you at
least that there are none with which you would have any right to be
angry.

I will revise the laws of the Medes and Persians, and write nothing in
April myself, but short notices.

Why does not New Zealand appear this time?[2] There would be hardly
room, however, as we have ten articles—one containing some original
poetry consisting of translations—by a native of a neighbouring Island.
This is F. MacCarthy's review of Ticknor,[3] which would make a decent
ballad article.

We have no foreign events, by the failure of two writers. There would
be the Congress, and the affairs of Germany.[4] I must do the latter as
well as I can—and I suppose the former too if your decision about
France is final. I am afraid, with so little room left, Belgium would be
almost superfluous.

I remain
Your's ever sincerely
J D Acton

---

[1] For 'Current Events'. Simpson wrote neither of these.
[2] It was never published.
[3] Denis Florence McCarthy, 'Old Spanish Ballads', *Home & Foreign Review*, IV
(January 1864), 79–102.
[4] Acton wrote both the 'Current Events': 'Denmark and Germany', *ibid.* 335–7,
and 'The Proposed European Congress', *ibid.* 337–8.

SIMPSON TO ACTON · 19 DECEMBER 1863

Dear Acton

I send you a few more short notices. I have no more books to look at.
Mudie keeps me too short.

As to France, I have not watched the papers, & my house is full of
visitors, so that I have not time to look up the history. Shall you say
a word about the condemnation of the 7 Bishops?[1] if so, I can give you
a note of V.D.B's.[2] Also shall you mention the decree modifying the
naval conscription?[3] if so I will get a note about it from Hall.

Ever yours faithfully
R Simpson

Clapham
Dec. 19. 63

SIMPSON TO ACTON · 23 DECEMBER 1863

Dec. 23. 63

Dear Acton

Here is Buck's note, w^h is worthless, & after a long talk with Hall on
the modifications of the Navy, he advises me that they are not important
enough to be included in the current events. They are a small concession
made to commerce, in hopes of restoring the marine traffic, & a specious
relaxation of the sailors conscription.

I will ask Block for French Agriculture.[4] You may count upon it, for
B. is a sure card. I wish that Spanish Ballads[5] could be kept back; the
whole middle is dry & rubbishing to a fearful pitch. Which is the light
article this time? I am afraid that Paley[6] comes nearest to the name,
but the Greek in it is frightful.

The article on New Zealand[7] was much below par, horribly provincial;
I have written to Carleton a long letter, explaining the kind of article

---

[1] Seven French bishops were condemned by the Council of State for 'abuse of authority' for having published a letter of advice to electors.
[2] Victor de Buck.
[3] In France.
[4] 'Agriculture in France.'
[5] 'Old Spanish Ballads.'
[6] 'Classical Myths in Relation to the Antiquity of Man.'
[7] Not published.

wanted—I think, by the evidence of his peroration, that he can do it; whether he will or not he has not yet told me.

Try to suggest some slight subject not unconnected with what I have read up for Shakespeare, for a light article for April.

Ever yours faithfully
R Simpson

A Happy Xmas to you

607

SIMPSON TO ACTON · 29 DECEMBER 1863

Dec. 29. 63

Dear Acton

Carleton, you see, will write on New Zealand—he promises the article in 6 weeks. I told him he might go beyond 30 pp, but begged him to try to keep within 40. He is to do an exhaustive article, & therefore we cannot grumble if it is exhausting.

I dont think that the Index is done well, so far as the analysis of the articles is concerned. Can we not, another time, give the Index[1] maker the analyses, & leave him only the names & paginations. E.G. look at your ultramontanism;[2] Gueranger & Perron, & the liberal view of the Reformation. I have struck all this out of the proof.

I wish that I could have seen your article[3] in Ms. It was written more in a hurry than is usually the case, & must have puzzled Wetherell sadly. He must have considerably relaxed his wonted tension of Editorial stupidity, in order to allow the meaning to glimmer on his mind. Perhaps he allows himself to understand more easily towards the end of the quarter.

Who does Thackeray for April?[4] Did you get a note I sent you from Froebel?[5]

Ever yours faithfully
R Simpson

[1] Of the 1863 Home & Foreign Review.
[2] 'Ultramontanism', in July.
[3] 'The Munich Congress.'
[4] Simpson wrote 'Thackeray', Home & Foreign Review, IV (April 1864), 476–511.
[5] Julius Fröbel (1805–93), German political writer.

ACTON TO SIMPSON · 30 DECEMBER 1863

Wednesday

My dear Simpson,

Carleton seems to promise very well. I hope you have made due corrections in my proof,[1] as Renouf and I are not very good at discovering the obscurities. W kept the article a week, so that I hoped he would make it what it ought to be. I got Fröbel's note, and was sorry to see that a letter containing moneys which I sent him from Munich was waylaid.

I put off writing to you because I could not think of any slight subject connected with Shakespeare, Do you think Thackeray would be such a light subject? He would be a very good one in other ways if he could be made to attract you, only there are some hard things to be said of him.

An article by Moule on Henry Tayler[2] is at the printers. It is not remarkably good, but represents 'Edwin the Fair' as a panegyric on the Medieval Church—which is an ingenious way of dealing with it. I don't know Tayler enough to say whether it is fairly done. If you do, I wish you would send to Robson for the MS.

Shall we have some notices of your's next time, and French events? Excepting New Zealand[3] and Poor Relief[4] we are not yet provided with political articles.

Spanish ballads[5] had all the middle taken out of them, all the mere account of ballads—preserving only the notice of Ticknor's new edition,[6] and so much of the prose as was wanted to explain the poetry.

I am just off to Coughton[7]—

A happy New Year to you—

Believe me
Ever faithfully Your's
J D Acton

---

[1] Of 'The Munich Congress'.
[2] Not published. Sir Henry Taylor (1800–86), civil servant and playwright, knighted 1869, was the author of *Edwin the Fair. An Historical Drama* (London, 1842).
[3] Not published.
[4] 'The Rise of the English Poor-Law.'
[5] 'Old Spanish Ballads.'
[6] Of his *History of Spanish Literature.*
[7] The seat of the Throckmortons.

ACTON TO SIMPSON · 8 JANUARY 1864

Friday

My dear Simpson,

Pray decide as you think best about this letter, and let me know what I had better write to Robson.[1] I suppose we shall be in no danger of having the printing interrupted, if we go on with him; and I think you always said the accurate correcting was due to Robson.

Are you looking at Thackeray, or have you some better subject? If the former, let me recommend Esmond to your most attentive study. I think it is a far subtler book than Vanity Fair.

What do you make of Moule's article?[2] You have seen I suppose what they have decreed at Rome about the Corpi Santi.[3] What do De' Rossi and De Buck say? Do you think the latter would notice the life of S. Dympna, by OHanlon,[4] in which he is respectfully mentioned?

Wetherell says your corrections to the Congress[5] came too late, which I am very sorry for. I fancy he kept the MS unnecessarily long from a superstition against printing later articles before those that precede them in order.

I remain
Ever Your's truly
J D Acton

Are there murmurs in arca?

610

SIMPSON TO ACTON · 9 JANUARY 1864

Clapham Jany 9. 1864

Dear Acton

If it will not damage us, let us by all means keep to Robson. He is honest, & much more up to his work than any other sender out of proofs that I have ever had to do with. I will call today, & know what guarantees he can give of being able to go on without interruption, &

---

[1] Robson and Levey, the printers, were breaking up their partnership.
[2] On Taylor.
[3] The dispute about the bodies of alleged martyrs in the Catacombs.
[4] John O'Hanlon, *The Life of St. Dympna, Virgin, Martyr, and Patroness of Gheel* ... (Dublin, 1863).
[5] 'The Proposed European Congress' in the January 'Current Events'.

to complete the printing, even though a mass of matter should come in just at the last, & will write on Monday to tell you what he says.

Can you lend me Esmond & Vanity Fair?

I have engaged a man to look all through Wilkins,[1] so as to get up for me the ecclesiastical development of the poor law. Did you see the article after I had rewritten it? W, I think, has it. I will write the second part a third time if the materials to be collected for me seem to require it.

Are you likely to want Deutinger[2] next time?

You see that for Robson's sake, if we go on with him, it will be even more indispensible than before to be early. How can a man, without a great establishment, provide for doing in three days what oppresses a large house to have to do in seven? I don't know whether he may not propose some commission—undertaking himself the composition, & paying another establishment to do the printing. Anyhow, it is for our comfort to have him preside over the composition, whether he sets up independently, or is obliged to contract for part of his work with other printers.

Tell me the decision about the Corpi Santi.

I will write to DeBuck to know what he says, as soon as you give me information. Also I will ask him if he will do S[t] Dympna.

Who in the world was S[t] Dympna?[3]

Ever yours faithfully
R Simpson

611

ACTON TO SIMPSON · 10 JANUARY 1864*

Saturday

My dear Simpson,

I am glad there is somebody who will say a good word for our Current Events. As to Notices I do not feel guilty this time of having written very many. Nevertheless I would try, if I was you, to get some Notices from DeBuck, and especially one on S. Dympna.

Block is so very sensible a man, and his politics are so sound, as I judge not only from the generality of the articles in his Dictionnaire, but

---

[1] David Wilkins, ed., *Conciliae Magnae Britanniae et Hiberniae*, 4 vols. (London, 1737).

[2] The unpublished article on German philosophy.

[3] An Irish saint, beheaded at Geel (now Belgium) in the 7th century, associated with cures of the insane.

* Gasquet, Letter CXLVIII, pp. 309–12, with omissions.

especially from the notes with which he occasionally corrects a digne confrère, that I would not, if I was you, lose the chance of getting his notices, on any books that interest him more particularly on France, politics and economy. Laboulaye's book[1] is very good indeed, but if he does not make certain drawbacks on his praise I shall be in a fix.

I do not see why Judaism is an objection to a man writing current events. Block would go into details, and give a real chronicle, with very accurate knowledge. Renouf expects to get M. de Circourt[2] to write for us, who is a very remarkable personage, and would be invaluable; but I do not anticipate that he will do Current Events. So if you will offer them to Block, and undertake to give them an H&Fical aspect, I think you cannot do better. We had better offer him a sum for it—as you like. By all means promise him an article (notice) on his Dictionary, whenever he likes. If you don't write it yourself I will, and the book deserves great praise.

Do you really think of two successive articles on Shakespeare? There would be many reasons of policy against it, and I should think internal objections too. Would you prefer doing Shakespeare altogether for April, putting away Thackeray, and getting somebody (which is easy) to translate Block?[3] I think the other arrangement would be better. Your article can be as long as ever you like, four sheets if necessary, and I am sure it will answer.

Are you so sure all the sonnets were written early? Nobody, who is a real poet, sits down to write a hatful of sonnets; they were produced occasionally—in intervals as it were of business. Bodenstedt[4] has arranged them in order by the resemblance of phrases &c to passages in his plays, and, though very vague, the plan struck me as plausible and ingenious.

Assuming that you care enough for Thackeray to do him, which nobody else is likely to attempt, I am sorry to say I have neither his books nor any good ideas about him. The former you must buy out of the public funds.[5] I have a vision of a clever essay on him by Henri Taine, in one of his volumes of essays. His views of history are surely very superficial and he is not in the first rank of literary critics. But he

---

[1] Edouard Laboulaye, *Le Parti libéral, son programme et son avenir* (Paris, 1863), reviewed in *Home & Foreign Review*, IV (April 1864), 724–5. This review is generally attributed to Acton.

[2] Adolphe Marie Pierre, comte de Circourt (1801–79), French diplomat and author, a liberal Catholic, later legitimist.

[3] Simpson's 'Thackeray' and Block's 'Agriculture in France' were published in April.

[4] Friedrich Martin von Bodenstedt, *Sonette; in deutsche Nachbildung* (1862).

[5] I.e., from the common funds of the *Home & Foreign Review*.

can go to the bottom of small minds, in a way which is wonderful because he was not a first rate judge of character among his acquaintances, and therefore often wanted tact. Lord Broughton[1] dined with him and there was a bottle of rare wine, of which one glass remained when all had partaken. Thackeray slapped the drunken old lord on the back saying "And this shall be for you, my good old friend." At which the other pulled a wry face, as having a sore back, and because he thinks he is not old and knows he is not good, nor wishes to be thought so. Thackeray himself was extremely sensitive in the great world. I certainly did not think him distingué.[2]

The marvel is how he knew the ladies of the great world so well, for that is his strongest department. Esmond, again and again I assure you, is a masterpiece for that sort of knowledge. Also in the Virginians the description of the growth of love in the two sisters for the two brothers. The old flirt in that book (Lady Maria) does not seem to me superior to Amelia Roper. Also in the Newcomes the matchmaking mammas, I could add a touch or two.

There are historians, like Thiers and Ranke, whose cleverness won't allow them to recognize the union of greatness and genius with goodness. Their great men are Richelieu, Frederick, Napoleon, without high moral virtue, and their good men are commonplace or else dupes. They require some compensation of this kind, and would be puzzled to draw the conventional Washington, or Burke. There is a point to be made here for those who read and love the lives of the Saints; and as you remember Thackeray's joke about the Dictionary, perhaps he w^d deserve it. For he is very like those historians. I suppose more poetry would have raised him above this defect, for Dickens is without it, although he is so far below Thackeray in his characters.

The resemblance to Horace which one of the reviews suggested may deserve following out. Is it not a fault in art to hold the mask in one's hand instead of on the face, and to be constantly looking round from behind it? To give him his place in literature you must read Tom Jones and Thackeray's essay on Fielding. Is he not quite incapable of the great effort of art which is so common in Shakespeare, and which Dickens imitates, of putting the comic perpetually as a foil to the tragic? He rather relieves the comic by the colloquial.

---

1 John Cam Hobhouse (1786–1869), M.P. 1820–33, 1834–51, president of the board of control for India 1835–41, 1846–52, created Lord Broughton 1851.
2 At this point, Acton wrote in the margin: 'I got 18 pages this morning, on our first article, from the subject of it. [Gladstone. The reference is to "Mr. Gladstone's Financial Statements".] He is intensely pleased, but will not suffer the budget of '60—to be attacked. It is a letter full of autobiography, and he promises to tell things unuttered yet to mortal ear about the formation of the ministry when we meet.'

There! I know it matters not whether one's ideas are true or false if one can set you a going. The fact is I only know Vanity Fair well. But you will find him often a congenial mind with your dining out self.

Arnold is recovering him of his illness, and will do his Northumbria[1] in April. He seems to have been cured by the H&F for January.

I remain
Ever Your's truly
J D Acton

Sunday

The account given by the Register of the last week of 1863 is that a commission,[2] on a report I think of Tongeorgi, decided that the old tests were satisfactory, and should be continued. I did not read it, but Renouf read it out. Perhaps it is a way of covering their retreat.

You shall know all about S. Dympna when DeBuck has sent his notice. Her biography was sent with a request for a notice by the author, who is a Maynooth Professor.

I am quite of your opinion about old Robson's merits, if you see your way to an arrangement. I have had a second note from him, after your visit, which I sent with the former to Wetherell.

I have your MS on Poor Relief,[3] and was going to send it up for printing, but I will wait till I hear whether it is go to you first for additions.

What do you make of Henry Tayler?

I remain
Ever Your's
JDA

612

SIMPSON TO ACTON · 11 JANUARY 1864

4 Vict. Rᵈ Jany. 11. 64

Dear Acton

Have you Bodenstedt's arrangement of the Sonnets? I dont think they were all written early, but also I dont subscribe to the last opinion that they all date between 1599 & 1603. Meares refers to them in 1598 —"his sugared sonnets among his private friends." It seems pretty

---

[1] 'The Colonisation of Northumbria.'
[2] This refers to the Roman decision on the bodies of martyrs in the Catacombs.
[3] 'The Rise of the English Poor-Law.'

clear that Shakespeare himself arranged them for publication in 1609; therefore the order in which he placed them has a meaning—either historical or Spencerian & mystical.

If you believe in the realistic exposition of Gervinus, tell me whether you think Sonnets 73 74 can refer to a dangerous illness contracted through being stabbed in a brawl

My body being dead
The coward conquest of a wretch's knife

(A common accident to players at that time) and whether sonnets 124, 125 can refer to Southampton's disgrace after the Essex row in 1601.[1] He assures his friend that his love is not the child of state, that it should fail when fortune changes, or fall under the blow of *thralled discontent* (as if he also was imprisoned for his share in the representation of Richard II w[h] was the preface to the outbreak). Then how would you explain the two lines

To this I witness call the *fools of time*
Which *die for goodness*, who have *lived* for *crime*—

In 125 guess what his allusions are—

What canopy did he bear to do honour—to whom?
What if his bases for eternity had failed?

What was he threatened with when he wrote

Hence thou suborned informer! a true soul
When *mort impeached*, stands least in thy control.

I am miserably off for Shakespearian literature, having only Massinger & Jonson, & Halliwells miserable life, besides Gervinus. Will you send me a list of what you have? I do not relish the Museum as I did when I was younger, & I much prefer working at home, if I can borrow the necessary books.

Rio[2] writes to me for full length moral portraits of certain actors in the Essex plot wth whom Shakespeare must have been on more or less intimate terms—particularly Rutland, Talbot, Pembroke & above all Lady Eliz. Vernon. He wants any book, history, biography, old peerage, or document of any kind where he c[d] find what he wants. Do you know, or must I go to Stephenson or Duffus Hardy?

I have written to Block to accept his notices & to ask him to help in the Chronicle.

I will try to do Thackeray for April, & Shakespeare for July. I have

---

[1] Henry Wriothesley (1573–1624), 3rd earl of Southampton 1581, was condemned but not executed for his part in the rising of the earl of Essex in 1601.
[2] Alexis François Rio (1798–1874), French author, was an active Shakespearian scholar.

not read Moule[1] yet. I am obliged to be my own man of business & collect my own rents. I am off to Mitcham for that purpose—

Ever yours faithfully
R Simpson

613

ACTON TO SIMPSON · 12 JANUARY 1864*

Tuesday

My dear Simpson,

I am afraid I dare not without book involve myself in the difficulties you propose. Some of the points are, I remember, dealt with in Bodenstedt's commentary, but I have not got the book. It is a little volume, 1862, well worth looking at.

I wonder how you reconcile the Dedication of 1609 with the idea that Shakespeare prepared the edition, and is responsible for the arrangement.

The fate of Marlowe and others would confirm your interpretation of sonnet 74. I can bring or rather send you Marlowe and Webster; I am not sure I have any others. Also you shall have Ulrici, who, I presume is not translated, in spite of his Protestantism.

I don't know whether you would care for Delius. Arnold says his notes are a weak reproduction of Knight's. He thinks all the Sonnets turn on matters purely imaginary.

There is nothing monographic that will suit Rio's purpose—at least unless the Record office people know of ought. That is your private period.

May your rents be successful, and mine too next week.

Ever Your's truly
J D Acton

614

SIMPSON TO ACTON · 12 JANUARY 1864

Clapham Jany 12.

Dear Acton

On opening my parcel from Robson, I find that Tayler[2] is printed—perhaps all of it—Any how I have proofs down the end of Edwin the Fair.

---

[1] The unpublished article on Henry Taylor.

* The first part of Gasquet, Letter CXLIX, pp. 312–13; the last three paragraphs omitted.   [2] Moule's article.

The whole paper is wretchedly superficial, and the criticism on the character of Dunstan seems to accept the wickedness imputed to him as normal conduct in a *saint* of the 10th century. This is surely quite contrary to the moral standpoint of the H.&F.?

The abundant quotations of passages which I remember quoted in Blackwood when I was a boy at school seems a little infra dig. of our honourable quarterly; and the tone of the review seems to show that the reviewer admired too much to be able to exercise his judgment. I see that W. has abated some of the more fulsome panegyric; but what is left is hardly justified either by the analysis or by the quotations given.

Wenham knows Tayler, who is a neighbor of his. I wish he (W) were not in Rome, else we might learn something about him (T) & his intentions & meanings. I suppose he is liberally inclined in religion, from the fact of his occasionally asking a Priest to dinner—

Try to give me a more tangible theory of the *genus* & *differentia* of Thackeray among writers—Does he teach, like Shakespeare, simply to use your eyes in the wider or narrower world of his experience, or does he provide you with peculiarly coloured medium through which to see the things he can show? So he is a humourist or a humanist (if that is the alternative)? I am going to Town to look for, & to cheapen, his works.

Ever yours faithfully
R Simpson

What is to be done with Moule. I have all the Ms. so the printers cannot go on with it till I send it back. About 14 pp are printed, out of say 24 or 25.

615

ACTON TO SIMPSON · 13 JANUARY 1864*

Wednesday

My dear Simpson,

Pray stop the printing of Moule, and I will write unto him. It won't do to have a weak Tayler by the side of Thackeray.[1]

The latter is not objective, if that is what you mean, as a glance at his perpetual moralizing will show you. He is hardly ever epic, but rather surgical. A writer of the first order discovers the mode of action and thought of his own characters when once he has clearly conceived them, rather than invents.

---

* The second part of Gasquet, Letter CXLIX, p. 313, with an omission.
[1] 'Thackeray' was published; the article on Henry Taylor was not.

He does not sit down to consider How *shall* my hero act or speak under these circumstances? But, How *does* he? Shakespeare passim. Which is caricatured by your friend Balzac,[1] who did not *give* names to his characters, but walked over Paris reading the names on shops till he *found* them. I don't think Thackeray ever got so high as this, unless in Esmond. I think Trollope does, and his glasses do not colour, but he does not profess to go so deep. Perhaps the slow and studious growth of Thackeray's powers contributed to this, or is connected with it. The Germans whom he studied would not raise him above this Euripidean method—nor probably any amount of mere labour.

But why do I talk? Have you not cheapened the original?

What do you say about Robson? I have not written to him, awaiting your better judgment, and I ought to answer his letters, if only to say how I appreciate his knowledge and care. I suppose Levey[2] keeps on, and will dish for us also.

I remain
Ever Your's truly
J D Acton

616

SIMPSON TO ACTON · 14 JANUARY 1864

Dear Acton

Block you see will do the events.[3] How many pp. shall we allow him, what shall we tell him is the last day, and what sum will you fix? Norgate was urging once more upon me the other day the necessity of letting the Review be in the publishers hands 48 hours before the time of publication. In fixing the last moment you must keep this in view, as also the exigencies of translators. It may be that I shall be too busy in the last days to translate, & I shall have to look for another person to do it In a quarterly chronicle, as in a drama, it is better to look to the completeness of the action than to the registration of the latest known steps in it, unless they seem something essential.

What if the chronicle stops at 15 (?) or 21(?) days before the end of the quarter? Give me your views, & I will send them on to B.

Ever yours faithfully
R Simpson

Jany. 14. 1864

---

[1] Honoré de Balzac (1799–1850), French author. It is not certain that 'your friend' is to be taken literally.

[2] The other partner in the printing firm, about to be divided.

[3] The 'Current Events' in the April number have not been attributed. Block wrote 'France', *Home & Foreign Review*, IV (April 1864), 769–76.

617

ACTON TO SIMPSON · 15 JANUARY 1864

Friday

My dear Simpson,

I have told Robson that you would make arrangements with him about our printing.

Block is very satisfactory. As to time, I think the 10th or twelfth of the month preceding the day of publication ought to be the term at which you ought to receive his MS. allowing him a week for any additional matter. The quantity, from four to eight, or even ten pages—You would, I suppose, mention this as a general guide, not as an actual limit. As to payment, whatever you think will induce him to do it well. Taking the rate at which I think you have been paying him and the highest limit, of ten pages, I suppose it would be about five pounds a number; but I pray you use your discretion, as you know the man.

Froude[1] writes angrily that Parker[2] calls his predecessor D. Cranmer, which means 'of blessed memory', as Stanley tells him. He has no other observation to offer, and is a fool.

I remain
Ever truly Your's
J D Acton

618

SIMPSON TO ACTON · 16 JANUARY 1864

Dear Acton

By some mistake in the Post your letter about the Printers[3] did not reach me till last night. I supposed that I had said enough in my first to show you that I voted for continuing with Robson—Levey has never been of any good to us, & only to Robson I imagine by the share of capital he brought in. He never did more than keep the accounts, & does not understand the technical part of the business. I will go up to see Robson this evening.

I do not like to set Moule aside for anything of mine, which very likely wont be half as good as his paper.[4] At any rate I will hold my hand for

---

[1] James Anthony Froude (1818–94), historian, author of *The History of England from the Fall of Wolsey to the Defeat of the Spanish Armada*, 12 vols. (London, 1856–70), very anti-Catholic.

[2] Matthew Parker (1504–75), archbishop of Canterbury 1559.

[3] Letter 615.   [4] On Henry Taylor.

a week, & read Thackeray, whom I have borrowed from Williams,[1] without prejudice to the common fund.

Ever yours faithfully
R Simpson

Saturday.

619

ACTON TO SIMPSON · 19 JANUARY 1864

Tuesday

My dear Simpson,

Moule wishes to try his luck with some other review, so pray send him his MS. addressed to H. Moule Esq. (I believe he is Rev? but have never recognized his orders) Dorchester Dorset.

I hope you are deep in Thackeray and have settled with old Robson. You must be thinking of a list of books for me to pack up for you when I come to town, especially as you are becoming faithless to the Museum.

I am in hopes of getting a good Irish article for April from a new contributor.[2]

Stevenson[3] has my MS life of Mary Stuart and is studying the subject, but he has not yet promised an article, and Brewer has not answered positively whether we are to have Wolsey[4] next time.

I remain
Ever Your's truly
J D Acton

620

SIMPSON TO ACTON · 23 JANUARY 1864

Clapham, Jany 23. 64

Dear Acton

The question of "humour" will occur in Thackeray, & may as well be treated. Coleridge has a little about it in his lectures on Shakespeare.

---

[1] The publisher.

[2] E. Dease, 'The Irish Exodus and Tenant Right', *Home & Foreign Review*, IV (April 1864), 339–64.

[3] Joseph Stevenson (1806–95), historian, formerly an Anglican minister, employed in the Public Record Office. He had secretly converted 1863, though Acton did not know this; he became a Jesuit 1877.

[4] Not published.

Has he any more about it in his Friend? Has it been treated by any of your Germans? If so, I should like to see some of them; & for curiosity's sake, I should like to read some French essay on the subject. Have you Swift in one Vol?—Has Delius a chronological order of the plays & sonnets? I cannot think of other books at present. When do you come up, that I may write again about them?

I have read Esmond & the Virginians, besides Sundry Miscellanies. I am very tired of them. Two or three amethysts are valuable stones; but a whole box of them! I had no idea he was so *narrow* a man. His *disjecta* membra covered a deal of ground, when, like one of the fantoccini, he threw his head at you one month, & his legs the next, & so on. But when they are gathered up & put together again, his body goes into a box not much bigger than the coffins of second rate men. I think I shall have a deal to say on him; I have already quarrelled with Wetherell about Beatrix, on whose behalf I am ready to bring an action of libel against her unnatural father & guardian. W. however believes all that T. says of her. I won't, & I hope you will or do or have agreed with me.

Ever yours faithfully
R Simpson

621

ACTON TO SIMPSON · 24 JANUARY 1864*

Sunday

My dear Simpson,

Delius does nothing for the arrangement of the Sonnets. I suppose you know Mrs. Bacon's Philosophy of Shakespeare, which I think is only an attack on his claim to be his own author. You shall have Swift in two volumes, and any German in whom I can find anything humorous. The Friend is not at all literary, but almost all political and philosophical. But the Biographia Literaria? DeQuincy? You shall also have the new volume of the Philobiblon with Bohn's foolish life of Shakespeare.

You are putting Thackerary in his box before reading Vanity Fair, which is premature, and the picture of this great world in Pendennis and the Newcomes is true to a considerable degree.

I shall not come up probably for a fortnight—So write for books any time next week.

Do you think it would be possible to get through Block a Spanish Current Events for April? There are ministerial changes and new party arrangements of which we all know nothing at all.

* Gasquet, Letter CL, pp. 314–15, with several omissions.

Talking of Spain I have suggested an article on recent Spanish Literature to MacCarthy, perhaps for July.[1]

My friend Dease[2] promises an Irish article for April, on Emigration and Landlordism. I have already seen the bulk of it and think him very sensible, honest, and fluent.

Bonamy Price offers Currency for July. Renouf shirks the Bible Dictionary, for fear of the Jews.[3]

Goodwin,[4] knocked down by the article on George Eliot, is anxious to write for us. I am afraid you have given Lathbury the impression that you are at dagger's drawn with Wetherell, not only about Beatrix. It will be very unfortunate if you give him or anybody that idea. He perfectly understands that you ought to see MSS subject to the same conditions as my seeing them is subject to; but he cannot admit that it is anybody's fault but your's if it has not always been so.

> I remain
> Ever Your's truly
> J D Acton

622

ACTON TO SIMPSON · 28 JANUARY 1864

Thursday

My dear Simpson,

Can Poor Relief go to press, or are you doing anything more to it? I will always try to post you up to what is going on on our side of the water—The state of the April case is thus:

Lord Palmerston
Emigration & Tenant right
New Zealand
The German Movement—I hope.
Poor Relief   Colonization of Northumbria
French agriculture
Thackeray   The University Question
Chemistry
Smiths Bible Dictionary ⎫ Renouf[5]
Religion of ancient Egypt ⎭

---

[1] Neither of these was published.
[2] Brother-in-law of Acton's cousin Emily Throckmorton Dease. Edmund Gerald Dease (1829–1904), M.P. 1870–80, a commissioner of national education.
[3] Both were published: Price, 'The Bank Charter Act', *Home & Foreign Review*, IV (April 1864), 402–32; Renouf, 'Dr. Smith's Dictionary of the Bible', *ibid.* 623–66.
[4] Perhaps Harvey Goodwin (1818–91), dean of Ely 1858, bishop of Chester 1869.
[5] Of these, there were published: 'The Irish Exodus and Tenant Right'; Julius

The difficulty with the Irish Bishops is the National School question. But I hope we can manage to do something there. The obvious resource, of having light articles instead of heavy, ought, I think, to be only adopted in the last extremity. Perhaps we might save money by printing fewer copies. One or two things occur to me that may be done. But the Westminster had equal difficulties to contend with for many years—although it had a physical basis, and we have only a metaphysical one.[1] Molesworth[2] used to say that the Keep of a review cost about as much as that of an actress, and that it was barely possible to have both at once. We must discuss this when I come up at Shrovetide.

I squeezed H&Fdom into the compass of a short speech at Dudley the other night,[3] and it was very well received by several of the Staffordshire clergy, who, I was told, do not take their bishop's[4] part against us.

I hope you are quite sure of Carleton.[5]

> I remain
> Ever Your's truly
> J D Acton

623

SIMPSON TO ACTON · 4 FEBRUARY 1864

4 St James' S^t
Feb. 4/64

Dr Acton

Buck will notice "S. Dympne"[6] if you will send him the book.

> M. l'Abbé V. de Buck
> College St Michel
> Rue des Ursulines
> Bruxelles

He is shocked at my levity, & wonders that I dont know him too well

---

Fröbel, 'The Schleswig-Holstein Movement in Germany', *Home & Foreign Review*, IV (April 1864), 365–78; 'The Rise of the English Poor-Law'; 'Agriculture in France'; 'Thackeray'; 'The Progress of Chemical Science'; 'Dr. Smith's Dictionary of the Bible'; and 'The Colonisation of Northumbria'.

1 The *Westminster Review* was a philosophical radical, not religious, quarterly.
2 Sir William Molesworth (1810–55), baronet 1823, M.P. 1832–41, 1845–55, cabinet member 1853–5, proprietor of the *London Review* 1835–7, of the *Westminster Review* from 1837.
3 Acton's speech of 26 January is reprinted in *Ignaz von Döllinger/Lord Acton: Briefwechsel 1850–1890*, ed. Victor Conzemius, III (München, 1971), 435–8.
4 Ullathorne.
5 The unpublished article on New Zealand.
6 The life of St Dympna was not reviewed.

to think that he should care more for the propagation of his own opinions than for the dignity of the congregations of the H. See.[1]

I have given Carleton to the 15th he has written an article of 100 pp. & he is going to compress it to the required amount. Ever y[rs] truly

R Simpson

624

SIMPSON TO ACTON · 6 FEBRUARY 1864

Dear Acton

I have not told Wetherell about the diminished sale of the H.&F. I was afraid that it might disconcert him; he was very much disappointed about the sale of the two first numbers. So it will be your business to tell him, or to let him remain in his happy ignorance.

I have been through our last printing bill with Norgate, who, when he saw our friends in the Gazette[2] wrote to tell me he could put me into the way of doing the thing cheaper. But he finds the bill perfectly fair, & thinks that we have done best in sticking to our old printers.

By printing only 750 copies[3] we may save £3.7 in printing, & £10.8. in paper. By looking over our Mss a little more carefully & correcting less in proof we ought to save from 10 to 15£ and by being earlier with our Mss we ought to save all the night work—from 14 to 20£. Making a saving of from 35 to 40 a number, or from £140 to £160 a year. This we ought to do, so I hope you will stick to the new rules, not as rules laid down to censure our friend, but as necessary reforms.

I read your Dudley speech in the Times.[4] Why dont you favour a larger audience at Westminster in the same way. It would be the best advertisement for the H&F. Even Capes, in his little way, found that lecturing at different towns was the best way of getting new subscribers for the Rambler. And what an opening you will have in German affairs this session!

Ever yours faithfully
R Simpson

Feb 6. 1864

I have borrowed Bodenstedt's Sonnets of Shakespeare. Dont forget to let me have what you think may be useful in that direction. You have not Chalmer's collection of the British poets have you? If so, lend me the volume with Davies on the immortality of the Soul—Vol 3 or 4 I think

---

[1] This refers to the decision on the bodies of martyrs in the Catacombs.
[2] The announcement of the dissolution of Robson & Levey.
[3] 1,000 copies were printed, but the sale did not exceed 750.
[4] *The Times*, 4 Feb. 1864, p. 12.

ACTON TO SIMPSON · 7 FEBRUARY 1864[*]

Sunday

My dear Simpson,

What you suggest will be a way of saving somewhat, and it would also be wise to restrict ourselves to 320 pages. I would not horrify W,[1] if it is not necessary, by reports of our small circulation, for several reasons. When he took an increased allowance he said it was on the supposition that money was beginning to come in; and he would therefore be disturbed to find it so little. Then he would easily despond; for he once wrote in such terms that I at once warned him very distinctly that there was no triumph in store for our doctrines and that the authorities could never adopt them or sincerely admit us to be other than rogues. To this he demurred very decidedly, I suppose because Newman dreams of a conversion in high places.[2] Now Newman has great sympathy with our cause, in as much as he is enlightened and liberal and highly cultivated, but I do not believe he really understands our theory, and certainly would no more admit it than DeBuck.

And I don't want Wetherell to bother me about pushing the review by advertisement and levity, nor, as you propose, by the aid of parliamentary discourse. If you still ignore the reason of this, I give you up altogether.

I have not Chalmers, and only bring you Marlowe and Webster, Ulrici, and a new book by Flathe rather in your line.

Thackeray[3] is getting on I hope. I shall be in the dreary Halfmoon[4] tomorrow.

I remain
Ever Your's truly
J D Acton

* The first part of Gasquet, Letter CLI, p. 315, with major omissions and alterations.
1 Wetherell (whose name was concealed by Gasquet).
2 A change of the bishops' attitude towards the *Home & Foreign Review*.
3 Simpson's article.
4 37 Half-moon St.

ACTON TO SIMPSON · 17 FEBRUARY 1864*

37 Halfmoon St
Wednesday

My dear Simpson,

Why don't you write an answer to Anglicanus in the Times[1] (who is Arthur Stanley) and sign it Romanus, and show the way in which we have an advantage over Anglicans, and how far Döllinger's words can apply to them, and preach up H&Fdom?

Carleton[2] is very provoking, for he carefully excludes the question which makes New Zealand interesting—the gradual formation of a free community.

Ever Yrs truly
J D Acton

627

SIMPSON TO ACTON · 24 FEBRUARY 1864

Clapham   Wednesday

Dear Acton

Among the things I wanted to say to you this morning & didn't was an enquiry whether you would give me 1£ for a girl, daughter of a good sort of woman, deserted by her husband, whom I have an opportunity of putting into a convent in Belgium for education for 500 francs down. I have collected almost enough, & only want about 2£ more, one of wh I make bold to ask you for—

Ever yours most sincerely
R Simpson

over

Dont send any money, only say whether I may put your name down or not—

---

* The second part of Gasquet, Letter CLI, p. 315.

[1] *The Times*, 17 Feb. 1864, p. 12, commenting on the vehemence of Anglican theological controversy and citing Döllinger's speech at the Munich Congress by way of favourable contrast.

[2] The unpublished article on New Zealand.

ACTON TO SIMPSON · 24 FEBRUARY 1864

Wednesday

Dear Simpson,

I hope you will put my name down for the two pounds yet wanting, and will claim the money next time we meet.

Thackeray[1] is indeed excellent. The want of groove and orthodox arrangement may disturb superficial readers, but the article is a triumph.

Ever Your's truly
J D Acton

SIMPSON TO ACTON · 25 FEBRUARY 1864

Thursday

Dear Acton

Thanks for the 2£.

Is not the arrangement[2] clear? I have

1. Introduction 2 pp. the last paragraph giving the programme of the article. Then

I. Thackerays theory, as developed

  1. in his criticism

  2 —————— history

  3 —————— art

  4 —————— philosophy.

II. His principle being a practical one, how does he carry it out? How does he manifest *himself*? & first morally

  1. in his characters

  2 in the circumstances with wʰ he surrounds them—

in wʰ he manifests

  α his various experiences

  β his sorrow

Which sorrow goes to explain

  a' his humour

  b' certain judgments & theories   { 2ᵈ marriages / 1ˢᵗ loves

---

[1] Simpson's article.

[2] Of 'Thackeray'.

3 (secondly intellectually) in his tastes
  α style of mind
  β critical preferences
  γ artistic forms
  δ literary feeling & laboriousness
  ε religion
III Peroration
  Instability of his philosophy, because without intelligent back-bone

---

If it the arrangement does not understand itself, let me have your notes; & I will see if I can correct it—If it is uncorrected, perhaps it w^d be as well to give the indexmaker this syllabus, w^h will do for the analysis of the article, & only wants the pages filling in.

Ever yours truly
R Simpson

Have you sent Buck Dympna?[1]

630

SIMPSON TO ACTON · 2 MARCH 1864

Dear Acton

With reference to the subject we spoke of yesterday,[2] first let me frankly & fully apologize to you & Wetherell for anything I have ever said which may seem rude & reflective upon your motives or acts— Without your knowledge or intention the new position in w^h I was placed in Decr 1862 caused a rankling wound in my mind, & anything that irritated it may very likely have caused intemperate expression—All which I hereby withdraw.

After this preface let me say what I think about the future, as growing out of the past.

I suppose I may say that before Decr 21, 1862,[3] You, Wetherell, & I formed as it were a cabinet, with the three offices of Editor, Subeditor, & Joint Proprietor—that these positions were publicly known, & that we each had a right to call himself what he was.

---

[1] The biography of St Dympna.
[2] This refers to a quarrel between Wetherell and Simpson. Simpson had altered an article which Wetherell had written for Block's *Dictionnaire politique*, dealing with the *Home & Foreign Review*, Apparently the alteration had been the insertion of Simpson's name in the list of the staff of the *Home & Foreign*, despite his nominal withdrawal in December 1862.
[3] Here Simpson draws upon his draft letter of 13 Dec. 1863 (Letter 601, n. 1) for his 'constitution' of the *Home & Foreign Review*. See also Letter 525, to which Simpson refers.

That when the office of Joint Proprietor was abolished, the Cabinet was not abolished. Wetherell had not "the least desire to lessen my real connection with or influence in the H.&F." And you only proposed "preserving my present position intact, & sacrificing only the name of proprietor". Everything else remained as it was—And I had really, though I did not exercise the right, because I did not see that I had it, a perfect right to say publicly that I was really as much as ever connected with the Review, but that I was no longer proprietor—i.e. that I was in the Cabinet without a portfolio, like the Whig Nestor[1]—

But to have acted on this right would have stultified the whole proceeding. I therefore understood the request made to me as a request to conceal & deny to the public that I had any real connection with the H.&F. I tried to carry out this. My only way was to suppose myself your *alter ego*, & in any correspondence I had about affairs to make a free use of your name, as if I was merely your agent. But this was manifestly incompatible with Wetherell's notion of separating us two as two mutually interchangeable evil genii like the damned in Malabolge. It only more clearly identified us. Neither was it ever accepted by you— for you saw no security for the new position in which I told you W's proposition placed me but my being paid for what I wrote—A proposal which I rejected absolutely.

But now, let me ask you, has this arrangement done the least good? Has it secured the success of the Review? has it rehabilitated me personally? In matter of fact I believe I get more abuse than ever I did— What has it done except to inflict a wound upon me, & to do that it was intended least of all to do—to lessen my real connection with & interest in the Review by putting me in relations to my colleagues & the world mutually incompatible, & which, when I attempted to carry them out honestly, I found to involve dishonesties which I felt to be degrading, for reasons which I felt to be insulting?

This is all subjective. So were my reasons for doing everything in my life that I am most glad of having done. The feeling that bridges over the abyss between the assent to a truth, & the will to make sacrifices for it is necessarily subjective. And I protest that the way in which I have hitherto understood and tried to carry out our paper constitution is impossible to me, & I henceforth renounce it.

But to return to where I was at first—I rejoice to believe that the *impossibilificating* point of the constitution is one merely interpretative, not really contained in it. I look in vain for any reason why I should consider myself bound to conceal the fact of my being in the Cabinet—

---

[1] Henry Petty-Fitzmaurice (1780–1863), 3rd marquess of Lansdowne 1809, Whig elder statesman, declined the prime ministry in 1852 but was a member of the cabinet without office to 1858.

I am bound to deny being Editor, Subeditor, or Proprietor. I am bound to confess having precisely the same power as I had when I was proprietor.

With this idea, if my colleagues allow it, the great weight will be taken off my mind. The cause which has made me jealous, cantankerous & disagreeable will be removed, & I shall be able to work with as much freedom as I could before Decr 1862. I ask for no conditions; I ask simply for the recognition that I am at liberty, on occasion, to state publicly, that though I hold no official portfolio in the management of the H.&F. I am really, in my own right, as much connected with it as ever I was.

I know that this is against the spirit of W's letter which I enclose. But it is not against the letter of my engagements, nor against the letter of the demands made on me parenthetically in that letter, w^h I enclose for your reading. And I submit that in odious matter the interpretation is to be made literally, & not extended according to its supposed spirit & purport.

I have written to Block to cut out all our names.[1] If Wetherell is angry, beg him from me to consider my note of Monday night as not written—I at first sent out word to the cabman that I would reply by post—He answered that he was told to wait an hour if necessary, but to insist upon bringing back an answer. I foolishly wrote in my natural irritation, & though I dont believe I said anything personally offensive, yet what I said *dixi in excessu meo*, & perhaps spoke venom.

On the other hand, I have no wish for publishing to the world the concerns of the H.&F.—or of talking of myself as one of its conductors— I desire however that if Block is to have a list of our personnel sent him at all, my name should not be omitted, when to him practically I am the H.&F. I am quite ready to make a mystery of the whole concern, but I am quite unwilling that I should bear the whole burden of the mystery—as if I was a wild beast, to be kept in a cage & under curtains, for fear of biting the public.

I sincerely hope that this will be a settlement of this *umbrageous* difficulty. *Umbrae me prohibent* is a fair motto for me. But in affairs of the mind shadows are more penetrating than substances.

Ever yours sincerely
R Simpson

March 2.

---

[1] From the article on the *Home & Foreign Review.*

ACTON TO SIMPSON · 3 MARCH 1864

37 Halfmoon S^t
Thursday

My dear Simpson,

Since I saw you I have had a note from Wetherell which I have since found that he wishes to have communicated to you. He has asked me to return it to him for that purpose if I was unwilling to do so, and I do not see that I have any right to refuse him, on the understanding that I am merely discharging the duties of the postman, and do not intend to enter into any personal aspects of a question which I have viewed only as it effects the Review.

There is an inconvenience which I have several times pointed out to you in bringing constitutional questions forward in the last month of the quarter. But you must not suppose that in saying this I am alluding in any way to words which might need an apology such as you express your willingness to make if there is occasion, and which, if there was occasion to make it, would be accepted without further words. If I once said something which suggested this, it was in order to deprecate a possible construction, not in reply to any hint coming from you.

I am anxious to remove one misconception in your letter, the existence of which I knew not before. I never had any doubt as to the possibility of your acting as my interchangeable *alter ego*, and the suggestion about payment for articles[1] did not proceed from any such feeling.

If we do not all understand that a paper constitution is vain, and that everything must depend on mutual confidence in arrangements such as our's, then it is too late to expect such insight to be granted to us.

Matters now stand thus: You reject the existing arrangement hence forward, and make certain proposals. I should much wish not to have to go into them now, with the stress of the number upon me. Pray think whether you can fairly allow me to postpone answering you on these points till the end of the month, interpreting meanwhile the matters in question as liberally as you think allowable.

I remain
Ever Your's truly
J D Acton

[1] In Letter 525.

SIMPSON TO ACTON · 3 MARCH 1864

My dear Acton

I send you by this post some additions to *Poor-law*,[1] & a conclusion, which perhaps are none of them worth inserting. Will you read them & do what you like with them.

I have finished Block,[2] & also gone through the article on Ireland[3] which I have translated from Irish to English where necessary. I was afraid at first that it was going to be a statistical account of Irish Agriculture & so a double of Block's article—which is the best he has ever sent. I have sent both to Wetherell.

I hope you remember that you have promised him (B.) a short notice of his Dictionary in this next number. If you are of opinion, on second thoughts, that having had one notice of it, you ought not to have another till the work is complete, tell me so, & I will tell him.[4] Otherwise, if I say nothing & the April N° does not mention him, I shall have to hide my face.

I am quite ready for your article,[5] if you wish me to do anything with it.

What current events have you in petto? I suppose that DeBuck's Belgian letter[6] had better be dropped. It would be absurd to notice the Flemish stick-in-the-mud in the face of such stirring doings elsewhere. Block's are to come on the 10ᵗʰ—he is to have 100 fʳ a number. My frugal mind has lopped off 4£ a year from your offer—

Ever yours truly
R Simpson

[1] 'The Rise of the English Poor-Law.'
[2] 'Agriculture in France.'
[3] 'The Irish Exodus and Tenant Right.'
[4] Block's *Dictionnaire politique* was not reviewed in the April *Home & Foreign Review*.
[5] On Frohschammer, which was being expanded to include both Lamennais and Frohschammer, and which eventually became 'Conflicts with Rome'.
[6] For the 'Current Events', not published.

ACTON TO SIMPSON · 4 MARCH 1864

Friday

My dear Simpson,

Your additions to Poor Relief seem to me all right, end and all.[1] I am afraid Dease[2] must have given you a deal of trouble. I did not know you had kept him.

Surely there has been no Notice of Block.[3] In any case I thought it would be best to defer noticing him till his book is complete, and did not therefore bring him to town, except one livraison. But I will do as you please. The book deserves the highest commendation.

Lamennais—Frohschammer[4] gets on and you shall have half of it soon. We shall incur excommunication for the review of Smith,[5] where we reject the greater part of Isaiah.

I expect Dano German events,[6] and at least a sheet of English. These and Block will do.

I remain
Ever Yrs truly
J D Acton

Pray don't forget Goldwin Smith.[7]

634

SIMPSON TO ACTON · 4 MARCH 1864

Friday Night

Dear Acton

Will you at your convenience read Block's current events,[8] wh I send herewith, and tell me whether it is worth while translating them all, eg. the antediluvian introduction—the tedious quotations from the Congress—letters—the humour as he calls it, which is really the tone of French journalism, the shrill sarcasm of a Becky Sharp afraid of the

---

1 'The Rise of the English Poor-Law.'
2 'The Irish Exodus and Tenant Right.'
3 The *Dictionnaire politique.*
4 'Conflicts with Rome.'
5 Renouf, 'Dr. Smith's Dictionary of the Bible'.
6 Part of 'Current Events', *Home & Foreign Review*, IV (April 1864), 761–9.
7 Goldwin Smith, *A Plea for the Abolition of Tests in the University of Oxford* (Oxford, 1864), was reviewed by Simpson, *ibid.* 730–3; not attributed in the *Wellesley Index*, I, 553.
8 'France.'

fists of a Rawdon Crawley. The only part that is new or good seems to be the analysis of the subscriptions to the loan at the end. Let me have your views upon it.

What do you think of Sullivan for the agricultural editor?[1] or of the man who wrote the Irish article?[2] or of Lathbury? I am afraid the pay will not be very great.

I have Block's first volume. If you would like to do that I will leave it at your rooms one day next week.

I send with Block's current events a short notice of Goldwin Smith.[3] Cut out all the end if you think it dangerous. I never yet succeeded in explaining to any body the doctrine that analogy is the great weapon by which the mind guards its supposed *interests*. That the intellect, finding a doctrine difficult, bases it upon a thousand fancied analogies, all of which become safeguards of the dogma, and are fenced about with a share of its sanctions. Real faith keeps divine dogma in its proper isolation from all earthly things. Sham faith brings it down, mixes it with false conceptions of those things, & places orthodoxity in strict adherence to these falsehoods. This is the real reason why faith is so supremely indifferent to speculation—because speculation cannot really touch it, however it may seem to do so. Or rather, the progress of speculation gradually destroys the analogies, which false faith loves, and if it does not prove the dogmas, at least shows that beyond its own sphere lies an infinite sphere which it cannot fill with its own ideas, & for which therefore it ought to be ready to accept the testimony of revelation. The empty infinite sphere is the formal God of pure reason, which revelation fills & vivifies with substance & life. Here is the difference between Smith & Mansel,[4] & here Mansel is right & Smith wrong. Then Smith is right against Mansel, when he insists that our moral nature bears the *positive* image of God – Here is the great question to be treated in all controversies with Smith, Kingsley & the like—How to reconcile our innate & natural conception e.g. of justice, with the power of moral definition & dispensation by an external authority? I expect it is a hard nut. Roberts ought to do it for us. Or why does not Newman do it, as an appendix to his correspondence?[5]

Ever yours sincerely
R Simpson

---

[1] Of the *Dictionnaire politique*.
[2] Dease.
[3] *A Plea for the Abolition of Tests.*
[4] This refers to the debate over Mansel's *The Limits of Religious Thought.*
[5] Newman had just published his correspondence with Charles Kingsley in the controversy which led to the writing of the *Apologia pro vita sua.*

ACTON TO SIMPSON · 6 MARCH 1864

37 Halfmoon S^t
Sunday

My dear Simpson,

I saw Wetherell yesterday for the first time since Monday and then discovered what it is that has so much disturbed the peace. As I thought I saw an easy way of restoring it, I venture to disregard your wish to receive no communication on the subject except from him; and to emerge from the merely mechanical action of postman.

He gave no such orders to the cab as you were told, and did not even ask for an answer. So the answer that came astonished him. Moreover his note to you was originally a telegraphic message. Hence its brevity, and therefore apparent discourtesy. Moreover he regarded the article as his property, and not changeable without consultation with him. Now the urgency which you had given him to understand existed for the speedy transmission of the article, caused him to suppose that he would never have another opportunity of seeing it, and that by sending it off with the alteration to Block you had intended that it should appear without his having the power of preventing it.

As I am utterly unable to reconcile the haste of Saturday with the slowness of Monday and Tuesday,[1] I cannot say that there was not a sort of palliation for this misconception.

I assured him that I could answer for it you would admit that you had *formally* no right to alter the article you had asked him to write, without previous consultation with him—quite irrespective, of course, of the particular alteration made; and that in sending it off to Block you had no idea of withdrawing from Wetherell's final control the form in which his article should appear.

If you will consider the extreme contrast between the precipitation on the Saturday, and the ultimate reality, you will understand the mis-understanding. Pray give me the assurance I have given him which is of course valueless coming from me.

I would omit much of Block's Events,[2] and have put signs of ? opposite all that seems to me most superfluous. The congress letters can all be described in five lines.

---

[1] On 27 Feb. Simpson had taken Wetherell's article for the *Dictionnaire politique*, altered it and sent it off. On 29 Feb. occurred the incident with the cabman.
[2] 'France.'

Sullivan would be, of all our friends, the best man for Block.

I remain
Ever Your's truly
J D Acton

636

SIMPSON TO ACTON · 7 MARCH 1864

Monday Evening

My dear Acton

Many thanks for your performance of a kind office. The haste of Saturday is easily accounted for. My request to Wetherell was occasioned by my finding say on Feb. 25 a letter of Block's dated Feb. 12. in which after telling me that he was writing an article for his Dictionary on English reviews he added Vous pouvez si vous voulez me donner avant la fin de Fevrier la valeur de 20 à 25 lignes sur la H.&F. 1° dates. 2° noms. 3 but on principles.

These words I copied in English & sent to Wetherell, because I was too busy to write the information, & because I knew Wetherell would do it much better than I. But at the same time I never intended to ask for an article—Block asked me for information. As he might accept or reject what I sent him, or add to it or take away from it according to his own opinion or knowledge, so I merely intended to ask Wetherell for the same kind of help, & should never have dreamed of treating what he wrote for me as a communication from him to Block—indeed if he had sent it to Block without showing it to me I should have considered an extraordinary proceeding.

But if he considered it in that light of course I had no right whatever to alter it. But however we may both have regarded it, I had never any intention of letting my alteration be printed without consulting Wetherell & you. I knew Block's habit of always asking for copy 10 days, sometimes three months before he wants it—At the same time he & I take a common pride in being punctual to our engagements to one another, & in letting one another have what we promise on the very day fixed. This accounts for the extreme apparent haste of my request for copy, & my certainty that there was plenty of time for corrections on Monday. This also shows then in sending Wetherell the paper with alterations I had no intention of merely telling him of a thing done without his power of preventing it, but that I meant to provoke discussion on the matter, so that we might find some means, if names were to be mentioned at all, of not making mine conspicuous by it's absence.

The misconception is my fault. I should have told Wetherell that there was time to consult about it when I sent him back his paper on Monday.

So you have my full authority for repeating to Wetherell the assurance you have already been kind enough to give him—

I remain
Ever yours faithfully
R Simpson

637

SIMPSON TO ACTON · 8 MARCH 1864

Tuesday Evening

Dear Acton

Do you remember how some two years ago I deluded you into taking a copy of Gravinas work on the Duomo of Monreale for the benefit of the Maidstone Mission? Father Emanuele now asks me to ask you for £11..4..0 which he says you owe him for 14 no^s delivered, & for 2 which he has in hand, & will send immediately he is told where to send them.

If you send him a cheque by post mind you scratch out *Bearer* & put *Order* instead, & cross the cheque. Don't be offended at my pedagogy— you confess your carelessness of these details.

His direction is

The Revd Ruggiero Emanuele

Grove House

Maidstone

Shall I get up an article on *proverbs*. I hope I shall be able to make more of it than of epigrams.[1] Do you see that Jeffs has on hand a lot of French novels at 8^d a vol? Would it be worth while to lay in a stock of Georges Sand[2] against the day of writing about her?

Ever yours faithfully
R Simpson

What is Sullivans Christian name & address? I want to give it Block.

---

[1] 'Epigrams' appeared in July 1863. The article on proverbs was not written.
[2] George Sand (Aurore Dupin Dudevant; 1804–76), French novelist.

ACTON TO SIMPSON · 8 MARCH 1864[*]

37 Halfmoon S[t]
Tuesday March 8
1864

My dear Simpson,

I send you a document,[1] received this evening, which will make it impossible for me to carry on the Review as hitherto with a good conscience.

The whole drift of the papal Rescript, beyond the direct attack on Döllinger, is to condemn the foremost principle of the Home and Foreign—one on which I believe there has never been any difference of opinion between us. Let me call your attention particularly to the passage in the second half of the first column on page 49.

This is an elaborate statement of opinions and intentions on a point practically fundamental which are incompatible with our own. I, at least, entirely reject the view here stated. If it is accepted by the H&F, the review will lose its identity, and the very breath of its nostrils. If it is rejected, and the proclamation of the Holy See defied, the Review cannot long escape condemnation, and cannot any longer efficiently profess to represent the true, authoritative Catholic opinion. In either case I think the Review forfeits the reason of its existence. It cannot sacrifice its traditions, or surrender its representative character.

There is nothing new in the sentiments of the Rescript, but the open aggressive declaration, and the will to enforce obedience, are in reality new. This is what places us in flagrant contradiction with the government of the Church.

My wish is therefore to close the career of the H&F with the next number, and to do so with your full consent and approbation, but on my responsibility alone. The article on Lamennais and Frohschammer[2] gives an opportunity of explaining, in a peroration, the motives of the step, and of defining once more the principles of the Review, and of vindicating the Catholicity of its conductors.

[*] Gasquet, Letter CLIII, pp. 317–18.
[1] A papal brief ('Tuas libenter') to the archbishop of Munich, dated 21 Dec. 1863 but published 5 March 1864, implicitly criticizing Döllinger's doctrine of freedom of scholarship in his address to the Munich Congress of scholars, and requiring submission, not only to dogmatic definitions, but also to the decisions of Roman Congregations and the common opinions of the theological schools, which must control the conclusions of the secular sciences.
[2] Now to be expanded into 'Conflicts with Rome'. Cf. Acton to Döllinger, 9 March 1864, in Conzemius, I, 335–6.

I will draw this up separately, and will send it to you on Thursday, to be judged and interpreted with your usual kindness, and handled with your usual freedom. If my impression of the probable consequences of this document do not seem to you justified by its language, I hope you will suspend your judgment till I have put together the grounds of my opinion. I will only say that, in reading the Rescript, the maxim restringenda odiosa would not be a safe guide. Remember also the public effect this attack on the Munich Congress will have. Pray return the paper when mastered.

I remain
Ever Y^{rs} truly
J D Acton

639

SIMPSON TO ACTON · 9 MARCH 1864

4 Victoria Road
Clapham
March 9. 1864

My dear Acton

You have my full consent and approbation for the course which you propose. It is clearly as impossible to carry on a professedly Catholic Review on our principles, as it is for us to change our principles at every wind of pastoral that may blow across the Alps. Literature for Catholics must clearly come out in a non Catholic form; we must give up our notion of Catholic literature as a bad job.

I am very sorry that I did not pocket my own discomforts a little longer, so that this cloud of personal feeling[1] should have been waiting at this time to be cleared up. Another regret I have had is that for my sake I allowed you to make the H.&F. the acknowledged successor of the Rambler, by which means we have been led into needless difficulties, & your purse has been too much drawn upon—for which I feel partly guilty. But I believe you do not think of this half so much as I have done.

Of course you will let it be clearly understood that we in no sense accept the views of Pio IX. Do notice the palpable lie that it was never the practice in the Church for theologians to meet and consult about doctrines without the impulse, authority & mission of the Bishop. Or rather draw up your own declaration as you like, & then if I have any suggestions I can make them.

I send you back the Pastoral-Blatt.[2] Will you let me have it again when you send your article. I will honestly return it.

---

[1] The quarrel with Wetherell.   [2] The papal brief.

I hope that Wetherell & I are not going to part in dudgeon. He has not written to me yet, but he sends me all the Mss, & so for the first time I am doing my work comfortably.

It will be a real sacrifice to give up literary work—and a much greater one to dissolve my literary partnership with you, which has given me nothing but comfort from the first day when I proposed it to you till now. If I can hereafter be of any use to you in this way you may always depend upon me.

Do you give an index with this number? If so, the maker ought to have the proofs, so as only to have to add the pages at the last moment.

I suppose also that for this time it will not be of much use to save £7 or 8 by printing 750 instead of 1000 copies.

Ever yours faithfully
R Simpson

640

ACTON TO SIMPSON · 10 MARCH 1864*

March 10 1864

My dear Simpson,

I am most grateful for your letter because I take it as evidence that you see the thing in the same light as I do, and are not making a concession to my scruples. In omitting all allusion to the two circumstances you speak of, the expense, and the differences which have arisen, I was guided by no other motive but that of sincerely informing you of the true grounds of my intention—with which they had nothing to do.

As to the first, I have never been disturbed by it, because the object of our experiment deserved some sacrifice. As to the other matter, I hope you know by this time that it no longer exists. On Tuesday evening I found Wetherell quite restored to an equal mind.

My Committee,[1] and the obligation of attending the Speaker's Levee, prevented me from writing above a page yesterday. Today, having your reply, I must write, privately, to those who have stood by us; the public need know nothing till the number appears. So that I cannot keep my promise of sending you the declaration today. I mean it to be as open and objective as possible. I shall write only for the purpose of making people clearly understand our motives, not in order to please, or to conciliate anybody; but I will give as little scandal, and say as little against Rome as possible. Of course it must be made as clear as daylight that

---

* Gasquet, Letter CLIV, pp. 318–20, with an omission.
[1] Of the House of Commons.

we do not accept the views of Rome on the subject. But I am unwilling to enter upon any part of the paper which may involve a defence of the Germans against whom it is directed—as nobody must be given an opportunity of attributing to them the same disagreement with Rome which we acknowledge. Keeping only this in mind pray modify what I shall send you, give it all literary form compatible with my signing it, and return it to me to be copied out.

I hope our literary partnership is not at an end. It has been often in my mind that you had larger things to do than to write articles, and that the pressing need of the hour kept you from more important work. If you and Renouf turn your thoughts to the composition of serious books, you will do more for the literary character of the Catholic body than the H&F could ever have done. For my part I will take the most selfishly liberal advantage of your friendship to consult you about the political philosophy of Catholicism, for which I have collected so much.

Believe me
Ever faithfully Your's
J D Acton

I have just received the enclosed.

641

ACTON TO SIMPSON · 14 MARCH 1864

Monday morn[g]

Dear Simpson,

I have just received Palgrave's MS[1] and have not time to read it between post delivery and my first engagement this morning—I send it to you with his letter.

In haste
Ever Y[rs] truly
J D Acton

642

SIMPSON TO ACTON · 14 MARCH 1864

Monday Morning

My dear Acton

Would not Renouf be the man to read over Palgrave? It should be some Orientalist. It would be good to print it, if possible, in order to say

---

[1] W. G. Palgrave, 'Asceticism amongst Mahometan Nations', *Home & Foreign Review*, IV (April 1864), 553–76.

that we had a jesuit writing such a theory of religion as he opens with—
a theory which certainly goes beyond any Catholic theory I have yet seen
in fundamental inconsistency with any absolute revelation.[1]

He will want a deal of doctoring: I have worked at a little of it, but
I should like Renouf's approval before I went on. Therefore write to
Renouf, & send his direction to me, & I will send him the article &
Palgrave's letter.

Why have I yet received nothing from you, except a few pages which
Wetherell has just sent me—I cannot begin working in the middle of it,
so I will wait till you send me the rest.

Under the circumstances, is it necessary to hold very strictly to the
day of publication? You may save 20 by suppressing night work &
taking two or three days more.

I am delighted to find that our literary partnership will not altogether
die. If some four or five of us can hold together we may perhaps be able
occasionally to make ourselves heard in the Edinburgh or National
Reviews—

Ever yours faithfully
R Simpson

643

ACTON TO SIMPSON · 15 MARCH 1864

Monday night

My dear Simpson,

I cannot recapitulate the impediments which have kept me from
finishing what I had begun.[2] I am very sorry for the delay, but the
house,[3] together with urgent private affairs, has taken up nearly all my
time. Lamennais was done before I heard of the Rescript. What relates
to it is nearly ready for your treatment.

Renouf is in town. Direct to him at 7 North Bank N.W. How can we
have twelve articles?

I hope you will consider several things. 1. The life of Campion.[4] 2. a
volume of Essays, from Victor Hugo downwards, when you have done
a few more, and especially Shakespeare, for some more fortunate publication. There is no better criticism than your Eliot and Thackeray, and
a volume of this kind ought to be successful. 3. a book on Metaphysics;
before publishing which you ought surely to read Hegel, whose

---

[1] 'Asceticism amongst Mahometan Nations' was published as a 'communicated'
article.
[2] 'Conflicts with Rome.'
[3] House of Commons.
[4] Published in 1867.

philosophy is, in many shapes, the subtlest pervading influence of the present day.

Not now, when it would be revengeful, but later, you might do something useful on the state of Catholic parties in England; and there is your essay on Newman to be completed.[1]

Whatever I send you pray make as thoroughly objective as possible, and remove every trace of personality.

Could you not prepare a paper for the Academia on some indifferent topic.

I remain
Ever Your's faithfully
J D Acton

A Jesuit would have been much gratified this morning to hear me disputing with Thirlwall[2] on the merits of the Society.

644

SIMPSON TO ACTON · 16 MARCH 1864

Tuesday Afternoon

Dear Acton

I send you back a few sheets,[3] which I have rewritten—If you will see whether I have succeeded in not sacrificing your meaning, & will then hand on the two copies to Wetherell we may at last attain to fluency.

No, do not let us have 12 articles; I will not send Palgrave[4] to Renouf. You must urge upon the Rev[d] F.[5] to publish it as a pamphlet.

I must obviously set to work to finish Campion. You will look over my Mss for me as hitherto, will you not?

Ever yours faithfully
R Simpson

---

[1] Of these projects for Simpson, only the essays on Shakespeare were published.

[2] Connop Thirlwall (1797–1875), ancient historian, Anglican priest 1828, bishop of St David's 1840, the most learned and liberal of the bishops.

[3] Of 'Conflicts with Rome'.

[4] 'Asceticism amongst Mahometan Nations.'

[5] Father (Palgrave).

ACTON TO SIMPSON · 16 MARCH 1864

37 Halfmoon S^t
Tuesday

Dear Simpson,

Palgrave[1] must be suppressed only if he is bad, not because of the number of articles. Lottner[2] was ready on Saturday, but has not arrived, and may be too late.

By all means finish Shakespeare while you are at it. I am afraid you are not aware of the singular power you have developed between Hugo and Thackeray,[3] and that you will have an incomparable success in that kind of criticism.

Renouf wants me to prepare Human Sacrifice and Adrian IV for the Atlantis,[4] and talks of adding a paper of his own on S. Ignatius his Martyrdom.

There is no money to be got there, and few readers—but hardly less of either than in the H&F. and we might make a first volume with Shakespeare and a paper of Sullivan. But that would only be if your Shakespeare is too Catholic for the Edinburgh or National.

I remain
Ever Your's truly
J D Acton

Renouf is highly approved by the Cardinal as Inspector,[5] and has been warned by him against the H&F. and advised to keep clear of it. Many thanks for Lamennais[6] in his new coat.

---

[1] 'Asceticism amongst Mahometan Nations.'

[2] Friedrich Löttner, 'Indian Epic Poetry', *Home & Foreign Review*, IV (April 1864), 512–52.

[3] 'Victor Hugo's *Misérables*' and 'Thackeray'.

[4] The *Atlantis* had been suspended. Discussions concerning its resumption or replacement went on for a few months.

[5] Renouf had been appointed an inspector of schools in March 1864. Letter 460 n. 1 (based on the *Dictionary of National Biography*) should be revised.

[6] 'Conflicts with Rome.'

ACTON TO SIMPSON · 23 MARCH 1864

Wednesday
1 o'clock

Dear Simpson,

I sent you a large piece of MS.[1] an hour or two ago, and now send the rest.

Perhaps there ought to be a brief recapitulation of our system at the end. I add a fragment which would have had to come somewhere in the part already sent; perhaps you may think it contains one idea not clearly put elsewhere.

I have been hoping to hear from Döllinger, in order that our cause may square with anything he may intend to do; but I suppose he is wasting his time saying masses for the late King, and preaching his funeral oration.[2]

Ever Y^{rs} faithfully
J D Acton

647

ACTON TO SIMPSON · 25 MARCH 1864*

Good Friday

My dear Simpson,

I sent you the exordium[3] yesterday. I now send all that remains to complete the story of Frohschammer—down to the beginning of our story. I have taken pains to make his progress in error intelligible, and, to be just, have separated the debateable part, much of which may be explained in two ways, from his pure heresy on Development. You will see at a glance what it is all about.

I send the Brief condemning him, which goes farther in the direction of Rationalism of any papal act—observe the words Dei *naturam*—Also my notes, when I meant to deal more at length with F. I don't know whether any part of them will suggest anything to you worth inserting.

---

[1] 'Conflicts with Rome.'

[2] Maximilian II (1811–64), king of Bavaria 1848, Döllinger's patron, died 10 March. Döllinger, as provost of the royal chapel, preached the funeral sermon on 15 March.

* Gasquet, Letter CLII (out of place), p. 316, misdated 'March 6'.

[3] To 'Conflicts with Rome'.

We must print the Rescript against us (shall we call it a Brief) after the article.[1]

I remain
Ever Your's truly
J D Acton

648

SIMPSON TO ACTON · 26 MARCH 1864

Saturday afternoon

Dear Acton

The exordium[2] has not come—Nothing came between what you sent on Wednesday afternoon, & the roll of F.[3] just arrived, with the brief against him. I have had in all 3 parcels of him. One sent by Wetherell, & two by you. I dont reckon the Postscript among these—Make sure that the exordium was sent—

Ever yours truly
R Simpson

649

ACTON TO SIMPSON · 29 MARCH 1864

Tuesday
Afternoon

Dear Simpson,

Wetherell has not yet finished his revision, and we shall not have a complete proof till the end of the week. There is therefore no pressing reason for you to come tomorrow. I am working a great patch of Adrian IV into a short notice of an Irish Church history.[4]

Ever Y^{rs} truly
J D Acton

[1] *Home & Foreign Review*, IV (April 1864), 691–6.
[2] To 'Conflicts with Rome'.
[3] Frohschammer.
[4] Sylvester Malone, *A Church History of Ireland*...(Dublin, 1864), reviewed by Acton, *Home & Foreign Review*, IV (April 1864), 708–15. The projected article on Adrian IV was never published.

650

ACTON TO SIMPSON · 31 MARCH 1864

Thursday

Dear Simpson,

The proofs of the article[1] are promised tomorrow morning and the number will appear on Monday. Can you meet me in Wetherell's rooms at twelve o'clock tomorrow for a final revision? We shall have time for our several corrections before meeting.

I remain

Ever Your's truly

J D Acton

651

SIMPSON TO ACTON · 12 APRIL 1864

4 Victoria Road

April 12

Dear Acton

It is about time to pay the piper. Robson's bill I have not recd; the Paper-maker's is 31£ minus discount. Block comes to 17£ (conveniently sent in 200f^r & a 5£ note) and the old balance due to me is 19£. Shall I tell the printers to send their bill in to you? This will obviate any fringes to the account. The rest comes to £64, allowing for the discount. The printers have sent in a bill for £20 for printing Campion.[2] Now as I used all the Rambler money for the H.&F. I think it would be fair if I took this amount out of the balance coming to you from Williams & Norgate, who owe for four numbers (say 160£). Then there is the whole stock on hand, which will be worth something. They have besides all that is left of the Rambler. I think that it had best be all sold, each of us reserving as many copies as he chooses to furnish himself with for future distribution.

I am diligently getting up the contemporaries of Shakespeare. When Rio[3] comes to your hands will you lend him me? Also have you Taine's History of English literature? It is reviewed in the Westminster, & the chapter on Shakespeare seems worth considering. Do you see that

---

[1] 'Conflicts with Rome.'

[2] A chapter of *Edmund Campion* left unpublished when the *Rambler* ended in 1862.

[3] *Shakespeare* (Paris, 1864).

Carleton has found a home in the Westminster?[1] Have you heard yet what is said about your farewell article?[2]

Ever yours sincerely

R Simpson

652

SIMPSON TO ACTON · 13 MAY 1864

Dear Acton

I trust that either you did not get my letter of about a month ago, or did not answer it with any enclosure. I gave you the state of the accounts, & asked for money to pay some that cried for payment. As I heard nothing I went to Williams & Norgate & got 50£ on account— So I am in no want.

Williams & N. want to get rid of the Rambler w^h is to them mere waste paper—I doubt if they have any perfect sets from the beginning —But if you want any numbers will you tell them. I think we had better ask them to keep 30 or 40 sets of the last (bimonthly) series.

I have put together a lot of books of yours—Shall I send them to Aldenham? I still keep some quarter of a hundred or more—with your leave. If you find Rio[3] at Aldenham will you bring him up with you.

I am busying myself with a commentary on Shakespeares sonnets,[4] but I dont think the form which it takes is publishable. How would it do to make it a Platonic dialogue between WS. & W.H?[5] Shakespeare was "Genio Socrates"—perhaps he was famed for his dialectic powers, & loved to talk Platonism as much as he loved to write it. Have you Crescembeni *della bellezza*, or any of the Commentaries on Dante? It is a long job to compare the sonnets with the Canzonieri of Dante & Petrarch, and a good commentary, w^h classified the things said w^d save a world of trouble.

Ever yours most truly

R Simpson

Clapham

May 13. 1864

---

[1] The articles are, respectively, William Fraser Rae, 'Taine's History of English Literature', *Westminster Review*, LXXI (April 1864), 473–512, and Carleton, 'New Zealand', *ibid.* 420–72.

[2] 'Conflicts with Rome.'

[3] Rio's *Shakespeare*, like Simpson's 1858 articles on 'What was the Religion of Shakespeare?', maintained that Shakespeare was a Catholic.

[4] *An Introduction to the Philosophy of Shakespeare's Sonnets* (London, 1868).

[5] 'WS' is William Shakespeare. 'W.H.' (identity uncertain) is cited in the dedication to the *Sonnets* as their 'onlie begetter'.

SIMPSON TO ACTON · 16 JUNE 1864

4 Victoria Road
Clapham
June 16

Dear Acton

The man whose card I enclose says that he left at Williams and Norgates', on the first of April, a Ms addressed to the Editor of the H&F. He is very anxious to have it back. I suppose it was sent to you. I know nothing of it.

I packed off to Aldenham some 10 days or fortnight ago a large box of books. I have some 10 or a dozen still here—

I wont send you any more accounts as you dont seem to take the slightest notice of them—I have done what I proposed doing in my notes to you

Ever yours truly
R Simpson

654

SIMPSON TO ACTON · 13 JULY 1864

4 Victoria Road
Clapham. July 13. 64

Dear Acton

I must transfer to you the task of winding up the enclosed accounts. On the face of the balance sheet there is a balance of £11.6.4 due to me. But I think that the sum of £13.3.6 w^h I have marked with a cross (the last payment in April 1863,) was paid to Robson for my Ullathorne pamphlet[1]—at least I can find no other payment to him on that account —That would make the balance a trifle the other way.

As to the sum of 85£ for Nos. 3 & 4 of the H.&F. I was careless enough to send you Williams' bill before I had put it down in my account—so though I feel pretty sure about the pounds, I have omitted all mention of shillings & pence. If you have the bill perhaps you would look to see how much it is, for I have a lurking idea that it was only £83 odd.

The Bill to Ford was on account of Wine w^h Wetherell asked me to order for him in 1862 or 3—before you had begun to pay him directly—

---

[1] *Bishop Ullathorne and the Rambler.*

If you like, either he can pay it, or, if it is better not to remind him of it, I will pay it next Christmas.

Of course, every thing that can be made of the Rambler & H.&F. as waste paper or otherwise goes to pay the £180 still due; but I am afraid that you must advance the money; for Spalding[1] & Robson will be clamorous before Williams and Norgate are prepared to pay more than 20.9.8 now due from them.

Am I ever to hear from you or to see you again? I have written three letters to you without moving you to an answer. I hope this will extract a line for old friendship's sake—

Every yours faithfully
R Simpson

Do tell me what you are about. My friends ask me to explain your vote last Friday;[2] I do not attempt to do so.

655

ACTON TO SIMPSON · 17 JULY 1864

37 Halfmoon S[t]
Sunday

My dear Simpson,

My mind is rather confused by the contemplation of your figures, and I am not sure whether the cheque I enclose bears a remote relation to the extent of the money due. If it falls ridiculously short, there will still be sums due from the Publishers to make up the deficiency.

Pray cause anything you like to be done with the remaining copies. Wetherell will perhaps wish for some, and some might be offered Renouf, who probably has not a complete set. How pretty it would be to send a neat copy, bound, to each of the Bishops.

I am afraid you will not derive much benefit from the sale.

Don't lose sight of the Liberal party. A good article on the subject[3] would do great good.

Here is the Mechlin invitation,[4] in case you have none, and think of going there.

---

[1] The paper-maker.
[2] Acton had voted against the Government on Disraeli's motion of censure regarding its conduct in the Dano-German war.
[3] I.e., the state of parties among the English Catholics. 'Liberal party' means Liberal Catholics.
[4] To the second Malines congress.

I hope you will stick to Shakespeare and make a book of it, for I am sure you would succeed admirably.

Believe me
Ever faithfully Your's
J D Acton

656

SIMPSON TO ACTON · 20 JULY 1864

My dear Acton

You sent me too much money. The account I gave you showed that we owed £180.7.3. to which I had to add Robson's bill for the Index[1] £7.12.6. making 187.19.9. You sent me 200 & Williams paid me yesterday 20.9.8. £220.9.8. Leaving £32.10.11. overplus. I reserve the 2.10.11 for possible calls, & I have paid £30.0.0. into your account at Herries & Farquhar's[2]—I have also told Williams & Norgate to put the proceeds of all the other sales, both of Rambler & H.&F. to your account —By this means I hope you will have back the £170 you have now advanced.

Give my best remembrances to Döllinger, and dont forget to ask him whether he can help me in Hecker's business[3]—If you could send back that letter before February I should be glad, for then I could give it such an answer as might be possible for me, in anticipation of what I might afterwards have to communicate from Döllinger.

Robson has got an excellent Printing Office close to the great Northern Station—He asked when he might expect your book—& he hoped you had mentioned him to Renouf & Sullivan. The old man seemed proceeding very well—I saw two new volumes of Carlyles Frederick, a new volume of Cathedra Petri, Dyces' Shakespeare, besides a lot of things for Burns on his forms.

I will try what I can do about the Liberal Catholics.[4] I have a kind of à priori frame work for it which you would thoroughly disapprove of, but I think I could work it up into something decent. O that you could find time to write a sheet of meditations about it—You know how much better I can do a thing under some sort of inspiration from you—either to contradict or to develop.

---

[1] To Volume IV of the *Home & Foreign Review*.
[2] A bank.
[3] It is not certain what this 'business' was.
[4] This article was never published.

Block 23 l'Assomption, Auteuil
Rio.   22 Rue Oudinot

Ever yours faithfully
R Simpson

Salute Block for me.

July 20. 1864

657

SIMPSON TO ACTON · 16 FEBRUARY 1865

4 Victoria Road Clapham
Feb. 16. 1865

My dear Acton

I write to you, in order to convey to you personally my "written embassage" of affectionate greetings, though the matter is rather for Wetherell. In the first place, then, I find that Manning took to Rome with him four sets of answers to the Bishops questions;[1] on the liberal side Allies' and mine, on the oscurantist, David Lewis' and another. On which Wetherell may make the following observations.[2] That I answered the questions on the supposition that there was a question of Newman's setting up a Hall at Oxford, and directed all my attention to recommending this intention for realization; that if I had known that there was no question of this, I should have applied myself to the defence of the next alternative, namely the sending Catholics to existing Colleges, and that I entirely adopt and adhere to all the arguments which Wetherell has drawn up in defence of this position retracting all that I said in my paper that may appear contrary to his arguments. It is quite possible that my paper may be used *against* the prayer of the Memorial;[3] so that it is worth while that Wetherell should have under my hand the foregoing declaration.

Next, he asked me to tell him what censures there were on people who hindered appellants to the Roman Curia. In the *Censurarum collectio* in Busenbaum (Vol. 2. ed. Rom. 1844 p. 260), in the first number, "Excommunicationes latae sententiae, ac Papae reservatae" the following are declared subject to it "Accessum ad romanam Curiam pro impetrandis apostolicis literis prohibentes (Bull. Caenae. ℈ 13)"—

---

[1] Concerning Newman's project of establishing a Catholic mission at Oxford. See *Letters and Diaries of Newman*, xxi (London, 1971), 346–8.

[2] Wetherell had taken to Rome (where Acton was also staying) a petition of a number of laymen urging that Catholics be allowed to attend the English universities.

[3] Wetherell's petition.

199

"Agentium in causis recursus ad rom: Curiam offensores (B. Caenae. ℣ 12; "In Rom: Curia collitigantium, vel procuratorum offensores denunciare omittentes: Bul. 11. Alex. VI. In *eminenti*".

Also will you tell Wetherell that as he seeks to deck his signatures in the grandest & most Cope-&-stole-like robes possible, he may describe my brother & me as "joint founders of the Chapel & School of Mitcham, in the diocese of Southwark." I suppose he received Mrs Renouf's[1] letter for Cardinal Reisach;[2] she posted it on the Saturday noon before he (W.) departed. She tells me that if Wetherell wants to gain Reisach's heart, he must tell him all the foolish stories about Talbot Manning, & such like obscurantists, that he can pick up.

Roberts tells me that the Cardinal Wiseman (who died yesterday) last Sunday week, when he protested his faith before his chapter, also declared to them on the word of a dying man, that he had not in any way sought to influence Rome with regard to his successor. That, so far as any recommendation of his was concerned, the Chapter were quite as free in their election as if he had never existed. &c. That of course Rome might or might not accept the Chapters nominee; but it would not be his fault if it did not do so. If this is true it takes away from Manning's chances—The chapter would as lief elect Beelzebub himself. Errington puts in his claim; he would be a regular scourge to the clergy & would have no chance except somebody bigger than Wiseman[3] dies too. Ullathorne & Clifford are spoken of as successors. Whoever comes, I think that the opportunity must not be lost of trying to make something of the Academy. Surely among all your collections you have materials for a paper to be read there.

This has been almost a lost year to me. In the autumn I was ill, & unable to do anything except Music—indeed the doctor forbad my looking at a book under pain of paralysis or some such vile result, & I had to take oceans of quinine—& I have so taken in the sweetness of doing nothing, that the spirit of idleness is being difficult to cast out. I am trying a rough method with it—namely compelling it to study the logic of Hegel of w^h one Stirling[4] has just published a partial translation, partial summary, with a great deal of elucidation that is more σκοτεῖνος than Hegels own indifference of light & dark. I must own that I had no business to publish my articles on the "forms of intuition" without having read this, and at the same time that even after reading it I should,

---

[1] Ludovika Brentano (la Roche) (1836–1921), a member of a famous German family, married Renouf 1857.
[2] Karl August Graf von Reisach (1800–69), bishop of Eichstätt 1836, coadjutor archbishop of Munich 1841, archbishop 1847–55, cardinal 1855, resided in Rome.
[3] Pope Pius IX.
[4] James Hutchison Stirling, *The Secret of Hegel: being the Hegelian System in origin, principle, form, and matter*, 2 vols. (London, 1865).

though with many modifications & developments, stick to the main principles of what I wrote.

I have just had a letter from A. Reichensperger—the more he reads in the H.&F. the less can he divest himself of the conviction that such doughty champions for the highest good of humanity cannot much longer withdraw themselves from the battlefield sulking in their tents. He harps upon one thought continually—namely that in the present crisis[1] we should not add to the Pope's sorrows, but join shoulders to attack the enemy. I reminded him that the Pope used his temporal misfortunes as a pretext for spiritual oppression, but he takes no note of the argument. It is a curious note of the time how duties are all made to turn on sentiments of personal attachment. E.G. at the end of our Lenten dispensations Tommy Grant[2] says not "According to the command, or dispensation, or decision of his Holiness, but "according to the *wish* of his H." Easter communions must be made within such limits of time. As if any body's *wish* bound my conscience. Reichensperger is much edified by the dutiful behaviour of the Correspondant in publishing the Encyclic[3]—though I cannot see much duty in accepting a document, salaaming to it, & then explaining it away, as the French & Belgian liberal Catholics do.

I wish somebody would write an article to exemplify the difference of the historical & scholastic systems by the respective conclusions each leads to with regard to the infallibility of the Pope. Ward often declares that he does receive the historical principle—but he certainly only argues upon the other, unless his forthcoming article on Galileo[4] is to be an exception; an article which Roberts is preparing to smash before it appears.

Have you been buying any Mss for the Lingard association that was to be? I have no doubt that you have been spending your time to good purpose abroad; at least by absence from England you have escaped the expense of many blushes which would have been due to appreciations of you[5] that have appeared in the Spectator &c &c, & now lastly in Dean Stanley's oration to the clergy of his deanery, on the theology of the 19th century, published in this month's Fraser.[6] At least when you next appear in print you will not have to struggle against the unbeknownness which was always a wet blanket to the H.&F. Your trumpet has been blown perseveringly, & any Ms you may take to Longmans will now I

---

[1] Of the Temporal Power.
[2] Bishop Grant, Simpson's diocesan.
[3] *Quanta Cura*, to which the *Syllabus of Errors* was attached.
[4] Ward, 'Doctrinal Decrees of a Pontifical Congregation: The Case of Galileo', *Dublin Review*, n.s. v (October 1865), 376–425.
[5] Reviews of 'Conflicts with Rome'.
[6] A. P. Stanley, 'Theology of the Nineteenth Century', *Fraser's Magazine*, LXXI (February 1865), 252–68.

have no doubt be accepted & the book pushed with all the energy of his standing machinery.

I dare say I shall have more to write either to you or Wetherell before you leave Rome, so I will shut up. Remember me to W.

Ever yours most sincerely
R Simpson

658

SIMPSON TO ACTON · 1 MARCH 1865

Dear Acton

One word of congratulation on occasion of the news[1] which Monsell has brought from Rome. I don't think any body observed the way in which you bore your long troubles with more respect & sympathy than I did, so I all the more heartily give you joy for the condign & congruous reward of a constant heart. So no more at present from

Yours ever, faithfully
R Simpson

March 1. 1865
Renouf sends his love

659

SIMPSON TO ACTON · 28 APRIL 1865

4 Victoria R^d Clapham.
Ap. 28.

Dear Acton

It was only yesterday that I heard you were back. If I was not almost certain of missing you I would call on you today—tomorrow I cannot— But if you are not disinclined to kill two birds with one stone, come out here & have lunch on Sunday at 2, & I will get Renouf to meet you. We have here besides Renouf one Lambert,[2] a Poor Law inspector, who draws most of the Bills for Villiers, & whom you would like to know— Him I hardly can get for next Sunday, but some future Sunday will do. Give me a line as soon as you can in order that I may secure Renouf—You

---

[1] Of Acton's impending marriage.

[2] Sir John Lambert (1815–92), Catholic solicitor, mayor of Salisbury 1854, poor law inspector 1857–71, secretary of the local government board 1871–82, knighted 1879, privy councillor 1885; active on various commissions and as a drafter of legislation.

are a horrid fellow for not giving me an inkling of your return; I would have tried to see you before this

Ever yours faithfully
R Simpson

660

ACTON TO SIMPSON · 28 APRIL 1865

32 St James's Place
Friday

My dear Simpson,

I will come on Sunday at 2 with the greatest pleasure. I have only been in town a few, busy days, and was very glad this morning to hear a good account of you as you appeared at dinner at Robert's.

When we meet I shall try to make up for my poverty of correspondence by telling you stories of foreign parts; meantime let me thank you with all my heart for your good wishes on an event the approach of which has already wrought a great change in my life.

Believe me
Ever faithfully Your's
J D Acton

661

SIMPSON TO ACTON · 10 JULY 1865

Dear Acton

I saw Hall yesterday, who told me he was somewhat in a fix through having no answer to the Duke's[1] letter to you (3 copies of w^h have been despatched to your different addresses)—and though he took your *vivâ voce* acceptance of the Commissions[2] & has sent up your name to the Queen, he wants your Ms. I told him how you were busied at Bridgenorth[3]—but perhaps it will be easier to steal five minutes now than later on.

I am delighted that you are standing for Bridgenorth—I give you all my votes; in spite of the hindrances you will have to the modern history

---

[1] Probably Edward Adolphus St Maur (1804–85), 12th duke of Somerset 1855, first lord of the admiralty 1859–66.

[2] This may refer to Acton's appointment as justice of the peace and deputy lieutenant for Shropshire.

[3] Acton had become a candidate for the parliamentary seat at Bridgnorth.

of the Papacy. Farewell—Faustum Felixque sit with respect to both events of the month[1]—

Ever yours
R Simpson

Clapham, July 10. 1865.

662

ACTON TO SIMPSON · 12 JULY 1865

July the 12th 1865

Dear Simpson,

The Duke's letters miscarried very strangely, but I will send him his answer.

We are in the midst of the election, which has never offered me the slightest prospect of success, and will not therefore interfere with my plans for the future. But I have so strong a party that the enemy has been fool enough to fall into certain traps which we provided for him— At the nomination I had it all my own way, and got the show of hands after a very theological speech, which my opponent compelled me suddenly to make.[2] We expect not to be beaten by a very large majority.

I remain
Ever Your's truly
J D Acton

663

SIMPSON TO ACTON · 21 OCTOBER 1865

Clapham, Oct 21. 1865

Dear Acton

Buck prays me to remercy you in his name for the present truly royal which you continue to make to arrive at him. Stewart it seems has just sent 27 more of the books of the Master of the Rolls,—a collection which already fills four rows in the Bollandist library.

Look in your Tablet of to-day, at the 2[d] correspondence from Rome. The author of the Statement comes in for much the same treatment as

---

[1] The other was Acton's marriage.

[2] See Acton to Marie von Arco-Valley [11 July 1865], in *Lord Acton: The Decisive Decade 1864–1874*, ed. Damian McElrath (Louvain, 1970), pp. 67–8, misdated 'June 1865'. Acton was declared elected by one vote but was unseated in 1866 on a scrutiny.

the Ox received at the hands of his Dublin butcher[1]—But why was the Ox so moved? or being moved, why did he not treat his subject in a way calculated to throw some light on the whole question of subjective criticism of objective argumentation, on which he might have written a page or two more true and as racy as the few paragraphs of the introduction to his philosophy of history which Hegel devotes to the "psychological varlets" who judge of the achievements of heroes by their real or supposed "morbid cravings." I remember during the Crimean war the Rev[d] H. Christmas,[2] F.S.A. or rather A.S.S. published a book on Nicholas I, proving that though great, the Czar could not be happy. Consoling doctrine! So Wetherell, though writing truth, yet writes against Bishops—therefore he must be conceited; therefore again he cannot be true. I am afraid the series ends there—At least I dont see how to make a recurring decimal of it, like the "Cretans always liars". The only conclusion that I can draw is that truth & falsehood are of very little importance, the one thing needful is to be submissive to Barnabo, & so far to feel the identity of being & nothing, as to be wide awake to the last telegraphic news about the "Becoming" at present in vogue at the Vatican—Greedy of eating the toads before they are cooked—to use not at all the most expressive of the old English sayings which occur to me, but the one least offensive to commit to paper.

I have now I think shaken off the numbness which the cessation of the H.&F. left upon me, & I am working hard at a reconstruction of those papers on the Forms of Intuition into a systematic shape, in w[h] they will come out quite in a different shape. But I am often chilled by the feeling that in these shadowy metaphysical regions nothing is easier than to follow a will-o'the-whisp—And I have not sufficient confidence in myself to form any judgment beyond this, that I seem to myself to apprehend a principle that will explain the discrepancies of rival systems, & allow the Hegelian & Positivist to shake hands on a middle platform. But my dreams may be rudely dissipated by the first competent critic who descends upon me as Brownson did, as one who "has the weakness to think himself a philosopher" without the shadow of a reason for so thinking. I often wish I had more material work—Cannot you employ me about some of your Roman documents, when you get them?

Buck gives me the Epitaph pronounced on the H&F. by P. Matagne,[3] the new Bollandist a man "vraiment savant, connaissant un nombre indefini de langues, qui a énormémant lu,—well "il considerait H.&F.

---

[1] W. G. Ward, 'Mr. Oxenham and the *Dublin Review*', *Dublin Review*, n.s. v (October 1865), 319–51.

[2] Henry Christmas (later Noel-Fearn; 1811–68), ordained 1837, journalist and numismatist. He published a memoir of Nicholas I in Shaw's *Family Library*, 1854.

[3] Jules Matagne (1833–72), entered Society of Jesus 1851.

comme une de plus fortes revues qui eussent jamais paru"—This I tell you for the sake of the Belgian Jesuits & the Bollandists in particular, whom one must distinguish from the Roman ones. Of course "he did not always approve the tone, & thought that with a little modification of form it was calculated to do immense service".

I have just written to Wetherell to ask him to dine on the 21ˢᵗ Wedding day—think of that you novice.

Ever yours
R Simpson

664

ACTON TO SIMPSON · 20 FEBRUARY 1866

22 Dover Sᵗ
Tuesday

My dear Simpson,

I have owed you a letter ever since I came back from Italy, and have cherished the debt which was not quite a new one when I got home and found your letter. So that there are grievous arrears of talk, which I want to make up, if you will give me the opportunity by coming to dine and make my wife's acquaintance on Thursday, at the Sᵗ James's, at 7.

Ever Your's most truly
J D Acton

665

SIMPSON TO ACTON · 21 FEBRUARY 1866

4 Victoria Road
Clapham
Feb 21.

Dear Acton

I am equally glad to see your handwriting again and vexed that I have to dine with Roberts tomorrow But I will take my chance of finding you at home on Friday afternoon to do my homage to Lady Acton and to begin liquidating some of our arrears of talk. Do not let me keep you in if you are going out, for I can call any other day—I would come before, but I have a friend staying with me—

Ever yours, most truly
R Simpson

666

ACTON TO SIMPSON · 2 MAY 1866

Wednesday

My dear Simpson,

Not knowing Renouf's direction I send you the Italian dissertation we spoke of, praying you to give it him at your convenience.

I made Dunne's acquaintance this morning who came with the Rector of the University[1] to talk about the charter. He seemed not a bad fellow but very like a country doctor.

Ever yrs.
J D Acton

667

SIMPSON TO ACTON · 8 MAY 1866

Dear Acton

Here are two letters from Norgate[2]—One you see informs you that you are to receive £5—to gain which you have spent £9 in advertising— However it is something towards the £170 which I flattered you you might recover from further sale of the Review—

Dunne wants to know when he may expect your promised contribution to the Atlantis—will you tell Renouf or Sullivan about it—I am going to the West of England & therefore want to have done with Dunne.

Did the cards that my wife & I left for you in Dover Street ever come to your knowledge, or had you already left for Germany?

Yours ever
R Simpson

May 8. 1866.

[1] Woodlock, rector of the Catholic University of Dublin.
[2] The publisher.

668

SIMPSON TO ACTON · 4 JULY 1866

Care of Capt Hall RN.
July 4. 1866

Dear Acton

I am far from the Museum,[1] & shall not be thereabouts for a month. Can you therefore, in memory of Buck's helps to the H.&F., get copied for him the three pages which he describes in the enclosed note, and have them sent to him, directed

M. Abbé Victor de Buck
College St Michel
Rue des Ursulines
Bruxelles.

do you see his dread of French annexation? Are you also frightened about Worms becoming Gallic?[2] or cannot the needle gun as easily protect Germany as tear it in pieces? Gladstone is now in the Purgatory you always desired to see him in[3]—how long do you give him to remain there?

This place is entirely out of the world, & leads nowhither. The G.W.R.[4] are of opinion that it is on the way to Waterford & Cork, but the public do not share the delusion. The main use of the steamers which profess to go to & fro daily is to bring over an Irish Salmon now & then, which perhaps they pick up from some wandering fisherman in mid seas. On the other side Hall has an excellent yacht & there is capital smooth water sailing in the Haven, & we get the Times every evening.

Ever yours
R Simpson

669

SIMPSON TO ACTON · 7 SEPTEMBER 1866

Friday

Dear Acton

I shall be happy to dine with you on Tuesday. I have heard nothing of Renouf. Would it not be worth while for you to have a note lying for

---

[1] British Museum.
[2] The references are to the prospect of French annexation of the left bank of the Rhine. Worms is near Acton's seat at Herrnsheim.
[3] Out of office.
[4] Great Western Railway.

him at the Privy Council office? He would probably fish out yours from the numbers waiting for him there. Absit omen, but your note was singularly like the text, go to, let us make us a name and a town before we be scattered abroad on the face of the earth. Perhaps the Memorial[1] will be only like Babel in the multitude of languages whose literatures are duly criticized there—

Ever yours
R Simpson

670

SIMPSON TO ACTON · 7 SEPTEMBER 1866

(No 2.)
Friday

Dear Acton

Buck writes to me that he has determined to put K. Alfred among the Saints of the Acta;[2] he believes he cannot get on without Kembles Codex Diplomaticus Aevi Saxonici. Have you those 6 vols? If so will you lend them to him? I will be responsible for conveying them over to him, & will concert measures with him for getting them back for you by next Summer. He does not think of writing a new life, but only giving Spelman's,[3] with notes. I should have thought Asser's with notes more to the purpose, should not you? & if such be your opinion, then it follows to ask you whether you have Petrie's Monumenta Historica Britannica, where, according to Duffus Hardy, the best text of Asser is to be found.

Buck flatters himself that the publication of the life in the Acta aiderait beaucoup pour faire reconnaitre son culte à Rome, and asks me to reflect a little, & the tell him what effect it would have at Oxford.[4] Innocent Buck!

If you happen to see any one who knows about Alfred & his times, or if you have any knowledge of them yourself, will you by Tuesday make a list of books which Buck ought to read mark learn & inwardly digest, before he fires off his double-barrel at Rome and Oxford. Are there any inosculations of European politics with English in those days which

---

[1] This probably refers to the weekly that Wetherell was projecting, to provide an organ for the former contributors to the *Home & Foreign Review*, but without any denominational character. It eventually appeared in March 1867 as the *Chronicle*.

[2] Alfred the Great (848/9–99), king of Wessex 871, was popularly regarded as a saint but never formally canonized.

[3] Sir John Spelman, *Ælfredi Magni...vita...*(Oxonii, 1678).

[4] I.e., influencing high Anglicans towards Rome.

are known to you? If there are write me a letter about them, which
I may give to Buck.

Ever yours
R Simpson

671

ACTON TO SIMPSON · 7 SEPTEMBER 1866

15a Hill S^t
Friday

Dear Simpson,

I will forward the Codex Diplomaticus[1] if it can be found in my
absence, which I doubt. I cannot remember where the Monumenta are.
It is a book our friends ought certainly to possess. It has also the best
text of Bede's Eccles. History.

You ought to do all you can to induce F. de Buck to write a proper life
of Alfred. The reprint of Spelman with notes will look like ignorance or
defiance of so many later labours. On the other hand a new enquiry into
so important a section of our history would glorify the Bollandists in
England.

There are grave questions of criticism to be settled about Asser, for
which indications are to be found in Potthast. But the chief sources are
Petrie's Monumenta, Kemble's Codex, Thorpe's Ancient Laws.

Strodl's Angelsächsische Kirche, Thorpe's translation of Lappenberg,
Wright's Literary History of the Anglo Saxons, Kemble's Anglo Saxons,
and the lives of Alfred by Weiss, a Catholic, and Pauli, a Protestant, are
the chief books written of late on the subject. I think something has
been done lately in the way of a new edition of Alfred's works, and
there is a new book on the Saxon chronicle. Worsaae and Haigh I have
never looked into.

Among the people one knows I think Arnold most likely to know of
the latest performances in Saxon studies; or Stevenson.

I remain
Ever Your's truly
J D Acton[2]

---

[1] J. M. Kemble, *Codex Diplomaticus Aevi Saxonici*, 6 vols. (London, 1839–48).
[2] There follows a line written by an unknown hand: 'Thorpe's ancient laws superseded by an edition by Phillipps of Munich.'

SIMPSON TO ACTON · 12 SEPTEMBER 1866

Wednesday

Dear Acton

I left you last night without ascertaining whether you can lend DeBuck Kemble's Codex. As for Petrie's Monumenta, Stevenson lends me a copy for him. If the former book can be found in your absence will you tell me, as in case of its not being forthcoming I must try to get it elsewhere. If it is to be found let it be sent to me by next Monday, as I may start on Tuesday.

Ever yours
R Simpson

673

ACTON TO SIMPSON · 12 SEPTEMBER 1866

Wednesday

Dear Simpson,

If the Codex Dip. can be found it will reach you before Monday. Pray carry my most cordial respects to St Michel.[1]

I have had a long talk with Stevenson, and we instituted a pleasing conspiracy. He spoke of his Catholicism, but retains the clerical garb,[2] and I direct to him accordingly. I suspect he is very low and lonely, and wants encouragement especially from Catholic friends.

If you and Lambert will fairly put your heads together, you will strike invaluable light for the coming labours of Reform.[3]

Don't neglect Shakespeare, I beseech you. I don't talk to you of my own workings out of respect for so great a promise.

Ever Your's most truly
J D Acton

Bedford Hotel, Brighton—Sept. 18
Hotel Westminster, Rue de la Paix. 25
Munich   October 10
Then, Hotel Serny, Rome.

---

[1] De Buck, at the Collège St. Michel in Brussels.
[2] Of an Anglican minister. Hence he would be addressed as 'Rev.'.
[3] Lambert had helped to draft the Liberal reform bill of 1866.

SIMPSON TO ACTON · 14 SEPTEMBER 1866

Friday

Dear Acton

Renouf turned up on Wednesday. He had been in London all Tuesday, but had not been to the Office[1] for his letters. He stayed with me till yesterday morning & then went to Coventry. He is now at the Oratory Edgbaston. He is full of two discoveries, one in Egyptian Astronomy, which demolishes much labour of Biot,[2] & another, more important, which enables him to connect the old Egyptian with the Indo European tongues, & to trace whole classes of roots & the rules of their transformation. also he has in his portfolio his pamphlet against Ward,[3] which he is going to publish at Longmans, having made it bitter after the style of Newman's Apologia. So you see he has not been idle in his Vacation—

Stevenson comes to dine with us & Wetherell at 2 on Sunday—Have you time to come & lunch?—There are trains from Victoria at 1.5, 1.12, & 1.20—If you come I will go & look after Lambert so that you may discourse about Reform, me listening.

Stevenson protests he shall not be able to give us any help in the *Truth-teller*,[4] as Renouf wants it Christened—He has too much on his hands already. Is this Anglo-Saxon for the scruples of a new convert at being invited to join old Home & Foreigners?

Ever yours most truly
R Simpson

Did you not tell me that you saw Davis[5] in prosperity lately? This morning my brother had a letter from him, to say that his wife had just been confined, & that he was at his wits ends to procure necessaries. He dates from 34 Carnaby St St James'. W. I tell you this as you may perhaps have some employment you could give him. I never saw the man in my life, I only know him from my brother's description—

---

[1] The Education Office. Renouf was an inspector of schools.
[2] Jean Baptiste Biot, *Recherches sur plusieurs points de l'astronomie égyptienne* (Paris, 1823).
[3] This does not appear to have been published.
[4] Wetherell's projected weekly (the *Chronicle*).
[5] A former copyist for Acton.

ACTON TO SIMPSON · 15 SEPTEMBER 1866

Bedford Hotel
Brighton
Saturday night

Dear Simpson

I did not sufficiently explain that I was leaving town, so that I have the disappointment of not being able to join your pleasant party tomorrow.

Renouf told me of his astronomical discovery which of course I could not understand—The other, which I know nothing of, seems truly important. No doubt Stevenson has scruples, as you guess, or he would not speak of Bergenroth as you say. The latter is a perfectly true man, with few beliefs, and no prejudices that I can discover—a state of mind eminently painful to the devout. Pray don't frighten Stevenson. He has principle, and will reveal all the truths he finds in history: only he will find none that exercise the mind much. I am intriguing very secretly to get him sent to Rome in the winter. He will work afterwards occasionally, when books are sent him for review, and the remuneration is made manifest to him.

(Private & confidential)

Reeve has accepted for January an Irish article by Dease.[1] Dease ought to send it to Wetherell in proof, not more for suggestions, than in order that W. may write a premature article on it in the Incendiary[2]— as I interpret Renouf's nomenclature.

J. M. Capes ought to contribute secular articles, and Sir John Lubbock,[3] pace Sullivan, a young scientific man of great attainments. Goldwin Smith distils exquisite wisdom in the Beehive,[4] as I see in today's Daily News.

I have marked, in several volumes of the Calendars of James I, very many papers I want copied—in most cases my marks indicate the part of the paper I care for; in others, the whole is wanted. If Davis is able to do this for me, and you don't mind setting him to work, and arranging terms—w^h I can't do being absent, I will cause the vols. to be sent from

---

[1] 'Tenant Compensation in Ireland', *Edinburgh Review*, cxxv (January 1867), 187–218. Attributed erroneously to 'James A. Dease' in *Wellesley Index*, I, 516.

[2] Wetherell's projected weekly.

[3] Sir John Lubbock (1834–1915), 4th baronet 1865, banker, naturalist and anthropologist, M.P. 1870–1900, created Lord Avebury 1900.

[4] Goldwin Smith published a letter in the *Beehive* (a radical periodical), 8 September 1866, on the Governor Eyre controversy.

Aldenham when you return. If you approve and think well to give him a couple of sovereigns beforehand, pray tell me, and I will restore the loan.

Ever Yours
J D Acton

676

SIMPSON TO ACTON · 21 SEPTEMBER 1866

Hotel de Flandre
Brussels, Sept. 21: 1866.

Dear Acton

Wetherell had a highly successful meeting with Stevenson last Sunday; Stevenson not only promised to write, but evidently took considerable interest in the work, & was beating his brains to think of other writers whom he might suggest. Among them was young Brewer,[1] whom he recommended for his intimate knowledge of art.

I find Buck rather in the dumps. He half fears, half hopes that the government will deprive the Bollandists of the 6000ffs. a year which they get now, and he has almost determined to announce the cessation of Bollandism, if such an opportunity is given him. His reason is not the money, (or rather the want of it) but the deficiency in the succession of men. His staff is incompetent; all three together do as much in 15 days as he does in one. And then he appears to be a slave to the printers. He is only going to give 6 or 8 weeks to the life of Alfred; when I suggested 12 or 16, and asked why not, he said it would throw so many workmen out of employment; that of the 600 printers of Brussels already 200 were without work, & that he would not add to the misery—All that I could say was that after he had laboured all his life, & had acquired the historical instinct so perfectly, Bollandism would easily last his time; that he was only 50, & might look for 10 years more, in which time he might work up 3 more volumes, & leave to Providence the succession. I think he has a sort of yearning for encouragement & if you would write him a letter from Rome you might do him good.

When you get to Rome could you inquire whether any records of Alfred's relations with the Popes are remaining there. He was twice at Rome, & he probably had some communication by letter with the people there. If you could furnish DeBuck with any original information it would add a glory to his life of Alfred which does not seem likely to accrue to it from the hasty half despairing way in which he is going to set about it.

[1] Henry William Brewer (1836–1903), archaeologist, artist and architect, a convert.

I came over on Tuesday, & had no time before starting to make inquiries about Davis. I will however write to my brother & tell him to go & see him, and if necessary make some advance for copying to be done as soon as I can set him to work for you.

You see that the reports of the Pope's going to Malta[1] get more frequent. Renouf guessed that the *Lord*[2] got the original report from his sister-in-law who is married to a doctor at Trêves, with whom Cardinal Reisach stayed when he was there.

When you get to Munich will you buy for me, & send to Buck Phillipps' edition of the Anglo Saxon laws, which Stevenson tells me has superseded Thorpe's,[3] and is probably cheaper. Your six volumes of the codex reached me on Monday; I found them on returning from London after a happily unsuccessful search for a copy—The two first volumes are worth about 3£. The 4 others about 7 or 8 shillings.

I suppose Wetherell knows about the Irish article in the Edinburgh[4] —Anyhow I will mention it to him when I write

I have called upon Gachard,[5] but I said nothing to him about the Incendiary;[6] I did however mention it to a sub in the Archives, one Alexander Pinchart,[7] whose hobby is the history of art which I suppose he pinches out of the Mss in his office. After talking to him I thought of Weale, who was not in your list, was he? I should try to see him while I am here. Remi de Buck[8] has had transcribed for you the Ms. life of Cardinal Fisher which he says you wot of. He is to give it me to carry over to England for you.

I hope you have had a happy passage over the channel. The sea on Tuesday night was playing a heavy game at pitch & toss, but we had gained so much experience in our yatching that we laughed at its attempts to upset us, mechanically or chemically.

Who is to get at Sir John Lubbock? I knew his father & grandfather, but I never saw him. I could more easily get at Joseph Prestwich,[9] whose sister I know very well; he would be an admirable help, being a bigger authority on Geology than Sullivan himself.

Ever yours
R Simpson

[1] For refuge.
[2] Not identifiable.
[3] Cf. Letter 671, n. 2.
[4] 'Tenant Compensation in Ireland.'
[5] Louis-Prosper Gachard (1800–85), director of the Belgian archives for 55 years.
[6] The projected weekly.
[7] Alexandre Joseph Pinchart (1823–84), historian, attached to the royal archives in Brussels from 1847.
[8] A relative of Fr de Buck.
[9] Sir Joseph Prestwich (1812–96), merchant and geologist, professor of geology at Oxford 1874–88, knighted 1896.

SIMPSON TO ACTON · 22 SEPTEMBER 1866

Hotel de Fland^{re}
Brussels. Sept. 22

Dear Acton

When I saw Buck again yesterday after writing to you he seemed to have got over his melancholy fit, & he told me by no means to say anything to any body, not even to you, of what he had told me about the cessation of Bollandism. So when you write, if you do so, make no allusion whatever to the idea—I did not tell him that I had already told you, because I knew that it only wanted a line written to you to make it as though it had never been said.

He mocked at the idea of your being able to find anything about Alfred in the Vatican, & went so far as to say that he thought the Burgundian library here more rich in historical papers (as distinguished from precious Mss) than the Vatican, which he thought had nothing to reveal after the labours of Assemanni[1] &c—

Ever yours
R Simpson

678

ACTON TO SIMPSON · 22 SEPTEMBER 1866

Hotel Westminster
Sept 22

My dear Simpson,

We gave the sea a day or two to calm itself, and crossed very successfully on Thursday. I have had two mornings at the Library,[2] and a good haul at the booksellers. We stay, I suppose, till Thursday next.

Are you sure that DeBuck is making the most of his talent by burying it in the Acta SS.?[3] The price, the bulk, the incompleteness, the worthlessness of parts, make it a book that only sturdy students seriously use. The past cannot be redeemed, and he cannot get rid of his pedigree. Much of his labour must be spent on matters not largely interesting, and secondary Saints.

Do you not think that if he was emancipated from that duty he would

---

[1] A Syrian Maronite family of orientalists, active in the Vatican library in the eighteenth century.
[2] Bibliothèque Nationale.
[3] *Acta Sanctorum.*

become a much greater and more available power in church literature, and would add more valuable matter to things known? I should think his energies and spirits would fly up like a cork if he got that old man off his shoulders. At any rate I write not to him till Rome, as you suggest, and perhaps you will think it useless.

Pray thank meanwhile in my name the other DeBuck (I knew not it was he) for his ready kindness in letting me have the copy of Fisher's MS. life. I asked them for it on their own statement of its merits.

Pinchart is an excellent man, more efficient and obliging, I have always heard than Gachard. It would be worth while to bring him definitely to book. Many parts of history he could criticize, and he would review his countrymen more freely in another country than if he was known.

There is also one Piot,[1] in the archives, I think, a friend of De Buck, and knower of MSS. who might help as well.

I don't know where I got the idea that Weale is averse to light, which made me forget to suggest his name.

Phillips published in 1827 a book on the Anglo Saxon legislation.[2] There is a recent edition of their laws published in Germany by somebody else, which I imagine Stevenson means, and I will seek it, as well as anything about Alfred in Rome—Unfortunately the notices of early MSS. are in books not to be found in Rome.

If you can get Prestwich, he is decidedly a most desirable man, and would help towards Lubbock.

I remain
Ever Your's most truly
J D Acton

I open my letter on Sunday morning, to say that I have received your's;[3] and it's all right.

679

SIMPSON TO ACTON · 26 OCTOBER 1866

4 Victoria Road
Clapham. Oct 26. 1866

Dear Acton

Mrs Renouf has visited the family Davis, & reports that they are in the last, or prae-Workhouse stage. Therefore I told her that I had your

---

[1] Guillaume Joseph Charles Piot (1812–99), archivist and historian, *archiviste général* of Belgium 1886.
[2] Georg Phillips, *Versuch einer Darstellung der Geschichte des Angelsächsischen Rechts* (Göttingen, 1825). Acton may have confused this with *Englische Reichs- und Rechtsgeschichte seit der Ankunft der Normannen im Jahre 1066*, 2 vols. (Berlin, 1827).
[3] Letter 677.

permission to set him to work at copying for you, when you have furnished me with the marked Indexes from Aldenham. Will you then direct that these be sent to me? As to the payment, I will get Stevenson to fix the tariff for you. He will do it fairly, & with more knowledge of the subject than I. But I should like to know what you do actually pay to your English copyists, so that I may not go beyond the mark. Also to what amount in the aggregate I am to employ him. I will advance whatever money is needful, & let you know when it gets up to a round sum.

I am working at the life of Campion.[1] There exists, I suppose in the Gesú, a letter of his to Acquaviva dated July 9, 1581, unpublished, but referred to twice by Bartoli who quotes scraps of it. You would do me a great service if you could get me a copy of it. There are also letters of Parsons to the same of about the same date, & so on till nearly the end of the year, also unpublished, on account, I suppose, of the evidence of his treasonable tampering with the English Catholics & with Mendoza which they contain. You would be amused if you could get to read them, & see whether any part of them ought to be copied.

I was lucky in my Belgian expedition. Besides Block & Reichensperger I have secured[2] Pinchart, Thonissen, Schollaert and Weale, besides the Bollandists, and now Buck has got for us a young advocate called Woeste, whom he most strenuously recommends. I had a long talk with De Neve,[3] the Rector of the American College at Louvain, who was a subscriber to the H.&F. & will do all that in him lies to recommend the Memorial.[4]

Lambert quite enters into your plan of writing joint articles on reform with me; but he quarrels atrociously with the name. He is now in Ireland, & promises a rich recital of the doings of a Tipperary election.

Whom have you for Russia? Buck could suggest none but Augustin Galitzin & Father Gagarin,[5] whom he promised to make write for us. he said that Count Orloff told him that the former knew more about Russia than any of the other ordinary writers in the Western Press—

---

[1] Published in 1867. Of the characters mentioned here, Claudio Aquaviva (1543–1615) was general of the Jesuits from 1581; Robert Parsons (1546–1610) entered the Society of Jesus 1575 and was Campion's fellow-missionary; Bernardino de Mendoza (1540/1–1604) was Spanish ambassador to England 1578–84, later to France.

[2] As contributors to Wetherell's new weekly. The list includes Jean Joseph Thonissen (1816–91), François Schollaert (1816–79) and Charles Woeste (1837–1922), Belgian Catholic lawyers and politicians.

[3] John De Neve (1821–98), born in Belgium, ordained priest 1847, served in the United States 1856–9, rector of the American College at Louvain 1859–71, 1878–91.

[4] The tentative name of the new weekly.

[5] Johann Xaver Gagarin (1814–82), Russian nobleman, converted 1842 and entered the Society of Jesus, in Paris since 1855.

who must then be very ignorant—Do you know any thing of Borette, the Minister of Justice in the present Dutch ministry? He is the only Catholic in the Cabinet, & I know intimately an intimate friend of his brother, Mgr Borette,[1] who (i.e. my friend) promises to use whatever influence she may possess with the said brother—but I dont like to move till I know that it might be useful. I forget what Dutchmen you have on your list.

I am in a controversy with Buck. I find that the first three couples of Jesuits sent into England consisted each of a dove & a serpent—a saint & a conspirator—the conspirator conspiring, & the saint always protesting that their arms were only preaching & prayer, & they never meddled in matters of state. I connected this with the polarity which seemed a natural force of the order, & which projected the doves into the partes infidelium, while it retained the serpents at the European courts. & I suggested that the same polarity was now exhibited in the Acta Sanctorum at Brussels & the Civiltá[2] at Rome. He wrote at first that it was a *bétise*, but then he said it was only a *bétise* if I erected it into a system, & gave me extracts which showed that in a mission the gifts of a superior were distinct from those of the active preachers &c &c—Do give me some references to shed a little light on this part of my subject—or have you any lights to impart?

Ever yours most truly
R Simpson

680

ACTON TO SIMPSON · 1 NOVEMBER 1866

Bologna 1 November

My dear Simpson,

I imagine that there would be fairly work to the amount of 15 or 20£ in my marked calendars. They shall be sent to you as soon as may be, and you may think it right to let the poor man[3] have a few pounds to start with. My copy of Panzani's Report[4] was made by a man ignorant of Italian almost faultlessly, at, I think, a shilling a page of 400 words.

---

[1] Eduard Joseph Hubert Borret (1816–67), Dutch advocate, member of parliament 1849, councillor of state 1853, minister of justice 1866. His brother was Theodoor Joseph Hubert Borret (1812–90), ordained priest and D.D. 1836, professor of scripture at Warmond seminary 1837, pastor at Vogelenzang 1854–88, dean of Noordwijk and canon of Haarlem 1858–70.

[2] The *Civiltà Cattolica*, which was more propagandistic than scholarly.

[3] Davis.

[4] Gregorio Panzani (d. 1662) was sent to England in 1634 to report on the state of the English Catholics. His report was acquired by the British Museum in 1854.

My Venetian copyist put 300 words in a page for half a franc. The quantities are not very large, and I will be buried by Stevenson's award.

I will fish discreetly and anonymously for the letters at the Gesú. You do not reckon on my being persona grata there, and part of their papers is in concealment, but there are generally ways and means at Rome.

I have no Jesuitica of the sort you seek. But I have found in all those things for which I have been curious, especially in their teaching and management of literature, that their policy has been definitely laid down by themselves. They were very indiscreet because they did not expect their archives to be pillaged. Have you examined the modern 7 vol. Oct° edition of their Institutes, the literae annuae, the Annales des Soi-disants Jésuites, their own Réponse aux assertions (a perfect Repertory of materials most honestly put together) and Arnauld's voluminous work on their morals and policy, where there is much about their missions? De Buck's explanation is surely more a confirmation than a denial of the truth of your theory.

Your Belgian expedition is truly a great success. Thonissen (not what is called an Ultramontane) ought to know modern Belgium better than almost anybody. I hope these men will work at once and send in articles for the start.

Buddeus promises to write on Russia. He has written the best books extant on the subject, but he is a political man, and the religious part may be usefully supplied by that excellent Gagarine. A Galitzine struck me years ago, as mediocre extremely. Pray tell Wetherell that Buddeus accepts, as I am not writing to him till I have more to say.

Albertingk Thym[1] was my Dutchman; but I don't feel sure of his active help, as he wrote me a die-away letter in the H&F. days. Do all you can to obtain counsel of Borette.

I hope you know of a better name than the Memorial—Aletherama?

We took our ease in Tyrol, and I spent three days at Venice joining my people here only yesterday. We remain till the 12th and go straight on to Rome.

Parsons would have been a better hero for you than Campion.

> I remain
> Ever Your's very truly
> J D Acton

De Strada. Essai d'un ultimum organon. 2 Vols. 1865

---

[1] Jozef Albert Alberdingk Thijm (1820–89), Dutch Catholic writer.

680A

SIMPSON TO ACTON · 11 NOVEMBER 1866

Dear Acton

Your charming Stevenson plot[1] has for the present wrecked against a rock that I think you may easily clear away. It appears that you have frightened Lord R[2] with the notion that more money is required than he has any chance of getting. Lately he had to apply for a little sum, and the Exchequer people told him that as Gladstone had economized by cutting down the grant by £1000 they could not possibly increase it without the gravest reasons. He felt sure that he could not get a grant of £1500, & therefore put off all application, & even all reply to your letter till you should come back, & he could talk the matter over with you. I asked my informant (who was not Stevenson—*he* knows nothing of this, but thinks that the project has been frustrated simply by the childish humour of Lord R. who has another butterfly in chase) whether he understood from your letter that it would take £1500 to begin at Rome, or whether that sum was not meant for the total cost of transcripts to be made in the course of three years or more—He said that Lord R. understood that that sum, plus £300 for Stevenson or whoever was to be the Rawdon Browne[3] or Bergenroth of the Vatican, was to be asked for the first year. That Lord R was as anxious as ever to get the Vatican papers—that even now he considers himself the first historiographer in Europe, & that the opening of the Vatican would be the cocks' feather in his cap. But with all his desire he had not face to ask for a grant of nearly £2000. w^h he knew would be refused.

I said I was quite sure that he had mistaken the drift of your letter— that if Lord R. would apportion to Rome the same sum that he apportioned to Venice or to Simancas I felt certain he might begin & that, once begun, he need be in no fear from the thing being starved for want of funds.—(Venice costs 400, Simancas 500 a year) I said also that it was letting the opportunity slip by not to begin operations while you were in Rome to introduce whoever was sent to the authorities; & I asked my man (who is one that forbids me to mention his name, but is, as you may see, one quite familiar with all this business, & who sees Lord R's letters on the matter) whether, if you were to write again to

---

[1] To secure government funds to employ Stevenson to copy documents in the secret Vatican archives.

[2] Romilly.

[3] Rawdon Lubbock Browne (1803–83), settled in Venice 1833, employed since 1862 to calendar the Venetian archives for the *State Papers, Foreign*.

Lord R, from Rome, telling him that you had made enquiries, & that such and such facilities were now open, that it would cost so much for the FIRST YEAR (the only place where the shoe pinches) & would take so many years to finish—whether Lord R would begin to move again on receipt of such a letter? He thought he might. Then I said—Suppose Acton were to get Gladstone to write about it? He answered, Romilly would at once take his letter to the Museum, & get the grant. For the only thing that keeps the government back is the fear of the great economist. Now it seems to me that as a literary man Gladstone is positively bound to assist this plot to this extent. Can you not persuade him? Or if not can you not communicate in some way with Romilly through Odo Russell? My informant thought that he would have great influence on Lord R., but Gladstone, whom I named immediately afterwards, quite eclipsed Russell, who, du reste, is a relation of Lord R.

All agree that Lord R is a great baby, vain as a peacock, & can only be got into work by judicious flattery. Withal obstinate as a mule, & so only to be touched with kid gloves on. Of course I tell you this that you may use the information to the best advantage of the cause; but you must not let out anything that could lead to the identification of my anonymous informant, who absurdly enough forbids me to mention his name to you, though I assure him that you are any number of times more diplomatic & prudent & secret than I am.

I have had your letter about Davis for some days, but have not received the Calendars from Aldenham. Stevenson awards 1/ for a folio of 430 words—I tried to cheapen him but he would not be cheapened. I have bought ruled white paper, foolscap size as near as I could find to the paper you usually write on—So I hope the copies will be satisfactory. Mrs. Renouf tells me she saw Davis copying at the British Museum the other day, & she supposes he has found a little work. She has told him you mean to employ him.

The letter of Campion which I asked you to get a copy of for me is signed, not Ed. Campion, but *Alexander Stribevius*—This might mislead a searcher, so it is as well to let it be known.

I am in some hopes of getting DeBuck to come over to England for a month next July—do you still intend to be back in England by that time?

Ever yours most sincerely
R Simpson

4 Victoria Road
Clapham Common S.
Nov. 11. 1866.

ACTON TO SIMPSON · 22 NOVEMBER 1866*

Hotel Serny Nov. 22

Dear Simpson,

I found your letter of the 11th on arriving here[1] this evening. It brings me more comfort than grief, for I have been beset with the fear of having gone too far without being quite sure how matters now stand. For Rome changes, and the disposition of Theiner[2] is like the surface of water.

Of course, Romilly[3] is a goose; and I spoke of 1200 or 1500£ as the whole copy value of the papers fit to take from the Vatican. I spoke of 400 or 500£ to be spent at once, and 300£ a year for two or three years. All these estimates however are very vague, and I am not sorry to have the opportunity of testing them while I feel my way as to the scheme itself. If I find Theiner and Antonelli amenable, I will talk to Gladstone. It is conceivable that he may dislike to press for expenditure in opposition which he cut down in office. But the fact will remain, that Lord R. need not ask for more than 500£ for 1867.

The Venice money, entre nous, is not going to be spent profitably, and it may be well if you will submit this part of my letter in strict confidence to Hardy or Stevenson. A sum, not very large, is awarded to Rawdon Brown for various copies. He will give them some of great value, for which, I believe, a special grant has been made, as photographs are involved in the matter. He proposes to send other copies, of papers not relating to England in any way, and even some translations, without copies, dotted with parentheses and notes of his own. I told him I thought that neither the one nor the other came within the definition of the documents for which copymoney is awarded. He did not much like my remonstrance, and I was afraid he would think I was trying to get these documents for myself. So I desisted.

But I should like to know what the Record Office thinks of the matter, and whether, while so much English history remains to be cleared up with documents, they will feel justified in paying for copies of reports on the Siege of Rome, and on the court of Borgia, and for translations, without copies of the text, of other papers more nearly concerning England. If they confirm my doubts, I pray them to say noth-

---

* Watkin and Butterfield, pp. 99–100.
[1] In Rome.
[2] The archivist, from whom Acton was attempting to buy copies of documents in the secret Vatican archives.
[3] Master of the Rolls.

ing, and I will convince our Venetian friend of his error, and induce him to look out for better things. I will also comfort him by offering to buy these things myself, so far as they do not suit the Record Office. And I will undertake, if I get hold of them, to submit them to Stevenson, or Hardy, or Brewer, that they may keep such of the papers as seem to have come into my hands by a too rigorous interpretation of their canons. Nobody will suspect Rawdon Brown of wishing to earn his pay unfairly, but he has worshipped his collections so long that he has lost the sense of discrimination. On the other hand his Calendars are compiled with infinite pains. If you think there is the least danger of my being misunderstood or awakening hard suspicions, pray exercise all possible discretion.

Ever Your's most sincerely
J D Acton

682

SIMPSON TO ACTON · 29 NOVEMBER 1866

4 Victoria Road, Clapham S.
Nov. 29. 1866

Dear Acton

I received your letter today, & went to the Record Office, where I fished out this history: early in the year Dr Russell[1] told Hardy that he thought he could get him into the Vatican; Hardy & Romilly empowered him to act in the matter, he obtained Cullen, Manning, & Talbot's support, Theiner was sounded, & Romilly was informed that here nothing could be done without money; Romilly who had just failed in getting some small grant feared to ask for this, & gave up the idea; this was in July. Then your letter[2] came upon him as a new revelation, he bent his thoughts that way again, but was again frightened by your estimate.

There are two points that Stevenson & I agreed were important, one with reference to Romilly, the other to Gladstone.

1. The owner of the Paston letters[3] the other day offered them to R. He said, he had no money to buy such things, that the British museum was the proper depository for documents of this kind, & that *there* there was fund for purchasing such things. This applies to Theiner's transcripts. The British museum is the place for them, the Trustees either have funds to buy them, or might obtain the money more easily than R. To which I may add that Lord Granville & Gladstone are infinitely

---

[1] Of Maynooth.
[2] See Acton to Romilly, 2 October 1866, in *Lord Acton: The Decisive Decade*, pp. 68–70.   [3] A famous 15th-century correspondence.

stronger men than Romilly, & you could more easily satisfy them of the importance of the papers than you could satisfy Romilly—Hardy agreed that if the millstone of the transcripts were taken from Romilly's neck he could not make much difficulty about going to Government for the annual grant for the maker of the Calendar.

2. As to Gladstone. He did not economise the £1000. The case was that the Scots put the screw on, & got him to transfer one of the three thousands from the M.R.[1] to a Scots commission for the publication of Scotch chronicles. The money is applied to the same purpose, but only differently administered.

But even granted that it is an economy, it only applies to the series of Chronicles, which is a different affair from the series of Calendars. There may be many opinions about the former, but no one doubts about the exceeding utility of the latter. Gachard said to me that it was the greatest historical work ever undertaken by any government. Now whatever interest is felt in our domestic Calendars, all agree that the Venice & Simancas Calendars are of much greater importance still (I speak with tongue of Hardy); and everybody knows that the papers in the Vatican are of infinitely more importance than those of the Signory or the Spanish archives. The Vatican calendar would be the crown of Romilly's success &c &c Wherefore, even if Gladstone had economized in the Chronicles, (which he has not done) he might still without any inconsistency extravagate in the Calendars, which stand on so completely different a footing

I mentioned to Hardy with due reserve what you said about Browne; he was at first disposed to fling about, but soon became quiet. Browne was too conscientious a man to &c &c; I pointed out that it was not a question of conscience but of judgment; B. knew too much about his commission which was clear, & the papers he had sent had all passed under Hardy's inspection; Has he never sent transcripts of irrelevant papers? I asked—Never he said—He has had too good a lesson; & the lesson turned out to be that he had calendared a certain number of documents which had not the least reference to English history, beyond mentioning the name of some Englishman. So I pointed out that it was not impossible B. might do the same thing in his transcripts. "Well if he does I shall say, My dear Browne, you dont call this a document of English history do you, & shall tell him to take it back" then followed a declaration of his conscience, & of his religious principles (a kind of mixture of Swedenborg & Spinoza)—So I did not mention your proposal to him; but I did so to Stevenson who fully appreciated the delicacy & generosity of it & applauded it highly, because he said if Browne sends any such papers to the Office they must be returned to his hands, &

[1] Master of the Rolls.

225

then will come a very disagreeable discussion about the cost of them. Hardy is a good sort of fellow but he has a very thick indian rubber habit of routine over him, & he tells me in strict confidence things that any one may read in parliamentary papers.

Hardy still sticks to his opinion of the transcendent importance of Gladstone's recommending Romilly to ask for the Grant.

No calendar from Aldenham; Davis asking Mrs Renouf where his work is; I throwing away a little money to stay his cries.

And so I take my leave—

Ever yours most truly
R Simpson

683

ACTON TO SIMPSON · 6 DECEMBER 1866*

Hotel Serny, Rome
December 6 1866

My dear Simpson,

Your letter of the 29th has only just come. Many thanks for your intervention about Rawdon Brown. I will try to keep him out of the impending scrape, and at the same time to secure his miscellaneous transcripts. Perhaps even if I fail, and the unbidden papers are sent to London, our friends will yet let me try to save Brown from sore disappointment, and to preserve the documents for literary uses. Brown has a particular friendship for Hardy and reliance on him.

Touching the Vatican let me begin with a retrospect. Early last year Theiner agreed to let me have, under conditions which were settled between us, some of the most important English papers from the Archives. Those on the Spanish match[1] I brought home at once. Those of the reign of James II were to be forwarded to me, and some others were to be got ready in transcript. The thing got wind. Theiner showed the James papers to Manning, who spoke of it, and it occurred to persons here that I was not of all people the one chosen to possess the secret revelations of the Vatican. Theiner had shown Manning grievous things against Father Petre[2] and his bad advice, consulting him whether they would give scandal. The old feud against Theiner was awakened, and it was said that he had sold me not only copies but originals out of the Archives, and that we were conspiring to damage the Jesuits.

---

* Watkin and Butterfield, pp. 100–1. They read 'Correo' as 'Conne'.
[1] The proposed marriage of Charles I to a Spanish infanta.
[2] Sir Edward Petre (1631–99), entered Society of Jesus 1652, succeeded to baronetcy 1679, adviser to James II, privy councillor 1687–8.

226

Theiner was alarmed, and wrote me word that he could not fulfil his promise.

I bethought me that the same objection would not lie against the Record office, and that if the negotiation was taken up by them, it would be possible to exhaust the English materials here, which would be much beyond my strength.

I took Gladstone to the archives, soon after your former letter came, and got him fully committed to approve the necessary expenditure. Thereupon, however, in a private interview with Theiner, I succeeded in renewing an old negotiation, and finding him open to persuasion, seized my opportunity, and took possession of the documents which interested me most. I must bore you with more conditions of secrecy, as Theiner is anxious that nothing should be known just now of the transaction. Between you and me and Stevenson, I have now on my table; 1° all the Pole[1] papers remaining in the archives; 2° the whole correspondence of Panzani and Correo; 3° the correspondence between England and Rome under James II. But I have urged Theiner to make a clean breast of it, and have asked for the acts of the Divorce suit, and everything else down to the XVIII cent. He is entertaining my proposal, and overhauling his archives. It is impossible that I should really exhaust this source of information on English history, or that I should have the means of knowing how nearly I have exhausted it. But if I go on as successfully as I have begun, there will be no occasion for Lord Romilly to do anything at the Vatican. I don't waste a word with you in showing that I should have been a fool after your letter, having no authority from Lord Romilly, if I had failed to use at once the advantage I had over Theiner, and given up a present certainty for a remote contingency. You may imagine Gladstone's joy at this victory of free trade over state subventions!

Ever Y[rs] truly
J D Acton

684

SIMPSON TO ACTON · 13 DECEMBER 1866

4 Victoria Road Clapham
Dec. 13. 1866.

Dear Acton;

Your letter of the 6th reached me on the 11th Yesterday I went up & told Stevenson the results; he congratulates you most warmly on your

---

[1] Reginald Pole (1500–58), humanist and Catholic reformer of royal descent, cardinal 1536, archbishop of Canterbury 1555.

success, & is of the same mind as Gladstone about the superiority of private effort over official routine, & free trade over government expenditure. I would not speak to Hardy, as I could not see by your letter whether you wished or not to interfere farther on behalf of the Record office. When you say "It is impossible that I should really exhaust this source of information on English history or that I should have the means of knowing how nearly I have exhausted it" you seem to give a reason for employing a man to Calendar—if such a man can gain admission. But when in the next sentence you say "If I go on as successfully as I have begun, there will be no occasion for Ld Romilly to do any thing at the Vatican", you leave it quite doubtful whether you would like to farther his man in getting admission there. Moreover I did not know how to tell Hardy that there was no longer any question of the purchase of transcripts—for they were sold—without as good as telling him that you had bought them—So I did not go near him. Stevenson however says this—If you see cause that a man should be sent to Calendar; & if you will get Gladstone to write a note of Ld Romilly, saying that he considers the expenditure should be made; then he has no doubt that Lord R will at once apply for the grant.

I sounded Jones at the British Museum about buying the transcripts. He was all alive to their value; & if there should be a mass beyond your strength, if you would give a general description of them & estimate of cost, of copying, he would at once apply to the Trustees to apply to the Treasury to apply to Parliament for a grant.

However, the affair rests very well as it is; unless you would like still to play Lord R. on your line, to the end that if Manning again frightens Theiner you may still have the same second navigation, without the trouble of knitting together the unraveled ends of the broken line— So direct me what to do, lest I unawares commit you farther than you like.

Do you remember, years ago, taking me into the Italian publishers shop opposite Stewarts, & showing me in some new book a curious sentence about the deliberations in the Council of Trent on the subject of Elizabeth & England? I have lost the reference, & have no idea of the name of the book, or of the substance of the extract, beyond what I have told you.

I have finished Campion,[1] & I am now busy in furbishing up text & notes. I hope to have it printed by February or March. The letter of Campion which I asked you about is referred to in Sacchini, Hist. S.J. lib 1: num 219. perhaps he tells where the original is kept. Do not bother about getting it for me, I am contented with what I have: only I think it possible from Bombinus passing it alto silentio, & Sacchini only giving

---

[1] The biography of Edmund Campion.

so short an extract, that the rest of it was not publishable—whether through defect of style (for Campion's friends were ashamed of his unequal Latinity, so splendid on occasion, so careless often) or through perilousness of matter I know not—only the latter is most unlikely, as he began his letter with complaints of the danger of conveyance & of so many of his having miscarried.

I have got rid of another plentiful source of idleness, for I expect back from the binders today my third & last volume of Shakespeares 154 Sonnets, all set to music with original tunes since 62. It is a monument of perseverance if of nothing else; but I hope that there are among them some songs that might live, if they ever attained the luck to be born. When I have got rid of Campion I hope to turn my hand to Shakespeare, which will be a subject of infinitely greater interest.

Ever yours faithfully
R Simpson

P.S. Stevenson suggests that Gladstone might be led to recommend a man from the Record office at Paris, to calendar the Anglo-French Papers, if the Vatican is sufficiently filled—I should have made you see that I as well as Stevenson congratulate you most sincerely for your success & quite agree with Gladstone about the superiority of (some) individual exertion over that of governments—

685

ACTON TO SIMPSON · 17 DECEMBER 1866

Rome Dec. 17.

My dear Simpson,

There is so much uncertainty in all things here, and my footing is still so precarious, that I am afraid of awakening new suspicions and difficulties by any formal proposal. I think the best plan, will be that I should go on quietly, making the most of my advantages as long as I can. I shall then know the ground well enough to judge whether anything else ought to be attempted, and I shall have a more exact notion of what there is in the Vatican. I find that only the most cautious management answers. The French government lately was left for months without any reply to an application for a copy of the acts of the canonization of S. Lewis. The MS. of Salimbene,[1] a rival Matthew Paris, is in the Vatican. A copy was sent to Parma ten years ago, where it was printed.

---

[1] Salimbene degli Adami (1221–88), Franciscan chronicler.

229

When I applied for the original, it had disappeared. Ways and means were however found to get at it, and I find that nearly half was omitted by order when the copy was taken. You may hear any day of my having been solemnly snubbed, and it would not be wise at this moment to risk anything upon my favour.

I hope therefore that Stevenson will not think it wrong that I should recommend delay in taking such steps as I proposed. I do not feel able to adopt the plan he mentioned to you, of having somebody sent to calendar here, when the best part of all that we know of is already in my hands. No doubt there is a great deal more, but I don't yet know what. I am busy now getting papers of a period when I did not expect to find any, after 1689. I have only dabbled yet in the sixteenth century.

I think it would be well to restrict your confidence to Stevenson in these matters. I don't know Hardy personally, and cannot tell how I stand in his eyes.

I am positively assured that the Gesù archives have been sent out of Italy. A discreet friend of mine will ascertain more about them as soon as can be. Parsons's correspondence would indeed be precious.

What the book at Molini's can be I cannot imagine. I have not been able to get any new light on the story of the Pope's insulting answer to Elizabeth's message, which Tierney denies in one of his prefaces. For the later affairs at Trent, have you seen Calini's letters in Mansi's edition of Baluze?

The idea of getting the Paris papers done is a very good one; but I fear Gladstone is hardly so generously disposed yet.

Long live Campion, Shakespeare and Wetherell! I cut short, to leave nothing legible through the envelope[1]—

Ever Your's truly

J D Acton

686

SIMPSON TO ACTON · 20 MARCH 1867

40 the Albany March 20

Dear Acton

Salutations &c! Here we are in the agonies of producing No 0.[2] And our spirit is greatly troubled with respect to Cartwright's[3] article on Monte Cassino. It has been suggested that some months ago a paragraph

---

[1] Acton wished to prevent the Roman authorities from reading his letters.
[2] A 'ghost' or rehearsal number of the *Chronicle*, privately printed a week before the first number.
[3] William Cornwallis Cartwright (1826–1915), M.P. 1868–85.

was seen in the *Times* saying that the government had determined to spare the place, that the Abbot was to become a Bishop, and Father somebody Royal Archivist, & that the whole place was remain a monument of the historical importance of Italy, & of the clemency of Ricasoli. Is this so? Is it any thing like the truth? For if so Cartwright is superannuated. Wetherell expects the answer in hot haste, so that the article may come in No 1, though it cannot show its face in No. 0.

Ever yours
R Simpson

The point is. Is the thing settled. or can the article now be used

T.F.W.[1]

687

SIMPSON TO ACTON · 22 OCTOBER 1867

Oct 22

My dear Acton

Will you be kind enough to have the new vol of the Acta SS. sent to me. I thought I had the parts of it necessary for a review but I have lost them. There is a curious account of Aethiopia in (I think) the XIIth century, & of the Feudal oeconomy of a Spanish Bishop in the XIIIth, each of which will make articles, besides a notice of the volume.

Will you also charitably send me notes for the current Italian events. I am taking two weeks for Lathbury,[2] & as I come quite fresh to the matter, & have not attended to the prior moves in the game, I am somewhat bewildered about the sequences of things. You can tell me about the possible combinations after Ratazzi's[3] resignation, the reason & the significance of Cialdini,[4] his character, & his policy. Also whether there is now any probability of the old threatened *coup d'etat* coming to the surface again, & with what modifications. Italy this week ought to be well done, & I am not in a position to do it well without private informations.

If Bismark supplied the money the present solution is a distinct defeat of B. by Napoleon, is it not? Or does B. woo the Italian nation as distinct from the Italian government?—Dividing & neutralizing that

---

[1] The postscript is by Wetherell, from whose residence the letter is dated.
[2] I.e., replacing Lathbury as sub-editor of the *Chronicle*.
[3] Urbano Ratazzi (1808–73), Italian radical politician, prime minister 1862, 1867.
[4] Enrico Cialdini (1813–92), Italian general, failed to form a government in October 1867.

231

which he foresees must be an ally of France in the event of a French-Prussian war?

Also have you a view about American affairs? What is the value of the reaction? Is it a protest against the equality of the races—European, Negro & Chinese—as the "Yankee" of the Spectator wills? Or is it a protest against the whole of the Radical policy?

I should never end if I had you to question. How about the Austrian Concordat, & how will *Non possumus* accept the new necessity?

I wont trespass upon your kindness any longer—nor will I apologize for so much—you have chosen to be a light & so you must shine.

Ever yours
R Simpson

I suppose now the Council[1] is a gloomy certainty.

688

ACTON TO SIMPSON · 23 OCTOBER 1867

My dear Simpson,

I have written to Allen to send you the Bollandists.

Rattazzi, having no encouragement from the Right, made offers to the Left, and as their terms were too high, formed a mongrel colourless ministry. His measure on church property alienated still more the Right, and he tried to conciliate the Left by fomenting the Roman invasion, or at least allowing the party of action to think that the moment would be favourable for action, under him. They, relying on his repulse from the Right, and believing that he would not repeat Aspromonte, (by encouraging the expedition tacitly and turning against it in the critical moment) set about the undertaking. It was well known that Napoleon could not tolerate a Roman revolution the moment his back was turned. It would have been such a blow to his reputation that he must have returned. A peace of nearly a year seemed enough to justify his departure, and it was thought he did not contemplate being permanently the Roman champion. This was also the view of the leading French statesman. You *must* be quiet for some time, said Rouher to Minghetti in the winter. (No names).[2] They however thought the stringency of the obligation would wear off in time. But Rattazzi's line was too flagrant to be

---

[1] Vatican Council I had been announced.

[2] These names were not to be mentioned in the *Chronicle* (26 October 1867, p. 721). Eugène Rouher (1814–84) was premier of France 1863–9. Marco Minghetti (1818–86), Italian prime minister 1863–4, 1873–6, was a relative of Acton by marriage.

tolerated. He is far the best parliamentary manager in Italy, but is not happy in wider combinations. His marriage, and other antecedents, keep him on the side of France, and make him inapt for a Prussian alliance, which I suppose certainly does not exist. None of the Italian leaders are Philoprussian. Bismark got Lamarmora turned out, and the way Prussia tried to make the Italians inglorious food for powder, and *compelled them to go to Lissa,* made them hateful. But among the people these particulars are not known, and the tangible grievances are against France.

Rattazzi must have relied on an Italian movement for Rome strong enough to carry him over the difficulties of his position. I suppose that the successes of the papal troops prove that the required steam was not got up. Italy will have to look to Prussia, or to Prince Napoleon,[1] for the deliverance of Rome.

I believe the country people in the Roman state, would welcome the Italians, though perhaps not the Republicans who want to exterminate the priests. In Rome itself the masses are not eager for change. The middle class is largely dependent on the upper clergy, and those of its members who would be dangerous are exiled or in prison to the number of many thousands.

Cialdini is much hated by both extremes. He is the regular officer, dynastic, disliking irregulars and democrats, disliking the clergy still more, and untouched by that liberality which Ricasoli and Minghetti adopted too late, in ecclesiastical affairs. He has ruthless energy, and courage to disregard outcry and the press. Though no debater, he can speak like a finished orator. Ricasoli expected that he would be his immediate successor. They accuse him of perfidy, at Castelfidardo. I believe that is spite, and the reproach belongs to others. At Gaeta they pretend that he fired on the hospital flag, and forced the queen to live in a casernate. It is probably a lie; but he is a hard strong man, and the clerical victory would not be worth much. The intriguers about the King would certainly work against him as against Rattazzi. Menabrea[2] would be the minister of that clique, and his nomination would at any rate imply an immense concession to Rome. He is an eminent man, a sort of Catholic Carnot. If he makes a ministry of unknown names, without his old colleagues, Minghetti, Feruzzi, Visconti, Pasolini, he means mischief. If Rattazzi comes back and remodels his ministry with these men, then the Roman question is postponed sine die. If he remains as he is, he cannot remain long.

---

[1] Prince Napoléon (1822–91), son of Jérôme Bonaparte, next heir to the French throne after the Prince Imperial, an eccentric liberal.

[2] Luigi Federico Menabrea (1809–96), Italian general and statesman, prime minister 1867–9.

In fact I know nothing about it. Still less about America. You have no idea how little I have read besides the Chronicle for months.

Ever Your's
J D Acton

689

SIMPSON TO ACTON · 28 OCTOBER 1867

Dear Acton

Many thanks for your letter—You see that I used it well. If you have time send me a few notes for the next number.

W.[1] is hungry & thirsty for short notices—That which was to have been the great feature in the paper has almost come to grief.

I send by this post the life of Fisher which the Bollandists gave me for you, & also the documents about Charles II & his son which you bought of F. Boero, together with my additions from the S.P.O.[2]

The Acta Sanctorum arrived safely on Saturday—many thanks—

Ever yours
R Simpson

Monday morning

690

ACTON TO SIMPSON · ?30 OCTOBER 1867

Dear Simpson,

The MSS. have come; many thanks for them. When one comes home after 18 months absence, one cannot find time for writing. I hope to have something this time, if Friday morning will do. The most significant thing in Menabrea's ministry, besides what you know, is the appointment of Gualterio.[3] He has long been my candidate for the Ministry of the Interior. This powerful and able man was formerly distinguished as a historian and is eminent, both in action and in literature. He has held successively all the most difficult posts in Italy. During the early and most violent period of the Italian revolution, he was prefect in Umbria, with seventeen bishops (I think that was the number) in his province.

---

[1] Wetherell.
[2] State Paper Office.
[3] Filippo Antonio, Marchese Gualterio (1820–74), Italian minister of the interior 1867–8. What follows is intended for use in 'Current Events', *Chronicle*, 2 November 1867, pp. 745–6.

He never had trouble or collision with anyone of them. The energy he displayed at Genoa nearly embroiled Italy with France, and will not make his appointment as minister acceptable to the Emperor. He went on board the ship that was taking the brothers La Gala, notorious bandits, to France; and arrested them, though their passports were quite regular.

It was he who, as prefect of Naples, inaugurated the work of reconciliation with the Pope. Prior to the change in Ricasoli's ecclesiastical policy in the autumn of last year, and then, independently of it, he carried on negotiations with the archbishop of Naples, Cardinal Riario Sforza,[1] who had settled at Rome, and was reputed not only one of the most austere, but one of the most uncompromising of the Cardinals. The proposals of the Marquis Gualterio established a modus vivendi satisfactory to both parties. The archbishop returned, and was received by the prefect with due honours. Each party afterwards bore testimony to the fidelity with which the terms of the agreement were observed by the other. There was a practical experimental solution of the administrative difficulties with which Tonello and his employers were vainly struggling.

The fall of Ricasoli isolated the prefect of Naples in his policy of moderation, justice and patience. He was induced at first to remain by assurances that the new ministry would maintain the concessions of the old. But when Rattazzi, after the failure of Ferraris, swerved into the pure anticlerical line, he took an opportunity to give Gualterio such a snub as compelled him to resign.

He is the only Italian statesman who possesses detailed and personal knowledge of parties and characters in Rome. At Naples, during many months, he held the threads of informal negotiations which promised to prepare an understanding more thorough than could be expected from those which were carried on with Florence. By his private correspondence, and his personal influence he was forming a party among the clergy—a thing impossible to Ricasoli. He becomes minister with the prestige of having restored religious peace in the most important and the most disturbed of the Italian cities, and of having gained the confidence of one who would be the most impracticable politically, if he were not also spiritually the most consciencious of the prelates. In the old oppressive times the Marquis Gualterio suffered impoverishment and almost ruin, by reason of his political liberality. Under Rattazzi he was deprived for the steadfastness of his religious liberality. He has made sacrifices both for a free state and for a free church. If the new ministry lasts the country will feel the change in the office by which

---

[1] Sisto Riario Sforza (1810–77), archbishop of Naples 1845, cardinal 1846, in exile 1861–6.

Italy is governed, from the intriguer whose art it is to over-reach himself, to a highminded straightforward man, who is not only faithful to his principles, but perhaps exceptionally ardent for their triumph. His character, like that of Menabrea, is a security against half measures; unlike Menabrea's, it is a security for the constitution. It is not in his nature, or in the circumstances, that he should be a popular minister. He will make his strong hand felt, and will probably draw rather tight the strings of the administration, neither neglecting nor wasting the resources of his power. It will perhaps appear that his Roman policy is inspired by the wish that the Church should not only enjoy liberty, but should adopt it; and that while he strives against the foes of ecclesiastical freedom he will strive also against the ecclesiastical foes of freedom. We should expect to find him averse from that system of sheer separation and mutual inacquaintance, borrowed from the example of America and the supposed example of England, which was promulgated in Italy by the eloquent pen of Minghetti. At least it is said that he has long been looked up to as their champion by that portion of the priesthood which is most impatient of the predominating influence of the Roman Jesuits. It would be a new feature in history of the Italian Kingdom, the government operating by dividing the Catholics instead of simply exasperating them. A settlement of the Roman question has been once or twice attempted by men sick of the long antagonism, by giving to the Church perfect corporate independence in the position of a private association. It is far more difficult, though it belongs to a higher order of statesmanship, to give her a position recognizing her as the church of the nation, while retaining the influence which may be claimed by a Catholic state. Real liberty is obtained not by the separation, but by the distinct and appropriate, but combined, action of church and state. The defined and regulated influence of the church in the state protects a sphere and a germ of freedom in political affairs, and supplies a separate and valuable sanction for laws. And the restricted and appointed action of the state in the affairs of the church gives security to the canon law, and prevents wanton innovation and the arbitrary confiscation of rights. Of the forces which restrain the papal power and preserve the traditions of church government, two, the episcopate, and the religious orders, have abdicated that function. A third, the Universities, is sinking under the coincident assault of the revolution and the Holy See. The state alone must remain. If the Italian state becomes consolidated and endures, the church will need statesmen of the type of the Marquis Gualterio. But if the conservative party breaks down, the Catholics will rue the evil day when the proposals of Scialoja[1] were rejected.

---

[1] Antonio Scialoja (1817–77), Italian economist and politician, finance minister 1865–7, unsuccessfully proposed a solution to the question of the church estates.

I see my letter has glided into the tone of our own correspondent. It will give you some points for the character of the new ministry. Gualterio was so poor that he sold his family papers now the Gualterio collection at the British Museum; and he was in communication last winter with persons very considerable indeed at the Vatican. It is essential to indicate the fact; but I am too much in the secret to say more than I said in the earlier part of my letter. Do not use anything in this paragraph. Gualterio is a bit of a theorist, and has doctrines about the developments of universal history which guide him in the Roman question, or as he calls it, l'assedio di Roma. Did you ever seen Laurence?[1] Gualterio has the same jaw, with a formidable biting and commanding power.

It may be well to say, among the things characterising his position towards Rome that he gave no countenance at Naples to the very obnoxious Cardinal d'Andrea.[2] *Between ourselves* I believe this was not of statesmanship, but from some unpleasant passages or resentments between the two. But before the world he must have the benefit of it.

Ever Your's
J D Acton

691

ACTON TO SIMPSON · 22 DECEMBER 1867

Aldenham
Sunday

My dear Simpson,

Do you know Davis's whereabout, and does not he owe you as much work as I owe you money on his behalf? If so, could you set him to look for the reply to the enclosed questions? I don't know the name of my friend at the B.M.[3]

The questions are Mr. Green's, and the answers are wanted to enable him to cover with confusion a very wicked man, a Protestant controversialist, a believer in the abuse of Indulgences. As the dispute has been going on in a weekly paper ever since June, it is desirable that it should close, and I do not see how I can hasten the end but by intreating

---

[1] Probably Sir John Lawrence (1811–79), administrator of the Punjab 1853–9, viceroy of India 1864–9, created Baron Lawrence 1869.

[2] Girolamo d'Andrea (1812–68), cardinal 1852, sympathized with Italian unification and left Rome for Naples.

[3] British Museum.

you to send the enclosed to some sufficient person. If the answer comes in time it will be used in next Saturday's letter.

A Merry Xmas to you, and happy New Year.

Ever Your's truly
J D Acton

692

SIMPSON TO ACTON · 24 DECEMBER 1867

Decb^r 24. 1867

Dear Acton

A happy Christmas and new year to you & yours. Your note followed me hither, & I have sent the questions to my brother Bob, whom I have exhorted to answer them on Thursday. I hope therefore you may get them (the answers) on Friday, in time possibly for Green's Saturday's letter—As for Davis I know nothing about his whereabouts. He has done nothing, for his beginning operations depended on the arrival of a marked Calendar from Aldenham, which never came, & could not be found. I advanced him in your name either one or two sums of 10/ shillings—Mrs. Renouf can tell which—But till I have asked her I cannot possibly say.

I am sorry for having called D'Andrea simply Andrea, in transcribing that life of Gualterio, which you sent me for the Chronicle. I am afraid it was marred in several parts by small changes, which were rendered necessary to save editorial "weighings" of words—judicial functions which take up a great deal of Wetherells too little spare time.

Have you any extracts ready written out, referring to the use or recommendation of Mahometan Jewish or Schismatic instructors, schools, or universities, by Catholics in the middle ages? Such things must be frequent. I looked for specimens in Roger Bacon & was soon rewarded by an ample harvest. I want to write another article on Oxford —W. has given me leave, but I suppose it will be dignified as "communicated."

Do you mind looking over the names & the extracts from the Narren Schiff[1] in the proof which I enclose, & then sending back the proof with its corrections to Lathbury. I have not the original Ms. here, & I can't be expected to evolve the true spelling of old German out of my own consciousness—I hope the corrections I have made are not too bad.

Has Darnell done the same as Newman—given notice that in consequence of the directions of the late Pastorals[2] his school does not

---

[1] The *Ship of Fools*, an allegory (1494) by Sebastian Brant.
[2] Disapproving the sending of Catholics to the English Universities.

henceforth prepare young men for the Universities of Oxford & Cambridge?

I talked to Wetherell about an article on a recently translated "Inner life of Lacordaire"; I proposed a psychological discussion of the subjective honesty of the objective contradiction offering at once an "impenitent liberal" and a proclaimer of the divine & infallible wisdom of the *Mirari vos*. If you have time scrawl down two or three sentences— The words of the wise are like nails in the wall says somebody in the Bible. Your wisdom must be great if it is measured by the capacity of your words for forming pegs of articles. I have lately gone in for rapid writing. I am proud of my two last feats. I wrote the article on "Claims of Catholic prisoners" in 1 hour 40 minutes, & that on Gladstone at Ormskirk in 1 h. 50 m. which fully accounts for their thorough emptiness. Addio.

Ever yours
R Simpson

693

SIMPSON TO ACTON · 21 MARCH 1868

March 21.

Dear Acton

Many thanks for your lecture[1]—why did you not have it printed as a pamphlet instead of a placard? Then it might have been kept, but now it can only be pasted into an album, instead of being bound up—Are you employing Davis! My brother saw him at the State paper office yesterday. Mrs. Renouf last year paid him 10 shillings at my request for work he was to do for you—(when I wrote to you at Christmas I did not know whether it was 10/s. or 1£.) So if you are employing him, it is open to you to count him your debtor to that amount. I am returning to my enquiries about Shakespeare's life & opinions. They lead me to a great charm in English history—viz—the true political import of Essex's rebellion— It is always treated as a kind of personal squabble between Robert Cecil, Walter Raleigh, & Essex,[2] determined by motives of personal ambition & of personal hate & revenge. What little there is left of Essex's writings show him to have been a regular Whig, & I dont think it would be

---

[1] 'The Rise and Fall of the Mexican Empire', a lecture delivered at the Bridgnorth Literary and Scientific Institution, 10 March 1868, reprinted in the Bridgnorth *Journal*, 14 March.

[2] Respectively, Robert Cecil (1563–1612), 1st earl of Salisbury 1605, secretary of state 1596, lord treasurer 1608; Sir Walter Raleigh (*c.* 1554–1618), explorer, author and courtier, condemned for treason 1603; Robert Devereux (*c.* 1566–1601), 2nd earl of Essex 1576, favourite of Queen Elizabeth, rebelled and was executed 1601.

difficult to trace the pedigree of the school from 1601 to 1688—Essex's chief tenets may be found in Shakespeare's historical plays & in the kindred book, Sir John Hayward's history of Henry IV, for which Hayward was near the gallows in 1600.[1] Is it not a saying of somebody that Shakespeare's plays are the soundest History of England! If you have any lights on this matter will you be kind enough to let me have the benefit of them. I suppose you have got nothing from Rome on the Essex affair—It kindled great hopes in those quarters—in the Spanish faction from the likelihood of civil war; in the more patriotic Catholics from Essex's promise of toleration. The man who for a whole year reconciled Puritanism & the Theatre, & made the London Corporation change places with the Council as the protector of players, might have worked 40 years earlier the toleration which afterwards characterized the Independents.

Raleigh is clearly an imperialist & despot—He believes in the universality of human law, like Aristotle (what it commands nor it forbids), & laments the discontinuance of slavery in England on the ground that some men are naturally slaves, & if not so externally will be thieves & vagrants instead—There is plenty of fundamental difference in view to account for the estrangement betweeen him & Essex, without putting it all down to personal jealousies & quarrels. Shakespeare was essentially of the Essex faction—Jonson alternated. In 1601, 1602 he was bitterly hostile—he made recantation in *Sejanus* in 1603, & returned to his courtly Theories in 1611 with *Cataline.* or rather in 1606, as may be shown by a letter of his to Cecil—It is wonderful what a new light some of Shakespeare's plays assume when all their minute references to contemporary political controversies are investigated. Collier & Halliwell[2] look only for references to personal affrays between Actors

Ever yours
R Simpson

Present my respects to Lady Acton—

---

[1] Sir John Hayward (*c.* 1564–1627), historian, dedicated his life of Henry IV (1599) to Essex.

[2] Two prolific Shakespearian scholars. John Payne Collier (1789–1883), journalist and barrister, edited texts, introduced forged marginal corrections, exposed 1859–61. James Orchard Halliwell (from 1872 Halliwell-Phillipps; 1820–89), librarian of Jesus College, Cambridge, biographer and editor of Shakespeare.

ACTON TO SIMPSON · ?9 SEPTEMBER 1868

33 Lower Grosvenor Street
Wednesday

Dear Simpson,

Will you read this document, and send me any points in answer that strike you? My people[1] seem to wish that there should be a reply, as it is said to proceed from a wellknown local dignitary, of high church proclivities; and I am anxious that the answer should not be mine. Perhaps you will not think it worth answering.

Ever Your's
J D Acton

694A

SIMPSON TO ACTON · 10 SEPTEMBER 1868

Sept. *10*

Dear Acton

I have been beating my brains to invent some form of reply to the ingenious liar who ironically calls himself Veritas, and accuses you of drunkenness because you will not endorse Disraeli's drunken speech about the Irish-Papist-& High Church-Ritualist conspiracy against the principle of Establishments. I fancy that a sort of Inquisitional paper of articles of confession to be ministered to you by Veritas would be the best kind of squib. I have scribbled a mere outline of such an affair, but it has not a single joke or point in it, & would have to be twice rewritten before it could do any good. I am obliged to send it off to you now, because I have to go at once to the city on business, & I fancied you might be in a hurry for my answer.

I dont think Veritas worth answering except so far as his personal attacks on you for dishonesty & breach of Xtian commandments are likely to have weight at Bridgnorth & these had better be answered by a dignified letter from you to the papers. His arguments are too futile to convince the reason, & too puzzle-headed to be intelligible to those who only look for cries.

Ever yours
R Simpson

---

[1] Acton's supporters in his second election campaign at Bridgnorth.

ACTON TO SIMPSON · 10 SEPTEMBER 1868

My dear Simpson,

Nothing, I see, brings you out like an election. I return the paper with 1000 hearty thanks in the hope that it will not bore you grievously to revise and sharpen it as you suggest. It matters not to a day or two when it appears. If you will, it will be an excellent squib, all the more for its good humour. As you have not sent back the original document, I hope you were prepared for my boring you so again.

Believe me,
Ever your's
J D Acton

Did I tell you that the man who facetiously signs himself Veritas is understood to be the chief literary parson of the place, and my very good friend?[1] He is also supposed to be the real author of the monstrous document, or at least of what is monstrous in it.

696

ACTON TO SIMPSON · 30 SEPTEMBER 1868

Dear Simpson,

My Bridgnorth friends are very anxious to have the Squib[2] put out, and suggest certain modifications. I send you the MS. not venturing to make them myself.

One writes: 'It seemed to me that 'by virtue of our inquisitorial office' or such like words might be wisely re-introduced in order to connect it with the heading 'Holy office', and that the officers of the court might be omitted or altered'.'

I hope it is not a great bore you to look it through once more. As soon as I get it back I shall take it to Robson.

Ever Your's
J D Acton

---

[1] This may refer to Horatio James Ward (d. 1894), B.A. (Cantab.) 1854, Anglican minister 1856, headmaster of Bridgnorth School 1859–77, vicar of Morville with Aston Eyre 1877–93. Ward supported his friend Acton, despite their difference in religion.

[2] Simpson's paper.

ACTON TO SIMPSON · ? OCTOBER 1868

Dear Simpson,

The paper is printed, and goes off to-day—Many thanks for it.

Wetherell will not be able to begin[1] in January, but looks forward to April. Shall you have at least two papers ready by that time?

A little newborn daughter[2] makes me write short letters, though all is well with us.

Ever Your's
J D Acton

Sometimes[3] like naughty rat catchers, I harbour the vermin 'tis my interest to destroy
In torrid zone my flesh with cold is creeping
My sours burn the tongues, & set eyes weeping
    (Chili)

698

ACTON TO SIMPSON · 22 OCTOBER 1868

My dear Simpson,

There is an outcry at Bridgnorth for more electoral writing by your hand. Are you disposed that way? With a view not to Bridgnorth merely, I think it would be very useful to have, in a short compass the annals of our party conflicts since 1865—or a history of the late parliament. It would be easy to put it together, keeping in mind the chief topics of popular interest, such as Reform, finance, Church Rates &c. Do you think it quite impossible?

If you see Lambert, would you ask him whether the story that the Tories paid the advertisements[4] double in their own papers, and were forced to do so to the others, is a certain fact?

I am off again on Thursday—

Ever Your's
J D Acton

---

[1] Arrangements were being made for Wetherell to take over the editorship of the *North British Review*, assisted by his Liberal and Catholic friends of the defunct *Chronicle*. His first number was actually October 1869, but Simpson contributed to the July issue.

[2] Anne Mary Catherine Georgiana Acton (1868–1917).

[3] The following lines are in Simpson's hand.   [4] Government advertisements.

SIMPSON TO ACTON · 23 OCTOBER 1868

Oct 23

Dr Acton

I send you herewith some lucubrations on your three points—not such a history as you suggest which would occupy a vast time. For I have no head for dates, and easily run aside after irrelevant details. Let me know on Monday whether this is, or may be made, of any use. Renouf turned up on Wednesday—he carries about with him a remarkable letter of Newmans on his Honorius[1] which you must see. He has taken lodgings here—55 Park Road Clapham SW I could tell you many things but my wrist is so tired with writing—I have scribbled all this at a sitting —that I must leave it—

Ever yours
R Simpson

ACTON TO SIMPSON · 25 OCTOBER 1868

My dear Simpson,

The papers are very good indeed and I should like to use them, if I may, in my next speech. You would do what you speak of extremely well. The Statesman's Year book, the Chronicle, Gladstone's late speeches would be a great help. There is no need to trouble yourself with a daily paper. The thing should be brief, sharp, with no more detail than you can help, and should tell by the arrangement of facts.

For 1866 and perhaps for 1867 there would be the Annual Register.

Before a small country audience that story of the newspapers[2] might have some effect. Do you think you could write to Cornwall, and ask Lambert to let me know, by return of post, whether I can tell it?

In greatest haste of canvass,

Ever Your's
J D Acton

---

[1] Renouf, *The Condemnation of Pope Honorius* (London, 1868).
[2] The double payment for government advertisements in order to subsidize Tory newspapers.

ACTON TO SIMPSON · 29 OCTOBER 1868*

My dear Simpson,

I hope it is not election work that has made you ill. I had rather attribute it to the subtle poison of the pink paper you write on.

I will vulgarize and stupefy your criticism of the Tories, and reduce it to the level of the new voters[1] whom I am to address on Saturday. What do you think of the perfect Reform of the future? All my friends here, even the better Tories, have become converts to the Ballot, which is my Palladium. I need not commit myself with women, as I am a favourite with them, and can express my sentiments in the form of a jocular compliment. And it is no use talking now of fancy franchises for the representation of groups of interests that are not locally defined.

Any ideas thankfully received up to Saturday morning, and after that also, for the hustings.

I see that your theory of Tory policy is right now, but I do not see so clearly how far it is sprung from real Tory roots, and how far it is the resource of the weaker party, and the unjust steward.

Will Disraeli have the courage to promote Wilberforce?[2]

If Lambert turns up, pray remember that Saturday is the day.

Ever Your's
J D Acton

702

SIMPSON TO ACTON · ?30 OCTOBER 1868

Dear A.

You will have already heard that the advertisement story is a piece of "confidential communication", so that bonne bouche is denied to the electors of Bridgnorth.

The Reform of the future evidently (for boroughs) comes in three things

1. Protection of the voter against corrupt influence.
2. Protection of the country against corruption of the voter.
3. Greater equalization of the voting power.

---

* The two sentences beginning 'All my friends here' are quoted in *Lord Acton: The Decisive Decade*, p. 17.
[1] Those enfranchised by the Reform Act of 1867.
[2] Samuel Wilberforce was a leading candidate for the vacant Archbishopric of Canterbury. He was not chosen.

1 For the first of these heads there is the material protection of the ballot; the personal protection of an enlarged & systematic national education; and the social protection of associations & combinations to ensure thorough publicity for all attempts at bribery or intimidation, & to offer mutual protection to persons threatened by landlords or others.

2 For the second; it was the second of Gladstones 10 points for the amendment of the bill of 1867—"omission of provisions against traffic in vote of householders of the lowest class by corrupt payment of their rates." This of course involved a proposal that occupiers of houses below some specified value should be excluded from the suffrage—a proposal that was to form part of Coleridge's[1] instruction (April 5), but which in consequence of the "tea-room" schism had to be dropped (It was again urged by Gladstone in his amendments of April 9, but the first of them was lost April 12 by a majority of 21, & so none of the others was pressed. It is to be noted that the majority was made up by 25 Adullamites[2] (out of 50) while of the 45 tea party only 8 voted with the ministry—so that it is to the old Whigs not to the radicals that we owe the final rejection of a hard & fast line of qualification for boroughs) But now this natural & easy principle for eliminating the semi-pauperized voter is gone for good, & no statesman could think of reimposing it.

The counter principle of the Tories was the "personal payment of rates". This is evidence of "possession of some property in the hands of a man who has earned it by his labour" & this again is "evidence of industry, of self-control, of good moral character". So spoke Lord Stanley on behalf of the Tory Ministry of 1859. You remember how the *personal payment of rates & two years residence* was exalted in 1867 as the test which should purge the constituency of all immoral elements. The real fact is that it was never supposed to be any such purge or test; it was simply intended to keep up the Tory policy of a personal & quasi paternal control over the constituency. Even after Hodgkinson's amendment (abolishing *compounding*) was accepted by government (May 20) Dizzy[3] wished to make the continuance of the system optional; by this means it would have been in the power of any landlord to disfranchise his tenants by insisting on paying their rates for them. The Tories hate any system that works mechanically; their wheels turn only by favour or privilege. It is thus that personal payment of rates seemed to them to promise so much in purging the electoral lists. And indeed if the rate was a fixed thing:

---

[1] John Duke Coleridge (1820–94), barrister 1846, M.P. 1865, solicitor general 1868, attorney general 1871, chief justice of common pleas 1873, lord chief justice 1880; created Baron Coleridge 1874.

[2] Liberal opponents of parliamentary reform.   [3] Disraeli.

if it was a fixed poll tax, due on the first of Jany. every year, & duly called for, or exacted by legal process within a month, then such a test would have nothing unfair in it. But the personal payment of rates has quite other elements in it. First, the poor rate is uncertain in amount, & uncertain in the time when it is required. Next the precise time of making it, & the circumstances of collecting it are in the power of parish officers; & these officers are elected by a plan of multiple voting which ensures that the great body of them should be representatives of the privileged classes. Overseers have before now, under the existing law, disfranchised whole parishes in boroughs, by making a rate (due on the day of its making) just before Jany 5, and not collecting it till after July. It was of course possible for each claimant to ascertain the fact of the rate having been made, to ascertain the amount due from him, & to convey the sum to the collector & obtain his receipt, & then to show the receipt to the overseer. But every one can see that there is hardly one Englishman in twenty that would take all the trouble; he might often enough resolve to do it, but some accident would put it out of his head, or put it off, the time would be over, & the vote lost. Rich persons are not in the same circumstances of disadvantage. Their rates are heavy enough to make it worth the Collectors while to beat them up. But when we come to little piddling sums of $1^s/3^d$ or $2^s/$ it is throwing a great additional charge on the ratepayer if we are to make the Collectors call once twice or thrice times for each rate, & then summon the defaulters. The personal payment of rates ensures the disfranchisement of large classes of voters through carelessness or forgetfulness on their own part, or through over work, desire of economy, or political corruption on the part of the collectors or overseers. For these reasons the rate-paying test must be done away with; and this is part of the Reform of the future. Shall we then have household-suffrage pure & simple in boroughs? We shall have honest household suffrage, not a corrupt one as now.

There will be the purge of reception of parish relief. If a householder or any member of his family has been during the year in receipt of relief as a pauper, the householder is off the register. Perhaps this might lead to a demand for greater publicity of schedules of persons & families so relieved within the year, alphabetically arranged, & stuck up on church doors with the electoral lists every year.

Again there will be the purge of householders of tenements from which no rates are collected on the score of poverty. Even after payment of rates is abolished as a condition of registration, the register must still be made up from the rate books, and tenements from which no rate is collected because of the poverty of the tenants will be crossed out in the rate book & will cease to give a qualification. Thus a use may grow up which in some future year may give us the hard & fast line which is still maintained in Scotland & Ireland, where tenements under 4£ value are not rated at all, & so give no vote. Mr Poulett Scrope's amendment to this effect was lost, but there is at present no legislation to prevent a custom of the kind arising in England. It would however be necessary to take from the overseers the power of excusing from rates those who did not wish to be excused. Such an immunity perhaps should only accrue after failure to recover rates by distress, or some equally potent test of the *bonâ fide* character of the transaction.

But at any rate, the borough voter ought now to be defined from the thrall of his own blundering forgetfulness, of the collector's carelessness, & the overseer's power, by the abolition of the personal payment of rates; especially since such abolition would revive the legislation for payment of rates by composition of the Parish with the landlord.

The other securities of the country against the corruption of voters are increased severity of the laws concerning bribery & intimidation, and perhaps compulsory education.

(One detail of the reform of the future for boroughs is the repeal of part of sect. 59, w^h provides, that though the town landlord whose houses stand on copyhold or freehold, has a county vote for his land, (besides the borough votes which the occupiers have) a landlord who has built on leasehold property (e.g. a 99 years lease) has no such county vote.—A mere matter of detail, though it is a disfranchisement of persons who previously had the franchise, & is in direct discord with sect. 56, which promises to repeal no existing franchise but only to add.

----

3 The great question of reform for the future is a greater equalization of the voting power.
Distribution of seats under Bill of 1867.

	Pop. 1861.	No. of representatives	Inhabitants to each member
Counties—	11,266,000 —	187 —	60,200
19 boroughs over 100,000 pop.	4,669,000 —	46 —	101,000
19 boroughs (50 to 100,000)	1,385,000 —	36 —	38,000
51 ———— (20 to 50,000)	1,567,000 —	77 —	20,000
49 ———— (10 to 20,000)	692,000 —	81 —	8,500
68 ———— under 20,000	420,000 —	68 —	6,100.
By addition			
89 boroughs ————	7,641,000 —	159	
168 ————————	1,112,000 —	149	

It is clear that the little towns get more than their fair share of political influence. A slight improvement was made by the disfranchisements of 1868 for the benefit of Scotland. But the whole problem is still to be solved.

		no. of
One more addition	pop.	rep.
19 boroughs over 100,000 —	4,669,000 —	46
all the other boroughs	4,064,000 —	262

The possible solutions for those difficulties & anomalies are infinite, & hardly to be touched in a speech. Perhaps on this part of the matter you might condemn the minority representation when only partially applied—perhaps if it were applied universally to electoral districts each sending 3 members it would be fair enough. But when we once talk of electoral districts we get into a wide subject, in which perhaps the best solution is Cobdens[1]—a multitude of districts each returning one member. The various local interests being sufficient to ensure representation in the collective house for each.

This* is I believe Gladstone's programme of the Reform of the future, so you will not run any risk by adopting it.

* (not the last paragraph).

I wish I had time to write an essay on the inner Tory & Liberal in every man's mind. For

> Two such opposed kings encamp them still
> In man—

One tends to equalization & the strict distributive justice of what is due both to man as man, & to man in respect of what he works. The other tends to privilege, through honour. There are patriotic services which no mere distribution of products can repay. These are repaid by privileges—The true Tory is perpetually repaying new sacrifices & new services with new privileges. The true liberal is perpetually levelling old worn out privileges which are no longer defensible as due acknowledgments of services rendered by the holder of them. The extreme Tory, formed by antagonism to the liberal, is the upholder of worn out privilege. The extreme liberal, formed by antagonism to the Tory, is the leveller even of well-deserved preeminences. Worn out privilege becomes to the corrupted Tory vested interest, and as such, has a claim upon justice. He enlarges the sphere of *vested interest* boundlessly. He is perpetually creating new vested interests. He has a feeling that the mere desire to retain an unjust advantage makes a man a Tory. Hence his

---

[1] Richard Cobden (1804–65), M.P. 1841–57, 1859–65, a leader of the free trade movement. His suggestion of uniform single-member constituencies was enacted in 1885.

patronage of all who have such advantage. Remember his persistent patronage of the freemen, the one class of borough voters from whom all corruption has flowed—corruption being clearly inherent in all those boroughs where the Tories of 1832 forced the Whigs to retain this nucleus of evil leaven. The freeman of a borough comes in at the back door of enfranchisement, because in most cases he is a mere nominee. Any man who choses to work may live in his own house & pay his own rates; but to make a man a freeman other people's consent is required. He must be voted for, or he must be received on a serviture by a freeman, or he must be the son of a freeman. The very consciousness of holding a privilege not self-gained but got by favour, is an element of Toryism in a man; it gives a preponderance to those ideas which carry him towards the Tory camp—just as the consciousness of having nothing & deserving no privilege naturally incline a man to liberalism.

If this is true. If Toryism would prop up failing privileges, it must do so by giving the persons aggrieved some equivalent. It must either create fresh privileges, or must pay the difference. The tory finance is a finance of privilege. Of course all the great lump sums of our national outgoings have long[1]

, & our smoothly enough, uninfluenced
deas. The peculiarities of each party are
ly in the side eddies & bye currents of the
it was a question of military economy, the
larizing the service by reducing the privilege of
are in his eyes something sacred, a vested
be unjust to touch. It would only remain to him
the common soldier without degrading the officer".
by abolishing flogging—for lets
officer's privilege?—or by really altering the
ranks—Nor even by opening the career of officer to the men— for is not that career almost a vested interest of the wealthy classes? But by giving an extra twopence a day. This is the solution which an honest man like General Peel[2] defends, as the right, nay as the only conceivable solution of the difficulty, certainly not because he cannot save the money by the suppression of officers—for such a compromise could not occur to him except to be scouted. It is not because his party is weak, or because he is an unjust steward that he does it; if his party was strong he would raise the soldier's pay to a still higher figure, & surround the officers' privileges with a yet stronger outwork of

---

[1] The left-hand side of the manuscript is mutilated at this point.
[2] Jonathan Peel (1799–1879), brother of the prime minister, entered Royal Army 1815, rose to lieutenant general 1859, sold out 1863, M.P. 1826–68, secretary for war 1858–9, 1866–7, resigned in opposition to the Reform Bill.

soldiers privileges. And whatever he did, he would do it as an honest man, in accordance with his own principles.

I have not time to develop this *ideé mère* any more; you may make a night mare of it if you please. Dizzy ought to promote Wilberforce, because W. has many of the elements which make Dizzy what he is; there is the same rotund rhetoric with inaccuracy of judgment, the same kind of literary merit, the same personal suavity & oiliness, &c &c. A fellow feeling surely unites the political & the Ecclesiastical adventurer. Probably he will keep the place open, & bestow W. as Abp on the nation with the last signature of his retiring hand.

It was not the work you gave me, nor the pink paper, that made me bad, but the common enemies of weak stomachs—*wittles & drink*—and unfortunately I can't do without them.

Ever y^{rs} RS.

703

ACTON TO SIMPSON · 4 NOVEMBER 1868

Dear Simpson,

My speech last Saturday was so desperately long that I have reserved the points you sent me for the hustings.

I wrote to sound Gladstone about the advertisements, as I remembered that Lambert told us he knew the story. Gladstone strongly urges me to deal wth the question, and says it will make it easier for him to put down the abuse afterwards. As I have his authority do you think Lambert ought to hold me still bound by his promise? I do not write to him on the subject because I cannot expect him to give me express permission. But could you not ascertain whether he would be displeased at my proceeding in the matter independent of his information?

Ever Your's truly
J D Acton

SIMPSON TO ACTON · 5 NOVEMBER 1868

Nov. 5.

Dear Acton

Lambert is again out for a week's shooting, but I expect to see him on Sunday or Tuesday, & then I will sound him. In my opinion, as you have the facts on Gladstone's authority the promise to Lambert no longer binds you, provided you are able, if your authority is asked, to refer to Gladstone, or at any rate to deny that L. is the authority on which you state the facts. I will however talk the matter over with Lambert, & try to get him to agree with my general principles first, & their special application afterwards.

I am getting better under a regime of prussic acid—The Renoufs have taken a house at Clapham. Is there going to be opposition to General Forester[1] at Wenlock as the Times hinted yesterday?

Ever yours
R Simpson

705

ACTON TO SIMPSON · 10 NOVEMBER 1868*

Aldenham
Tuesday night

My dear Simpson,

I have Gladstone's authority to use the fact, (and indeed his urgent request to bring the question forward), not his testimony to the truth of the story. I assumed that he knew it, in writing to him. Therefore I do not know it from a separate source, as you seem to suppose. I shall not use it until I hear from you again, and am sure that Lambert has made his position secure.

The story, as I remember it, is this:—the Tories paid double for the government advertisements in their own newspapers. Some of the Liberal papers found it out, and compelled them, by threat of exposure, to pay them also double. Is that the true version? Its importance to me is that my opponent[2] is a Lord of the Treasury.

---

[1] George Cecil Weld Forester (1807–86), entered Royal Army 1824, retired as general 1877, M.P. for Wenlock 1828–74, 3rd Baron Forester 1874.

* The second paragraph is quoted in *Lord Acton: The Decisive Decade*, pp. 17–18.

[2] Henry Whitmore (1813–76), M.P. for Bridgnorth 1852–70.

Let me beseech you to turn your mind very seriously to the appropriation of the Irish endowments, and to read the last Spectator on the subject. The party has no plan, and I can't tell which Gladstone will think best in Solon's sense. Have you not perceived that the great chief is not an inventor of schemes, but only of arguments? Like a great 3 decker, he wants to be towed into action, and then he does the fighting in a superior way.

Gladstone's letters to me do not contain any facts interesting to Villiers, and still less any idea of my amending the address, for I have told him that my return is at least very uncertain. There has, however, been a change to-day.

The glut of Tory money is felt in this County, and has turned a seat at Shrewsbury already.

Gladstone means, I know, to keep the two measures separate, and will be glad to do something like what you propose. The fight with the Lords will be an episode in this contest, and ought to precede appropriation.

I know the story of Whitmore's album, and a friend has written a parody on Horatius concerning it, which is rather good. He will not greet me since my calling his friends homines trium litterarum.

Our local paper is grievously Tory, and generally gives my opponents an opportunity of making fools of themselves every week. It also refuses my friends the same advantage. On the whole I have no right to complain.

Ever Your's most truly
J D Acton

706

SIMPSON TO ACTON · 12 NOVEMBER 1868

Nov. 12

Dear Acton

I am afraid the enclosed stops your mouth upon the advertisements, except in a very general way—as a question to be put rather than an assertion to be made—Your version is quite correct.

I have just read the last Spectator and I do not agree with it, on the simple ground that poor rates ultimately fall on Landlords, & that any rate in aid of the poor rates is ultimately a rate in aid of the Landlords. The plan then could only be adopted if accompanied with a stringent land law. In which case the Spectator might see in the tythe merely the compensation to the Landlords for the rights taken from them.

The rights taken from them must be—uncontrolled eviction—and uncontrolled accumulation & retention of land in great estates. A fancy has possessed me lately that if succession duties were simplified & increased—e.g. 5 per-cent for relations & 10 per cent for strangers in blood—& the government was permitted, if it chose, to demand payment in kind—i.e. that the heir of 100 acres must give up 10 (at his own selection, but of average value) to the government, there would be both means of breaking up the estates, & using them for some of Bright's projects. Fancy the effect of the London companies having to part with one tenth of their land every 30 years—or T.C.D,[1] with its fabulous acreage—But I suppose nothing of this sort can be effected except under a House of Commons elected by Ballot. There is a book just published I am told which traces a very large proportion of the great estates of Ireland to Church Property. In this way. The Bishops had immense incomes, & were almost the only residents of great means & power. The penal laws continually wrought changes in the tenures of Catholic lands, & the Bishops were always present both to put those laws into movement, & to take advantage of them when moved. Hence the numbers of Irish families founded by Bishops. Surely their estates ought to be pared by means of succession duty paid in kind. Then Gladstone's old question of the liability of charitable funds to taxation comes up again.

For the Ecclesiastical secularized money some semi-secular means of employment must be found, which cannot be made into a job for the landlords—(who by the bye, as they no longer collect the tythes for the parsons, ought to have reimposed on them the 25 per cent given them by Lord Melbourne)[2]—I dont see why the money should not go thus.

1. Invested in Railroads.
2. Expended in
   a. Hospices & Hospitals.
   b. Increasing the stipends of Primary schoolmasters, & building schools—
   c. Inspection of, & provision for the secular instruction in middle & upper schools
   d. Provision for all the secular part of University education—leaving the faculty of theology for the different confessions, & the moral training for different colleges in the university, or different boarding houses for the college

The Irish are fully aware that they will not get their way about denominational education. It is in their method—to demand more than they want. They were quite sharp enough to interpret Brights ominous silence at Limerick on all matters of education. I think we must apply

---

[1] Trinity College, Dublin.
[2] William Lamb (1779–1848), 2nd Viscount Melbourne 1828, prime minister 1834, 1835–41. His Irish Tithes Act (1838) transferred the payment of tithes from tenants to landlords but reduced the amount by 25 %.

ourselves to a separation of the secular & spiritual *elements* in a combined education, & while we allow government to provide the first, get it to guarantee & guard perfect denominational liberty in the second—Each denomination to find its own funds for the purpose, unless the principle of paying Army & Prison chaplains is admitted, and head money is allowed for religious instructors—

I suppose & hope that Tuesday's change was a bettering of your prospects—quod felix faustumque sit

Ever yours
R Simpson

707

SIMPSON TO ACTON · 13 NOVEMBER 1868

Nov. 13.

Dear Acton

It struck me yesterday Evening that you might write to Gladstone, tell him you had your advertisement story from Lambert, who forbids you to mention it on his authority, ask G. if he can give you an independent authority for it, & if you can use it on this authority. G. could telegraph to you in time for your Hustings speech on Monday.

What is the explanation of the non-performance of Ld Stanley's promise to explain his position in a speech? And why is his brother[1] made secy. of the Admiralty, if the Derby connexion is still as strong as it was through the elder brother? Is he going to rat? And does this explain Gladstone's compliments to him at Liverpool? If he does rat, farewell to the Tory party; the smash his desertion would make would reconcile one to having his detestable presence in Gladstone's cabinet—

Is it not a good omen that Whitmore ceases to salute you? I have sometimes thought that if you would give three weeks to the study of the question you might make yourself an authority in the House about Dockyard & ship-building expenditure. The subject lies almost in a nutshell. Childers & Stansfeld[2] have adopted wrong views. If Hall coached you, you might give a most valuable support to the comptroller of the Navy, whose views will not be represented in the next ministry, & through

---

[1] Frederick Arthur Stanley (1841–1908), M.P. 1865–86, secretary for war 1878–80, for the colonies 1885–6, governor-general of Canada 1888–93; Baron Stanley of Preston 1886, 16th earl of Derby 1893.

[2] Sir James Stansfeld (1820–98), radical, M.P. 1859–95, held minor offices 1864, 1868–71, president of the poor-law board 1871–2, of the local government board 1872–4, 1886, active in the movement for women's rights.

whom you might get information on matters of detail which would establish you as a master on that subject.

Ever yours
<u>R Simpson</u>

708

SIMPSON TO ACTON · 16 NOVEMBER 1868

Monday

Dear Acton

Lambert owns that he has not the semblance of a right to ask you to abstain from mentioning a story which you have on independent authority.

Nevertheless he asks you not to mention it till after Wednesday. On that day he is going to see the person from whom he had it, who he says is an invaluable retriever, & who very possibly told Gladstone as well as him (Lambert) the story. By this means it will not be in print till L. has had an opportunity of assuring the golden egg-layer that it is not through him that the hidden deeds of darkness come to light.

Lambert had just had a long talk with C. Villiers. V. was in a state of the greatest discomfort, which it appears is shared by many of his equals, because Gladstone has not had the slightest communication with any body about the coming Cabinet. He had heard that Bright was to come in with 4 nominees, & Villiers comforted himself that he might be one—But he wondered that Lord Granville had as yet heard nothing from his future chief.

It appears that the Tory candidate for Merthyr Tydvil is a large owner of mines there, who lately in the interests of his men & of the little tradesmen abolished the truck system. Now he threatens to reestablish it if his men & the said small tradesmen do not vote for him.

It is said that such a glut of Tory money for the elections is collected, & the agents are so shy in spending it, that Colonel Taylor[1] is thinking of stimulating a liberal opposition in Dublin County to afford him the opportunity of spending out handsomely that the memory may stand him in stead at some future election or elections.

Brande[2] says that the Irish Church question will be the death of two ministries after this one is kicked out. He fancies that the distribution

---

[1] Thomas Edward Taylor (1811–83), in Royal Army 1829–46, lieutenant-colonel in the militia, M.P. for county Dublin 1841–83, chancellor of the duchy of Lancaster 1868, 1874–80.

[2] Probably Sir Henry Brand (1814–92), M.P. 1852–84, Liberal chief whip 1866–8, speaker 1872–84, created Viscount Hampden 1884.

& appropriation of the funds will divide the party. Surely however at present it is more a question of investment than of spending; the funds will come in so slowly that it may be years before there is a great round sum to deal with. In the meantime the accumulating capital might be invested in Irish Railways. I hope that the Measure, like Reform, will be divided into two bills; one enacting disestablishment, disendowment, & a commission for receiving & investing the funds; & the other for their appropriation.

Renouf's & the other Reports will show that there are national schoolmasters in Ireland who nominally receive only 14£ a year, really but £7. And that in one place the schoolmaster & his wife occupy a stable—one stall being bedroom, the other their drawing room.

Renouf makes out with arithmetical certainty that the only safer denominational system for Ireland is the present national system. The Protestant owners of 8/9^{ths} of Ireland can now get no government aid for their proselytizing schools, & in consequence they are dwindling to nothing. Under a denominational system they would of course get grants, & their schools would flourish as they did some five or six years ago.

Thanks for your speech—have you seen the Daily News upon it? I have not, but have heard of it. You should get the article reprinted, for it flatters a constituency to find its candidate treated as one of the torchbearers of intellectual progress in the centre of national movement.

Wallis has been performing a feat. He closed the old Tablet with a Tory manifesto, & is the author of a Liberal manifesto in the new one (I believe) signed *a Liberal Catholic*.[1] He will have some ado to explain himself. He is a wise rat, & we always knew him to be *in utrumque paratus*.

Send me a report of your Hustings exhibition; how is it you don't convert your Journal? or are its leaders, liberal when its chief reports are Tory?

In an article in one of the Pall Malls of last week—Our *own irreproachable press*—is a sentence about "the partiality of Government (the French) functionaries in distributing those douceurs which are so handsomely disguised in most civilized States as Government advertisements". I don't know whether it indicates a knowledge of the story on the part of the writer; perhaps the sentence is worth quoting as an introduction to your tale.

Is Bright to be Irish Secretary, as some one says in a speech in today's Times? And are you going to propose or second the amendment on the address?

[1] In fact Wallis (a Tory) had sold the *Tablet* to Herbert (later Cardinal) Vaughan, who supported Gladstone in the 1868 election.

I hope all my news is not either stale or fabulous. Wishing you all good luck I am

Ever yours
R Simpson

Deane who knows your opponent told me a propos of his present of his photograph to every elector that he once found on the table of a young lady friend of his a *carte de visite* album, each portrait of which was described My self, *pris a gauche*; Myself in profile—Myself exhibiting my back hair—Myself's dog—Myself's favourite breech loader—Myself's nephew &c &c—every entry beginning with the same modest word. Deane wondered that such a gorilla should have amassed such a heap of ugliness; but that he should lend it abroad, to lie in public in women's drawing rooms, provoked his spleen. Of course the Myself was Whitmore.

709

SIMPSON TO ACTON · 19 NOVEMBER 1868

Nov. 19.

Alas! Alas!—but you will have more time for the Quarterly. Is there no bribery, no intimidation, no corruption that will justify risking the 1000£ you will have to deposit for preliminary expenses?[1] or is the gorilla to sit till the end of the Parliament?

Ever yours
R Simpson

710

ACTON TO SIMPSON · 20 NOVEMBER 1868*

Dear Simpson,

You may suppose how we liked being beaten by such an opponent, with the No Popery cry, and how strongly we begin by believing in the corruption as well as the iniquity of the Bridgenorth majority.

Our grand point was to get me seconded by a clergyman, Mr Ward, master of the grammar school. He takes some subordinate part in the services at St Leonard's where Mr. Bellett,[2] a great Tory, is parson.

---

[1] Simpson assumed that Acton would challenge his opponent's election.
* The opening sentence is quoted in *Lord Acton: The Decisive Decade*, p. 18.
[2] Probably George Bellett, born *c.* 1798, B.A. (Dublin) 1820, listed as 'of Bridgnorth, Salop, cler.' when his eldest son George, aged 19, matriculated at Oxford in 1854.

Bellett now tells him that his parishioners declare they will leave the church if Ward officiates any more.

Ward offers to stay away one Sunday, but no more, unless Bellett himself requests him, which he has not yet done. But he says that in that case he will make the thing public. He asks me whether I can make him sure of access for the story in the press, to which I shall say yes— and therefore write to ask you to promote it in any way you can, if we do send you the story for publication.

By this letter I am only fortifying myself, to be able to tell him that he may be sure of publicity, if he resolves to use it. At present he only wants it as a threat to Bellett.

Ever Your's
J D Acton

711

ACTON TO SIMPSON · ?20 NOVEMBER 1868

Dear Simpson,

Ward now says that Bellett has not yet asked him, personally, to stay away; but he thinks his hands might be strengthened to resist the pressure which he admits to be unjust, by some expression of public opinion. The only blame due to Bellett is for having truckled to his parishioners and asked his friend to submit to it. If you can get a word or paragraph said on the subject any where, it would be a very desirable thing for the peace of this borough.

In great haste,
Ever Your's
JDA.

712

ACTON TO SIMPSON · ?20 NOVEMBER 1868

Dear Simpson,

Here is a third letter. Ward is very anxious for a statement of the case in a letter from you to the Times. Could you do that with the materials you have? He has been lending his aid in the Church, of St Leonard's, for 12 years in a friendly way, helping when help was wanted. It is fully admitted that the complaint is due *only* to the fact that he proposed a Catholic and a Liberal—Bellett himself allows this. A letter stating these facts, and ending by wondering whether the Revd G. Bellett has yielded to his fanatical parishioners, or has had the courage to stand by his friend, and his own opinion—might be of great service. Perhaps you could do it sending this enclosure to the Editor. It would be a great joy to us.

Y^{rs} ever truly
JDA

713

SIMPSON TO ACTON · 21 NOVEMBER 1868

Nov. 21

Dear Acton

I have put the facts together & sent them with your note to Delane,[1] & I hope the letter will appear on Monday.[2]

Should you be any more sure of Bridgenorth with ballot? Have you even considered De Grey's notion of life peerages, & what you would do if Gladstone offered you one? I fear me for the prospects of Catholics in the English or Scottish side of the Dom Com.[3] We routed the chairman of the Protestant association in E. Surrey yesterday. On Tuesday Mid Surrey comes on. The danger is that Marsh Nelson[4] is a third liberal candidate. He is a servant of Rothschild,[5] who suffered in the City through the desertion of the stricter Jews who are scandalized at his wet Judaism. Julian Goldsmid[6] is one of these and Rothschild is said to furnish Marsh Nelson with 10,000 to filch votes from Goldsmid—

Poor Hartington—Bruce—Gibson—Mill—Acton[7]—now the list of killed and wounded mask the triumph. We were discussing your chances of this and that last week, & I will not tell you what we—Wetherell & I —concluded on—

Ever yours—& all the more in disappointment—

R Simpson

---

[1] John Thadeus Delane (1817–79), editor of *The Times* 1841.
[2] *The Times*, 23 November 1868, p. 9, signed 'R.S.'.
[3] House of Commons.
[4] Marsh Nelson was last in the poll, with an insignificant number of votes.
[5] Baron Lionel de Rothschild (1808–79), financier, M.P. 1858–74.
[6] Sir Julian Goldsmid (1838–96), 3rd baronet 1878, barrister, M.P. 1865–8, 1870–80, 1885–96, privy councillor 1895, active in London University and Jewish affairs.
[7] Liberal candidates defeated despite the general Liberal victory.

SIMPSON TO ACTON · 14 DECEMBER 1868

Clapham Dec. 14

Dear Acton

I had a talk with Wetherell upon the subject of a literary article for April fool's day[1]—We discussed Bulwer—too long—Other people too short—or too something else—At last Kingsley seemed the only available one for the present continuation of the course that began with the Miserables & ended in Thackeray.[2] But we were both so full of objections, that the discussion would never have ceased, but for my lucky thought of referring to you. Can you think of any body else, or better than Kingsley. Bulwer & Trollope would take too long reading. And if we decide on Kingsley, can you lend me any of his novels or other books that ought to be read? And have you any ideas about him that you will lend me? He is not much of a fellow whose *genius* to discuss, but perhaps he is a peg to hold up an article—

I saw the short account of the dinner at Bridgnorth, & your Member's speech—was he drunk? Or is it his nature to? Bestow on me half an hours consideration & believe me

Ever yours
R Simpson—

When you see Chancellor O'Hagan[3] urge upon him the release of the Fenians[4]—It would so clench Gladstone's popularity in Ireland.

715

ACTON TO SIMPSON · 17 DECEMBER 1868

Aldenham
Thursday

My dear Simpson,

In deciding the claims of Bulwer Trollope & Kingsley, I think you ought not to be influenced by the amount that there will be to read. In that respect Kingsley will be easiest, Trollope not difficult, and Bulwer the work of about 10 days.

---

[1] For the April issue of the *North British Review*, which Wetherell was expected to edit. This article was never published.
[2] Articles in the *Home & Foreign Review*.
[3] Thomas O'Hagan had just become Lord Chancellor of Ireland.
[4] Irish republican nationalist rebels, several of whom had been imprisoned.

Trollope will be the one least congenial to yourself, except in the matter of parsons and bishops. He is not a great thinker, or an influence among men who think. He is interesting as an artist, and so far worthy of dissection, but there are not many ideas to trace, and there is a certain monotony in his methods. I think you would find him a topic for recreation, not for an article of mark. Some day a recreative paper, pure and simple, may be much wanted. But not at first.

I hardly know Kingsley, and have not been attracted by what I know of him. But he has a view, a message, as they say, in which there is something definite and a purpose. I conjecture that he is a focus of various views and doctrines that pervade society, and so may be made a text. As he is an enemy he also requires dissection.

But if he has a system, it is not to be found in his novels only. It would be necessary to take him in all his manifestations—his lectures, his books on the Teutons and the old régime, probably his sermons. And the man would be incomplete without his attack on our priests, and his infelicitous selection of Newman as their representative.

So that if you deal with him, you might almost as well be dealing with Mill or Carlyle.

Bulwer's philosophy is in his novels, and he is superior as a subject to the rest, because he has developed, and reveals several distinct phases. Only his message was to a generation now a little gone by. I don't believe he is much of a force at present. That may be taken as a reason why he should be treated like a corpse.

Is not Dickens the richest subject? His views of life are concealed under his art, and he has a touch of the divine spark.

I have none of Kingsley's books, nor of Bulwer; but most of Trollope, and nearly all of Dickens.

O'Hagan forced me to admit that it will not be safe to let out all the Fenians; but he promises to weed them at once, and to restore the Habeas Corpus as soon as parliament meets. He says Gladstone is confident of beating the Lords.[1] I am afraid our member has not the genial vice of drunkenness, like his chief.

Ever Your's

J D Acton

Pray tell Renouf that Odo R.[2] says his pamphlet[3] is denounced to the C. Indicis.[4]

[1] On the disestablishment of the Irish Church.
[2] Russell.
[3] *The Condemnation of Pope Honorius*, which was placed on the Index of Forbidden Books.
[4] Congregation of the Index.

SIMPSON TO ACTON · 19 DECEMBER 1868

Clapham, Dec. 19.

Dear Acton

I think I will try Bulwer. If he is longest, he is also I fancy simplest. Do you mind now telling me, if you know—1. What are his typical novels—for I cannot read them all—it would overload me too much with detail. 2. What are the best & most comprehensive articles written about him. For I ought to know what my predecessors have said, if I aim at planting my pole a few inches further in space than they have planted theirs. Have you any notions about Bulwer in general that you could give me? It is so much easier to go in to a man with some chart, even though its lines have all to be drawn over again. So your roughest impressions would be thankfully received.

I shall see Renouf tomorrow & will tell him what O Russell says.

Have you read Dilke's *Greater Britain,* or *Grant Duff's* Survey of politics?—or Bholanauth Chunder's *Travels of a Hindoo* in Bengal?[1] The last is a very curious book, out of which a man may learn more about a Bengalee's turns of thinking than out of all other books that I have ever looked at.

Ever yours
R Simpson

717

ACTON TO SIMPSON · 20 DECEMBER 1868

Aldenham
Sunday

Dear Simpson,

Pelham[2] shows the capital with which Bulwer started, Eugene Aram contains his Psychology. E. Maltravers and Alice are his most thoughtful work in the earlier period. The Last of the Barons his greatest historical novel. Athens shows his learning, and a remarkable power of translating. Zanoni is an anticipation of his absurd Strange Story.

---

[1] Respectively, Sir Charles Dilke, *Greater Britain* (London, 1868); Sir Mountstuart Elphinstone Grant Duff, *A Political Survey of Europe, Asia and Africa...*(London, Edinburgh, 1868); and Bholanauth Chunder, *The Travels of a Hindoo to various parts of Bengal and Upper India,* 2 vols. (London, 1869).

[2] One of the first (1828) of Edward Bulwer's novels, which are discussed here.

The Caxtons begin a new phase, and yet it is not original—So that most of his progress is the effect of real study, but is governed by outer influences. You hardly trace the development of a mind but rather a succession of studies.

His best works, showing him at his height, are My Novel and What will he do with it. Then the inventive and constructive faculty seems to have been exhausted.

You cannot read less than all these; and I suppose Pelham, E. Aram, Maltravers, and the Caxtons, mark the stages best.

Höfer (Didot)'s Dictionnaire refers to the following criticisms, which I have not looked out: Edinburgh, vols. 53, 55, 57, 61, 64, 65. R. 2 Mondes[1] especially January 1839. Quarterly, 1847.

Don't overlook his England & the English, and his Reform Speech in May 1861. Observe his mystical tendency, and what has it to do with religion? Absence of passion and ill temper, in most of his books, his high idea of art, in plot and style, and in the toning down of all asperities. Momentary fondness for rogues, and desire to see the good in them. I suppose a reminiscence of the Satanic school. Serenity of his later novels.

In fact I know very little of him, being repelled by his foppery, his unreality, his want of robustness, his pretentious learning, and his way of using reminiscences of other men's books. You almost always smell the lamp, until you come to the Caxtons, and often after.

I am afraid you will ruin some of the fibres, if you don't look at his other novels.

Grant Duff has sent me his idlebook, but I can read nothing. I am to write about the German historians, of whom there are 300, who write 30 volumes each.

Ever Your's
J D Acton

718

ACTON TO SIMPSON · 6 FEBRUARY 1869

Dear Simpson,

I have already done what was in my power to obtain the Tasmanian appointment for F. Weld.[2] There is a horrible story about to the effect that Monsell is wasting power in getting colonial offices for every Irishman he can think of—which is sure to produce a reaction in the

---

[1] *Revue des deux Mondes.*

[2] Frederick Weld was appointed governor of Western Australia in 1869; he received the Tasmanian governorship in 1875.

office[1] sooner or later. I hope not before Tasmania gets the right governor.

I can send you most of Dicken's novels, but I have nothing of Browning, except an impression that he is not the wisest of men. Tortures won't make me read his poetry. But he is a very apt and congruous subject.[2]

Barring a Catholic speech in the Potteries on Monday, I shall be kept in town all next week. Do you frequent the B.M.?[3] I met the condemned but finally impenitent accuser of Honorius[4] there yesterday.

I will try to help forward W's[5] plans while I am here, and mean to call on Glyn[6] today.

Ever Your's
J D Acton

719

ACTON TO SIMPSON · 27 FEBRUARY 1869

Thomas Hotel
Friday night

My dear Simpson,

Wetherell says that he has sent you Sigerson's[7] paper of suggestions. Sigerson wished it published in the Times, but we got him to consent to its being made into a letter of moderate compass. Wetherell is knocked up, and I cannot get time, as we remain only 2 days more in town, and I have much to do. Will you try it? It will make a very good letter, and I think I can get it admitted. If you have a couple hour's leisure, do see what you can do, and meet me at Wetherell's on Sunday afternoon at 4 or 5 o'clock.

I cannot tell you how upset I was by the news of Bergenroth's death yesterday.

I remain
Ever Your's
J D Acton

---

[1] Colonial Office.

[2] Simpson wrote 'Mr. Browning's Latest Poetry', *North British Review*, n.s. xii (October 1869), 97–126.

[3] British Museum.

[4] Renouf, who had revived the condemnation of Pope Honorius I (625–38) for Monothelite heresy as an argument against Papal Infallibility.

[5] Wetherell.

[6] George Grenfell Glyn (1824–87), 2nd Baron Wolverton 1873; banker, M.P. 1857–73, paymaster-general 1880–5, postmaster-general 1886.

[7] George Sigerson (1838–1925), physician and scientist, professor of botany at the Catholic University of Dublin.

SIMPSON TO ACTON · 20 APRIL 1869

Ap 20.

Dear Acton

What do you think of getting up a subscription for the Bollandists to supply partly the loss of their subvention? Buck leaves it to me to do or to forbear—he has thrown cold water on offers from the Emperor of the French, & on a subscription begun in the Brussels Chambers on the ground of their being political protests, & on a Tyrolese subscription on the ground of the poverty of the people, & on a subscription begun by one of the Belgian Bp[s] on the ground that the subscribers might think they had a right to use the Bollandist library as a reading room. But if *I* (R.S.) thought, says Buck, that an English subscription would be neither a political manifesto, nor a measure calculated to interfere with the complete independence of the Bollandists, then I might try & get one together—What do you think of it? And if you approve, will you give say £4, which looks better as 100 francs? If we could get a few literary names, & a few heads of literary departments, such as Duffus Hardy & Winter Jones, it would take away all political appearance from the subscription.

Buck is in correspondence with various heads of the ritualists, & is labouring to find documents not yet much known on which he can base proposals[1]—I can furnish him with a paper of Feckenham,[2] Abbot of Westminster; have you the instructions of the Nuncios sent over to, but not received by, Elizabeth, in the first years of her reign? Also among your papers relating to Cardinal Pole do you know of his commission to the Dean & Chapter of Westminster (Feckenham was this very Dean) authorizing them to give faculties to conforming ministers to minister in suis ordinibus, etiamsi ab haereticis et schismaticis episcopis, etiam minus rite, dummodo in eorum collatione ecclesiastica forma et intentio sit servata—And have you, or do you know of, any evidence of ministers ordained by Edwd VI's bishops being licensed in accordance with the tenor of this commission? Evidently the point is important.

Buck writes—"D'après tout ce que j'apprends—et j'apprends les choses de très-bonne source—les idées les plus modérées triomphent à Rome et ailleurs aussi. Quelques evêques français, peut-être une dixaine, proposeront de proclamer l'infaillibilité du Pape; mais ils n'ont absolument aucune chance de réussir.......Malheureusement Dupanloup est

---

[1] In connection with the movement for corporate reunion of the churches.
[2] John de Feckenham (*c.* 1515–84), dean of St Paul's 1554–6, abbot of Westminster 1556–9, deprived and imprisoned.

pour le moment quasi-aveugle; mais les medicins lui ont promis qui [sic] bientot il pourra lire de nouveau. Il travaille avec une ardeur infatigable l'episcopat allemand et français pour les rendre indulgents envers les orientaux et les anglicans."—

Salutem ex inimicis.

Have you looked at Lecky on Morals?[1] Not a single German author quoted in his notes—I shall have a multitude of questions to ask you upon him, when I begin to write, which I have promised W. to do for October. I studied the matter for certain articles in the Rambler suggested by Montalembert's Monks of the West, so the subject is not entirely new to me, but I am sadly to seek in it.

Renouf hears from Mainz that the theologians there are much disturbed at the rumour of acclaming infallibility at the Council; that the German ultramontanes (not the Jesuits) say it shall not be, even if they have to protract the Council to 18 years—Longman has asked him to reprint Honorius.[2] The Index has clearly given a push to the sale.

Ever yours
R Simpson

721

ACTON TO SIMPSON · 22 APRIL 1869

Aldenham
April 22

My dear Simpson,

I cannot find the things you speak of in Pole's time. I have sent to Paris for an extract from the Acta Consistorialia of Paul IV, in which he speaks of his nuncio sent to Elizabeth, and declares that if Pole was living, he would have him tried. But they will not, I think, furnish what you want.

You shall have my hundred francs whenever you choose to call for them, for the Bollandists. If you can get a certain number of names to start with, will it not be well to publish a letter, asking for the subscriptions of studious men? I don't think it likely that England will make up the 6000 francs of the Belgian government. It does not seem wise of DeBuck to reject the other sources that might avail him. If he chose, he could have subventions from the Emperor of the French and

---

[1] W. E. H. Lecky, *History of European Morals*, 2 vols. (London, 1869). It was reviewed in the *North British Review*, n.s. XI (July 1869), 381–405, not by Simpson but by Charles Merivale.

[2] *The Condemnation of Pope Honorius.*

from the King of Prussia at the same time—without any political preference. Multiply 100 francs by the number of copies of the Acta in England, or by the number of people who use them—in neither case will the sum be large. The Oxford people ought to do something.

I bought Lecky at Parker's on Monday, and have not received him. There cannot be a richer subject for an article, as the comparison of pagan with christian ethics belongs to it. Looking through Lecky will suggest some books to send to you for the purpose.

If Renouf reprints his pamphlet, I suppose he will work his additions up in it, and make a very complete thing. I only wish I could be sure that he would not condescend to his opponents, and would take no notice of the Index.

I hope it will prove to be possible to get a large number of people for the Notices in the NB. It will be impossible to keep up that department with only a few writers, and there is nothing men like doing less.

Ever truly Your's
J D Acton

722

SIMPSON TO ACTON · 24 APRIL 1869

Ap. 24

Dear Acton

Many thanks for your letter—I write this to save you trouble about Lecky. Douglas has an article about him from Merivale which will appear in June. So all my preparations are useless, & I won't be guilty of letting you lose time in the same cause.

Renouf has nearly finished enough[1] to send his first instalment of copy to Germany for the press—I am afraid that he will benigger & befool his opponents—but he will pass over the Index in high silence. I am to look over the proofs. Why does he not let me see the Ms? He will do short notices for the NB. Can you prevail on Sullivan to do again what he did for the H&F?

I have undertaken the political article for June,[2] & have not an idea of what is to be its main line—have you any counsel to give?

Ever yours
R Simpson

---

[1] Of his reply to his critics, *The Case of Honorius Reconsidered with Reference to Recent Apologies* (London, 1869).
[2] Simpson, 'The Irish Church Measure', *North British Review*, n.s. XI (July 1869), 568–601.

SIMPSON TO ACTON · 12 MAY 1869

May 12.

Dear Acton

Blessed is the man in whom the will sufficeth for the deed. Buck writes to stay the subscription—He has made arrangements with Palmé,[1] his Parisian publisher, who bears the expenses, & even goes somewhat beyond, as a business speculation—Therefore instead of asking you for 4£ I offer you a thousand thanks—

Renouf sent off this day a packet of copy of his "Case of Honorius reconsidered in reference to recent apologies" to printers in Germany— I have seen some of it, & got him to strike out epithets & imputations which are sufficiently understood in the argument without articulation— He tells me that he has generally confined his fierceness to his notes. Like the purified editions of the classics which Byron describes in Don Juan—

The Merivale who does Lecky is I think a Mrs Merivale, & not the historian—At any rate his name is not in Douglas' list of contributors[2] —

Ever yours
R Simpson

ACTON TO SIMPSON · 13 MAY 1869

Aldenham May 13

My dear Simpson,

I am very glad our friends have made an arrangement with Palmé. He is a most enterprising man, and nobody knows how he gets his funds, or how long he will last.

You did well to tame the fierceness of the Renovian text, but I always think that a thing fit to last is spoilt by personal animadversion, and fear that the notes will scarcely be worthy of the occasion.

Are you really going to waste your fragrance on the 100th NB?[3]

---

[1] V. Palmé, not further identifiable.

[2] Simpson is in error. The Douglas list (cited in *Wellesley Index*, I, 693) gives 'Dr. Merivale'. David Douglas was publisher and editor of the *North British Review*, 1863–9.

[3] The July *North British Review*, the last issue edited by Douglas.

Without detriment, I hope, to September? Do you never think of working out and testing the doctrines you sent me sketches of last October, touching government expenditure? There is nothing they would be more grateful for than an essay seriously strengthening their economic hands, and they would supply you with information.

What are you going to do for September? It is a dull time of year at which the NB. is not used to awaken many echoes. Has not Deutsch published his article on the Talmud[1] in an enlarged shape? It might be a good nut for Renouf some day.

Who the juice, I wonder, is Mrs. Merivale? It seems like defective editorship to give Lecky to her.

Wetherell writes that he has opened communications with Sullivan. I am persuaded he will join the goodly throng.

Ever Your's

J D Acton

725

SIMPSON TO ACTON · 17 MAY 1869

May 17.

Dear Acton

Till you wrote I never spent a thought on what to write about, politically, for September. But you have given me a hint which may, Wetherell being propitious, be happily carried out. Have you by any chance preserved those papers? And will you let me have them if you have? plus whatever notes & queries you have or might have annexed to them?

The other papers I thought of were one on Browning's *ring & book*.[2] One on the navy, which will be Halls—on the causes[3] which have hitherto made our sailors the best fighters in any navy, & on the tendencies in modern reform which threaten the navy as a school of personal superiority. Then I have already written an article on genealogical researches on Shakespeare. These three, plus a political article, will be more than enough of me, & W will have something to hold over for Xmas, when I hope to be in Naples. You must tell me what is to be done there.

I have heard rumours of Deutsch being published separately. Certainly it would be nuts to Renouf, who longs to pitch into the man's

---

[1] Emanuel Deutsch, 'The Talmud', *Quarterly Review*, CXXIII (October 1867), 417–64.

[2] 'Mr. Browning's Latest Poetry' (a review of *The Ring and the Book*) was the only article Simpson published in October.

[3] Simpson originally wrote 'reasons' at this point.

shallowness; & I suppose you give him rope for personalities in a Quarterly. W. I think hopes to get some little birds & beasts[1] out of him, that he may garnish his first dish with a few of the unintelligibles that he so loves & admires, without wondering at them in the least.

We are going to spend a couple of days with Prestwich the geologist tomorrow. I hope to book him, but I doubt—A paper by him on the water supply of London might be appropriate to a thirsty autumn, such as some weather-prophets foretell, with the Thames so dry as to be forded at London Bridge at low water—on stilts, I presume, of no length in particular.

Renouf came across a nun teacher last week who not liking to teach her infants A for Ass had changed her alphabetical lore into A for Donkey.

Ever yours
R Simpson

I forgot to tell you that my taskmaster has made me write the political article for this coming number—It will be jolly bosh—on the Irish Church Bill & debate[2]—

726

SIMPSON TO ACTON · 2 JUNE 1869

June 2.

Dear Acton

Renouf, who is on an inspecting tour, has received his first proofs, & is profoundly desirous to know what his motto is, & which of the Greek philosophers it was that enunciated the sentence "strike but hear"—What are the Greek words, & what the reference to Diogenes Laertius—whom I have turned over in vain—or elsewhere—Can you give me this school-boy's information, & if so, will you do so by return of post as Mrs R. is impatient to send the proof to Germany.

Ever yours
R Simpson

[1] Hieroglyphic characters, which Renouf included in his Egyptological reviews.
[2] 'The Irish Church Measure.'

727

ACTON TO SIMPSON · 3 JUNE 1869

Ἐπαραμένου δὲ τὴν βακτηρίαν ὡς πατάξοντος, ὁ Θεμιστοκλῆς ἔφη "πάταξον μέν, ἄκουσον δέ."

Plutarch. Themistocles cap. II.

Dear Simpson,
Of course you could not find it in Diogenes. Moreover it was never spoken, for Herodotus has not got it.

Ever Your's
JDA

Aldenham
Thursday

728

SIMPSON TO ACTON · 5 JUNE 1869

June 5

Dear Acton
Many thanks for the quotation which Renouf had all right—a doubt must have across him just as he was starting on his journey, & that doubt has cost me at least some hours of Diogenes.

Will you tell Wetherell that I intended to send him the article[1] today, but that I have not had time to do the erasing part, which is almost as much trouble as the positive building up. It is finished as far as the House of Lords allows it to be.

Ever yours
R Simpson

Many thanks for your sketch of an article. Block would be the man to do the statistical part of it.

[1] 'The Irish Church Measure.'

SIMPSON TO ACTON · 16 JUNE 1869

Friday June 16

Dear Acton

I ascertained today that you were back again, but failed to find out on what day it would be convenient to you to meet Hall. What say you to Tuesday the 27th or Thursday the 29th? Either day would suit the Halls, so in consideration of your possible engagements, will you let me give you your choice of the day? If you can come, I trust that Lady Acton will be able to come with you. Hall would prefer the 27th to shirk the ball at Buckingham Palace. For the hour let us say 7.30.

Forgive this unwieldy kind of invitation, & believe me

Ever yours
R Simpson

729A

SIMPSON TO ACTON · 16 AUGUST 1869

Aug. 16.

Dear Acton

As October draws near I begin to feel that I ought to have some ideas about a political article. I am not strong enough in finance. Wetherell proposes a subject—the new position of the Tory party—the modifications in its policy, power, & aspirations introduced by its conduct of Reform, & by its acceptance of the Irish Church Bill.[1] That seems not a bad subject, but it seems also to be a part of the general modification of parties. It seems to take in the sketch you gave for the Prospectus of the New Series of the NB. My object then is to know, whether you propose doing an article on that subject—for if you ever intend doing it, I should be most sorry to mar your work by my very unequal previous effort. My next object is to ask your charity to lend me some topics— just jot down some of the things you think ought to be treated, & I will consider whether I am in a position to write on them, or to get them up. I shall be thankful for any hints or suggestions.

Next, I want to ask another favour. I think of spending next winter at Naples, where of course I shall have to work for Wetherell. But I could make myself twice as useful if you would put me up to places &

---

[1] Not published.

persons where & of whom I might procure proper information—I suppose you know all about the present aspect of your native place, & so might suggest what to look after in the interests of the Review.

These two things seem enough to ask you in one letter, but there is a third—a message from Roberts. He says, O that you could get a copy of the process against Galileo. He is soon going to publish his paper about him, but I suppose would hold his hand if he saw a chance of consulting the original of a document of w^h he has only been able to collect disjecta membra.

Renouf sends off his last sheet of Honorius[1] today. I am apprehensive of a rupture between Wetherell & him; R. has wrapped himself in Bull's hide, & has been impervious to W's questions about Orientalism—thinking that a man who never heard of the nail head characters[2] cannot know much even of the alphabet of the subject. & W. thinks that the absence of answers has amounted to "brutal insolence". I have not let Renouf know a syllable about W's state of mind, for of course he would at once cry off the whole affair, & on the other hand I don't see how I can avoid it, for R. has goodnaturedly undertaken to advise Wetherell on Oriental subjects generally, to tell him what book ought to be done by what man etc; This W. does not altogether accept, but insists on R's taking a "department" as he calls it, undertaking, in words, a responsibility which no one, not paid for editorial work, will fulfil in act—when I read a passage out of W's last letter to me, he happily professed not to understand it—otherwise I am afraid he would have rejected it, & then W. would have rejected him, & made an everlasting breach. It is a rent to be patched with cloth of any colour. In the mean time condole with me on the delicacy of a negotiation which to my undiplomatic habits is a grievous nuisance.

Ever yours
R Simpson

When shall you be up in Town?

729B

SIMPSON TO ACTON · 7 SEPTEMBER 1869

Sept. 7. 1869

Dear Acton

Mrs Renouf has sent me the enclosed with a request that I would send it on to you at once, as Renouf is somewhere in the Black Country, inspecting.

---

[1] *The Case of Honorius Reconsidered.*   [2] Cuneiform.

When I wrote last to you I did not know you were out of England, & you have wisely abstained from troubling yourself with answering my questions—For the political article Wetherell has been putting me through a course of Disraeli, to make me get him his anti-Conservative Tory theory, so as to talk about the new basis of the party when it can reorganize itself. I have also had the grace to write an article on Browning[1] which Wetherell professes not to be able to understand, & thereupon suggests a rearrangement without rewriting. He seems very much behind hand with his short notices, & anticipates that his first number will be a failure. But he is an adept in the art of encouraging his fellow workmen by trying to inoculate them with his own sanguine despondency.

Gladstone was very ill reported of by Lambert before he went down to Walmer. A chronic diarrhea which the Doctors feared depended upon some mischief in the train, and a kind of presentment that he was not destined to survive sixty—Let us hope this has all gone. Lambert called on Dizzy[2] just at he end of the Session, & had from him a most amusing account of the history of Cairns'[3] *coup d'état* in the concluding scene of the bill—I will not write it, partly because it is too long, & partly because I Dont know that L. would allow it. Gladstone has now commissioned him to get up the land question in Ireland—thither therefore Lambert has gone, & so I have not the benefit of his talks in getting up my political article—It seems absurd for me, with my secluded habits, & without any body to talk to, to be expected to get up the political article for what the Editor is pleased to call the party Review. I dont see that W. has received any of the information which you confidently anticipated we should get. And if we get none the article will only be a critical, theoretical affair, which readers will attribute to the influence of the silly season.

Ever yours,
R Simpson

---

[1] 'Mr. Browning's Latest Poetry.'
[2] Disraeli.
[3] Hugh McCalmont Cairns (1819–85), barrister 1844, M.P. 1852–66, solicitor general 1858–9, attorney general 1866, lord chancellor 1868, 1874–80; created baron 1867, earl 1878. As Tory leader in the Lords, Cairns accepted a compromise on the Suspensory Bill without consulting his party.

ACTON TO SIMPSON · 18 SEPTEMBER 1869

Herrnsheim
Sept. 18

Dear Simpson,

I have been too bad in my correspondence. Wetherell has held me in such a vice that I have neglected the duties of life in a truly shameful way. The Museum business[1] thrusts the NB. aside for today's post.

I am rather far off to take the initiative not knowing what may be doing from day to day. I have written to Lowe, inserting a poisoned arrow touching the state of the B.M. library, which is sure to work. But the best thing will be to get Lord Granville or Gladstone to refer to me for testimonia, which I should give in a way that will be decisive. If they can only be got to ask for my opinion, I think Renouf is safe. They both labour under a profound delusion which will be highly salutary.

Touching Galilei. There is no chance of my seeing the MS. The Oct. NB.[2] shuts the door of the Vatican archives against me. But, it has been seen by L'Epinois,[3] and minutely described. I don't think much more can be learnt about it. L'Epinois added a supplement in the Revue des Sciences Historiques.

In grievous haste and trouble,
Your's ever sincerely
J D Acton

When shall we meet? I am going to Munich and Austria, and hope to be at Venice between the 16 and 20 of October, and at Rome by Nov. 3. Shall you take Rome on your way?

---

[1] An attempt to secure the position of keeper of printed books at the British Museum for Renouf. See Acton to Renouf, 18, 19 and 30 September 1869, in *Lord Acton: The Decisive Decade*, pp. 74–7.

[2] Acton had two articles in the *North British Review*, n.s. XII (October 1869): 'The Massacre of St Bartholomew', 30–70, and 'The Pope and the Council', 127–35.

[3] Henri Charles Fernand Ernest de Buchère, comte de l'Epinois (1831–90), French historian, had access to the Vatican archives.

730A

SIMPSON TO ACTON · 3 OCTOBER 1869

Oct 3.

Dear Acton

Renouf, who has just started for month's inspection, is in a fix. Birch[1] told him some days ago that he did not envy Watts'[2] successor because his time was wholly taken up with settling feuds between the assistants; & yesterday he had two corroborative communications—one public, an article in the Spectator, which said that the duties were impossible, that Watts had killed himself by devoting his nights as well as days to the work, & recommending a modification in the arrangements before the appointment of a successor. Another a private letter from Bruce,[3] recommending him not to try for so laborious an office, & telling him that it was only administrative & that he would to manage 100 subordinates. Mrs Renouf spoke to me in despair this morning. As I first led him into the mess, & think it my duty to do what is possible to get him out of it, I went to see him for a few minutes before his departure this morning, & asked him whether he would consent to my writing to you to tell you this. He was glad of the offer. I then said, it seems to me that you should only demand a slight modification—that the head assistant who now has 450£ a year, should have 500£ & take off your hands all the work connected with the readers & the reading room; & that you, with the ordinary salary should have all the other departments—namely the development of the library—its arrangement—& the cataloging. He thought that he should be only too happy to get this. Any how, the office as Watts had it, would leave him less leisure than the one he has now, & would not be a bit more literary. Jones & Watts had no idea of the development of a library quâ library, & save all their energies to the perfecting the reading department, leaving the higher function to take care of itself. It is time now to change all this—to leave the administrative arrangements to administrators, & to let the scholar have proper scholar's work. If this cannot be done—or is not promised to be done on Renouf's accepting the office, he would rather remain where he is.

I hope you are right about the majority of English Bishops going against Manning. Brown of Newport certainly would be glad to do so.

[1] Samuel Birch (1817–85), Egyptologist, entered British Museum 1844, keeper of oriental antiquities 1861.

[2] Thomas Watts (1811–69), keeper of printed books in the British Museum 1866.

[3] Henry Austin Bruce (1815–95), M.P. 1852–68, 1869–73, vice-president of the council for education 1864–6, home secretary 1868–73, lord president 1873–4; created Baron Aberdare 1873.

He encouraged me to abuse the Archbishop, & told me how, in the meeting of Bishops, he propounded the doctrine that all the property left in trust to the Bishops for Catholic purposes, was the private property of the Pope, in such sense that they were bound, at his command, to supersede the uses for w^h the property was devised, & to apply it to such purposes as he directed—This he agreed with me was abominable, & ought to raise a storm in the country. Don't mention either his or my name if you make use of this information. B. however thinks that a way may be found to define the Pope's personal infallibility.

Ever yours
R Simpson

Have you ever read Paul IV's Bull "Cum ex Apostolatus Officio" Cherubius Vol 1. p739 & tried to fancy the effect of putting into action ¶5 for a single day?

731

ACTON TO SIMPSON · 8 OCTOBER 1869

St Martin, Ried, Upper Austria
Oct. 8

My dear Simpson,

If so small a change would satisfy Renouf, I think he will be able to get the first assistant made supreme in the Reading Room,[1] but subject to him. In several of the letters I have written, I have spoken of the necessity of great reforms in the book Department, so that, if Renouf is appointed, they will be quite prepared for some such proposal from him. But the separation of the library and the reading room cannot be made complete. The supreme authority over all these subordinates will still be in Renouf's hands, and there will be some unwillingness to deprive readers of all help from him. I don't think Winter Jones spent much time in the Reading Room when he was Keeper.

If Renouf means to make the proposal as a condition of his accepting the office, he ought to know his case well before hand, so as to explain it to the Trustees, and make them see what they would gain. Watts was a man of no sort of authority.

I have never said anything about the English bishops, as I know nothing, and believe that not one of them would be proof against the strong inducements to submit to Rome.[2] What I heard was that only two were

---

[1] At the British Museum.
[2] On the issue of Papal Infallibility.

quite Manningite, and the others open to treatment. Your description of Dr Brown is what I should call thoroughly Roman. The only real division is between those who think it somewhat possible, and those who think it utterly impossible. Rome has nothing to fear from bishops who question the opportuneness of the thing. Nevertheless I still feel very confident that the thing will not be done.

What are your own plans and movements? We expect to be at Venice about the 23^d and at Florence about the 28^h

Ever Your's
J D Acton

732

SIMPSON TO ACTON · 9 NOVEMBER 1869

4 Victoria Road
Clapham Nov. 9.

Dear Acton

I have but just returned from the W. of Eng. where I have been the last month; but I hope I am not too late in telling you that Mrs Renouf thinks that the Speaker's reply to you shows the necessity of trying to get Winter Jones at least to acquiesce in R's nomination. She says that you were to get Ld Granville to speak to Panizzi. Could he not add speech to Winter Jones? or if W.J. is not thus approached will you write to him? or should R. get Grant Duff[1] to see him?

Mrs Renouf also begs me to remind you of Stevenson & Gladstone.

I have taken the liberty of giving a New Yorker a Note of introduction to you. You have often heard of him from me & you will find him excellently posted up in all the politics of his country & craft. I was going to write much of what he will say to you, but what need, when you will soon see him?

The Egyptologue's second part[2] is not out yet, though the printers have had the last proof more than a month. I hope you will have it in time to notice for the January NB. M^{rs} R was speculating on the least costly process of sending you copies—Whether through Spitzover? or in any other way direct from Germany, when it is printed. Wetherell has told me that you had smelt out the undigested sediment of old note books in my article[3] in the current number—& laid to my charge some

---

[1] Sir Mountstuart Elphinstone Grant Duff (1829–1906), M.P. 1857–81, undersecretary for India 1868–74, for the colonies 1880–1, governor of Madras 1881–6; diarist with a wide range of acquaintances.

[2] Renouf's reply to his critics, on Pope Honorius.

[3] 'Mr. Browning's Latest Poetry.'

grievous historical blunder, which I hope is not mine but Browning's own—as a critic I ought to have corrected it & not adopted it, but sometimes Homer nods, especially if it is not Homer but a very ignorant rhapsodist. Did you have the grace to read R's little beasts & birds, or the Babylonian nail-heads?[1] Wetherell gave Smith,[2] the writer of the last, a breakfast yesterday. He has promoted him to the Assyrian department, & given him Lepsius on the points of contact between Assyrian & Egyptian chronology to do for the next number.[3] The man drops his H's, & W. thinks—he is a Jew. W. will have a large collection of Hebrews on his staff. If Salisbury[4] succeeds in thrusting Contarini Fleming[5] out of all hopes of regaining the first portfolio of Trinacria, perhaps he may join, & accept the imaginative department. I suppose you have seen the article in the Quarterly[6] which does penance for the tactics, not for the principles, of the party. There he is plainly pointed at as the most infamous of men, who has aimed at sham power for the show of power, & sacrificed all principle in the pursuit. The *Times* is still in his interest, & only this morning, a propos of the Lord Mayors dinner speeches, sneers at the ministry of all the Virtues,[7] which it contrasts with the audacious exhibition of last year. W. wants me rather to err on the other tack, & to exhibit Conservatism as founded on Ignorance, selfishness, & cowardice, & its reverse on knowledge, generosity, & bravery—which may be true in the abstract, but is so untrue in the concrete that its assertion could hardly keep clear of the farcical, & the eleven men in buckram.[8] But perhaps so it behoves the Organ of All the virtues to speak, in spite of the laughter of the groundlings.

Once more commending the New Yorker to your attention when he turns up, I conclude

Yours ever

R Simpson

---

[1] Cuneiform characters.

[2] George Smith (1840–76), self-trained Assyriologist, entered British Museum 1867, discovered Chaldean account of the deluge 1872, led expedition to Nineveh 1873–4.

[3] Smith's articles were 'Babylonian and Assyrian Libraries', *North British Review*, n.s. xii (January 1870), 305–24, and 'Assyrian Annals', *ibid*. xiii (July 1870), 323–65.

[4] Robert Arthur Talbot Gascoyne-Cecil (1830–1903), 3rd marquess of Salisbury 1868, M.P. 1853–68, secretary for India 1866–7, 1874–8, foreign secretary 1878–80, prime minister 1885–6, 1886–92, 1895–1902. In 1869 he was opposed to Disraeli as leader of the Conservatives.

[5] Disraeli. *Contarini Fleming* was an early (1832) novel by him.

[6] Salisbury, 'The Past and the Future of the Conservative Party', *Quarterly Review*, cxxvii (October 1869), 538–61. Simpson responded to this with 'The Repentance of the Tory Party', *North British Review*, n.s. xii (January 1870), 478–508.

[7] Gladstone's ministry, 1868–74.

[8] 'O monstrous! eleven buckram men grown out of two.' *King Henry IV, Part I*, ii, ii.

SIMPSON TO ACTON · 9 NOVEMBER 1869*

4 Victoria Road
Clapham. Nov. 9.[1]

Dear Acton

I have but just returned from a month in the West, so I am rather late in answering your last. Mrs Renouf thinks that the Speaker's reply to you shows the necessity of bringing to bear some influence on Winter Jones to make him at least acquiesce in Renouf's candidature. She says also that you were going to get Lord Granville to speak to Panizzi— would it not be even more to the purpose if he spoke to Winter Jones? Or if W.J. is not communicated with in that way can you write to him, or can you name any one who could influence him?

Mrs Renouf also begs me to remind you of Stevenson.

I have taken the liberty of giving Father Hecker, the Paulist of New York, a letter of introduction for you. You will be very glad to know a man of such energy of character. He has great influence with the Episcopate of the U.S. & of Canada, & he thinks that the former at least will go the right way, & withstand to the last any innovation. He and the Archbishop of Halifax[2] dined with me on Sunday. Renouf met them. He has every confidence in Hecker, & much confidence in the Abp. whose acknowledged ignorance might make him dupe of men like Manning. But he has at present the grace to think Manning an impostor if not a hypocrite. The US. Bishops want to hold caucus meetings at the American college, & to secure some German Bishop as their Spokesman. Hecker asked me about it, & I said that I thought character was more than erudition in such matters, & I would rather trust the Abp of St Louis[3] than Hefele[4] to stand stiff against the allurements & terrors of the Curia. Anyhow Hecker would be glad if you would introduce him to the Bishops you know.

---

* Most of the two paragraphs beginning 'I have taken the liberty' is quoted in Con-zemius, II (München, 1965), 8, n. 10. A few other lines are quoted by Hugh A. MacDougall, *The Acton–Newman Relations: The Dilemma of Christian Liberalism* (New York, 1962), p. 115.

[1] This letter (which overlaps Letter 732) had not been received by Acton when he replied with Letter 734.

[2] Thomas Connolly (1815–76), Irish-born Canadian priest, bishop of St John 1852, archbishop of Halifax 1859, opposed the definition of Papal Infallibility.

[3] Peter Richard Kenrick (1806–96), Irish-born American priest, coadjutor bishop of St Louis 1841, bishop 1843, archbishop 1847, retired 1891; one of the strongest opponents of Papal Infallibility at Vatican I.

[4] Karl Joseph von Hefele (1809–93), professor of church history at Tübingen 1837, bishop of Rottenburg 1869.

Renouf's second part has probably been long printed, but he has received no copies. The Archbishop of Halifax is willing to have 20 sent to him—& to distribute them, but only on the condition that the question of infallibility is mooted. I have told R. that I thought it would be better to have them sent to you through the Bavarian Minister, or in some such way as will do away with sinister chances of confiscation & you would distribute them more intelligently, & without the condition of the Abp of Halifax. I have entreated the last named to take in tow some of our poor English sheep—especially recommending to his care Vaughan,[1] who came in on Sunday under the wing of Coffin. I think that the English & Irish Bishops should be acted on through the Americans who are perfectly misunderstood at Rome—they have the art of hiding an uncompromising resistance under the show of the most hearty loyalty, & so they are more listened to than we are, who if we resist, generally resist without that show. Hecker as a missionary, with a vocation to convert the semiliterary class in the U.S. puts this truth into the first place—that it is impossible to believe against evidence, & not only impossible but wicked to attempt it—So he is toto caelo opposed to the Jesuit school, whose triumph he thinks would be the greatest of calamities. I see that I have forgotten to tell you that he is procurator at the Council for the Bp of Columbus Ohio.[2]

Wetherell is somewhat in despair at the special papalism of the NB —at which I on the contrary rejoice. He declares he does not see his way to more than 40 short notices this time—Can't you find some one to send him a batch of Italian books? Also cannot you hasten your notices so that he may publish on the 1st as putting it off to the 15th is highly noxious to the sales teste Douglas?

Brown of Newport is, or has been teazing Newman to go with him as his theologian. N is rather sorry now not to go. But having first refused the Pope, & then Ullathorne on the ground of that first refusal, he does not think it expedient to yield to the 2d thought. U. said to one of Oratorians lately—Honorius spoke ex cathedra, & decided wrong. So if he is properly strengthened & backed up he will probably go right. Passages of his pastoral are clearly taken from the Memorandum & others as clearly directed against Manning. Blennerhasset[3] tells me that all the Irish Bishops will probably go wrong, except M'Hale,[4] who is too strongly committed in his published lectures to be able to say that

[1] William Vaughan.
[2] Hecker became Kenrick's theologian.
[3] Sir Rowland Blennerhassett (1839–1909), Irish baronet, studied under Döllinger and at Louvain, M.P. 1865–74, 1880–5, president of Queen's College, Cork, 1897–1904; had helped to finance the Chronicle.
[4] John MacHale (1791–1881), coadjutor bishop of Killala 1825, archbishop of Tuam 1834, a stubborn and idiosyncratic nationalist.

he can witness that the Church has always taught what he there says is a question of the schools, only affirmed by the most obscure theologians. But direct the Yankee battery upon them & who knows what may come of it? Hecker spent a few days in Ireland on his way & was quite satisfied with what he heard & saw.

I wish I knew your distinct address—& I hope this will reach you unopened.

Ever yours <u>R Simpson</u>

734

ACTON TO SIMPSON · 19 NOVEMBER 1869*

74 Via della✠
Nov. 19

Dear Simpson,

I have done nothing lately about the B.M. because he[1] seemed so fearful of success. My word would not weigh with W. Jones, whom I hardly know. It will be well to get somebody at home to see him, after ascertaining whether he is neutral or hostile.

I expect your New York friend, still perfectly ignorant of his name, which keeps up a pleasing excitement.

Wetherell says Stevenson has not left the R.O.[2] Is it so? Do you think Stevenson would like to help me with his infinite knowledge of the sources of English history, for my collections on Cardinal Pole? I am rather anxious to complete them this year, and hope to complete the sweeping of the continent before I come home. Would Stevenson like to gut the English libraries for the purpose? There would be the B.M., R.O., Lambeth, Canterbury, Bodley, Cambridge, and perhaps Middlehill, and one or two other places. He probably knows exactly where things are to be found, for I think he told me that the Lambeth papers are worthless. If you think, knowing circumstances, that I could make it worth his while to spend a couple of weeks in this way, between this and Midsummer, do let me know.

I used to think the Chronicle fairly avoided the semblance of partiality, except in Buddeus's articles, so it may surely be done now, equally well. I remember Felix Holt[3] was indignant that the people who were in the right were no better than those who were in the wrong. If you go to the bottom of things, Toryism is fed by all manner of vices, and by

* Watkin and Butterfield, pp. 103–4.
[1] Renouf.
[2] Rolls Office, i.e., the staff of the Master of the Rolls.
[3] *Felix Holt* (1866), a novel by George Eliot.

feeble virtues. But many vices contribute even to pure Whiggism...
Your treatment would have to be quite impersonal, and being impersonal, need not be unjust.

I continue to say Whiggism, but the age of historical Whiggism is past. The problems coming now are beyond its reach, for it regarded, chiefly, the relations between the subject and the state. They are not a fit motive now to fill man's lives with passion. I beseech you, examine the two parties in relation to political economy, and the condition of the poor, and of those who are liable to become poor. Have a talk with Lambert. The juridic phase of Whiggism is gone, and the economic is in full swing, and the social is at hand. As they glide easily into each other, the continuity is in a way preserved. There is a common temper which the true Whig retains in all three.

Why is there no Shakespeare? The article on Browning[1] was delightful, but very provoking. I thought you had no more sympathy with him than who should have with an old curiosity shop.

Blennerhassett, starting early in December, would bring me anything needful.

Ever Your's
J D Acton

734A

SIMPSON TO ACTON · 30 NOVEMBER 1869

Nov. 30

Dear Acton

First my hearty congratulations.[2] As there is no man living whom I honour & respect more than yourself, there is a feeling of reality & solidity about the new way I have to direct to you that is quite delightful.

I hope Hecker has called on you, & by this time relieved you of your pleasing excitement.

Stevenson is still at the R. O.[3] nominally, but he is on his travels, being employed in the Commission to examine the archives of private families for historical materials. Ld Arundell of Wardour wd not submit to the search, unless it was conducted by a Catholic; so S. was named *ad hoc*, & since he has been sent to other Catholic houses. He is now in Scotland, where I cannot tell—But I have consulted Mrs. Renouf who has constituted herself mother & daughter to him since his widowhood,

---

[1] 'Mr. Browning's Latest Poetry.' Simpson later wrote 'The Early Authorship of Shakespeare', *North British Review*, n.s. XIII (April 1870), 69–92, and 'Ben Jonson's Quarrel with Shakespeare', *ibid.* (July 1870), 394–427.

[2] On Acton's elevation to the peerage.

[3] Rolls Office.

& she answers for him that he will delight in the commission you offer to him. I have copied out that part of your letter to me w^h. refers to him, & given it to Mrs R. who will ask him the question as soon as she comes to know his direction.

I did not like to tell you all that H.[1] told me; I hope you have seen himself by this time. Instead I wrote all the bosh I could think of, in hopes of cooking a dish of poison for the censure of the past. Was my charitable intention fulfilled, or did I simply put you to trouble?

I had some time agone been preparing a discussion something like that w^h you suggest on Whigs & Tories; but I had not gone far when I saw that I should have infinite difficulties with W. So I resign myself to write an article on his scaffoldage,—only I wish he would not change his mind every week. I am only waiting to be clear of him to cross the Channel, tending to Naples *via* Rome, where I hope I shall see you, & talk over the projected article, which will not appear till you are in Engd. again. W. is very ill, & I dont see how he is to get through his work. He is being employed this week on official work that he can do at home & so has not to go to the W. O.[2] But he has to give 6 hours to that work before he can begin the NB,[3] which in his state is fatal. I wish that Gladstone could be got to employ him in some way that would take him in a similar way from the W. O. & yet be easy to him.

The second part of the Egyptologist's book[4] has come astray—It was sent from Leipsic 4 weeks ago, & has not arrived yet. So I shall not be able to send it by Blennerhasset.

I have given W. an article on Shakespeare, but he probably will not want it this *no*. I promise him another and a better for April.

I think it was you who put me out of all countenance with regard to sympathy with Browning. You said you would rather lose a leg or arm or some member or other than read him. So it is to you that I refer in the last sentence but one of the article.[5] I am glad that St Bartholomew[6] is getting more notice here now. I hear with satisfaction of his approaching translation.

Ever yours
R Simpson

Is Lady Georgiana[7] at Rome? I told Mrs Chirol[8] to direct to her there, care of Plowden & Cholmeley.[9]

---

[1] Hecker.   [2] War Office.   [3] *North British.*
[4] Renouf, *The Case of Honorius Reconsidered.*
[5] 'Mr. Browning's Latest Poetry.'
[6] 'The Massacre of St. Bartholomew.'   [7] Fullerton.
[8] Harriet Ashburnham, married Rev. Alexander Chirol, who converted 1847 but returned to the Church of England later.
[9] English bankers at Rome.

734B

SIMPSON TO ACTON · 8 DECEMBER 1869

Dec. 8.

Dear Acton

I send you 6 copies of Renouf's 2nd part.[1] Will you make the wisest (width & wisdom it must be remembered go together, & wisest may be widest) use of them you can. Wetherell boned one, so I send a cut copy in the place of one destined for you originally. I was a few hours too late on Blennerhasset, who started at an unearthly hour on the 1st, & so verified the proverb which we heard Ld Dundreary[2] give out "The early bird gathers no moss.

I hope things are going well at the Council—and that you have been able to concert with Hecker some plans for making the American Bishops represent in a body that the infallibility has never been taught on their continent. Hecker & the Archbishop of Halifax[3] were with me before they left England. They had just read Manning's pastoral. The Archbishop asked me whether he could be in good faith—I think I persuaded him that he was either an impostor or a hypocrite or both. He (Halifax) said that he had always been brought up to believe the infallibility, but that the more he considered the *ex cathedra* the more he was convinced of the impossibility of defining it—& agreed that it was impossible to define anything about it, till all the letters of Popes had been examined by the Council, to see whether or not they contained errors in faith. The Redemptorist fathers here are preaching daily sermons on the infallibility, & will be left high & dry on the sands of the grills if the question is not defined at all—I wish some one would propound the difficulty that it would be a sin against the Holy Ghost to say that the Holy Ghost had any share in the politico-moral teachings of for instance Paul IV's Bull *Cum ex apostolatus Officio*. I would as soon cut off my right hand as own it—

Ever yours
R Simpson

---

[1] *The Case of Honorius Reconsidered.*
[2] A fictional character in Tom Taylor's *Our American Cousin* (1858).
[3] Connolly.

SIMPSON TO ACTON · 23 JULY 1870

Pembroke Dockyard
July 23. 1870

Dear Acton

I hope this will reach you through all the intervening blood & thunder.[1] Wetherell wrote to me just one week ago, announcing the end of his labours of the quarter, & the deficiency in result, mainly from his own illness, & in part, in that he had nothing from either you or Renouf. He said he was going to write to you to bring home to you the position that as you I & he were the contracting parties on one side, if he failed, by being disabled, Douglas[2] would be entitled to come upon us. This of course is more or less a sick man's dreams. But it is of consequence to determine whether, having now possessed ourselves of an organ, we have any thing to say—For my part, with regard to anything I have said, I would just as lief have left it unsaid—But I had always hopes that I might contribute to furnish stuffing & floating corks, while you & Renouf furnished the substance & cargo of the Review. But if you have no substance to contribute, wherefore, except just to keep W. in the Albany,[3] should we cudgel our brains to produce so many pages of copy a quarter? I wish you would review the position & tell me, in confidence or communicably as you choose, how you feel & intend with regard to the future of the Review. Surely you might want it for an exposition of foreign politics; or for the literature of the Council; or for some of the historical questions on which you are primed. But if not, let me know, that we may see how to bring our connection with it to a timely & peaceable end.

We have only the telegraphic news of events in Rome,[4] which seem dismal enough. Have you any better information? What is Döllinger going to do? & what the Hungarian Bishops? Schism is better than heresy, & an Antipope than an Antichrist—

I shall stay here a week longer, & then return home by a zigzag. So please direct to Clapham.

I hope your domestic events are proceeding favourably & untroubled, in the midst of this storm—as for the Admiralty, my friend here[5] has had a hint from head quarters to ask for a squadron of the turret ships,

---

[1] The Franco-German War. Acton was in Germany.
[2] The publisher of the *North British Review*.
[3] Wetherell's residence.
[4] The recent definition of Papal Infallibility.
[5] Captain Hall.

to test their comparative value in an Atlantic cruize from October to Feb (when he will probably become Controller)—instead of acting on the hint he has simply put himself, because of the political tension, at the disposal of the 1st. Lord, who has "cordially" accepted the position. So he may go from this any day. I mention this, because there is a talk of my going with him, in which case W. would not have a line from me for the Xmas No, if it still comes out under his auspices.

With all desire to see you safe back in England at the soonest, believe me,

dear Acton
Ever yours
R Simpson

Dont mention about Hall—

734D

SIMPSON TO ACTON · 12 AUGUST 1870

Gloucester Aug. 12

Dear Acton

Your letter of the 2nd did not reach London till the 8th, & I got it in Wales on the 10th. So I have not had much time for consideration of your questions—

1. About the Pope. He is generally considered a weak-minded old man, fond of flattery, readily believing what his sycophants tell him, & turning a deaf ear to disagreable informants. It is not an uncommon form of senile bigotry to profess that you will not hear anything that would alter your views about persons or things. In addition he is a devot, and a fanatic. And his fanaticism takes a turn typical in this age. The characteristic of the age (theologically) is ignorance. This leads to the explicit denial of the direct & immediate use of truth in doctrine. Protestants deny it explicitly, & sum up all religion in sentiment & action. Ultramontanes deny it implicitly, and make dogmas not an illumination for the intellect, but a charm or a spell to give greater efficacy to prayer. Hence the unintelligent desire to be always right in the formula, for fear of loosing devils, instead of drawing down grace by uttering it. Hence a wish again for simplifying the forms, at the same time that you define rigidly the means for ascertaining them. Hecker (who is half & half) said he should like to make a clean sweep, & to have nothing binding but the Apostles' creed. The Ultramontanes act in an analogous way when they explain away the heresy of Honorius' language, & make his ideas all one with those of his orthodox opponents. There is a thorough contempt for the substance of dogma, and an interest only in its acciden-

tal efficacity as a conjuring formula. And who is to guarantee this efficacity? Of course no intellectual enquiry could determine whether "abraxas" or "hocus pocus" were the properer form for cleaving Eildon Hills in three only authority can determine the question. And the authority shall be the Pope's. Pio IX took this view of the use of dogma when he declared his expectation that the definition of the Immaculate Conception would keep him in Rome. Dogma is not for the intelligence, it is simply for practical purposes; it is magic, or hocus-pocus. I hear ignorant women rejoicing that now doctrine has fresh definiteness, now we know what to believe, which we did not know before—It is the apotheosis of ignorance & superstition, and the Pope is the natural representative of the tendency. He is an epileptic medium.

2. Newman's state of mind is to me utterly unknown. He has said that he accepted the opinion of Papal infallibility as an opinion; he has also expressed the deepest disgust at the fraud & tyranny of those who would force on the definition. I have not here his books to refer to. In one place I remember he says "How often have the Popes spoken since Trent? Once, perhaps twice". So that he would surround the act with forms which would almost preclude its exercise. Again I know a place where he explicitly denies that the Church is committed to the medieval principle of persecution &c. But his language is effusive in its exaltation of the Popes' authority & his own submissiveness, intellectually & practically. What his state of mind is now I cannot tell you— & no one else can tell you either, probably.

3. Manning I consider to be an ambitious man, cock-sure of his own practical wisdom & infallibility, who sees that his only chance of action & influence is, to hook himself on to Rome as a satellite, & be carried up the hill by the borrowed force. At bottom he has the modern disdain of dogma as a matter to be understood. He stood by me in my controversy with the Cardinal[1] about original sin, on the express ground, not that I was right, but that I was not condemned by Rome, & that a man was safe while he tethered himself to Rome & looked only to Rome for the ultimate & decisive information. As if the intellectual tendency to heresy was of no matter, while it was checked by an external profession of readiness to believe all that Rome might define. Manning's position seems to be a contempt for the intelligent development of doctrine (hence his contempt for truth & logic in reasoning about it) combined with a sovereign fear of the material consequences of false doctrine. Hence his feeling that the one remedy for the tendencies of the age is on one side to snub all religious thought, & on the other to exaggerate a centralized dogmatic authority. Coffin, a good foolometer of Manning's mind, told me that he has it on good authority that

---

[1] Wiseman, in 1856.

Döllinger had lost his faith. I insisted on knowing how & why he considered himself justified in saying so. It reduced it to this. D. had said to a lady in Munich,—how can Pio IX know anything of theology, seeing he has not read five books of theology in his life? Talbot (now mad)[1] preached three times one Sunday in London, for the purpose of reading at each sermon a letter of Pio IX to him, which he prefaced by saying that "when the Pope speaks it is Jesus X^t that speaks." The letter was "I hope you are well. I hope that Cardinal Wiseman is better" —But if the words were only "bow-wow", it would be all the same—it is the magic of the voice of God, thunder on the left hand, birds on the right, healthy intestines in the victim, or any other unintelligent magical form, but not dogma. Once more the apotheosis of ignorance.

Both Manning & the Pope have the ambition to leave their names on the history of the Church as Athanasius[2] did. When Pio IX first became Pope, I remember he said that he hoped his pontificate would be distinguished by the reconciliation of the East, which he at once proceeded to render more impossible than ever.

4. Your fourth question, "state the case for Rome," is ambiguous. Do you mean from the point of view of a man who sympathises with Rome, or from that of a liberal Catholic seeking reasons why he should not leave the Church? The ultramontane view reduced to terms of intelligible language, or the liberal view? My reason now for being a Catholic is, that I have as good right to the sacraments as the Pope; & that I in my measure am as much answerable for the custody of the *depositum* as he is. I take the traditional view of the Church to be— a community which (1) does not contradict, or tolerate the contradiction of any point of the faith—(2) maintains in its integrity the sacramental system—& (3) offers good security that it administers the sacraments validly. These notes are only found in the Roman body in the West, therefore we ought to remain in it if possible, & we have a right to remain in it, and we may be useful if we remain, for there is a principle of recovery in it while these notes remain in it which is not to be found elsewhere in the West. We must fight for the Sacraments & not leave them to the Jesuits. If schism is necessary to keep clear of falsehood, then let the schism take the medieval form of an antipope, not follow the Reformation type. A Pope, driven from Rome, might perhaps be supplanted by one who would listen to reason. We cant have too much of a good thing, so if Popes are so good, let us have two. this is Renouf's formula.

[1] Talbot had been declared insane in 1868.
[2] St Athanasius (*c.* 295–373), bishop of Alexandria 328, chief opponent of Arianism.

(Aug. 13.)

As for the Ultramontane view, the Bishops here seem to confine themselves to thankfulness that a burning question is taken out of the sphere of controversy. Ullathorne has discovered a new truth—that the independence of the Hierarchy is established for ever by the definition of Papal autocracy. A Te Deum tomorrow probably throughout England for the definition. In Clifford's diocese[1] it is simply for the return of the Bishop, & Dr. Case, with whom am staying here intends to call his people's special attention to the fact that this is the sole reason for the Te Deum.

Of DeBuck I have heard nothing, nor of the Americans. Ryder[2] told Renouf that Hecker's journal has not ceased to be rabidly ultramontane even since his return, accusing all liberals & Gallicans of mortal sin &c. I dont think Hecker has anything to do with this. It was through Oakeley that the Chapter of Westminster once refused to send a petition of the definition. Now however he advertizes in the Times that Manning will Pontificate in his Church during the Te Deum for the definition tomorrow. The enclosed address of the London clergy is cut out of the *Standard* of yesterday. He has caved in; so has Lockhart. And there is great danger of a regular rout of our little band, unless you Germans move up quickly. Time is precious. Whether any Priest stands except Case, Trappes,[3] & Roberts I am quite ignorant. It is of much more importance that we English should know what you Germans are doing, than that you should know our doings. Our only chance is to tack ourselves on to you. There is a deal of smothered discontent among the laity which I think might flare up.

Here must end my lucubrations on the affair. Except this question. Does not the German triumph give good hopes that the Pope will soon have to leave Rome & would it not be possible to set up another Pope on the ground that *this* is a heretic?

Renouf, on whom W. depends for short notices will fail him he says. "I do not mean to write any more for the NB except occasional short notices of philological character.....I shall write nothing which bears in any way upon theology, since W. is such.....as not to understand in what objectivity consists. He would have a perfect right to complain if I wrote from a partisan point of view. But I defy any man to tell from my notices whether I am Catholic, Protestant, or nothing at all. The plain truth has to be spoken &c &c.....

[1] Clifton.
[2] Henry Ignatius Dudley Ryder (1837–1907), joined the Birmingham Oratory 1856, ordained priest 1862, superior of the Oratory 1890. A theologian, Ryder opposed Ward's extreme views on Infallibility.
[3] Michael Trappes, a Yorkshire priest.

"Even in such matters as hieroglyphics W's alterations are intolerable. He seems to have no notion of the extent to which doubt or mere opinion are unavoidable in a scientific progress, & must be expressed when necessary. Of this necessity & of the mode of expression W is utterly incapable of judging."

So you see Renouf is lost to us. What W will do for short notices next time I cannot conjecture. I cannot write more than a dozen for him. He hopes if you write to Renouf you will move him to short notices, not to an article.

You must be prouder now of being a German than of being an Englishman. I hope I may soon have the opportunity of congratulating you on domestic matters as heartily as I do on national ones.

Mrs Renouf writes that Duffus Hardy tells her that Thorpe[1] having just died his annuity of £200 is vacant & might do for Stevenson, if you would at once write to Gladstone about it. She also wants to know if in the event of your coming to England you could take charge of her boy?

> I am, dear Acton
> Ever yours
> R Simpson.

Write to Clapham, for though I shall not be there till the end of the month, I cannot say exactly where else I shall be at any particular day.

734E

SIMPSON TO ACTON · 2 SEPTEMBER 1870

> Dartmouth, Sept 2.

Dear Acton

You asked me about DeBuck. I have just had a letter from him. The phrase he refers to was somewhat like this. "The chastisement for the crime of July 18[2] is coming more swiftly than its perpetrators could have imagined." Here is his comment.

—Vous percez mon cour d'un glaive de douleur en me parlant de la decision du conc. de la maniere dans laquelle vous le faites.... Vous êtes très-mal informé de ce que c'est passé à Rome. Ainsi que l'Archevêque de Paris l'a dit a son clergé après son retour, tous les journaux n'ont fait que mentir, plus (je pense) par aveuglement et passion que par mauvaise foi. Il etait impossible qu'il en fut autrement. Les journaux qui

---

[1] Benjamin Thorpe (1782–1870), Anglo-Saxon scholar, given a pension of £160 in 1835, raised in 1841.
[2] The definition of Papal Infallibility.

s'imaginaient defendre la majorité ne savaient rien de ce que voulait la minorité, et *vice versa*. En verité, *ce sont les journaux qui ont fait tout le mal*. Je pense que, à Rome, il n'y avait que deux hommes qui sussent ce que l'on voulait à droite et à gauche, savoir de Rossi et moi. Nous seuls avions des relations avec des eveques de la majorité et de la minorité. *Premier fait.* Il est faux que le concile a été assemblé pour condamner le gallicanisme a) au mois de Juin 1869 pendant que j'etais à Rome tous les hommes de quelque autorité etaient contraires à l'introduction de cette question; b) quand elle à été introduite, on à été pris au dépourvu. On n'avait pas de formule au bout de 15 jours, la commission a proposé une formule faite et refaite par elle-même, en declarant qu'elle etait incomplète. Aussi cette formule a été, après, remaineé bien six fois. c) C'est Maret qui, en posant la question devant le concile, a été la vraie cause de son introduction. *Second fait.* Ce ne sont pas les jesuites qui ont poussé cette affaire. La *Civiltà* est de fait et quasi de droit indépendant de la Compagnie et n'exerce sur personne moins d'influence que sur les Jesuites de Rome Notre Père General s'est completement effacé; souvent il n'assista pas aux congregations; il evitait toute relation avec les évêques de la majorité et de la minorité; il n'a signé aucune addresse &c &c. Certainement—et je suis un témoin bien informé—s'il eût pu empêcher l'introduction de la question, il l'aurait fait. Moi, son theologien, on m'appelait le théologien de la minorité—Dans la Commission, Mgr. Steins,[1] notre Abp. de Calcutta, a été incontestablement l'homme plus modéré de tous. Le P. Perrone qui y a été appelé souvent était toujours du côté des plus modérés. Le P. Franzelin item. Il n'y avait que le Père Schrader qui se montra ardent, mais il n'avait avec lui que deux évêques de la commission. La transformation du premier schema *de preambulis*, que les impies mêmes n'ont pas osé attaquer, est due au P. Peters ou Kleutzen.[2] *La liberté de la science* qui y figure a été introduite à la suite d'un discours de M. Genouilhac,[3] sur des notes que je lui avais communiqués. La declaration que la commission a faite par rapport à l'inspiration des livres saints, savoir que le décret définit l'inspiration, mais ne tombe pas aux ques-

[1] Walter Steins (b. 1811), Dutch Jesuit 1832, went to India 1853, became Vicar Apostolic of West Bengal, left Calcutta 1867. The *Dictionary of Indian Biography* erroneously gives 1867 as the date of death.

[2] Those mentioned were all Jesuits. Johannes Baptist Franzelin (1816–86), S.J. 1834, professor of theology at the Gregorian University, Rome, 1850, cardinal 1876. Klemens Schrader (1820–75), S.J. 1848, professor of theology at Louvain 1850, Rome 1853, Vienna 1857–63, Poitiers 1870, a member of the preparatory commission for Vatican I. Joseph Kleutgen (1811–83), entered the Jesuits 1834 under the name of Peters, a philosopher and theologian.

[3] Jacques Marie Achille Ginoulhiac (1806–75), bishop of Grenoble 1852, archbishop of Lyon 1870. (It is not clear whether de Buck misspelled names or Simpson mistranscribed them.)

tions *de ratione inspirationis* ni surtout à l'opinion de Lessius,[1] a été faite à la suite de demarches de notre General, a qui, ainsi qu'à plusieurs autres, j'avais remis des notes. Voila en quel sens ont agi les Jesuites.

Troisième fait. Dans la minorité il n'y avait tout au plus que cinq Gallicans. Beaucoup étaient contraires à la opportunite; d'autres voulaient une forme plus précise; d'autres enfin ne voulaient pas d'anathème; mais il n'y avait quant au fond, que 5 tout au plus qui fussent gallicans. Ainsi Dupanloup, Genouilhac, Kettler, Melchior,[2] &c &c admettaient la doctrine de Bellarmine, de Thyrsus Gonzalez, de Gregoire XVI. L'Abp. de Paris disait pendant l'hiver, après avoir étudié la question pendant deux mois: "L'opinion ultramontaine me parait la vraie, mais je ne la crois pas mûre pour une decision." J'avais fait un scheme tiré de Bellarmin, de Benoit XIV, de Gregoire XVI, de Melchior Cano et de Muzzarelli. Les chefs de file de la minorité étaient prêts à le signer. De son coté Mgr. Dechamps[3] a fait tout un discours pour la defendre. Malheureusement mon schema venait trop tard que quelques jours; celui de la commission était deja imprimé. Toutefois on a pris de mon schema une partie tres-importante, sauf qu'on a changé la forme. Ayant trouvé deux compagnons pour retourner en Belgique, j'ai quitté Rome le 20 June. Avant mon départ, j'avais mis en relation Mgr. Steins et Mgr. Dupanloup: apres explication, tous les deux étaient d'avis qu'on s'accorderait. A peu près toute la minorité était unanime à dire "Il est impossible de refuser du Pape l'infaillibilité dans certaines conditions. Nous lui accordons le droit de confirmer et d'infirmer les conciles par consequent il reste le juge suprême. Dire que ses jugements ne deviennent irréformables que par l'assentiment de toute l'Eglise, c'est ne lui accorder pas plus de droit qu'au dernier, des evêques. Tout ce qui a été donné aux Apôtres a été auparavant promis et donné à Pierre, et les promesses come les dons de Dieu sont sans repentance. N'est donc impossible de dénier au Pape le *charisma* de l'infaillibilité. Mais le Pape comme les conciles n'agit pas par inspiration, mais avec l'assistance divine. Il doit dont examiner et faire examiner l'Ecriture et la tradition, dont le depôt est confié à tout l'Eglise. Cet examen est ce une condition, ou est-ce seulement un devoir? Est-il possible, que Dieu permette que la Pape ce tente?.... (sic) Puisque tout le monde est d'accord que cet examen est un devoir, la minorité eût voulu que cela fût mis dans le secret. Mal-

[1] Leonhard Lessius (1554–1623), Jesuit theologian.
[2] Wilhelm Emmanuel Freiherr von Ketteler (1811–77), ordained priest 1844, bishop of Mainz 1850, a pioneer of social Catholicism. 'Melchior' is probably Paul Melchers (1813–95), ordained priest 1841, bishop of Osnabrück 1857, archbishop of Cologne 1866, exiled 1875–85, cardinal 1885. These bishops, de Buck insists, were traditional ultramontanes.
[3] Victor Auguste Dechamps (1810–83), Belgian Redemptorist, bishop of Namur 1865, archbishop of Malines 1867, cardinal 1875; an ardent Infallibilist.

heureusement, les mots qu'elle mettait en avant, *nisus testimonio ecclesiarum* ou *conscius testimonii ecclesus* etaient mal choisis [(note) Quand je suis parti de Rome, j'etais tout heureux. Depuis je l'ai regretté. Si j'etais resté, il me semble que, connaissant ce que l'on voulait des deux côtés, j'aurais trouvé moyen de la dire] et prouvaient, dans la pratique, ouvrir la porte à une foule d'inconvenients. La commission jugea donc à propos de laisser cette question de côté, et de mettre simplement dans le caput par manière d'exemple, comment les Papes, avec l'assistance des conciles généraux, des conciles particuliers, ou en consultant tous les évêques, avaient exercé leur prerogative d'infailllibilité. Aussi, trés-probablement, le decret, tel qu'il est, aurait été voté à l'unanimité si dans la troisième chapitre on n'avait pas introduit d'une manière peu régulière les *mots plenitudinem potestates, non autem potiores dumtax at partes.* La minorité avait adopté la *plenam potestatem* du concile de Florence; les mots ajoutés n'etaient qu'une explication pour condamner le Febronianisme, mais on les introduisit, ou les ôta, ou les remit d'une manière peu conforme au reglement; et voila contra quoi les évêques de la minorité ont voulu protester.

—Pour le reste, la commission a procèdé avec la plus grande moderation, et le Pape—je le tiens de Mgr Steins—n'a jamais pesé sur elle ni directement, ni indirectement. Le Cardinal Bilio[1] agissait avec tant de moderation que je l'ai entendu appeler par des fanatiques un hérétique, un ambitieux qui cherchait à capter les voix des cardinaux français et allemand pour devenir pape &c &c. Un certain nombre d'hommes ardents ont presenté au Pape une supplique pour que le concile declarât que le Pape est infaillible dans la discipline general, la canonisation des saints, et les faits dogmatiques. Le Pape a remis la supplique à la commission sans racommandation aucune, et la commission l'a tout simplement écartée. À deux reprises différentes on a voulu introduire dans le décret que le Pape est infaillible même dans les condamnations avec des notes inférieures à celle d'herésie la commission deux fois à l'minorité moins deux voix, a rejecté la proposition, et n'a admis l'infaillibilité que dans les choses *fidei et morum conformement à l'Ecriture sainte et à la tradition,* c'est-à-dire dont la contradictoire est heresie. Aussi ai-je vu des gens ardents entrer dans une sorte de colère. Ils disaient. "Quand le Pape parle-t-il *ex cathedra* selon la commission? Les bulles contre les jansenistes, la Bulle *Auctorem fidei* et la bulle sur l'immaculeé conception dont les seuls documents modernes qui semplissent ces conditions! Ce que nous perd, ce ne sont pas les hérésies proprement dites—ce sont tant d'autres erreurs qui on propage. Si l'on ne voulait que cela, il ne valait pas la peine de saisir le concile de cette question! Une bulle dans

---

[1] Luigi Bilio (1826–84), Barnabite theologian, cardinal 1866, bishop of Santa Sabina 1873; president of the dogmatic commission at Vatican I.

chaque siecle, et cela au milieu des erreurs qui nous inondent!" La commission ne se laissa pas émouvoir.

Je suis persuadé que de tout cela vous ne savez rien.

La liberté n'a pas non-plus manqué au concile; il y en a en trop, &c.

—"The differences were rather political than theological.

—"I have submitted, therefore submit you......

Les Papes, même depuis le gallicanisme a surgi, ont constamment agi comme s'ils etaient les juges supremes des questions de fois, et par consequent infaillibles. Côté de cette pratique, il y avait l'ecole gallicane, existant plus de mon que de fait. Ne valait il pas mieux qu'une fois de droit fût mis souverainement d'accord avec la pratique?

Such is Buck's letter. It may give you some anvil to hit, so I transcribe it. It seems singularly weak as a persuasion. Great congratulations, domestic and national—[1]

Ever yours, R Simpson   T.O.

I hope you got my letter from Gloucester a fortnight ago.

734F

SIMPSON TO ACTON · 23 MAY 1871

May 23. 1871

Dear Acton

I enclose a letter to Döllinger—will you kindly give it him?

Mrs Renouf called here last night, & was in despair that Renouf had written to you exactly what he should not have written about her brother[2]—I was in despair about understanding a distinction which she failed to make her husband comprehend, & so begged her to write herself to you to explain. You will have time on your passage to Ostend to read her letter. Dont forget the bottle of milk. Qn. after the champagne will the product at all resemble milk-punch? Are you likely to call on DeBuck at Brussels? If you do, & he asks about me, tell him that I said the chief difference between myself & him was that whereas he said the doings of June 17 was a malheur I said it was a crime—He believing it to be the work of the Holy Spirit, I not so believing—In his letter to me he said over & over again what modifications he had wanted in the decree, which "unfortunately" were not adopted.

I am dear Acton

Ever yours
R Simpson

[1] The birth of Acton's son and the German victory at Sedan.
[2] Either Lujo or Franz Brentano.

734G

SIMPSON TO ACTON · 31 AUGUST 1871

Freiburg i/B
Zäringer Hof
Aug 31

Dear Acton

A vehement hailstorm reminds me to ask you to allow an umbrella which I left at Herrnsheim last Saturday, to be packed up with yours & taken to England on your return & left somewhere in London where I can call for it. I do not venture to ask Wetherell to take it—the poor fellow is hardly capable of looking after his own.

I wrote to tell Hall how ready you were to get up the Naval questions —(in a properly generalized form)—which might sooner or later prepare one "to be a successor of Göschen's[1]—Hall I know will be prepared to administer the doses as soon as you are ready to receive them, & that both in his own department of materiel, as in that of naval discipline, upon w^h he wrote that prophetic article in the H. & F. You know that of the 7 or 8 recommendations then, all were carried out under the Duke of Somerset, but that Packington[2] would not allow the gradual abolition of the Masters to proceed further—This now has given occasion to the Agincourt business, whereupon everyone demands the immediate abolition of the whole class—It is quite clear that a man with so prophetic an insight most thoroughly understands his business —& a first Lord under his guidance might be the v Roon[3] of our Navy.

I dont think you could arrive at equally decisive constructive results from Lambert's advice. I fancy that Göschen's plans for the new incidences of local taxation were Lamberts. They were received very coldly—Something prevented my reading Göschen's great speech, but almost all the comments I saw upon it seemed to be favourable. But it is clearly a matter which has to be got up, for the increasing local taxation cannot for much longer be levied only on real property, without some corresponding reduction in the share borne by that property in the imperial taxation—perhaps it was only the prevision of the deficit, which

---

[1] George Joachim Goschen (1831–1907), banker, M.P. 1863–86, 1887–1900, president of the poor law board 1868–71, first lord of the admiralty 1871–4, 1895–1902, chancellor of the exchequer 1886–92; created viscount 1900.

[2] Sir John Pakington (1799–1880), baronet 1846, M.P. 1837–74, secretary for war, 1852, 1867–8, first lord of the admiralty 1858–9, 1866–7; created Baron Hampton 1874.

[3] Albrecht Theodor Emil von Roon (1803–79), Prussian minister of war 1859–71, reformed the Prussian army.

made the House so indifferent to the proposed transfer of the house tax to the Overseers & Local Boards.

Hall proposes to come to meet us somewhere on the Rhine. I have suggested to him that he might find time for a few days talk with you at Herrnsheim.

Tell Lady Blennerhasset that I will not forget to ask Mivart[1] to review Huber's book,[2] if she does not forget to let me have the book.

With my best remembrances to her & all your party, believe me

dear Acton
Ever yours
R Simpson

735

SIMPSON TO ACTON · 7 JANUARY 1872

Jany 7. 1872

My dear Acton

I am working at three old plays,[3] one of which is certainly an early work of Shakespeares, the next probably so, the third possibly. The first is not historical. The second is so; it is about the Siege or rather Sack of Antwerp in 1576. I have found two English pamphlets on which the play is chiefly founded; but there are multitudes of details which I find in neither of them—I am in correspondence with Schollaert about contemporary pamphlets on the subject in collections in Belgium. Perhaps you also may among your Spanish collections have some Spanish account of the exploit. E.G. were Roda's letters published in Spain? If not how did Champagny get hold of them to put them into his *Recueils d'Arétophile*, Lyon, 1578. if you could give me, or tell me where to look for, the bibliography of contemporary literature on the subject, English, Spanish, French, Flemish & German, I should be much obliged.

The third play is on captain Thomas Stucley.[4] I am making a biography of the man to prefix to it. He went to Pius V in 1570, he was at Rome again in 1572, again there with Don John of Austria in 1576, & again in 1578, when Gregory XIII made him Marquess of Leinster,

---

[1] St George Jackson Mivart (1827–1900), English Catholic scientist and critic of Darwin, excommunicated 1900.

[2] Johannes Nepomuk Huber, *Die Lehre Darwin's kritisch betrachtet* (München, 1871).

[3] For a series of reprints of Elizabethan dramas, which appeared as *The School of Shakespeare* (London, 1872); revised ed., 2 vols. (London, 1878).

[4] Thomas Stucley (c. 1525–78), English Catholic soldier of fortune, projected invasions of Ireland.

Vicount this & Baron to this, & sent him to Ireland with 1000 men—but Sebastian at Lisbon persuaded him to turn aside, & he perished at Alcazar.

What detailed annals of Pius V & Gregory XIII ought I to look into, to find traces of such occurences? What Roman correspondence of the period is published?—besides Theiner—Am I likely to find such things mentioned by Gabuzio, Bzovius, the Bollandists, or Feuillet on Pius V? Catena does tell me something about Stucley. What of Agatio di Somma, & his French translator, Félibien? or Labbe? or Muratori? I want you to tell me the likeliest reading for my purpose—which is, to find a needle in a bottle of hay.

Stucley was evidently a great favourite with Emmanuel Philibert D. of Savoy whom he served in the campaigns of 1553 & 1554. Are there any detailed accounts of these campaigns w^h w^d be likely to speak of the English auxiliaries? I dont think Stucley can have joined till after the capitulation of Hesdin in 1553

One more question of a different kind. Do you think it likely that your servants brought back my umbrella from Hernsheim? If so, I shall find it in London after the Session has begun.

A very happy new year to you & all yours.

Ever yours
R Simpson

In Stucley's life, such delightful rascality of Maurice Gibbon,[1] or Fitz-gibbon, or Reagh comes out! Frailty, thy name is Bishop!—the mot serves for those times as for these—

735A

SIMPSON TO ACTON · 19 JANUARY 1872

Jany 19. 1872

My dear Acton

Many thanks for your note. I hope that the cause which hindered your concentration has happily passed away, & then I hope you will not give yourself needless trouble about my Stucley. When I have written my sketch of his life perhaps I may make bold to ask you to read it over, & then your memory or your indexes may more easily help you to help me, if you have much that I have not. My question now is, have you among your Spanish collections got any thing about the Knights of

---

[1] Maurice Gibbon was Roman Catholic archbishop of Cashel 1567–78, dying in exile in Portugal. He thwarted Stucley's efforts in Spain and informed the English government of his plans.

Calatrava? I find that when Stucley went to Spain, he was received for a while at court, then a house was taken for him for 22 weeks at Arosso, said to be a village 3 leagues from Madrid, where he had his deed defrayed by the King "being accompanied by a knight of the Order of Calatrava, called Don Frances Merles of Catalonia"—At the end of the 22 weeks, Jany 22 1571 Stucley was Knighted by Philip. Does not this look like a kind of noviciate, ending with his admission into the Order.

Immediately after he went to Rome, was almost royally received by Pius V "ubi cum Pio consiliis pluribus agitatis, de restituenda religione; tandem ex sententia facinus quod suo loco narrandum erit, generoso animo aggrediendum suscepit"—so Laderchi[1]—but I do not find that he fulfils his promise. It is probably only S's offer to seize Scilly, & to burn Elizabeths ships in the Medway, as related by Catena in a parenthesis.

Stucley is afterwards said to have been in command of 3 gallies at Lepanto—have you any originals or reprints of contemporary accounts with details?

Then it seems he went with Don John the year following to the capture of Tunis.

All this looks like a Knight of Calatrava, & his acta might possibly find a place in the registers of the Order. If you dont know where to look for such registers, I will ask DeBuck.

Ever yours
R Simpson

I have the umbrella—Many thanks.

736

ACTON TO SIMPSON · 26 JANUARY 1872

Aldenham Friday

Dear Simpson,

I sent you this morning a highly unceremonious telegram intreating you to come down. You will find Miss Charlton[2] one of your wildest admirers, and we shall be able to see what can be found about Stukeley.

We have been so shut up all the winter, with nursery troubles, that the sudden arrival of our visitor is the first chance we have had of

---

[1] Jacobus Laderchi (c. 1678–1738), Italian Oratorian, continuator of Caesar Baronius' *Annales Ecclesiastici* (Rome, 1728–37).

[2] Probably Mary Charlton, afterwards Marchesa Pasqualino.

asking any friends to Aldenham. We hope you will be able to spare us a few days.

I remain—waiting for my shillingsworth of answer.

Ever Your's
Acton

737

SIMPSON TO ACTON · 27 JANUARY 1872

Jany 27, 1872

Dear Acton

I was out when your telegram arrived yesterday, & when I got back it was too late to telegraph. And I found that I should have to set off at 9 o'clock this morning, as the 10 train is the only available one that I can make out. So I telegraphed this morning that I would come on Monday (by that train) if it was convenient to you; dont scruple to say if it is not so; your letter will reach me before I start on Monday, quite in time to stop me.

I quite agree with you that any one that admires me must be eo nomine *wild*. I am only afraid that my presence may so far tame the patient that at rate the symptom of wildness that strikes you may be considerably relieved.

I am like the French Abbé—I have done my Stucley, and I hope I shall not find any thing to contradict me—if so, so much the worse for the contradictors.

Ever yours
R Simpson

737A

SIMPSON TO ACTON · 28 JANUARY 1872

Jany 28. 1872

Dear Acton

I hope you won't think me very cool—But this morning my courage failed me, & I shivered at the idea of so long a journey today to be repeated on Wednesday. I suppose my shivering came from a cold I caught on Saturday, for which cause my pusillanimity found plenty of domestic encouragement. As I said on Saturday, my Stucley is done— I dont think much more could be added till in the lapse of Ages the Spanish Calendars for 1570–78 are printed, & till Brewer has favoured

301

some coming generation with the concluding volumes of Henry VIII. Talking of Brewer I proposed to Hamilton,[1] one of the men at the Record Office, that a temporary calendar of the remaining years, no fuller than Lemons,[2] and only referring to the papers in the record office should be at once printed. Hamilton wished I would get some man of influence to make the proposal to Duffus Hardy. He also said it would be grateful to Brewer.

I wish I could find some series of Gazzetti Italiane for the years 1570–78. The Roman news letters for that period are almost entirely wanting in the Record office—For these reasons I have been obliged to content myself with much secondary information out of Fuller[3] & the like, the originals of which, if they exist now, have hitherto baffled my search—Stucley is the third of the dramas I want to publish so there will be time for the revolution of accidents to turn up fresh information before I print. But I have got together so very much more than any one before me that I feel as if my collection were equal to the occasion, as the man, after all, is of very little significance beyond being a popular hero with balladers & playwrights

Ever yours
R Simpson

738

ACTON TO SIMPSON · 23 FEBRUARY 1872*

Aldenham
Feb. 23.

Dear Simpson,

A scruple occurs to me after returning your squib[4] to Wetherell.

You say that nearly all the bishops who protested have since given way. Is not this saying too much? There are some who gave way distinctly, like Ginoulhiac and Haynald[5] and Maret. But many others have

---

[1] Hans Claude Hamilton (1811–95), assistant keeper of the Public Record Office 1855–88; or William Douglas Hamilton (d. 1894), clerk in the Public Record Office 1855–92.

[2] Robert Lemon and Mary A. E. Green, eds., *Calendar of State Papers, Domestic* 12 vols. (London, 1856–72). Probably only the early volumes are referred to.

[3] Thomas Fuller (1608–61), author of *The Church History of Britain* (1655) and *The History of the Worthies of England* (1662).

* Watkin and Butterfield, pp. 104–5, dated 1874 on the strength of a note apparently in Simpson's hand. But the context indicates 1872: see note 4 and the next letter.

[4] A reply to a work on Infallibility by Franz Xaver Weninger (1805–88), Austrian missionary to the United States. See Acton to Döllinger, 23 February 1872, in Conzemius, III (München, 1971), 48. But see also the next letter.

[5] Ludwig Haynald (1816–91), bishop of Transylvania 1852, archbishop of Kalocsa 1869, cardinal 1879.

pursued a course which they think different from actual surrender and consistent with a state of mind that is not internal acceptance of the dogma.

They say—to themselves—that it will yet be explained away, or got over somehow. Schwarzenberg,[1] the Primate of Hungary,[2] the bishop of Marseilles,[3] MacHale, the late Darboy,[4] and, as I understand him, Clifford, are of this kind. My notion is that they ought not to be all branded, like Moriarty or Scherr[5] or Förster,[6] and that it would be enough to say 'most of them'.

I was very sorry not to see you here, but you were quite right not to come so far, and I ought not to have bothered you so in opportunely. I hope Shakespear is getting on well.

The business of getting Stevenson sent on a—perfectly idle and irrelevant—mission to Rome has been so delicate that I am afraid to propose other expenditure just now to Romilly. But a plan ought to be devised to enable Brewer to do all Henry[7] himself, that is, to direct and manage the whole. I fancy there is little chance of that, at the present rate, unless the papers become more scarce, as the printed matter no doubt does after 1535.

Ever Your's

A

739

ACTON TO SIMPSON · 26 FEBRUARY 1872

Dear Simpson,

You must have thought me mad. I called today, hoping to dispel the error, but in vain.

An anonymous MS. was sent to me for suggestions. It contained remarks on Wenniger's tract,[8] intended for the meanest comprehension. I cannot imagine why I thought it was your writing.

I went through it today with Wetherell. It is not exceedingly forcible.

---

[1] Friedrich, Prince zu Schwarzenberg (1809–85), archbishop of Salzburg 1836, cardinal and archbishop of Prague 1842.

[2] Johann Simor (1813–91), bishop of Raab 1857, archbishop of Gran 1867, cardinal 1873.

[3] Charles Philippe Place (1814–93), bishop of Marseille 1866, archbishop of Rennes 1878, cardinal 1886.

[4] Georges Darboy (1813–71), bishop of Nancy 1859, archbishop of Paris 1863, shot by the Commune.

[5] Gregor von Scherr (1804–77), abbot of Metten 1840, archbishop of München and Freising 1856, excommunicated Döllinger in 1871.

[6] Heinrich Förster (1799–1881), prince-bishop of Breslau 1853.

[7] The state papers of Henry VIII.

[8] Probably *On the Apostolical and Infallible Authority of the Pope*...(New York and Cincinnati, 1868).

Both W and I think that the writer, on the whole, would do better to let it alone.

Would anything induce you to write a short, parallel, and excessively plain and popular exposure of the Wenninger tract? It seems that there are people who want it.

It does not seem difficult, as each proposition in the Tract is directly contrary to truth, and all subtlety and compromise with conscience has been carefully avoided by the author.

Ever Your's
A

740

ACTON TO SIMPSON · 31 MARCH 1872

Dear Simpson,

I sent some remarks on that lecture,[1] but the points you raise escaped me, and I cannot find the Report. I forward your remarks, with some developments of my own.

Paul's[2] violent language was used after the Acts of Supremacy and Uniformity were passed—so that it was not the mere question of legitimacy that influenced him. But in the vague, tolerant, uncertain position in the summer of 1559, I imagine the attitude of the Pope as an enemy of the realm must have given help to the Protestant minority to overcome and bind the Catholic majority.

Would not Arnold do what you want at the Bodleian?

In Hosack's Mary Stuart preface,[3]—which I have not got at hand— you will find the name of a Danish professor who looked up documents for him. Perhaps, ingeniously approached, he would do the same for you on Shakespeare. Foreign ambassadors in England at the time you speak of are to be found, I think, in the papiers d'Etat de Granvelle, in Vertot's Ambassades de Noailles, in Friedmann's Michiel, in Gachard's Philip II, in Gonzalez's paper on Elizabeth in the Memorias di la Academico, w[h] have been partly translated by Spencer Hall, in Froude, in Schlossberger's paper on the Archduke Charles in an early vol. of the Forschungen zur Deutschen Geschichte, and in other places I don't remember.

Ever Your's
Acton

Aldenham
Easter

---

[1] One of Döllinger's lectures on church unity. Simpson's remarks on it were forwarded to Döllinger.   [2] Giampetro Carafa (1476–1559), Pope Paul IV 1555–9.
[3] John Hosack, *Mary Queen of Scots and her Accusers* (Edinburgh and London, 1869).

ACTON TO SIMPSON · 11 MAY 1872

Dear Simpson,

Your suggestion is extremely valuable, and I should be glad to get any information that can be got in the matter.

My present impression is that Clifford and Kenrick's argument[1] is quite just as a résumé of English Catholic history, but that a link is wanting in George IV's time to make it decisive in the way they put it.

Pray do what you can.

Ever Your's
Acton

741A

SIMPSON TO ACTON · 7 JUNE 1872

June 7

Dear Acton

I am sorry I have kept no notes of the missing books. One which I noted some 20 years ago Roberts tells me has since been procured. My late studies have been in Elizabethan literature, in wʰ it is of very little use to note deficiencies, for the books missing may be almost unique.

But I have often wished that manuscripts of some of these unique books wʰ are in the Bodleian, or *penes* Sir Thomas Isham,[2] or elsewhere might be procured for the Museum. It is one good feature of Dyce's library at South Kensington[3] that you may find there a small parcel of transcripts which save you the trouble of applying to the Revᵈ Mr Corser,[4] or other private collectors. If the Museum would spend some moderate sum annually on obtaining such transcripts, & would have

---

[1] Concerning the pre-Emancipation assertions of English Catholics about Papal Infallibility and the Pope's authority in England.

[2] Sir Thomas Isham (1657–81), baronet 1674, kept a Latin diary, published 1875, the original being kept in private hands.

[3] Alexander Dyce (1798–1869), literary scholar, bequeathed his library, rich in Elizabethan materials, to the South Kensington (now Victoria and Albert) Museum.

[4] Thomas Corser (1793–1876), ordained 1816, rector of Stand 1826, edited *Collectanea Anglo-Poetica* (1860 ff.), collector of books. F.S.A. 1850.

a separate catalogue for them, it would be a great boon to London students of our old literature, & would not, I think, be very expensive.

Ever yours R Simpson

No more yet from Pownall *in re* Blounts MSS & printed documents. We were on our way yesterday to enquire about Lady Acton, but the weather cut us short. I hope all goes well; & accept our congratulations on your new boy[1] or joy or both.

742

ACTON TO SIMPSON · 11 JULY 1872

Dear Simpson,

If you see the papers, the point I don't understand is this:—

Was any declaration touching the Infallibility of the Pope ever made by any party, or by any official person, a condition of supporting the Catholic Claims?

And is there proof that the declarations made concerning that question contributed to the passing of the Emancipation Act?

Were, therefore, the declarations by which the Catholics committed themselves, really efficacious for their purpose?

I remain

Ever Your's
Acton

742A

SIMPSON TO ACTON · 17 JULY 1872

Wednesday July 17

Dear Acton

I saw the papers last Friday, but I was so interrupted that I could go through only a small part. Before I go again I write some particulars, to know whether it is of any use to do so.

1. The papers are all of them publications of the Catholic Association, or of its "Defense Committee". If you have them, there is an end.

2. From what I saw, I am sure that your questions in their present form cannot receive any categorical answer. The condition you speak of (the declaration touching infallibility required as a condition of

---

[1] John Dalberg Acton, b. 30 May 1872, d. 16 April 1873.

306

supporting the Cath. claims) was understood, but I dont find it expressed. It was understood on both sides that Catholics would have but little chance of emancipation if they still were as they had been. Hence the anxiety of their friends & themselves to show that they were changed.

eg. Wm Pitt to King Jany. 31. 1801 "those principles, formerly held by Catholics which made them be considered as politically dangerous, have been for a course of time gradually declining, &, among the higher orders particularly, they have ceased to prevail."

Brownlow,[1] speech in H. of Commons Ap. 19 1825

"The R. C. religion has freed itself from the corruptions of the Roman Curia. The R. C.s of Ireland consider the Pope the chief Pastor of their Church.....but as such, they recognize in him a pure spiritual supremacy & nothing more". He quotes Dr. Doyle,[2] who, if the Pope interfered with his allegiance "would oppose him by every means in his power, even by the exercise of Spiritual authority."

On the other side the Catholics vied with each other in making this appear to be so. If there is no English declaration of Infallibility, this is because the doctrine was not even imputed to them. Bossuet was the theologian they always quoted, but he appears to have been accepted by both sides as the expositor of the modern & moderated popery. But they made declarations w^h are utterly subversive of the Vatican doctrine. e.g. a publication of the "Defense Committee" "charges brought against the R.Cs of G^t B. & Ireland, & their defense".....It is said that the Popes on several occasions have claimed and exercised the right of temporal power. We acknowledge it, & we lament it. But the fact is of little consequence. No R.C. *now* believes that either Pope or Council or both Pope & Council acting together, have, or ought to have, any right to interfere by any form or mode, either of temporal or spiritual power, in civil concerns; or to interfere, by any form or mode of temporal power in spiritual concerns. This the Irish, Scottish & English RCs have sworn, & they act up to their oaths".

2. Surely the statement by friends of emancipation, in speeches in Parliament, that the Catholics had become moderate & had changed, & had given up certain doctrines, is proof enough that Catholic declarations contributed to the passing of the act, & that they were really efficacious for their purpose.

Write & tell me whether you want me to proceed. And whether proofs of the kind I have given will satisfy you.

Ever yours
RS.

---

[1] Charles Brownlow (1795–1847), M.P. 1818–32, created Baron Lurgan 1839.
[2] James Doyle (1786–1834), ordained priest 1809, bishop of Kildare and Leighlin 1819.

SIMPSON TO ACTON · 22 JULY 1872

July 22. 72.

Dear Acton

I enclose a few extracts I made today from the papers you wot of. Of course I read much more than I took notes of. My conclusion is that the arguments for Emancipation were of two kinds. At first, to gain the Liberals, the Catholic religion was represented to be thoroughly changed from what it had been, liberty of conscience was said to be the form it took in all Catholic countries, & the race of Papists who would constrain the conscience was almost extinct. This game was played out in 1826, & then it became evident that the Liberals by themselves could not carry the measure. It was necessary to gain the Tories. This could not be done by an appeal to reason—nor by an appeal to any honest passion. An appeal to fear was the only resource left. "You will certainly lose Ireland" was the argument used alike to the mobs of Kent & Devon by the liberal speakers, & the converted Tories, and to the H. of Lords by the Duke of Wellington.

The declarations made by the Catholics were judged by themselves at the time to be really efficacious for passing the act. And surely they were right. For by them they had consolidated the liberal opinion in their favour, and unless they had persevered in them they would have chilled that great assistance.

The threat of civil war was only efficacious because the opinion of England had been thoroughly divided, & nearly half of it had gone in first for the justice of the Catholic claims, & next for the necessity of conceding them as a measure of liberal policy, to strengthen the hands of the liberal party. With England divided, & hotly divided, United Ireland was able to threaten. But what had first divided England was the opinion that it was 1. just, & 2 safe to concede the claims. And neither of these points could have been made plausible without the Catholic declarations. There was indeed a kind of contemptuous pity for the Catholic Church. It was gone or going. There was no fear of its being again strong enough to hurt. But then the reason for this was that it was an Empire indeed, but one of opinion only. And the opinion of all Catholic countries was strongly in favour of toleration, liberty of conscience &c, and as strongly set against all the pretensions of the Curia, so that they could never rise again from their grave.

So I conclude

1. The liberals as a body would not have supported (at first) the

Catholic claims unless they had been convinced that Catholics had become liberal.

2. The declarations made by the Catholics did in fact convince the liberal party this was truth.

3 And therefore were efficacious in gaining the support of that party, without which, even at last, the bill could not have been carried.

Ever yours
R Simpson

743

ACTON TO SIMPSON · 31 JANUARY 1873

Aldenham January 31 1873

My dear Simpson,

I am quite alive to the calamity of Renouf wasting his powers on such inferior objects, and the Museum always seemed to me the right place for him. Cole's[1] retirement has long been forseen, wished for, and provided for. Birch[2] is getting old, and I do not know who else can succeed him. But before he retires Rawlinson[3] will probably be a Trustee, and would be much consulted by the three men with whom the choice will rest. Birch will have something to say to it himself.

Is there any chance of R.S. Poole[4] being a competitor? Birch, I know, does not believe in him, and does in Renouf. And I don't know that the office is better than his own.

If you can, let me know how Renouf stands with these men—although his is but an uncertain contingency.

I shall be at the meeting next week. My only Shakespearian friend is Clark[5] the Cambridge editor once P.O.[6] but now vacant. You can write to him invoking my name. He is a good scholar, and a good fellow, and is to be found at the Athenaeum.

[1] Sir Henry Cole (1808–82), patron of industrial design, organized the 1851 Exhibition, secretary of the department of science and art 1852–73, director of the South Kensington (later Victoria and Albert) Museum 1857–73, knighted 1875.
[2] Renouf succeeded Birch only in 1885.
[3] Sir Henry Creswicke Rawlinson (1810–95), in East India Co. service 1827–55, mainly in diplomatic positions, deciphered the Behistun stone (cuneiform) 1846, knighted 1855, M.P. 1858, 1865–8, member of the India Council 1858–9, 1868–95.
[4] Reginald Stuart Poole (1832–95), entered British Museum 1852, keeper of coins and medals 1870–93, Yates professor of archaeology, University College, London, 1889–94.
[5] William George Clark (1821–78), fellow of Trinity College, Cambridge, 1844–73, public orator of the University 1857–70, edited the Cambridge Shakespeare (1863–6).
[6] Public Orator.

My poetical friends are Browning,[1] Arnold, and Palgrave[2]—If you don't know them and think them worth consulting do by all means.

I shall look forward to your article greedily. Don't suppose that people whom it concerns do not know your authority on Shakespeare. I will suggest the putting the MS. into a place of honour.

I am constantly coming on points of the XVI century that I should like to ask you about. Don't be surprised if I give you some trouble one of these days.

Believe me

Your's ever truly
Acton

744

ACTON TO SIMPSON · 1873?

Dear Simpson,

I should be grateful for any notes on the wants and gaps of the British Museum library, as I may have to raise a discussion on them next Saturday.

Ever Your's
A

745

SIMPSON TO ACTON · 1 JANUARY 1874

"School of
Shakespeare"

I return to Clapham tomorrow or Saturday, I cannot tell which

Jany 1. 1874

My dear Acton

A happy new year to you & yours, & many another in due succession. I heard from Wetherell of the anxiety you have had to go through;[3] and I believe you heard from him of that which I inflicted upon my wife

---

[1] Acton is not known to have been a friend of the poet Robert Browning (1812–89). Perhaps this refers to Oscar Browning (1837–1923), fellow of King's College, Cambridge, 1859–1923, assistant master at Eton 1860–75, lecturer in history at Cambridge 1880–1908; he wrote lives of Dante and Goethe and introductions to editions of Robert Browning.

[2] Francis Turner Palgrave (1824–97), examiner (later assistant secretary) in the education department 1855–84, professor of poetry at Oxford 1885–95.

[3] Acton's wife and two of his children were seriously ill in the autumn of 1873.

by nearly giving up the ghost once in May & twice in September. I am pretty well again now, but my heart is too weak to allow of much work, and I am under strict discipline so that I have very few opportunities of working. However, such, as they are, I am moved to tell you of my doings, because, as I am precluded from the Museum, perhaps I may be bold enough to get you to help me to a few books—A request which does not come very well from me, who have had about a dozen books of yours packed & ready to send to you for three years past, till a few weeks ago, when I undid the package to take out two volumes of Tierney's Dodd. But I keep your books separate, & if anything happens to me, you shall have them all right again.

My idea was this—As Geo: Eliot makes much of the background of her novels, the social medium in & by which her characters are developed, so, thought I, it might be interesting to look up the lives of the gentry who lived about Stratford in Shakespeare's time—And when I began to look into it, I found such a constellation of interesting people that I thought a good volume of Elizabethan biographies might be made of it. The men are of various kinds; the Throqmortons, about whom I suppose you can help me—the Ardens Somervilles, Giffords, & Bishops, most of them recusants, some traitors, others leading men in the quarrels between the Secular Priests & the Jesuits, & one, William Gifford,[1] Archbishop of Rheims, about whom you might help me with the French memoir of his life, the funeral sermon preached upon him, the funeral sermon he preached on his predecessor Cardinal Louis of Guise in 1621, & monographs on the City & University of Rheims, which contain a lot about him. Some 10 years ago I saw at Rheims a MS. local history, one volume of w^h was almost all about Mg^r de Archidal (Gifford) & I found that much was printed by two local historians, whose names I have in my note books at Clapham.

Then there are the Grevilles—both branches—at the head of the elder Ludowick Greville the murderer, a wonderful country squire, about whom lots of things are to be found in records of chancery &c, & about whom I have many collections—at the head of the younger branch Sir Fulke, the father of Fulke the younger, afterwards Lord Brooke.

Then Sir John Conway, governor of Ostend in 1587, 88, about whom I have searched Van Meteren almost in vain, but concerning whom memoirs must exist somewhere. About him also much is to be gathered from law records—

Then there is Sir Thos Lucy the Puritan, Shakespeares Shallow—Sir William Catesby & his son Robert the gunpowder plotter, with his friends Grant & Bates—

[1] William Gabriel Giffard (1554–1629), English Catholic priest, entered Benedictine Order 1608, coadjutor archbishop of Rheims 1618, archbishop 1621.

Then there is a rascally lawyer called Bott, about whom I have much, a wonderful thief, alderman of Stratford, & turned out of office to make way for John the father of Wm Shakespeare.

There are many other possible names on my list, eg. the Porters, ending with Endymion P. but at present I will only ask you whether you have anything about the Throqmortons—(Sir Nicholas is a little too early, & would take me too long, & besides was connected rather with the West than with the midland counties)—Francis, Sir Robert, Sir George, Edward, Clement &c &c—

And secondly, whether you have anything about William Gifford, Bishop of Archidalia in partibus, afterwards Abp of Rheims.

In 72 I wrote a biography of Thomas Stucley, as an introduction to an old play upon him;[1] but the first specimen of my "school of Shakespeare" sold so badly that I am not much encouraged to go on. If any Society would publish, they should be welcome to my MSS.

Ever yours
R Simpson

746

ACTON TO SIMPSON · 8 JANUARY 1874*

January 8 1874

My dear Simpson,

Your letter has been the most welcome New Year's greeting I could have received, after all the anxious accounts we had of your illness in the summer. I do most sincerely hope that the discipline you speak of is a salutary one, and that you are gaining strength surely, and without losing prudence. If the apprehensions of last September had been unfortunately realized I should not only have had to bear the grief of all your friends, but especially my own, for having never expressed, nor I fear, shown, how great a part of the good things of many years of my life had come to me from your true and generous friendship, or how much reason I have had to thank God for it. And also for having been of so little help and comfort and edification to you in former troubles, for which it cannot be inopportune now to ask your forgiveness.

Since your letter came I have had to watch one of my children through a threat of scarlet fever—Lady Acton being disabled; and this, now happily over, has delayed my search among my books. It has not been fruitful of results, for Abp Gifford. The most I can find about him

---

[1] Part of *The School of Shakespeare*.
* The first paragraph is printed by Gasquet, Letter CLXX, p. 357.

is in Marlot's history of Rheims, of which there are two original texts, one in Latin and one in French. The latter seems the fullest, and shall be sent to Clapham. This French work has been only lately published, and may possibly be what you saw in MS.

I think there must be information about Conway elsewhere than in Meteranus which I will look for, but most of your topics are altogether out of my depth.

I believe there are some Throckmorton papers of the 16th century at Coughton. An ancient priest, Mr. Brownlow, made a compilation out of them, which I have seen, and it leads to very little. But I will try to ascertain whether the papers themselves are in any such order that it would be possible to communicate the necessary bundles to you.

Have you seen the reports of the Historical MSS. Commission? They give some notions from family papers, but I don't remember any curious Warwickshire matter. If you have not got them, I will send them to you.

Clearly, much the most of your materials must come from un-published MSS. But why do you devote yourself so much to the back-ground of the drama, and keep us waiting so long for the chief Character?

Believe me,

Your's very truly
Acton

747

ACTON TO SIMPSON · 22 JANUARY 1874

January 22
1874

My dear Simpson,

I have been away from home in Birmingham and London. I sent off the worthless Anquetil[1] as soon as I came home but I fancied I had a duplicate of the MSS report. I find that I have it only of the two first volumes which pray retain. The third seriously damaged with my own marks pray return at some distant day. All this I am afraid will supply you with very little matter and it is not worth while to tire yourself with these things as long as you have to be on your guard against the internal enemy.[2]

I hope you will never think of me as the external enemy, for in that way you would be unjust; but I do very sincerely thank you for your reply to the question of my last letter.[3]

---

[1] Probably Louis Pierre Anquetil, *Histoire civile et politique de la ville de Reims*, 3 vols. (Reims, 1756). [2] Illness. [3] Missing.

What has become of Brentano?[1]

I am so unreasonably dispersed over literary clubs, societies and spending or subscribing institutions, that I should like best to give my name and tribute to Furnivall[2] in his Shakespeare Society, if you will manumit me from the two others.

Believe me

Your's most truly
Acton

748

SIMPSON TO ACTON · 24 JANUARY 1874

Jany 24. 1874

Dear Acton

Many thanks for 1 Marlot 2 Anquetil, & 3 the Ms Commission w^h arrived this morning, & which shall be duly returned after I have looked through it & duly extracted it. I hope, when I am well enough, to be allowed to hunt among Tierneys MSS at St Georges, where I expect to find transcripts of letters of Abp. Gifford, & other documents that will suit me. I see that there must be many things in the Commission; but what a pity that Lord Salisbury's papers should be so barely catalogued, without an indication of what they are about.

I have told Furnivall that you will subscribe to the SK[3] society & he replies, wanting to know whether you will allow your name to be on the list of Vice-Presidents. I might give you the same reason for it as Dr Merrion[4] once gave me for his satisfaction at your having the H.&F. "It can't do any body any harm, if it does no good." But he was no Solomon, & his proverbs are not worth preserving.

I really am very thankful for all the trouble you are taking about my probably useless researches. But my Shakespeare lucubrations may come to something now. I have made some progress in converting Furnivall to those of my views which I have argued out, & his energy will get a hearing for them. His enthusiasm is a phenomenon. It is quite amusing. He is a tee-totaller, but the heat of his liver has made his nose as self luminous as Bardolph's. With such a torch to lead it how can the

---

[1] Franz Brentano (1838–1917), ordained priest 1864, taught philosophy at Würzburg 1866–73, left the Roman Catholic Church 1873 (his opposition to Papal Infallibility leading to a critique of basic Christian doctrines), professor of philosophy at Vienna 1874–80. He was Renouf's brother-in-law.

[2] Frederick James Furnivall (1825–1910), philologist and editor of texts, a founder of the New Shakespeare, Early English Text and several other societies.

[3] Shakespeare.

[4] Simpson's physician.

new Society lose its way? If I can but get him to carry it the way I should like!

Some time ago you said you had something to ask me to do about Elizabeths times. It is possible I may have an answer among my papers. If so I could give it you. If not, I am afraid my searches at libraries &c are over for a year or two at least, if I can ever resume them.

Ever yours most truly
<u>R Simpson</u>

749

ACTON TO SIMPSON · 31 AUGUST 1874

My dear Simpson,

Many thanks for the two extracts, which are precious. You named Persons in connection with the second—I suppose from some other source.

Case promises to lunch with us tomorrow, but without farther details, by telegraph.

Don't bring Tierney: he is not at all wanted at Aldenham.

Ever Your's
Acton

750

SIMPSON TO ACTON · 3 SEPTEMBER 1874

Sept 3

Dear Acton

I have written a paper on the political allusions of Shakespeare's historical plays.[1] Furnivall has read it, & does not agree, but says he is ignorant. I am very loth to trust to my own judgment on the matter, & so venture to ask whether you will read it over, & give me your candid opinion upon it—whether it proves anything or not. Backed by you, I would stick up; but if you agree with him I should withdraw. Tell me whether I may send it you for your opinion. It is only as long as a short H.&F. article.

Case went this morning, having settled the draft of his letters. He will send you a copy of them tonight.

[1] Probably the supplement to the general introduction of C. M. Ingleby, *Shakespeare Allusion-Books* (London, 1874).

315

I send you an extract from Tierney's Dodd which I mentioned to you last Friday.

> Ever yours
> R Simpson

751

ACTON TO SIMPSON · 15 SEPTEMBER 1874

> Aldenham Sept. 15

My dear Simpson,

I have been laid up, and am still incapable and plugged, but I will read the paper with delight if it can still be of any use.

Many thanks for the extract. Case I should hope will not now be specially molested again, but of course other difficulties may arise in his path from episcopal action.[1]

Wetherell, writing on the 10th seemed to feel himself much better, and was starting from his mountain tops for Austria.

> Ever Your's
> Acton

752

SIMPSON TO ACTON · 16 SEPTEMBER 1874

> Sept 16.

Dear Acton

I am grieved that you are ill—please do not bother about the paper I send with this till you can do it without any difficulty.

My difficulty is that I have to deal with such an absolute ignoramus as Furnivall. I send you his letter, & you will see his pencil comments on my paper. What I want to know is this—Is it sufficiently detailed to prove or to "ought" to prove, its point to decently informed persons? If there is any sense I am more especially wanting in, it is the historical sense. I can never tell a story or put forth an historical argument decently. I either enter into too much detail & twaddle, or expect people to know more details than they should know, & liken myself to the dark philosopher.

---

[1] Case (a priest) had difficulty in submitting to the Vatican decrees. Acton and Simpson helped him work out a formula to satisfy both his conscience and his bishop.

I can certainly furnish adequate authors to all Furnivall's pencilled questions. But probably he has not hit on the really weak parts. If you would criticize you would do me a great kindness—& not with your own good-nature, but rather with the editorial severity of a Wetherell.

Case was at first very unhappy after finding the Bishop[1] so pleased. He thought he had been entrapped into sacrificing to idols. & now he is haunted with a morbid fancy that he may, in transcribing his letter, have said *full* where he meant to say *due*. He was cool enough while the strain lasted, but now it is over I am afraid he feels it very unpleasantly.

With hardest wishes for your speedy complete recovery

Yours ever
R Simpson

753

ACTON TO SIMPSON · 23 SEPTEMBER 1874

Aldenham September 23
1874

My dear Simpson,

A trip with my little girl has delayed my answer longer than it is worth waiting for. Nobody can seriously doubt that you are right in saying that there is a political current in Shakespeare, and that he belonged to the opposition you describe in the days of Elizabeth. The allusions in King John would bear more development, at least that part did not seem to me so decisive as what you take from the later plays. Surely you would be able to carry the thing over into James's[2] reign. If you do, you will make the impression one gets from your paper more definite.

Ever Your's truly
Acton

754

ACTON TO SIMPSON · ? SEPTEMBER 1874

I think it will be very difficult to get a date out of the allusion.[3] There was war in 1589, after the murder of Guise, for the definite purpose of excluding Navarre from the succession.

---

[1] Clifford of Clifton.

[2] James I (1566–1625), king of Scotland 1567, of England 1603.

[3] This note appears to be associated with Letter 753, although a date in 1872 is

But while Henry III lived, the war was waged, primarily, against him.

In 1590, 1591 the war was carried on against Henry IV directly. Would it be very irregular to call him the heir while he remained unacknowledged by Paris, by great part of the people of France, and by Catholic Europe?

While a succession is in dispute, may not a claimant or pretender be called the heir?

There was also war before the death of Guise, but the exact dates I don't remember; the Athenaeum is closed, and I cannot get to the Museum today.

755

ACTON TO SIMPSON · 4 NOVEMBER 1874*

Most private   Aldenham
                                                                         Nov. 4

My dear Simpson,

Pray consider what follows most secret, and discuss it only with your inmost self.

Ten days ago Gladstone wrote to me about his article on Ritualism[1] besides other things. In my answer I said that the reproach of Ultramontanism is too grave to be lightly addressed against anyone without definite reason. He thought what I said just and suggestive and asked to consult me about his next step. I went to him, and found that he has written an elaborate and careful pamphlet,[2] which amounts to this: You[3] got emancipated by declaring yourselves good subjects and decent people in 1826. But you also declared, for the same purpose, that you disbelieved Infallibility. This declaration has become false. What proof have we that the other is still true?

Assume that the evidence in support of this dilemma, of this challenge, is fairly and fully put. The result is, to demand of the Catholics security

possible. In Simpson's handwriting are the words: 'This note of Ld. Acton refers to a passage in Comedy of Errors—France in the girl's "forehead, armed and reverted, fighting against her heir." ' The references are to Henri de Lorraine (1550–88), duc de Guise 1563; Henri III (1551–89), king of France 1574; and Henri IV (1553–1610), king of Navarre 1572, of France 1589.

* Gasquet, Letter CLXXI, pp. 358–9.

[1] W. E. Gladstone, 'Ritual and Ritualism', *Contemporary Review*, XXIV (October 1874), 663–81. The article contained the words: 'no one can become [Rome's] convert without renouncing his moral and mental freedom, and placing his civil loyalty and duty at the mercy of another.'

[2] The first draft (the first four chapters) of *The Vatican Decrees in their Bearing on Civil Allegiance: A Political Expostulation* (London, 1874).

[3] The English Catholics.

against political Ultramontanism under pain of losing their claim to liberal, to national respect and support—in reality, under pain of a tremendous No Popery cry.

Objections in detail were attended to, but to all political, spiritual, and other obvious arguments against publication he was deaf. I ended by saying that though not one of those attacked, I was one of those challenged, and that I should meet his challenge on my own account. I only obtained a promise that I shall see him again before he publishes. I want to have your views on this grave business.

Do you think it right for me to reply? Do you see your way to a good reply? I have made a sketch, and have plenty to say. If I do prepare a letter to the Times I shall be anxious to bring it to Clapham and talk it over with you.

Ever Your's
Acton

756

SIMPSON TO ACTON · 9 NOVEMBER 1874

Nov. 9. 1874

My dear Acton

I remember what a light you gave me once when you showed how many of the Ecclesiastical sins arose from—the greedy pursuit of Ecclesiastical *interests*. Should you not make a point of this—that in *universal principles* (not simply commands to the Italians to refrain from the poll, or to the French to murder the Hugenots, or the English to dethrone Elizabeth) the Pope cannot suddenly alter all the catechisms & manuals; & that these things rule the faithful; that only partial regard is paid to his commands which refer only to the interests of the Church—for interests luckily always clash with other interests, & not much sacrifice is to be expected either for Ecclesiastical or other interests which do not coincide with the interests of the State, family, or individual—Hence, whatever is said, the obedience really rendered to the Pope will always be on points in all catechisms—& it does not matter to the world whether there is an immaculate conception more or less,—& never,—except locally, in such measure as a strong state may easily crush,—on matters of mere Ecclesiastical interest & expediency.

I have not seen Renouf this morning; Mrs Renouf protests against your letter[1]—It is, she says, as if you were waiting for the opportunity to say all the disagreeable things you could against the Vatican decrees —& she compares it to Mannings paragraph against Döllinger[2]—This

---

[1] *The Times*, 9 November 1874, p. 9.   [2] In his letter, *ibid.*

perhaps is the woman's view, in whom the Ultramontane heart is scarcely protected by the reasonable historical mind. I quite applaud the letter; Shall you not point out to the Times that it is (in the eyes of Rome) one thing to repudiate a decree, another to point out that it is exactly as much & no more operative than certain superannuated & dormant definitions which now no theologian troubles his head about?

I talked to Lambert on Sunday; he was terribly vexed with Gladstone, & thinks it a terrible blow to the party. His wife was present so I did not dare to anatomize his ideas—But he told me a good story— He met Bob Lowe last year (I think) returning from a visit at Hawarden; To enquiries about Gladstone Lowe answered that he was as holy as ever, getting up betimes to go to Church every morning; but Mrs Gladstone had informed him that her husband worked hard all Sundays, so there *was some hope of his being damned yet.*

I suppose that Gladstone will point out that Manning's answer is precisely of that character which he anticipated, & by anticipation proved to be insufficient.

Ever yours
R Simpson

757

ACTON TO SIMPSON · 17 NOVEMBER 1874*

Aldenham
Tuesday

My dear Simpson,

I was so very sorry to be nervous and ill the other day at your house, and hope you will not remember it against me. Your drops did me great good.

Manning writes,[1] amiably as to my answer to his first question and the suppressed letter. But he knows not what I mean to be taken as the answer to the second, "unless you intend to describe yourself as one of 'those who adopt a less severe and more conciliatory construction' of those decrees. If I am right in this inference, I would still ask

---

* The first part of Gasquet, Letter CLXXII, pp. 359–60, with omissions.

[1] Acton's letter had given offence by its criticisms of the Church and raised doubts as to his submission to the Vatican decrees. Manning began a correspondence which might lead either to Acton's submission or to his excommunication. Manning's first letter, 12 November, asked whether Acton had any heretical intent and if he accepted the decrees. His second letter, 16 November (discussed here), and Acton's reply, 18 November, are printed in *Selections from the Correspondence of the First Lord Acton*, ed. J. N. Figgis and R. V. Laurence (London, 1917), pp. 151–3.

you to enable me to understand what that construction is."..."Let me be able to reassure the minds of a multitude who &c &c."

You see, of course, the opening. I think of saying that I did not answer a question there seemed to be no occasion to ask. But that I must resist the inference he draws from my letter to him, as I really have no interpretation of my own, but am content to wait the constructions of others, in absolute reliance on God's providence in the government of His Church &c.

The great question is whether I ought to say that I *submit* to the acts of this, as of other Councils, without difficulty or examination—(meaning that I feel no need of harmonizing and reconciling what the Church herself has not yet had time to reconcile and to harmonize). Or ought the word *submit* to be avoided, as easily misunderstood? I mean to be very short, to save the old ground, of his having no business here, to deal only with the meaning applied by him to my words about conciliatory construction, and to meet that, in 10 lines, so fully, as perhaps to meet the difficulty.

Please see Renouf, if possible, and telegraph to me your answer as early as you can. I must reply tomorrow.

Ever Yr.
Acton

758

ACTON TO SIMPSON · 17 NOVEMBER 1874*

Telegram[1] Nov. 17, 1874
Acton Shrewsbury to Simpson Clapham

He[2] repeats question, and asks what my conciliatory construction is. This is a new start. Shall I take the opening he gives me and say with reference to this special question that I submit to this and all other acts of Church authority without difficulty, having no private construction of my own but confidently waiting the interpretation of others? please answer fully by return of post.

* The second part of Gasquet, Letter CLXXII, p. 360.
[1] Copied by Simpson.
[2] Manning.

SIMPSON TO ACTON · 17 NOVEMBER 1874

Nov. 17.

Dear Acton

You contrasted the rigid interpreters of the decrees (vz. Manning & the Ultramontanes) with those who adopted a conciliatory construction, namely, such liberal Catholics as submit to, & shelve, the decrees.

I understood you to mean by conciliatory construction that literal interpretation which is always given to the words of a law, the taking the utmost care that more shall not be attributed to those words than is really in them; and that where their meaning admits of any doubt, such interpretation should be followed as can best be reconciled with previous legislation.

The conciliatory construction is one therefore which takes the Vatican decrees not as an isolated phenomenon, but as something to be incorporated & reconciled with the decrees of Trent & Constance—They do not stand alone, but have due order & subordination in the corpus of Ecclesiastical decisions. They do not supersede or change what was before.

The rigid construction on the other hand looks at these decrees alone, and refrains from tempering them with the historical corpus to which they belong; it uses them as weapons to bang opponents with. It says— "There is no change, & yet the decrees are Ultramontane; therefore the Ultramontanes alone are Catholics—down with all gallican liberals & other heretics."

Now perhaps one or the other Gallican tenet is inconsistent with these decrees—And if so I renounce that or the other tenet. But as the decrees have not introduced a change, though they have erased a line or two of Gallican theology (as the decree of the Immaculate Conception erased a line of dominican & Thomistic theology)—yet the Gallican spirit and the Thomistic spirit are alive in the Church, and have their right & their place there; & the conciliatory construction, among other things which it does secures them this place.

After this explanation there can be no difficulty in saying 'I accept the Vatican decrees, as I accept those of Trent & Constance; and where party spirit makes apparent contradiction with history, I trust to time & the conciliatory working of theologians, to reduce the contradictions to proper unity.

Is this your meaning when you propose in reference to the special question of the conciliatory construction to say "I submit to this (?)

and all other acts of Church authority without difficulty, having no private construction of my own, but confidently waiting the interpretation of others"?

Considering that we suspect all Councils to be reformable by a plenary agreement of the whole Church, surely we may say what I propose to say. In your formula I do not quite see what *"this"* means. If you mean the Vatican decrees, you put the submission much more strongly than I do. The explanation of *conciliatory* naturally introduces the mention of Trent & Constance; & to receive the Vatican decrees *as* you receive *those* surely is quite compatible with your conscience. It is with mine. We have forced Case to do as much. We must do it ourselves. Why are we to be excommunicated more than Ricasoli & Schollaert?

I had written the accompanying letter to the Times.[1] As I have the opportunity of submitting it to you, will you read it over & see whether you agree with it. If you do, it surely makes our "conciliatory" policy more easy, & at the same time justifies the step we take & intend to take, of a full publication of historical difficulties.

I was unfortunately out this morning when your telegram came. But this letter is the fruit of as much reflection as I could squeeze into the after dinner hours. I shall take it to Renouf, to catch, if possible, his opinion before Post time, which is here at 5 PM.

Ever yours R Simpson

760

ACTON TO SIMPSON · 3 DECEMBER 1874*

Dec. 3.

My dear Simpson,

Manning asks whether my letter means that I adhere &c. repeating his question and sending me his pastoral.[2]

Meantime I have had a correspondence with my bishop,[3] who is very angry, but admits that nothing I have said touches the Council, and that I have shown that I so understood it.

My first letter to him was rather strong.

The second, after his explanation that he admits the principle of telling no lies, very civil.

Now, how do you think in again telling Manning that his question is

[1] Not published.
* Gasquet, Letter CLXXIII, pp. 362–3, postscript omitted.
[2] Reprinted in *The Times*, 30 November 1874, p. 8.
[3] Brown of Shrewsbury.

not justified and will not be answered. I can employ the testimony of my own bishop?

"My explanation referred only to a suggested interpretation of a passage in my letter to him. I meant to say that no such question could be admitted to arise from my letter to Gladstone. Confirmed in this view by the fact that that is not questioned by my bishop—I should regret if that was not, on consideration, also his opinion."

Pray suggest what occurs to you, and say how far I ought to hint that my own bishop is most to the purpose. I want your answer by return of post if possible.

Ever Your's
Acton

I have not time to write to Renouf—see him if you can.

761

ACTON TO SIMPSON · 10 DECEMBER 1874*

Dec. 10
1874

My dear Simpson,

My bishop, getting angry at last, asks me whether I reject the decrees or accept them.

Please to consider this formula and all we said to Case.

The question is motivé by the unsatisfactory nature of my letters to him. Inasmuch as I said it is a pity to be a liar, and, at last wrote him a very civil answer indeed. So that it is not motivé at all. Besides he has admitted that, in public, I said nothing heterodox.

Is not his case so weak that it ought to be resisted?

I cannot admit questioning on that ground, I should gain nothing if I did, as the same thing would begin again. Dr. Green has written to a local paper to say that I never, even critically, attacked the Council. He is my confessor, and so has some claim to an assurance.

I have thought of writing to thank him for his letter, and then saying to him everything I can say, or should say in the confessional if questioned: namely—I do not reject—which is all the Council requires under its extreme sanctions.

As the bishops who are my guides have accepted the Decrees, so have I.

They are a law to me as much as those of Trent, not from any private interpretation but from the authority from which they come.

The difficulties about reconciling them with tradition, which seems

* Gasquet, Letter CLXXIV (in part), pp. 362-3, with an omission.

so strong to others, do not disturb me, a layman, whose business it is not to explain theological questions, and who leaves that to his betters.

The bishop then, in refusing me the Sacraments, would be doing it solely on the ground of my refusal to be questioned à propos of my letters by one who admits their orthodoxy, not at all on the ground of heterodoxy.

Please to think all this over. I will try, if I can, to see you between $4\frac{1}{2}$ and 5 tomorrow, Friday, unless you send a message to the Athenaeum to say that the hour will not do.

Ever Your's
Acton

762

ACTON TO SIMPSON · 11 DECEMBER 1874

My dear Simpson,

Pray send me, at Aldenham, the paper of suggestions you showed me this morning—and would you mind telling me nearly what it was that you were asked to say when you were very ill?

I went to my Tierney[1] for a passage you told me of, but could not find him. If he is at Clapham, may I ask for the loan of him?

Ever Your's most truly
Acton

763

ACTON TO SIMPSON · 12 DECEMBER 1874*

My dear Simpson,

My bishops' answer to my note, asking in what way I was to interpret his former letter—as he did not seem quite consistent with himself—is moderate, friendly, does not actually repeat his question, does not resent my last, and distinctly prefers the milder interpretation without sacrificing his solemn duties &c. He says it is all to be considered a privileged communication—as if he thought I was ready to say more to him than to the public. In this there may lurk a snare. But it is evident he does not want to force a quarrel.

One element in considering it is that it was written after a special visit of Dʳ Green to Shrewsbury—Dʳ Green being as well disposed as

---

[1] Tierney's edition of Dodd's *Church of England*.
* Gasquet, Letter CLXXV, p. 365, with omissions.

one can be when grievously shocked, and preferring probably to end his days here in peace.

I send the letter to Wetherell, asking him to forward it to you, the first thing. Pray return it to me with all your remarks by tomorrow's post if possible.

Ever Your's
Acton

Many thanks for your letter of this morning. I will try it on Gladstone.[1]

764

ACTON TO SIMPSON · 19 DECEMBER 1874*

My dear Simpson,

I have followed your suggestion and here is the result.

Pray consider what should be done if the bishop, through indiscreet friends, (for he has described our correspondence as strictly private and confidential) should announce that I have accepted, or submitted, or retracted, or adhered.

Ever Your's
Acton

765

SIMPSON TO ACTON · ?20 DECEMBER 1874

Dear Acton

The oftener I read your letter[2] the more I approve of it. We do believe and behave in a way entitling us to be Catholics, and we have the right, as it is our duty, to assert our position. It is I think impregnable.

As to what may ooze out. You are hardly in a position to make Brown give you what Bellarmine[3] gave Galileo—a certificate that he had not retracted anything—But you are in a position to say, that you retracted nothing, that you satisfied Brown that there was nothing in your public

---

[1] Simpson's letter dealt with Gladstone's remarks on the subject of civil marriage. It was enclosed with Acton to Gladstone, 16 December 1874, in *Selected Correspondence of Lord Acton*, pp. 48–9. This led to correspondence between Gladstone and Simpson: see Damian McElrath, *The Syllabus of Pius IX: Some Reactions in England* (Louvain, 1964), pp. 268ff., 350ff.

* The first sentence of this letter is the first sentence of Gasquet, Letter CLXXVI, p. 366. The full letter is given by Watkin and Butterfield, p. 105.

[2] A draft letter to either Brown or Manning, enclosed with Letter 764.

[3] Robert Bellarmine (1542–1621), entered Society of Jesus 1560, cardinal 1599; canonized 1930, a doctor of the Church.

letters on which he could found a doubt of your orthodoxy, and by a further declaration you satisfied him that you had incurred no ban or anathema, but were a good Catholic—And this declaration was received by him with the "deepest gratitude."

Haneberg[1] has written to the Renoufs to send him Gladstone, & Acton, and all that has appeared on the Controversy. Mrs. Renouf wanted me to ask you whether she might say anything of your correspondences with Manning & Brown. I told her I would not ask you that, but would give you this information, in order that you might (or might not) write to him, to tell him what you chose to tell about matters which do not appear in print. So she is to say nothing, nor to hint that she could say anything.

Now the next step is to choke off the Manning correspondence with Brown's assurance of satisfaction. I should think that might be done, even if Manning perseveres in his interrogatories—But I dont see how any one can ask more than a formula like this—

To whatever is universally imposed as a condition of communion under anathema I submit, totidem verbis—

To any deduction from, extension of, rider to, corollary of it &c &c I refuse to say either yea or nay, as neither faith nor obedience can justly be asked for to such deduction, extension, &c

Ever yours
R Simpson

A happy Christmas. Shall you let Case see in what terms you have answered your B^{p}? It might comfort him.

766

ACTON TO SIMPSON · ?21 DECEMBER 1874[*]

My dear Simpson,

If you like, let the second sheet of this letter be sent to Haneberg.

Gladstone writes:[2]—"I agreed with *every word* of R.S. till I came to 'G. should own himself mistaken, like a man.' But it seems to me that

---

[1] Daniel Bonifaz Haneberg (1816–76), professor of Old Testament at Munich 1844–72, abbot of St Boniface 1854–72, bishop of Speyer 1872.

[*] The first part of this letter (to the first signature) is printed as the latter part of Gasquet, Letter CLXXIV (dated 10 December), pp. 364–5, with an omission. The second part (the 'second sheet' to be sent to Haneberg) is Gasquet, Letter CLXXVI (except the first sentence), pp. 366–7, misdated 18 December.

[2] Gladstone to Acton, 18 December 1874, in *Selected Correspondence of Lord Acton*, p. 147, in response to Simpson's letter which Acton had sent to Gladstone. Gladstone to Simpson, 26 December 1874, in McElrath, *The Syllabus of Pius IX*, p. 350, indicates that Simpson replied on 21 December in a letter which Acton forwarded to Gladstone.

I am exactly right. I put 13 to illustrate 14.[1] I complain of 14. and simply because it condemns civil marriage as per se null and void—or as the Pope calls it in his marvelous speeches, un sozzo concubinato. I manifestly cannot confess an error which I do not see."

Certain serious Italians want to prefix a short statement, from a truly Catholic point of view, to a translation of Gladstone's Appeal. He passes it on to me. I cannot do it. Shall I pass it on to you?

Gladstone also sends me a long correspondence with Coleridge,[2] which I advise him to send you, on the point treated in your letter. You are quite right that I cannot ask the bishop for a certificate of consistency. But do you mean, because he could refuse it? If you do, my letter must be misleading. It was suggested that the word 'inconsistent' might imply assent; and so I said that if any word *contradicted* the doctrine, it was against my real meaning, and must be blotted out. If you have a misgiving, let me know. I could still explain myself to the bishop, without danger, as to consistency with my letters.

Ever Your's
Acton

What I want people to understand is this:—Gladstone's Appeal could not be met by denying that political consequences could be drawn from the Council, or that any interpretation of that sort could be right or authentic. My reply to him was that, as an English statesman, he exaggerated the practical danger, and that his way of imputing to Catholics all the consequences constructively involved in the Decrees admitted of a reductio ad absurdum. Avoiding everything that might seem to touch on the present system, such as Inquisition and Liguorian Ethics, I chose my instances from an order of things that is quite by gone and inoperative. This enabled me to give truth its due by bringing out the fact that Gladstone had not darkened the dark side of the question, whilst adhering to my view that the Council did not so directly deal with those matters as to exclude a Catholic explanation, or so that no authentic gloss or explanation could ever put those perilous consequences definitely out of the way. For I could not take my stand, for good or evil, as an interpreter of the Decrees, without risk of authoritative contradiction.

Although this was no attack on the Council, it was an attack on Ultramontanism, and altho' I carefully distinguished the system I attacked from the Decrees which I declared harmless in these matters,

---

[1] Citations from the *Syllabus of Errors* in Gladstone's *Expostulation*.
[2] Henry James Coleridge (1822–93), converted 1852, ordained priest 1856, entered Society of Jesus 1857, editor of the *Month* 1865–81. For the Coleridge–Gladstone correspondence, see McElrath, *The Syllabus of Pius IX*, pp. 335–50.

it was at once assumed that a statement of facts derogatory to the popes must amount to a statement of opinions inconsistent with the Council. Therefore, in my second letter, I stated that the facts I dealt with were undogmatic and could not involve my collision with authority. When Manning asserted the contrary, I not only disclaimed the intention, but showed that it would have vitiated my whole argument. Having given him this explanation, besides what I said in public, I was obliged to decline the dogmatic question, which my letters did not raise, and which belonged to my Diocesan. When my own diocesan then raised the question, I proved to him that my letters were perfectly orthodox, that I did not at all dissociate myself from the bishops of the minority, or disobey the Apostolic Constitution, or incur any anathema; and that my argument was directed against a totally different point, namely, the theory that it is not well to let history speak out or the truth be known. I told him that, if a single word in my public or private letters contradicted this declaration, I would blot it out. The bishop admitted that there was no such contradiction, and, without admitting the truth or propriety of my letter, declared himself quite satisfied as to the Catholicity of the position I have taken up.

It would also be right to point out that a misquotation contained in my letter to the Times was corrected as soon as it was pointed out, and that one of the bishops having expressed doubts about my account of Fénelon,[1] I showed, without determining the guilt or innocence of Fénelon, that I had not touched that question.

Ever Your's truly
Acton

767

ACTON TO SIMPSON · 6 JANUARY 1875*

Jan. 6

My dear Simpson,

Manning, in a letter which you will receive from Wetherell, with my comments enclosing it, says he must leave the thing in the hands of the Pope, as everybody tells him I don't believe the V.C.[2]

He means, it seems to me, that he simply asks Rome to excommunicate me—a thing really almost without example, and incredible in the

---

[1] François de Salignac de la Mothe Fénelon (1651–1715), archbishop of Cambrai 1695, censured for Quietism 1699. Acton's letters to *The Times* had discussed Fénelon's public submission and private resistance.

* The first part of Gasquet, Letter CLXXVII, p. 368, with a small omission.

[2] Vatican Council.

case of a man who has not attacked the C. who declares that he has not, and that the Council is his law, though private interpretations are not, and whose own Diocesan has, after enquiry, pronounced him exempt from all anathema.

If he meant some farther application he would have said so.

Still the action of Rome may not be peremptory and final, but they may ask me for some further declaration.

If that should be, it may be best to write such an answer as I could then appeal to. Pray think it over, against afternoon post. If you write tomorrow early, I shall have your letter here on Friday morning. But you can hardly get W's communication in time for that, and then I hope to find your answer on Friday afternoon at Brown's Hotel, 22 Dover St. W.

Ever Your's
Acton

768

SIMPSON TO ACTON · ? JANUARY 1875*

You have now a right to state your own case and to demand that the statement should go with the other papers to Rome.

1. You published your letter in the London *Times*.

2. Manning thereupon asked you two questions: (a) your intention in the letter; (b) your private belief.

3. You distinguished his right and authority as having published the letter in his diocese. You (a) disclaimed all schismatical meaning in the letter; (b) evaded all reply to the second, since he, not being your diocesan, had no right to ask it.

4. Manning professed himself glad to receive the reply (a), but insisted on an answer to his second question.

5. Meanwhile you had satisfied your own bishop as to your orthodoxy.

6. Manning having ascertained this, begins with a new charge, that you had given public scandal in his diocese, and must publicly retract it.

7. Your reply to this might be:

(1) You have publicly, in your second letter to the *Times*,[1] repudiated the only explanation of your letter which could justly give scandal.

(2) That if scandal still exists, it is either reasonable or unreasonable.

---

* The second part of Gasquet, Letter CLXXVII, pp. 368–70, headed 'Simpson's Suggestion for Acton's Answer, Jan. 1875'. The original of this letter is missing. It is not absolutely certain whether this is the reply to the previous or a draft for Letter 770.
[1] 24 November 1874, p. 6.

If the former, let the passages be produced on which the reason is founded, and you will either explain them, or if necessary retract them.

(3) But having had it already acknowledged by Manning that he believed you had no schismatical intent in the letter, and having satisfied your own bishop and other theologians that your letters do not in any way attack the doctrine of Papal Infallibility, it is absurd to ask you so to confess that doctrine as by that confession to repair any alleged scandal arising from your letters. Reparation of scandal can only be given by a reply exactly corresponding to the scandal. To utilize an alleged scandal to demand an explanation already owned to have nothing to do with the matter whence the scandal arises is illogical, unjust, and a false pretence.

You therefore proceed to demand

(4) What are the passages in your letter (No. 1) which are not covered by your general disclaimer in letter No. 2, and from which the scandal is said to arise, viz., that they are inconsistent with your belief in Infallibility.

769

ACTON TO SIMPSON · 16 JANUARY 1875*

> Thomas's Hotel
> Berkeley Square
> Jan. 16

My dear Simpson,

Here is more light thrown on the matter.

I thought of saying to Manning that he would do well to remind them at Rome that he was wrong on both the points he raised—the sense of my letter—and my reception of the definition. Wetherell also thinks it would be well to point out that he now confines himself to my letter which I have already explained to him, and which he does not attempt to pick a hole in, or to connect with disbelief in Infallibility.

The ground is much cleared, at any rate, by this, and by the discovery that Pius V is at the bottom of it.[1]

I fear I am too late for post, and so send by hand—hoping to have your united and matured opinion on Monday morning.

> Ever Your's
> Acton

---

* Gasquet, Letter CLXXVIII, p. 370, with omissions.
[1] This refers to Acton's statements, in his letters to *The Times*, that St Pius V had ordered and justified the murder of heretics.

SIMPSON TO ACTON · ? JANUARY 1875*

I published a letter in your diocese, on which you took occasion to ask me two questions.

Whether I had a schismatical intent in it.

Whether I believed certain doctrines.

The first question I answered, because I considered you had some right to the assurance.

The second I did not answer, because I did not acknowledge, & do not now acknowledge, your right to ask it.

The same questions were afterwards put to me by my own bishop, & I at once satisfied him on both points, as you know, and might therefore rightly conclude that I do not reject, but on the contrary receive ex animo the Vatican definition.

Thus it is within your knowledge, though you personally have no explicit statement of the second point from me, that I have given to the two parties who had a right to ask me severally satisfactory answers to both the questions on which you sought information.

You know both by my explicit declaration to you of my intention & meaning, & by what you have learned from my bishop, that my letters to the *Times* had no reference whatever to the Vatican definition, which God forbid that I should contradict.

Therefore you know that whatever scandal has arisen from my letter or letters, to the effect that the writer of them does not receive the Vatican definition, proceeds from false assumptions & misunderstandings, which ought to have been scattered to the winds by the declaration prefixed to my second letter in the Times. After so many public & private declarations no one has any right to conclude that my letters emanate from a mind that rejects a doctrine with which they have nothing to do.

If it could be shown that any passage in my letters contradicts, or is inconsistent with the definition; or if any passage can be pointed out that is otherwise heretical, I will at once retract & modify it, and express my sorrow for it.

If it can be shown that any reasonable scandal has been founded on any passages of any of my letters, I will seize the opportunity of explaining myself when I know what those passages are, & what sinister meaning has been attributed to them. But I repeat, apart from all defects

---

* Printed as the third part of Gasquet, Letter CLXXII, pp. 360–2, misplaced in November 1874. A date of 16 January 1875 or later is established by the reference to the reception of Newman's pamphlet, published on 14 January.

of style & tone which I am ready to acknowledge & deplore, I do not believe that there is a sentence in my letters which any ingenuity can twist into an heretical meaning. And in this view I am strengthened by observing that Father Newman has in his reply to Mr Gladstone[1] made use of the many of the same facts, without thereby incurring the slightest suspicion against his orthodoxy.

771

ACTON TO SIMPSON · 21 JANUARY 1875

Thursday 3.30 P.M.

My dear Simpson,

Many thanks for the two extracts.[2] Foule's certainly does rather disturb my confidence in my own mistake.

The persistent illness in the nursery, by depriving me of night rest, has kept me from answering Manning, which can be done only à tête reposée. But if nothing worse intervenes I shall be delighted to come to lunch on Sunday.

I remain

Ever Your's
Acton

772

ACTON TO SIMPSON · 1 FEBRUARY 1875

Feb. 1

Dear Simpson,

I shall be delighted to meet you at the Athenaeum on Wednesday afternoon. Let me know at what time you will come. If I don't hear from you, I shall be there from 3. I don't propose to morrow because I have still one serious invalid to care for, who, I trust, will be better in a day or two.

Meantime I will forward your letter[3] to Hawarden.[4]

Ever Your's
Acton

[1] Newman, *A Letter Addressed to His Grace the Duke of Norfolk on Occasion of Mr. Gladstone's Recent Expostulation* (London, 1875).
[2] This refers to a lost letter of Simpson's, the contents of which are not clear.
[3] Cf. Simpson to Gladstone, 8 February 1875, British Museum Add. MS. 44446 f. 172: 'I wrote a letter to Acton on the 31st of Jany. which he said he would forward to you. It was to ask your name in setting up a Girls High School at Clapham.'
[4] Gladstone's residence.

773

ACTON TO SIMPSON · 9 FEBRUARY 1875

My dear Simpson,

I wrote to Hawarden enclosing your letter, but am still unanswered. I should apprehend that the fear of Greenwich[1] will make your plan impossible. He comes to town in a couple of days.

Things are more prosperous with us since yesterday.

Ever Your's
Acton

774

ACTON TO SIMPSON · ? 1875

Dear Simpson,

We have seen and heard nothing of you, so I fear you are at home again.

This is to say that the Abbé Michaud[2] is a most excellent and intelligent priest of Paris who, coming from Munich, and spending a few days here, is on his way to England, to see the people who can help him to see light in the present darkness.

He can tell you—from a Left point of view—all that passed at Munich the other day.

Ever Your's
Acton

774A

SIMPSON TO ACTON · 18 MARCH 1876

Hôtel d'Amérique, Rome
March 18. 1876.

Dear Acton

We only started from home on the 8th of last month, and reached this place on the 16th, being continually delayed with sickness, first at home, then at Boulogne, then at Turin, then at Florence. There however I gave four mornings to the Archives, with some little result.

[1] Gladstone was M.P. for Greenwich, not a safe seat.
[2] Eugène-Philibert Michaud (1839–1917), French priest, wrote against the Vatican decrees in 1872, professor at the Old Catholic faculty of theology at Bern 1876.

Guasti[1] I found charming, and ready & able to tell me anything I wanted. So I did not look at the papers of Lotti or his successor, which are all copied out, & in the British Museum. I only read the miscellaneous volumes, in one of which, mixed up with papers of 1603–15, is a begging letter of Ridolfi[2] to Gregory XIII, recounting his services in England, and asking repayment of his losses by confiscation. It is evidently a copy sent to Florence for verification of the man's representation of his mercantile position. I have copied the whole of it, and I will have a copy made for you when I return. Meanwhile I give you an analysis.

He says that Pius V from 1566 to the end of his life employed him, first as secret Nuncio in England, where no public nuncio was received, & where numbers of the chief nobles were continually offering the pope their services to do some great thing for Christendom & for Mary Stuart. Ridolfi thereupon received instructions to prevent open war between England & the crowns of France & Spain, & to discover all the doings of the Protestants who resorted to Eliz: from France & Flanders. By the aid of sundry great lords he completely succeeded in these two businesses.

He next made up a league among the Lords with the Duke of Norfolk[3] at the head of it, who was to marry Mary, & so make himself King of England. The enterprise was quietly proceeding, when the rising in the North in 1569 interrupted it. Norfolk & Ridolfi were both imprisoned, & the latter examined on 25 articles, the least of them enough to cost him his head 25 times—but by means of hard swearing & the grace of God he escaped. Having given an account of all this to Pius V whom he told that the conspirators who were not discovered were more ardent than ever in the cause, the Pope ordered him to renew the plot, & to be magnificent in promises. The lords thereupon renewed the league, & gave Norfolk & Mary the power to form & order the rising at the time they might think fit, with the permission of the Pope & the K of Spain. Upon this the Pope determined to publish the Bull,[4] of which he sent 80 copies to Ridolfi, who had one posted to the gates of the Bp. of London, & the rest dispersed in Court & Country. Upon this Norfolk & Mary, seeing that haste was necessary, sent Ridolfi to Rome, to obtain approval of their marriage, & to get the necessary aid. From Rome the Pope sent him to Spain, with the countenance of bearing the articles of the league against the Turk, but really to induce the King to agree to the marriage, & to send immediate help. By the aid of the Cardinal of

[1] Cesare Guasti (1822–89), head of the Italian State Archives at Florence.
[2] Roberto Ridolfi (1531–1602), Italian merchant in England, plotted against Elizabeth I.
[3] Thomas Howard (1538–72), 4th duke of Norfolk 1554, executed for treason.
[4] The excommunication and deposition of Elizabeth.

St Marcellus he readily obtained the consent of Philip. But then began the difficulties. Alva,[1] who had favoured the design, & intended his son to be leader, when he found Vitelli placed at its head began to suggest numerous obstacles, & to squander time; then he asked that Ridolfi might be sent to him at Brussels, & while Ridolfi was there the Duke of Norfolk was found out & beheaded, & the whole plot blown. He could not return to England, & the goods & credits he had accumulated in his nine years residence were confiscated. He then recounts the promises made to him by Pius V, & calls as witnesses Cardinals Allessandrino & Rusticucci, & appeals to the copies of the instructions given him, existing in the secret archives.

I will try whether I can get at any of these instructions, when I am well enough to make the essay. But unless they have been copied by Theiner I don't know how. I have sounded Stevenson, but he has only access to Papers of the time of Henry VIII.

I have not yet presented any of the letters you so kindly gave me, & indeed I am not now in a presentable state myself. And the slippery condition of Minghetti's tenure of office I suppose now occupies the minds of people to the exclusion of other matters. So I shall wait for more strength & a better opportunity.

Stevenson tells me that there are 48 conventual libraries now at the Collegio Romano, where a Commission is forming from them one great library, & separating duplicates for sale. This is being done in a manner both perfunctory & ignorant. It is probable that among the rejected books will be a whole library of the literature Father Parsons & his successors circulated in Italy, to give an account to the Italian contributors of the successes of the missionaries whom their charity helped to send into England.—By the bye, I found a letter of Parsons at Florence, of 1602, protesting by all the gods that he had never favoured the Spanish succession, & never opposed the Scottish!—If you could set somebody upon Bonghi[2] you might have a famous haul. I wish I had health to do it; but I cannot undertake it, unless it falls into my mouth like a ripe cherry. I will have a talk about it at the Valicella when I can go there.

I think I shall be able to prove that the Earl of Leicester[3] was in Ridolfi's plot, that he intended also to get the English Crown by his marriage with Mary, & that he was privy to the rising of 1569, & only shirked at the last moment. Ridolfi's letter certainly implicates a whole

---

[1] Fernando Alvarez de Toledo, duque de Alba (1507–82), Spanish soldier, governor of the Netherlands 1567–73.

[2] Ruggiero Bonghi (1828–95), Italian scholar and politician.

[3] Robert Dudley (1532/3–88), earl of Leicester 1564, favourite of Elizabeth I.

host of unnamed counsellors, & both *Leicester's Commonwealth* & *Watson's Quodlibets*, & the conversations of Westmoreland[1] in Exile fix upon Leicester as one of them. It will be as extraordinary a fact, if it turns out to be a fact, as the negotiations of Sir Henry Sidney[2] with Philip which the Spaniard (I forget his name) revealed some 50 years ago.

I am afraid that I shall not get to Venice—If I change my plans I will write, & in that case I will readily undertake any matter that I can do for you. Also I will take charge of anything that may be sent you from the Vallicella. Please let me have any suggestions that may occur to you about the books.

Renouf I am afraid returns from Egypt with broken health. His wife is in Germany, & he alone with his son in London. I saw her at Florence on her way to Munich.

We shall stay here about three weeks, & then pay a visit to Naples, if I can with prudence travel any further. I was condemned by an excellent doctor at Turin, Pachiotti, to 2 months in the Summer at Vichy or Carlsbad, if I wanted a cure.

Ever yours

R Simpson

---

[1] Charles Neville (1542/3–1601), 6th earl of Westmorland 1564, a leader of the Northern rising of 1569, fled into exile.

[2] Sir Henry Sidney (1529–86), lord deputy of Ireland 1565–71, 1575–8.

APPENDIX A

295A

SIMPSON TO ACTON · 7 MARCH 1861

Tuesday Evg

Dear Acton

I have been looking through the files of the Times for the American events—They are of two classes—1. the successive secessions—& 2. the successive proposals made diverse persons to patch up matters—The warlike demonstrations, as they have led to nothing, do not signify much—You will find a useful summary of the 2ᵈ class in a letter to which I have put three marks (111 ×) in my second index paper, which you will find in the roll I send with this—

That roll contains your papers—an index to the *nos* of the Times where you will find the information about America—if you want it—& a suggestion of Burns about the unfairness of the title Neo-protestantism of *Oxford*[1]—rather of the Universities—but perhaps the title is borne out in the body of the Article—

I enclose a note on the term "lay magazine", the idea of which I got from Brownson in an article in the Freeman's Journal of Feb 9. I forget what the Cardinal's is to wʰ he refers, but I fancy it must be some document connected with Veuillot's appeal to Rome[2]—Do you remember?—

I got to Victoria yesterday just in time to see the train go —however there was another at 4.30.—ten minutes after—

Ever yours
R Simpson

A certain Edw. Tudor Scargill has sent an article upon the Doctrinal Changes of the Establishment in the 17ᵗʰ Cent.[3] I have not read a word of it—I don't know that it is a bad subject—but I think I have read some effusions of the same Scargill that were decidedly bad—

---

[1] Oxenham's article. One of the Essayists and Reviewers was a Cambridge man.
[2] In 1853 the archbishop of Paris condemned Veuillot's *Univers*. Veuillot appealed to the Pope, who supported his lay magazine against the archbishop.
[3] Not published. See Letter 296 n. 4.

301A

Dear Acton

Some Scotch writer has been making a book about the gates of knowledge—to wit, I suppose, the 5 senses—I maintain there are six—I add that gate whereby in our youth knowledge is injected clyster-wise to the brain by means of the birch. This gate in me having been obstructed during the last week by a carbuncle has shut up the field of my ideas so much that I could neither read nor write & I dont know when I shall be able to do it again—

However I have read enough of Hennessey[1] to see that it is a very indifferent article, & absurdly pseudo-scientific in its verbiage—It is worthy of the social science association (w^h he mentions openly & talks of having "alluded to") but hardly of the R, however, I suppose we must have it—I certainly think that the decimal humbug shd be cut out, but that does not remove the root of the evil, for the whole gist of his article is that true political liberty is there where the whole nation like a flock of sheep follows the prescriptions of the social science physicians, & carries out its social life by geometric scale, under the guidance of a philosophic tyrant—That is very well for France, or perhaps Ireland, but I hope it will never do for us.

Wetherell is very ill. He is up & about but he writes like an old man, & the doctors have forbidden him to write a page under pain of paralysis. So we shall have a short notice of Montalembert this time,[2] & probably no current events from him—

He has not yet got Ward's letter,[3] nor have I, though Burns regularly sends to me what is sent to the R.—consisting chiefly of a long letter a week from Finlayson, w^h of course I do not look at, as no one w^d think of decyphering his handwriting without being paid for it.

Wetherell has still my second edition of Ward.[4] I have been carefully over the whole ground again, & find that I have kept well within the mark with regard to severity—still I have cut out all the passages which were at all railing, & have left the facts to speak for themselves through a thin mist of courteous language.

I hope to be able to get up to see you on Tuesday or Wednesday, for I can walk or stand though I cannot sit—

Ever yours faithfully
R Simpson

Sunday

---

[1] An unpublished article.   [2] No short notices were published in the May *Rambler*.
[3] 'Catholic Education.'   [4] The second draft of 'Dr. Ward's Philosophy'.

APPENDIX B

E. MARY SIMPSON TO ACTON · 9 APRIL 1876

Chez il Conte C. Smithe de Heritz
Villa Sciarra
Fuori di Porta Salara
Roma
Italy
Sunday Ap. 9—1876.

Dear Lord Acton

I write to give you heavy news—I lost my dear husband last Wed^y. We came out here by the kind invitation of our friends hoping that the country air and food might help him to recover from the bad attack which began after we had been in Rome a week. But he did not appear to improve in strength or to get relief from the pain, and on Tuesday evening he was seized with a violent fainting fit & sickness—this returned at 9—and again at 5 in the morning. After that he never rallied nor spoke though he was not unconscious the whole time till 11 when he breathed his last—He did not feel to be dying he said—after the second attack, but wished for the last sacraments as safer—The parish priest lives a long way off & did not arrive in time for him to speak—but he heard some of the prayers that were going on. He had been to Confession & Communion on Ash Wed^y. I know you will sympathize with my sorrow. The whole journey has been too much for him, but as it is not certain that the longer he lived the more he would have suffered, I think that everything has happened by the mercy of God.

I have the manuscript that he copied for you at Florence[1] & will send it to Aldenham when I get home—Mr Stevenson has most kindly offered to be my escort and he has also provided me with money for immediate expenses. We leave Rome on Easter Monday & shall be in England on Friday morning. I write hurriedly not wishing you to hear from anyone else first[2]—but I have so many letters to write that I can scarcely get through them.

Believe me
Y^{rs} Very Sincerely
E. Mary Simpson

[1] Ridolfi's letter.
[2] Döllinger heard the news from Mrs Renouf by April 11 and informed Acton. See Conzemius, III (München, 1971), 164–5.

BIBLIOGRAPHY

This does not purport to be a complete bibliography of works by or about Acton and Simpson. It incorporates three elements: a complete list of non-contemporary works cited in these volumes; a list (not complete) of works of reference frequently consulted by the editors, which will indicate the evidence on which the footnotes are based; and a limited list of other works relevant to this subject. A nearly complete bibliography of Acton's writings is supplied by Shaw, followed by Hoselitz in Acton's *Essays on Freedom and Power*; for works on Acton, a thorough list is appended to Himmelfarb's biography (1952), and ample lists are in the later bibliographies of Conzemius and of McElrath–Holland, *Lord Acton: The Decisive Decade*. For Simpson, see McElrath's biography. Attributions of authorship of articles in the *Rambler, Home & Foreign Review* and other periodicals are drawn from *The Wellesley Index to Victorian Periodicals*. It would be useless, and it would add unnecessarily to the cost of this volume, to reproduce bibliographies which can be found in these sources.

MANUSCRIPT SOURCES

Birmingham Oratory, Papers of Cardinal Newman.
British Museum, Additional Manuscripts (Gladstone Collection).
Cambridge University Library, Additional Manuscripts (Acton Collection).
Downside Abbey: Papers collected by Cardinal Gasquet, chiefly letters of Lord
    Acton to Richard Simpson and T. F. Wetherell.
Mitcham Public Library, Simpson Collection.
Pembroke College, Oxford, Archives (Renouf Papers).
Salop County Council Archives, Shrewsbury.
Westminster Archdiocesan Archives, 1847–65.
Woodruff MSS: Correspondence of Lord Acton in the possession of Mr Douglas
    Woodruff; now located in Cambridge University Library.

PRINTED SOURCES

Abercrombie, Nigel. *The Life and Work of Edmund Bishop*. London, 1960.
Acton, John Emerich Edward Dalberg Acton, 1st Baron. *Essays on Church and State*. Edited by Douglas Woodruff. London, 1952.
    Essays on Freedom and Power. Edited by Gertrude Himmelfarb, with a Bibliography of Acton's writings by Bert F. Hoselitz. Boston, 1948.
    Historical Essays and Studies. Edited by J. N. Figgis and R. V. Laurence. London, 1908.
    The History of Freedom and Other Essays. Edited by J. N. Figgis and R. V. Laurence. London, 1907.
    Letters of Lord Acton to Mary, Daughter of the Rt. Hon. W. E. Gladstone. Edited by Herbert Paul. London, 1904. (2nd edition, London, 1913.)
    Lord Acton and his Circle. Edited by Abbot [Francis Aidan] Gasquet. London, 1906. (Reprinted, New York, 1968.)

Selections from the Correspondence of the First Lord Acton. Edited by J. N. Figgis and R. V. Laurence. London, 1917.

Allgemeine Deutsche Biographie. Edited by Rochus von Liliencron and Franz Xaver von Wegele. 56 vols. Leipzig, 1875–1912.

Allibone, Samuel Austin. *A Critical Dictionary of English Literature and British and American Authors Living and Deceased.* 3 vols. Philadelphia, 1858–74. Supplement by J. F. Kirk, 2 vols. Philadelphia, 1891.

Altholz, Josef Lewis. 'Bibliographical Note on the *Rambler*', *Papers of the Bibliographical Society of America,* LVI (1962), 113–14.

    The Liberal Catholic Movement in England: The "Rambler" and its Contributors, 1848–1864. London, 1962.

    'Newman and History', *Victorian Studies,* VII (March 1964), 285–94.

    'On the Use of "Communicated" in the *Rambler*', *Victorian Periodicals Newsletter,* I (January 1968), 28–9.

    'The Political Behavior of the English Catholics, 1850–1867', *Journal of British Studies,* III (November 1964), 89–103.

Auchmuty, James J. 'Acton's Election as an Irish Member of Parliament', *English Historical Review,* LXI (September 1946), 394–405.

Biographie Nationale [de Belgique]. 28 vols. Bruxelles, 1866–1944.

Boase, Frederick. *Modern English Biography.* 3 vols., 3 suppl. vols. Truro, 1892–1921.

British Museum. General Catalogue of Printed Books. 263 vols. London, 1959–66.

Burke, John Bernard. *A Genealogical and Heraldic History of the Peerage and Baronetage of the British Empire.* London, 1843–9ff.

Butterfield, Herbert. *Lord Acton* (Historical Association, General Series, IX). London, 1948.

Campbell, Lily B. *Shakespeare's "Histories". Mirrors of Elizabethan Policy.* Berkeley, Cal., 1947.

Casartelli, Louis Charles. 'Our Diamond Jubilee', *Dublin Review,* CXVIII (April 1896), 245–71.

Catalogue Générale des Livres Imprimés de la Bibliothèque Nationale. 211 vols. Paris, 1924–72.

The Catholic Directory, Ecclesiastical Register and Almanac. London, 1860–5.

The Catholic Encyclopedia. 15 vols. New York, 1907–14.

Chadwick, Owen. *The Victorian Church.* 2 vols. London, 1966–70.

Crone, John S. *A Concise Dictionary of Irish Biography.* Revised edition, Dublin, 1937.

The Dictionary of National Biography. Edited by Leslie Stephen and Sidney Lee. 63 vols. London, 1885–1900. *Supplement I.* 3 vols. London, 1901. (Both reissued, 22 vols. London, 1908–9.) *Supplement II, 1901–11.* London, 1920. *Supplement III, 1912–1921.* London, 1927.

The Dublin Review. Vols. XLI–LIV. London, 1856–64.

'The Dublin Review. General List of Articles. Vols. I–CXVIII (1836–1896)', *Dublin Review,* CXVIII (April 1896), 467–520.

Enciclopedia Cattolica. 12 vols. Rome and Florence, 1948–54.

Enciclopedia Universal Ilustrada. 70 vols. Barcelona, 1907(?)–30.

Encyclopedia Britannica. 24 vols. 14th edition, various printings. Chicago, 1929ff.

Fasnacht, G. E. *Acton's Political Philosophy*. London, 1952.

Foster, Joseph. *Alumni Oxonienses: The Members of the University of Oxford, 1715–1886*. 4 vols. London, 1886–7.

Gillow, Joseph. *A Literary and Biographical History, or Bibliographical Dictionary of the English Catholics*. 5 vols. London, [1885–1903].

Gorman, W. Gordon. *Converts to Rome*. London, 1910.

Grand Larousse Encyclopédique. 10 vols. Paris, 1960–4.

La Grande Encyclopédie. 31 vols. Paris, 1886–1902.

Hansard's Parliamentary Debates, 3rd series. 356 vols. London, 1830–91.

Himmelfarb, Gertrude. *Lord Acton: A Study in Conscience and Politics*. Chicago, 1952.

Holland, James C. 'The Education of Lord Acton'. Unpublished Ph.D. dissertation, Catholic University of America, 1968.

The Home and Foreign Review. 4 vols. London, 1862–4.

Ignaz von Döllinger/Lord Acton: Briefwechsel 1850–1890. 3 vols. Edited by Victor Conzemius. München, 1963–71.

Kayser, C. G. *Vollständiges Bücher-Lexikon, 1750–1910*. 36 vols. Leipzig, 1834–1910.

Knowles, M. David. *Cardinal Gasquet as an Historian*. London, 1957.

Lally, Frank E. *As Lord Acton Says*. Newport, R.I., 1942.

Library of Congress. *Catalogue of Books Represented by Library of Congress Printed Cards*. 167 vols. Ann Arbor, 1942–6.

MacDougall, Hugh A. *The Acton–Newman Relations: The Dilemma of Christian Liberalism*. New York, 1962.

McElrath, Damian. *Richard Simpson 1820–1876. A Study in XIXth Century English Liberal Catholicism* (Bibliothèque de la revue d'histoire ecclésiastique, Fasc. 55). Louvain, 1972.

'Richard Simpson and Count de Montalembert, the *Rambler* and the *Correspondant*', *Downside Review*, LXXXIV (April 1966), 150–70.

'Richard Simpson and John Henry Newman: The *Rambler*, Laymen, and Theology', *Catholic Historical Review*, LII (January 1967), 509–33.

'Richard Simpson on Shakespeare', *Dublin Review*, CCXL (Autumn 1966), 261–74.

The Syllabus of Pius IX: Some Reactions in England (Bibliothèque de la revue d'histoire ecclésiastique, Fasc. 39). Louvain, 1964.

'Your's Ever, J. D. A.', *Interest*, III (Fall 1967), 10–16.

McElrath, Damian, James C. Holland, *et al. Lord Acton: The Decisive Decade 1864–1874* (Bibliothèque de la revue d'histoire ecclésiastique, Fasc. 51). Louvain, 1970.

Mathew, David. *Acton: The Formative Years*. London, 1946.

Lord Acton and his Times. London, 1968.

The New Catholic Encyclopedia. 15 vols. New York, 1967.

Newman, John Henry. *On Consulting the Faithful in Matters of Doctrine*. Edited by John Coulson. New York, 1961.

The Letters and Diaries of John Henry Newman. Vols. XI–XXII. Edited by Charles Stephen Dessain *et al*. London, 1961–72.

The Rambler. 1st series, 12 vols. London, 1848–54. New (2nd) series, 10 1/3 vols. London, 1854–9. New (3rd) series, 6 vols. London, 1859–62.

Ribner, Irving. *The English History Play in the Age of Shakespeare*. Princeton, 1957.

Roe, W. G. *Lamennais and England: The Reception of Lamennais's Religious Ideas in England in the Nineteenth Century*. London, 1966.

Shaw, William Arthur. *A Bibliography of the Historical Works of Dr. Creighton, Dr. Stubbs, Dr. S. R. Gardiner, and the late Lord Acton*. London, 1903.

The Times. London, 1858–75.

Ward, Wilfrid. *The Life of John Henry Cardinal Newman*. 2 vols. London, 1912.

Watkin, Aelred, and Herbert Butterfield. 'Gasquet and the Acton–Simpson Correspondence', *Cambridge Historical Journal*, x (1950), 75–105.

The Wellesley Index to Victorian Periodicals 1824–1900. 2 vols. Edited by Walter E. Houghton. Toronto, 1966–72.

Who Was Who. London, 1919ff.

INDEX OF PERSONS

Carnot, Lazare, 233
Carpentier, Edouard, *HF*, *27*
Cartwright, William Cornwallis, *C*, *230*–1
Case, George, *I*, *201n*; *HF*, 123; *HF* censure controversy, 24; Vatican Decrees, 291, 315–17, 323–4, 327
Castlerosse, Gertrude Thynne Browne, Lady (later Countess of Kenmare), 92
Castlerosse, Valentine Augustus Browne, Viscount (later Earl of Kenmare), *WR*, 124
Castro y Rossi, Adolfo de, 11
Catena, Giovanni Girolamo, 299–300
Catesby, Robert, 311
Catesby, Sir William, 311
Catherine II (the Great), 115
Centlivre, Susanna, 117–19
Chalmers, Alexander, 171–2
Champagney, Frédéric Perrenot de Granvelle, Seigneur de, 298
Charles I (England), 226n
Charles II (England), 38, 59, 234; *HF*, 16, 40
Charles V (Holy Roman Empire), 146
Charles, Archduke, 304
Charlton, Mary (later Marchesa Pasqualino), *300*
Cherubini, Laertius, 278
Chevalier, Michel, *II*, *306n*; 131, 134
Childers, Hugh Culling Eardley, 255; *HF*, *92*, 111, 122
Chirol, Alexander, *285n*
Chirol, Harriet (née Ashburnham), *285*
Christie, Albany James, *I*, *124n*; 128
Christmas, Henry (Noel-Fearn), *205*
Chunder, Bholanauth, 263
Cialdini, Enrico, *231*, 233
Circourt, Adolphe Marie Pierre, Comte de, *HF*, *159*
Clarendon, George William Frederick Villiers, 4th Earl of, *HF*, *92*, 103n
Clark, William George, *309*
Clifford, Bishop William Joseph Hugh, *II*,*302n*; 200; *HF* censure controversy, 22–4; Vatican Decrees, 291, 303, 305, 317
Cobden, Richard, *249*
Cochin, Pierre-Suzanne-Augustin, *I*, *150n*; 4
Coffin, Robert Aston, later Bishop, *I*, *77n*; Döllinger's alleged loss of faith, 289–90; *HF* censure controversy, 3, 15, 20–3, 41, 43, 57; Vatican Council, 282
Cole, Sir Henry, *309*
Colenso, Bishop John William, 53; *HF*, 95, 98, *99*–100
Coleridge, Henry James, S.J., Vatican Decrees controversy, *328*
Coleridge, Sir John Duke, 1st Baron, *246*
Coleridge, Samuel Taylor, 119, 146, 167
Coles, Cowper Phipps, *HF*, *74*, 109
Collier, John Payne, *240*
Collingridge, Peter, *I*, *70n*; *HF*, 49–50

Colombière, Claude de la, *59*
Comte, Auguste, 120, 125
Connolly, Archbishop Thomas Louis, on Manning's pastoral, 286; Vatican Council, *281–2*, 286
Conway, Sir John, 311, 313
Conzemius, Victor, 27n, 82n, 90n, 103n, 170n, 185n, 302n, 345n
Cornthwaite, Bishop Robert, *HF* censure controversy, *28*
Correo, 227
Corser, Thomas, *305*
Cousin, Victor, *HF*, 131, 134
Cranmer, George, *37*
Cranmer, Archbishop Thomas, *64*, 166
Cromwell, Oliver, 36–7, 119
Cullen, Archbishop Paul, later Cardinal,*I*, *83n*; 32n, 224; *Freeman's Journal*, 130
Cumming, Dr John: *HF* censure controversy, *54*
Cyprian of Cordova, 107

D'Andrea, Cardinal Girolamo, *237*–8
Dante Alighieri, 195, 310n; *HF*, 119, 122, 130, 134
Darboy, Archbishop Georges, Vatican Council, 294; Vatican Decrees, *303*
Darnell, Nicholas, *I*, *99n*; 131, 238–9; *HF*, 7, 12, 46
Darwin, Charles, 101n
Davies, John, 171
Davis (copyist), 212–13, 215, 217, 219, 222, 226, 237–9
Dean, Edward, *II*, *253n*; 258
Dease, Edmund Gerald, *ER*, 213; *HF*, 167, *169*, 180–1
Dease, Col Sir Gerald Richard, *142n*
Dease, James A., 213n
Dechamps, Cardinal Victor, Vatican Council, *294*
Delane, John Thadeus, *260*
Delarue, Gabriel-Jules ('DeStrada'), 220
DeLisle, Ambrose Phillipps, *II*, *173n*; 22
Delius, Nikolaus, 163, 168
Dembinski, Count Henryk, *100*
DeNeve, John, *C* and *HF*, *218*
Denison, John Evelyn (later Viscount Ossington), *92*
DeQuincey, Thomas, *HF*, 50
Derby, Edward George Geoffrey Smith, 14th Earl of, 246
Derby, Edward Henry Stanley, 15th Earl of, 255
DeRossi, Giovanni Batista, *II*, *20n*; *HF*, 78, 83, 85, 90, 118, 157; Vatican Council, 293
Dessain, Charles Stephen, 32n
Deutinger, Martin, *II*, *325n*; *HF*, 20, 29, 38, 57, 73, 82, 110, 115–16, 121–2, 129–30, 132–4, 158
Deutsch, Emanuel, *QR*, 270–1
Devereux, Robert, 2nd Earl of Essex, 162, *239*–40
Dickens, Charles, 119, 160, 262, 265

Gladstone (cont.)
249, 251–6, 260–2, 275–6, 279, 280n, 285, 292; *HF*, 111, 116, 119, 122, 131, 142–4, 160n; Vatican Archives project, 221–3, 225–9; Vatican Decrees controversy, 318, 320, 324, 326–8, 333–4
Gladstone, Mrs W. E. (Catherine Glynne), 320
Glyn, George Grenfell, 2nd Baron Wolverton, *265*
Gneist, Heinrich Rudolf Hermann von, *142*
Godefrid of Winchester, 107
Goethe, Johann Wolfgang von, 91, 119, 125, 146, 310n
Goldsmid, Julian, *260*
González de Santalla, Thyrsus, 294, 304
Goodwin, Harvey, *169*
Gortchakov, Prince Aleksandr Mikhailovich, *118*
Gordon, Lord George, 71
Gordon, Mary, 49
Goschen, George Joachim, *297*
Goss, Bishop Alexander, *104*
Graham, Sir James, *HF*, 110, 116
Grant, John, 311
Grant, Bishop Thomas, *I*, *112n*; 65–6, 201; *HF* censure controversy, 21, 23, 71, 134
Grant Duff, Sir Mountstuart E., 263–4, *279*
Granvelle, Cardinal Antoine Perrenot de, 304
Granville, George Leveson-Gower, 2nd Earl, *I*, *183n*; 44, 47, 52, 83, 224, 256, 276, 279, 281
Grässe, J. G. T., 108
Gratry, Auguste-Joseph-Alphonse, *I*, *194n*; 4
Gravina, Domenico Benedetto, 184
Green, Mary Anne Everett (née Wood), 302n
Green, Thomas Lewis, *II*, *157n*; 16, 20, 22, 121, 125, 131, 237–8; *HF* censure controversy, 13; Vatican Decrees controversy, 324–6
Gregory VII, Pope, 26
Gregory XIII, Pope, 298–9, 335
Gregory XVI, Pope, 294
Greville, Ludowick, 311
Grey, Sir George, 121
Grimm, Jakob and Wilhelm, *HF*, 122, 142, 144
Grosseteste, Bishop Robert, *HF*, 11, 20, 28
Gualterio, Filippo Antonio, Marchese, *234–8*
Guasti, Cesare, *335*
Guéranger, Prosper Louis Pascal, 155
Guise, Henri de Lorraine, duc de, *317–18*
Guise, Cardinal Louis de, 311
Guizot, François, 146
Günther, Anton, *I*, *176n*; 29, 133
Guy, Robert Ephrem, *II*, *302n*; *HF*, 38

Haigh, Daniel S., 210
Hall, Captain Robert, *II*, *199n*; 203, 208, 255, 270, 273, 287–8, 297–8; *HF*, 74–7, 88–90, 93, 95–6, 99–100, 104n, 107–9, 154
Hall, Spencer, 304
Halliwell-Phillipps, James Orchard, 162, *240*
Hamilton, Hans Claude, *302*
Hamilton, William Douglas, *302*
Hamlet, 146
Haneberg, Daniel Bonifaz, *327*
Hardy, Sir Thomas Duffus, *75*, 107–8, 162, 209, 292, 302; *HF*, 76–7; *NBR*, 266; Vatican Archives project, 223–6, 228, 230
Hartington, Spencer Compton Cavendish, Marquess of, 260
Hasting, Joseph, *35*
Hay, Sir John Charles Dalrymple, *88*
Hayd, Heinrich, *HF*, 29n
Haynald, Archbishop Ludwig, later Cardinal, Vatican Decrees, 302
Hayward, Abraham, *HF*, 91, 103; *NBR*, 103n
Hayward, Sir John, *240*
Hecker, Isaac, *I*, *25n*; 21, 23, 198; Vatican Council, 280–6, 288, 291
Hefele, Bishop Karl Joseph von, Vatican Council, *281*
Hegel, Georg Wilhelm Friedrich, 189, 200, 205
Heine, Heinrich, *122*
Held, Friedrich von, 21
Helfenstein, Jacob, *II*, *274*; *HF*, 73, 110, 112, 152
Henry II (England), 26, 71n
Henry III (France), *318*
Henry IV (England), 84, 240
Henry IV (France), 317–*18*
Henry VIII (England), 64, 84, 106, 110n, 302–3, 336
Henry of Lincoln, 107
Herbart, Johann Friedrich, 133
Herbert, Sir Arthur James, *43*, 46–7, 52
Herbert, Elizabeth A'Court (Lady Herbert of Lea), *88*, 93
Herbert, Sidney (Baron Herbert of Lea), *I*, *197n*; 88n
Herodotus, 272
Herries and Farquhar (bank), 198
Hilary, St, 55
Hodges, Nicholas William, *I*, *16n*; 123
Hodgkinson, Grosvenor, 246
Höfer, Ferdinand Jean Chrétien, 264
Hohenlohe-Schillingsfürst, Chlodwig Karl Victor, Prince of, 282
Holland, James C., 204n
Homer, 114, 280
Honorius I, Pope, 244, 262n, *265*, 267, 268n, 269, 274, 279n, 282, 285n, 286n, 288
Hooker, Richard, 37

355

Macaulay (Irish editor), 3
Macaulay, Thomas Babington, 1st Baron, 37, 86n, 89
MacCabe, William Bernard, *II, 255n*; *HF*, 38, 141n, 150
McCarthy, Denis Florence, *HF*, 153, 169
McClellan, General George B., 18
McDonnell, Thomas Michael, 26; *Catholic Magazine*, 32
MacDougall, Hugh A., 281n
McElrath, Damian, 204n, 326n, 327n, 328n
MacHale, Archbishop John, Vatican Council, *282–3*; Vatican Decrees, 303
Macmullen, Richard Gell, *I, 13n*; 31, 33–4, 39, 44, 74–5; *HF* censure controversy, 71
Madden, Sir Frederick, *II, 69n*; *HF*, 30, 38
Maguire, John, *I, 30n*; 26
Maintenon, Mme de, 119
Malachi, St, 107
Malone, Sylvester, 193n
Manning, Henry Edward, later Cardinal, *I, 9n*; 22, 35, 39–40, 79, 199–200; *DR*, 44, 127–8, 130, 135; *HF* censure controversy, 12, 33; Vatican Archives project, 224, 226, 228; Vatican Council, 277–8, 281–2, 286, 289–91; Vatican Decrees controversy, 319–23, 326n, 327, 329–31, 333
Mansel, Henry Longueville, *I, 168n*; 181
Mansi, Giovanni Domenico, 230
Manzoni, Alessandro, 119, 135n
Maret, Archbishop Henri Louise Charles, *I, 194n*; Vatican Council, 293; Vatican Decrees, 302
Marisco, Adam de, *28*
Marlot, Guillaume, 313–14
Marlowe, Christopher, 146, 163, 172
Marshall, Thomas William, *I, 13n*; 14, 65–6; *DR*, 44
Martial, 91
Martínez Izquierdo, Narciso, *118*
Martynov, Ivan Mikhailovich, *88*
Mary of Modena (Mary Beatrice), 59n, 106
Mary Stuart, Queen of Scots, *106*, 119, 304; *HF*, 57, 110, 167, 335–6
Massinger, Philip, 162
Matagne, Jules, *205*
Maurice, Frederick Denison, 106, 109
Maximilian II (Bavaria), *192*
Melbourne, William Lamb, 2nd Viscount, *254*
Melchers, Archbishop Paul, Vatican Council, *294*
Melun, Armand de, *4*
Menabrea, Luigi Federico, *233–4*, 236
Mendoza, Bernardino de, *218*
Meres, Francis, 161
Merivale, Charles, *92*; *NBR*, 267n, 268–9
Merivale, Louisa A., 269–70
Merles, Don Frances, 300

Merrion, Dr, 314
Meynell, Charles, *I, 5n*; *HF*, 98n, 99, 104
Michaud, Eugène-Philibert, *334*
Mill, John Stuart, 103, 260, 262
Milman, Henry Hart, *93*; *HF*, 111
Milner, Bishop John, *25–6*, 36n; *HF*, 20n, 22n, 31n, 32, 34, 38, 44n, 46n, 51, 52n, 56n, 57n, 65, 68n, 70–1, 72n, 74n, 75n, 77n, 79n, 80n, 83n, 93, 95n, 96
Minghetti, Marco, *232–3*, 236, 336
Mivart, St George Jackson, *298*
Molesworth, Sir William, *170*
Molinari, Gustave de, 132
Monsell, William, *I, 181n*; 202, 264; *HF*, 38, 56, 60, 73; *WR*, 123–4
Montalembert, Charles, Comte de, *I, 39n*; 32, 267; *Correspondant*, 94, 99, 131–2; *HF*, 131, 135, 140–1; Malines Congress, 128, 131–2; *R*, 342
Monteith, Robert, *I, 168n*; *WR*, 124
More, St Thomas, *HF*, 112, 122, 131
Moriarty, Bishop David, *HF* censure controversy, *63*; Vatican Decrees, 303
Morris, John Brande (Jack), *I, 13n*; *HF*, 7, 14, 17, 22
Moule, Henry, *HF*, 80n, *81*, 111n, 116, 122, 156–7, 163–4, 166–7
Mudie and Smith (lending library), 30, 64, 83, 107, 109, 113, 127n, 136, 152, 154
Muratori, Lodovico Antonio, 299
Muzzarelli, Alfonso, S.J., Vatican Council, 294

Nägelsbach, Carl Friedrich, 90
Napoleon I, 93, 160
Napoleon III, *I, 8n*; 6n, 100, 231–2, 235, 266–7
Napoléon, Prince, *233*
Nelson, Marsh, *260*
Newman, John Henry, later Cardinal, *I, 47n*; 23, 26, 30, 32, 36, 51, 60, 63n, 70–1, 85, 99, 104, 144, 181, 190, 212, 244, 262, 281n; Catholic university in England, 116n, 146, 199, 238; *HF*, 117, 172; *HF* censure controversy, 3, 12, 42–3, 46–7; *R*, 67; Vatican Council, 282; Vatican Decrees, 289; Vatican Decrees controversy, 332n, 333
Nicholas I (Russia), 205
Nicholls, Sir George, 83
Niehues, Bernhard, 69
Noah, 27
Noel, Baptist Wriothesley, *HF*, *105*
Nolan, Michael, 83
Norfolk, Henry Fitzalan-Howard, 15th Duke of, 333n
Norfolk, Thomas Howard, 4th Duke of, *335–6*
Northcote, James Spencer, *I, 78n*; Colenso pamphlet, 98n, 104; *HF*, 3, 41, 43, 85
Norton, Caroline, 117

Oakeley, Frederick, *I*, *13n*; Vatican Decrees, 291
Oedipus, 91
O'Ferrall, Richard More, *I*, *189n*; *WR*, 123
O'Hagan, John, *I*, *217n*; *HF*, 7, 16, 31, 38, 40n, 56, 57n, 73, 87, 97, 111n, 112, 116; *London Review*, 44, 46n
O'Hagan, Thomas, *II*, *88n*; 261–2; *WR*, 123, 132
O'Hanlon, John, *HF*, 157
Oliphant, Margaret, *HF*, 35
Oliver, George, 26
Orlov, Prince Nikolai Alekseevich, *118*, 218
Owen, John, 91
Owen, Sir Richard, *HF*, 101
Oxenham, Henry Nutcombe, *II*, *60n*; 26, 64; *DR*, 205; *HF*, 83; *London Review*, 46; *R*, 341; *WR*, 123
Ozanam, Antoine Frédéric, *HF*, 30, 38, 52, 56

Pachiotti, Dr, 337
Paine, Thomas, 80
Pakington, Sir John, later Baron Hampton, *297*
Paley, Frederick Apthorpe, *II*, *279n*; 26; *HF*, 7, 16, 38, 56, 78, 122, 130, 133–4, 144, 154
Palgrave, Francis Turner, *310*
Palgrave, William Gifford, *HF*, *120*, 188, 190–1
Palmé, V. (publisher), *269*
Palmerston, John Temple, 3rd Viscount, *HF*, 141, 151, 169
Panizzi, Anthony, *II*, *64n*; 279, 281
Panzani, Gregorio, *219*, 227
Paris, Matthew, 229
Parker, J. H. and J. (publisher), 268
Parker, Archbishop Matthew, *166*
Parsons, Robert, S.J., *218*, 220, 230, 336
Pascal, Blaise, 144
Pasolini, Giuseppe, 233
Passaglia, Carlo, *56*
Patrick, St, 40n
Patrizi, Cardinal Constantino, *118*
Paul, St, 85
Paul III, Pope, 5n
Paul IV, Pope, 267, 278, 286, *304*
Pauli, Reinhold, 89, 210
Pearson, Charles Henry, *II*, *276n*; *HF*, 141n, 142, 150–1
Peel, General Jonathan, *250*
Peel, Sir Robert, 2nd baronet, 86, 89, 250n
Peel, Sir Robert, 3rd baronet, *112*
Peele, George, 146
Pembroke, William Herbert, 3rd Earl of, 162
Périn, Charles, *HF*, 38, 52, 56
Perraud, Adolphe, *HF*, *4*, 7n, 44n
Perrone, Giovanni, S.J., *55*, 155; Vatican Council, 293

Peter, St, 106, 294
Petrarch, 195
Petre, Sir Edward, later S.J., *226*
Petre, William Bernard, 12th Baron, *I*, *67n*; *WR*, 124–5
Petrie, Henry, 209–11
Philip II (Spain), 300, 304, 335–7
Phillimore, John George, 109, 112
Phillips, Georg, 210n, 215, 217
Pinchart, Alexander, *C*, *215*, 217–18
Pinda of Hanenberg, 107
Piot, Guillaume Joseph Charles, *217*
Pitra, Jean Baptiste, *85*
Pitt, William (the Younger), 307; *HF*, 56, 73, 80–2
Pius V, Pope St, 36, 298–300, 335–6; Vatican Decrees controversy, 331
Pius IX, Pope, 10, 21, 27, 32, 56n, 87, 91n, 145, 200–1, 215, 235, 326n, 328; *HF* censure controversy, 5n, 63n; *S*'s evaluation of, 288–91; *Syllabus*, 328; *Tuas libenter*, 186; *Univers*, 341n; Vatican Archives project, 106; Vatican Council, 282, 294–5; Vatican Decrees controversy, 329
Place, Bishop Charles Philippe, later Archbishop and Cardinal, Vatican Decrees, *303*
Plowden, Francis Peter, *71–2*
Plowden and Cholmeley (bankers), *285*
Plutarch, 272
Pole, Cardinal Reginald, *227*, 266–7, 283
Pollen, John Hungerford, *II*, *312n*; *HF*, 57, 73
Poole, Reginald Stuart, *309*
Pope-Hennessey, Sir John, *I*, *182n*; *R*, 342
Porter, Endymion, 312
Potthast, August, 210
Pownall, Assheton, *104*, 306
Prat, Jean Marie, *HF*, 5
Preller, Ludwig, 86
Prendergast, John Patrick, *II*, *189n*; 3–4
Prestwich, Sir Joseph, *C*, *215*, 217; *NBR*, 271
Price, Bonamy, *HF*, *57*, 73, 114, 169
Price, Edward, *Dolman's Magazine*, 32
Priestley, Joseph, *63*
Proudhon, Pierre Joseph, *HF*, *61*
Pufendorf, Samuel, *79*
Pythagoras, *HF*, 9, 34, 44, 46, 57, 71, 81–2

Quaritch (bookseller), 11

Rae, William Fraser, *Westminster Review*, 195n
Raine, James, *HF*, 113
Raleigh, Sir Walter, *239–40*
Ranke, Leopold von, *II*, *25n*; 161; *HF*, 82–3, 91
Ratazzi, Urbano, *231–3*
Rawlinson, Sir Henry Creswicke, 1st Baron, *309*

Reed, Sir Edward James, *109*
Reed, Henry Hope, 146
Rees, William Jenkins, 9
Reeve, Henry, *II, 240n; ER*, 103, 213; *S*'s projected *ER* article, 16, 20, 22, 24, 29–31, 33
Reichensperger, August, *I, 173n; C*, 218; *HF*, 201
Reisach, Cardinal Karl August, Graf von, *200*, 215
Renan, Ernest, *HF*, 144
Renouf, Sir Peter le Page, *II, 321n;* 26, 202, 207–9, 215, 217, 252, 271, 296, 314n, 319, 337; *A*'s evaluation of, 139; British Museum post, 276–8, 281, 283, 309; *C*, 212–13; Catholic university in England, 144, 146; *HF*, 7, 27, 57, 65, 73, 77, 85, 92, 95–6, 111, 115–17, 119, 122–4, 127, 130–2, 135, 139, 142, 147n, 150–2, 156, 159, 161, 169, 180n, 188–91, 197–8; *Honorius* pamphlets, 244, 262–3, 265, 267–9, 271–2, 274, 279, 282, 286; *NBR*, 270, 280, 287, 291–2; School Inspector, 212, 257, 271, 274, 277; Vatican Council, 267; Vatican Decrees, 290; Vatican Decrees controversy, 321, 323–4, 327
Renouf, Mrs (née Ludovika Brentano), *200*, 222, 226, 238–9, 252, 274, 284–5, 292, 296, 337; British Museum post for her husband, 277, 279, 281; *Honorius* pamphlet, 252; *S*'s death, 345n, Vatican Decrees controversy, 319, 327
Ricasoli, Baron Bettino, *II, 167n;* 231, 233, 235, 323
Richard II (England), 162
Richard of London, 107
Richelieu, Cardinal Armand Jean du Plessis de, 106, 160
Ridolfi, Roberto, *335–6*, 345n
Riethmüller, Christopher James, 9n, 10, 31–2
Rio, Alexis François, *162–3*, 194–5
Ripon, George F. S. Robinson, Earl (later Marquess) of, *II, 55n;* 76, 260
Roberts, John William, *II, 212n; 12n*, 200, 203, 206, 274, 305; *DR*, 201; *HF*, 17, 19, 24, 29, 33, 39, 75–6, 110, 112, 115–16, 121–2, 181; *HF* censure controversy, 3, 6, 11–13, 33, 44, 56–7, 71; Vatican Decrees, 291
Roberts, T. W., 12n
Robson, Charles, 21, 72, 157–8, 161, 163, 165–7, 194, 197–8, 242
Robson and Levey (printers), 16–17, 19, 42, 58, 62, 65, 72, 104, 122, 136, 141, 156, 157n, 171n
Roda, Hieronimo de, 298
Romilly, John, 1st Baron, *75*, 106, 303; Vatican Archives project, 221–8
Roon, Albrecht Theodor Emil von, *297*
Roscher, Wilhelm Georg Friedrich, *HF*, 38, 52n, 56
Rothschild, Baron Lionel de, *260*

Rougemont, Abbé A., *II, 254n;* 91
Rouher, Eugène, *232*
Ruinart, Thierry (Théodore), 85
Russell, Arthur Tozer, 102n
Russell, Charles William, *I, 61n;* Vatican Archives project, 224
Russell, Lady William (née Elizabeth Anne Rawdon), *91*
Russell, Lord George William, *91n*
Russell, Odo William Leopold, later Baron Ampthill, 91, 262–3; Vatican Archives project, 222
Rusticucci, Cardinal Gerolamo, 336
Rutland, Roger Manners, 5th Earl of, 162
Ryder, Henry Ignatius Dudley, *291*
Ryley, Edward, *I, 179n; HF*, 19, 57, 114

Sacchini, Francesco, 228
Sadoleto, Jacopo, *II, 37n;* 85
St John, Ambrose, *I, 8n; HF* censure controversy, 42
Sainte-Beuve, Charles Augustin, 119
Salimbene degli Adami, *229*
Salisbury, Robert Arthur Talbot Gascoyne-Cecil, 3rd Marquess of, *280*
Salisbury, Robert Cecil, 1st Earl of, *239–40*, 314
Sand, George (Aurore Dupin Dudevant), 117, *184*
Sandeau, Jules, 117, 119
Santos, Don Emilio de, *23*
Sapieha, Prince Leon, *101*
Savonarola, Girolamo, *HF*, 19
Scargill, Edward Tudor, *II, 129n; R*, 341
Schédo-Ferroti, D. K. (Baron H. E. C. F. E. W. von Fircks), *118*
Scherer, Edmond, 122
Scherr, Archbishop Gregor von, *Tuas libenter*, 185n; Vatican Decrees, *303*
Schiller, Friedrich von, 91
Schlegel, August Wilhelm von, 91, 119, 146
Schollaert, François, 298; *C, 218;* Vatican Decrees controversy, 323
Schopenhauer, Arthur, 133
Schrader, Klemens, S.J., Vatican Council, *293*
Schwarzenberg, Cardinal Prince Friedrich zu, Vatican Decrees, *303*
Scialoja, Antonio, *236*
Scrope, Poulett, 248
Sebastian, King of Portugal, 299
Sfondrati, Celestino, 55
Sforza, Cardinal Riario, *235*
Shakespeare, John, 312
Shakespeare, William, 66, 117, 122, 160, 164–5, 167–8, 171, 240, 309n; *NBR*, 284–5; *S*'s writings on, 144–6, 155–6, 159, 162–3, 189, 190n, 191, 194–5, 198, 211, 229–30, 239, 270, 298, 303–4, 310–12, 314–15, 317
Sidney, Sir Henry, *337*

Sigerson, George, *265*
Simor, Archbishop Johann, later Cardinal, Vatican Decrees, *303*
Simpson, Elizabeth Mary (*S*'s wife), 207, 310; on death of husband, 345
Simpson, Robert, 200, 212, 215, 238
Smiles, Samuel, 40
Smith, George Adam, *NBR, 280*
Smith, Goldwin, *II, 225n; HF,* 180–1; *Beehive,* 213
Smith, Dr John Pye, *HF,* 169, 180; *HF* censure controversy, *54*
Solomon, 314
Solon, 253
Somers-Cocks, John, *I, 24n;* 100; *WR,* 123
Somerset, Edward Adolphus St Maur, 12th Duke of, *203–4,* 297
Southampton, Henry Wriothesley, 3rd Earl of, *162*
Spalding (paper manufacturer), 197
Spedalieri, Nicola, *80*
Spelman, Sir John, 209–10
Spinoza, Baruch, 225
Spohr, Ludwig, *79*
Staël, Germaine de, 117, 119
Stanhope, Philip Henry, 5th Earl of, *HF, 16,* 56, 73, 82n, 86n, 89, 97
Stanley, Arthur Penrhyn, *II, 58n;* 106, 166; *Fraser's Magazine,* 201; *HF,* 98; *Times,* 173
Stanley, Frederick Arthur, *255*
Stansfeld, Sir James, *255*
Steins, Mgr Walter, S.J., Vatican Council, *293–5*
Stevenson, Joseph, later S.J., 162, *167,* 210–11, 215, 217–18, 220, 222, 279, 281, 283–4, 292, 345; *A*'s evaluation of, 213; *C,* 212, 214; *HF,* 141n; Vatican Archives project, 213, 221, 223–5, 227–30, 303, 336
Stewart (bookseller), 11, 64, 78, 85, 90, 100, 103, 204, 228
Stirling, James Hutchinson, 200
Stokes, Scott Nasmyth, *I, 12n;* 26, 31; *HF,* 7, 104, 138; *WR,* 123
Stucley, Captain Thomas, *S*'s biography of, *298–302,* 312
Suarez, Francisco, S.J., 79–80; *HF* censure controversy, *54*
Sullivan, William Kirby, *I, 117n;* 198, 215; *Atlantis,* 207; *C,* 213; *Dictionnaire politique,* 181, 183–4, *HF,* 38, 56–7, 60, 64, 73, 101, 111n, 116, 122, 130–1, 151, 152n, 191; *NBR,* 268, 270
Sunderland, Robert Spencer, 2nd Earl of, 106
Swedenborg, Emanuel, 225
Swetchine, Anna Sophie Soymonoff, *HF, 127*
Swift, Jonathan, 168

Taine, Hippolyte Adolphe, 159, 194

Talbot, Mgr George, *II, 239n;* 93, 200, 290; Vatican Archives project, 224
Talbot, John, 162
Talleyrand-Périgord, Charles Maurice de, 119
Taylor, Henry, *HF,* 141, *156,* 157n, 161, 163–4, 166n
Taylor, Colonel Thomas Edward, *256*
Telford, John, *HF* censure controversy, *105, 125*
Temple, Frederick, 143–4
Tennent, Sir James Emerson, *HF,* 104
Teulet, Alexandre J. B., 36, 38
Thackeray, William Makepeace, *HF,* 155–7, 159–60, 162, 164–5, 167–9, 172, 174, 189, 191, 261
Theiner, Augustin, *II, 26n;* 299, 336; Vatican Archives project, 106, 223–4, 226–8
Themistocles, 272
Thiers, Adolphe, 160
Thijm, Josef Albert Alberdingk, *C, 220*
Thirlwall, Connop, *190*
Thompson, Edward Healy, *I, 35n; DR,* 44, 123n
Thompson, Harriet, *DR,* 123n
Thonissen, Jean Joseph, *C, 218,* 220
Thorpe, Benjamin, 210, 215, *292*
Throckmorton, Clement, 312
Throckmorton, Edward, 312
Throckmorton, Emily (later Dease), *142–3,* 69n
Throckmorton, Francis, 312
Throckmorton, Sir George, 312
Throckmorton, Sir John, *36–7*
Throckmorton, Sir Nicholas, 312
Throckmorton, Sir Robert (*A*'s uncle-in-law), *17*
Throckmorton, Sir Robert, 312
Thynne, Lord Charles, *9–10,* 39
Tichnor, George, *II, 122n; HF,* 153, 156
Tierney, Mark Aloysius, *I,* 26, 38, 57, 62–3, 230, 311, 314–16, 325
Tillemont, Sebastien le Nain de, 85
Tocqueville, Alexis de, 135
Todd, William Gowan, *I, 4n;* 67; *HF* censure controversy, 33
Tonello, Michelangelo, 235
Tongiorgi, Salvatore, S.J., 161
Toovey, James (bookseller), *I, 82n;* 136–7
Trappes, Michael, Vatican Decrees, *291*
Trollope, Anthony, 119, 165, 261–2; *HF,* 5
Turnbull, William Barclay, *I, 51n;* 75

Ullathorne, Bishop William Bernard, *I, 27n;* 134, 145, 200; *HF* censure controversy, 29, 40–7, 49–55, 57–9, 62, 63n, 68, 71, 75, 79, 81, 170, 196; Vatican Council, 282; Vatican Decrees, 291
Ulrici, Hermann, 146, 163, 172
Ursula, St, *HF,* 141, 152

Valdevedus of Saragoza, 107

Van Meteren, Emanuel, 311
Vaughan, Herbert Alfred, later Cardinal, 129n; *DR*, 127n; *HF* censure controversy, 130; *Tablet*, 257n
Vaughan, Roger, *129*
Vaughan, Bishop William: *HF* censure controversy, *24*; Vatican Council, 282
Venn, Henry, *HF*, 60–1
Ventura di Raulica, Gioacchino, 79
Vernon, Lady Elizabeth, 162
Vertot, René Aubert de, 304
Veuillot, Louis, *I*, *31n*; *Univers*, 341
Victor Emmanuel II, *II*, *325n*; 233
Victoria, Queen, 203
Victoria, Princess Royal of England, later German Empress, *HF*, *91*
Villari, Pasquale, *HF*, 19, 123
Villiers, Charles Pelham, *II*, *121n*; 202, 253, 256
Vinet, Alexandre, *I*, *37n*; 119, 142; *HF*, 131
Visconti-Venosta, Emilio, 233

Walker, Henry Martyn, *II*, *99n*; 123
Wallis, John Edward, *I*, *116n*; 31; projected merger of *Tablet* and *WR*, 126; *Tablet*, 32, 257
Ward, Francis, *WR*, 123
Ward, Horatio James ('Veritas'), 241, *242*, 258–9
Ward, William George, *I*, *3n*; 22, 24, 35, 79–80, 122, 212; *DR*, 44, 126, 201, 205; *HF* censure controversy, 27–8; *R*, 342; Vatican Decrees, 291n
Washington, George, 160
Waters, Robert Edmund Chester, *II*, *319n*; *HF*, 17, 20, 24, 29, 33, 36, 39, 57, 72–4, 76–7, 86n, 92, 97, 101, 103, 112, 116, 119, 122, 125, 127–8, 131, 142, 152; *HF* censure controversy, 39–40; *WR*, 126
Waterworth, William, S.J., *II*, *276n*; 26; *HF* censure controversy, 123
Watkin, Dom Aelred, 19n, 20n, 302n, 326n
Watson, Christopher Knight, *I*, *125n*; *HF*, 22
Watson, William, 337
Watts, Thomas, *277–8*
Weale, William Henry James, *C*, 215, 217–18, *HF*, *57*
Webster, John, 146, 163, 172
Weedall, Henry, *26*
Weiss, Johann Baptist, 210
Weld, Alfred, S.J., *59*
Weld, Charles, *I*, *4n*; 31, 44, 59
Weld, Frederick, *264*; *HF*, 121–2
Wellington, Arthur Wellesley, Duke of, 308
Wenham, John George, *I*, *94n*; 164; *DR*, 44; *HF* censure controversy, 33–4
Weninger, Franz Xaver, *302n*, 303–4
Werner, Karl, 80
Westmorland, Charles Neville, 6th Earl of, *337*

Wetherell, Thomas Frederick, *I*, *192n*; 26, 136, 196–7, 199–200, 202, 205–6, 212, 215, 260, 265, 283, 286, 297, 302–4, 310, 316–17; *C*, 209n, 213–14, 218n, 220, 230–1, 234, 238–9; *HF*, 4–5, 7, 9–10, 13–15, 18–20, 24, 28, 34–5, 38–40, 50, 52, 56, 59–60, 62, 71, 73–4, 76–8, 83, 89, 99, 108–10, 112, 115, 120, 124, 126–31, 133, 135, 141, 155–8, 161, 164, 171–2, 179, 189–90, 193–4; *HF* censure controversy, 6, 29, 58, 62; *NBR*, 243, 261, 267, 270–6, 279–80, 282, 285, 287–8, 291–2; *R*, 3–4, 342; Vatican Archives project, 106; Vatican Decrees controversy, 329–31, 336; Wetherell–Simpson conflicts, 46–7, 63–4, 66–70, 137–9, 147n, 148n, 149–51, 168–9, 175–8, 182–4, 186n, 187, 285; *WR*, 123–4
Whewell, William, *I*, *96n*; *HF*, 103
Whitgreave, Francis, *II*, *311n*; 66
Whitmore, Henry, *252–3*, 255, 258
Whittall, Sir James William, *81*, 91
Whitty, Robert, S.J., *31*
Whitworth, Sir Joseph, *II*, *27*; 104n
Wilberforce, Henry William, *I*, *13n*; 3–4; *HF*, 6; *WR*, 5, 13–14, 123, 126, 128
Wilberforce, Robert Isaac, *I*, *66n*; 26
Wilberforce, Bishop Samuel, *II*, *146*; 245, 251
Wilkins, David, 84, 158
William I (Prussia), *19*, 268
William III (England), 106
Williams and Norgate (publisher), 3, 8, 18, 21, 42, 64, 96, 103–5, 120, 128, 132, 134, 136, 147n, 165, 167, 171, 194–8, 207
Wilson, John (Christopher North), 50; *Blackwood's Magazine*, *49*; *HF*, 49, 60
Wilson, Thomas, 106
Wingfield, William, *123n*
Wiseman, Cardinal Nicholas, *I*, *16n*; 25, 26n, 31, 35–6, 51, 104n, 145, 191, 290, 341; *DR*, 111, 126; *HF* censure controversy, 5–6, 11–12, 15, 20–4, 27–8, 33–4, 39–40, 42–3, 61–2, 75–6, 125; on his successor, 200; *R*, 289
Woeste, Charles, *C*, *218*
Wolsey, Cardinal Thomas, 106; *HF*, *110–11*, 152, 167
Wood, Charlotte, *125*
Wood, William, *125n*
Woodlock, Bishop Bartholomew, *II*, *296n*; 207; *HF*, 40, 86–7, 97n, 128n
Woodruff, Douglas, 83n
Worsaae, Jens Jacob Asmussen, 210
Wright, Thomas, 210
Wuttke, Karl Friedrich Adolf, *90*

Xavier, St Francis, *HF*, 60–1

Yonge, Charlotte, *HF*, 103n

Zamoyski, Count Andrzej, *100–1*
Zamoyski, Count Wladyslaw, *98*, 100n

INDEX OF BOOKS
AND ARTICLES

N.B. Unless otherwise stated, the articles named in this index were published in *The Home and Foreign Review*. Where appropriate and feasible, biographies and correspondence pertaining to an individual have been indexed under the last name of that individual.